Praise for TEACHING MATH TO CHILDREN WITH DOWN SYNDROME AND OTHER HANDS-ON LEARNERS

"I learned to use the calculator. I really love the talking calculator. I can figure out the bills when they come—so we all pay our share. The class is mostly fun. I like the games best."

—Scott Hayes, a young adult with Down Syndrome
who was taught using the TEACHING MATH program

~~~

"I have seen how much the guys learn just sitting down at the kitchen table doing math, using real things, money and games. It really helps when they go to the store. I am sure that the book will help others learn math the same way."

—Betty Frazier, Supported Living Provider for "the guys from North Street,"
a group home where Scott Hayes and his roommates live in Worthington, Ohio

~~~

"Deanna Horstmeier is perhaps the most experienced 'parent-scholar' in the area of developmental delays that I know. She has been both an intimate coach for her son Scott for over 30 years, as well as a voracious student of what children with delays need. I recommend the book to all parents of children with learning delays as well as Down Syndrome."

—James D. MacDonald, Ph.D.
Director of Communicating Partners program, professor emeritus
Ohio State University.

TEACHING MATH
to People with
Down Syndrome
and Other
Hands-On Learners

■ Basic Survival Skills ■

DeAnna Horstmeier, Ph.D.

WOODBINE HOUSE ◆ 2004

All rights reserved. Published in the United States of America by Woodbine House, Inc., 6510 Bells Mill Rd., Bethesda, MD 20817. 800-843-7323. www.woodbinehouse.com

Library of Congress Cataloging-in-Publication Data

Horstmeier, DeAnna.
  Teaching math to people with Down Syndrome and other hands-on learners / by DeAnna Horstmeier.— 1st ed.
      v. cm.
  Includes bibliographical references and index.
  Contents: bk. 1. Basic survival skills
  ISBN 1-890627-42-9 (bk. 1 : pbk.)
  1. Mathematics—Study and teaching. 2. Down syndrome—Patients. I. Title.
  QA11.2.H67 2004
  510'.71—dc22
                                                                            2004011436

Manufactured in the United States of America

10 9 8 7 6 5 4 3 2 1

*Dedicated to Scott Allen, who inspired this book,
and to my husband, Heinz, who made this book possible
(along with P.J. sub sandwiches)*

Table of Contents

Introduction to Teaching Basic Math Survival Skills

Chapter 1 / Questions to be answered:

1. Why is there a need for this book?

2. Who will this book help?

3. What sets this book apart from other math books?

4. Who may teach the lessons in this book?

5. In what settings?

6. What areas of math are covered?

Why Is There a Need for This Book?

Scott Allen Horstmeier, my fourth child, was born with Down syndrome in 1970. At that time in the Midwest where we lived, people in general had very low expectations for people with Down syndrome. I was an elementary school teacher, however, and eager to look into the early "infant stimulation" research that was just starting to paint a more hopeful picture for children like my son. Using what I learned, I worked with Scott regularly. He was also able to go to both a typical and a special education preschool for some time.

In the meantime, I had entered the Ohio State University to get further education so I could help Scott and other children like him. My early work concentrated on speech and language. As part of my graduate work, I visited the University of Washington, where preschool children with Down syndrome were being successfully taught to read. Encouraged, our adventure with Scott and academic learning began. During his school years, I continued to teach him at home and worked hard to have him included in appropriate general education classes, especially in reading. (The first special education law, PL 94-142, was passed just when he was old enough to go to public school. I insisted on a public school placement, and Scott was the first child with Down syndrome to go to public school full time in our district.)

Scott learned to read quickly and uses his reading skills daily—especially to read the ads for pizza places, the TV schedule, and the current movie listings in the newspaper. The whole family supported his development, and Scott has been surprising us with his learning for over thirty years.

Although I worked hard with Scott on his reading, I really didn't pay very much attention to math. The school never indicated that math was especially a problem, and they seldom sent home math homework that taxed his abilities. Looking back at those school years, I realize that Scott had very little need to learn math skills involving money. We freely gave him any items that he needed or desired. He did not need to save money or use it in stores. Now he is a young adult, living with three of his friends in a supported living situation and working in the community. To my consternation, I found that he was handicapped more by his deficits in math than by any other factor. He knew some single-digit addition and subtraction facts but never tried any mental math at all. We had given him a calculator, but he really didn't know how to set up the problems to use it—and his budget was a disaster! He spent any money that he had, regardless of the need to pay bills. He once spent $90 for a robot toy!

By the time I discovered how inadequate Scott's practical math skills were, I was working as a consultant at a special education regional resource center in Ohio. I started to conduct some classes with Scott and his roommates on how to use the calculator. After a short time I discovered that the young adults needed much more than simple instruction in the use of the calculator. Some of the basic understandings that underlie the use of mathematics had flown—if they ever really understood them. I started searching the literature for current research on teaching early number concepts and computation. Since the young adults in Scott's group were visual, concrete learners, I found out that a hands-on approach was essential. In addition, they were adults who didn't want to go to school again in any sense. Therefore, using games was the most effective way to have them learn and practice. Since they were paying for rent, utilities, food, and other necessities, I used their own experiences in working with addition, subtraction, and budgeting as the basis for my instruction.

Eventually, we worked with Scott on a budget that required his household bills to be paid with a joint checking account that we monitored. Now we give him his discretionary money weekly so he is able to handle the money with minimum damage when he makes a mistake. I fully expect him to be able to handle his earnings by himself one day.

I began to record the progress and activities that I used with Scott's group so that I could share them with other educators at the professional development classes that I teach. I discovered that many of the concepts and activities I used with the young adults could help students who were still in school, and could possibly give them a better chance at a fulfilling life. I then began giving regular workshops to teachers on teaching math to students who are concrete or hands-on learners.

Parents and classroom teachers have given me many ideas and have told me when I made mistakes. We have found that children, including those with Down syndrome,

Caption: *The four young men who inspired me to write this book: Scott Hays, Steve Langhirt, Scott Horstmeier, and Bryan Hiveley. Photo reprinted courtesy of the* Columbus Dispatch.

are pretty frank about what works for them … or doesn't. The *"survival skills"* approach in this book emphasizes:

- Hands-on-activities where the students touch and manipulate physical materials
- A focus on the essential concepts, rather than just drill work with numbers
- Games and other activities that enable the students to enjoy the additional practice that they need to make sure the concepts make it into long-term memory storage
- Ideas for parents and teachers to make sure the skills are used in meaningful, everyday activities
- Examples, hints, and teaching strategies that have already proved useful for other students
- Motivation for the students by beginning with success steps (activities that allow them to show how much they already know) and by encouraging the instructors to give interesting and varied lessons

Who Will This Book Help?

There has not been a great deal of research into the math abilities of children with Down syndrome. However, now that children with Down syndrome are routinely expected to go to school and learn academics with their peers, there is growing recognition that many of these children have a great deal of difficulty acquiring math skills.

In the book, *A Parent's Guide to Down Syndrome: Toward a Brighter Future* (Pueschel, 2001), H.D. Bud Fredericks, a professor at Western Oregon University and the parent of a son with Down syndrome, cites a study of the academic skills of a sample of students with Down syndrome. In reading, the older students (ages 10-

13) had achieved more than a third grade level, which gave them access to many science and social studies materials, as well as works of fiction. In math, however, the same students (with the exception of one) had not achieved even a second grade level. While my personal experience has been that some students with Down syndrome can achieve at higher levels than his figures suggest, most authorities agree that students with Down syndrome have real difficulty with the abstract concepts of mathematics (Klein & Arieli, 1997; Nye & Bird, 1996; Broadley, 1991; Buckley & Sacks, 1987). A poor understanding of simple math concepts and money skills is also hindering many adults with Down syndrome in their quest for independent living. More explanation for these difficulties will be given in Chapter 2.

In addition, many other individuals who do not have Down syndrome, but who are concrete thinkers, also have difficulty with the abstract concepts of mathematics. (By "concrete thinkers," I mean individuals who are in the concrete operational learning stage; see the "Piaget Primer" on page 5.)

Much of the teaching of math concepts in school is done at the abstract level (formal operational learning stage). This book, however, is designed for the concrete thinkers who need hands-on, practical activities to learn. This includes individuals (including some on the autism spectrum) who have difficulties with using abstract math skills in a meaningful way. The book's focus on the functional uses of math in daily living can motivate those individuals to learn and practice useful skills.

In short, this book is helpful for:

- **Students with Down syndrome from early preschool through the elementary grades.** It is also especially good for older secondary students who have not mastered computation and basic number concepts. I have tried to suggest teaching materials that are not "babyish" with these individuals in mind.

- **Other children and young adults who are concrete thinkers, including some students with autism spectrum disorders.** Some students on the autism continuum may be able to memorize the math facts and perform calculations, but have difficulty knowing how and when to use these skills.

- **Young adults with cognitive disabilities who are handicapped in their independent living by lack of math and budget skills.**

- **Any elementary or secondary school students who have substantial difficulties with math computation and concepts.**

- **Young children, who need deliberate, concrete instruction in early math concepts.** (When I conduct professional development workshops, teachers have told me that young children with and without cognitive delay find the concrete experiences and game format of this book a pleasant way to learn the basic concepts of number sense. They are also progressing as concrete thinkers who can see concepts easier when taught at their level.)

A Piaget Primer

Jean Piaget, a Swiss psychologist, describes the growth of a child's cognitive skills by the stages of:

- **Sensorimotor learning** (infancy and toddlerhood)—where the child learns through touching, feeling, and using his senses, in addition to moving and exploring the environment.

- **Preoperational learning** (approximately ages 2-7)—where a child develops make-believe skills (representational learning) along with some illogical thought. For example, if a child has two clay balls with exactly the same amount of clay, you might roll one ball into a long snake shape. The preoperational child will think that the snake shape has more clay than the round ball. He probably focuses on the longer shape and feels that it has more clay.

- **Concrete operational learning** (usually ages 7-12)—where the child is able to solve problems through mental thought according to logical rules. However, this problem solving can only be done when the child is dealing with concrete information that he can perceive directly. For example, if the child can see the strawberries on his brother's plate and the strawberries on his own plate, he can count the berries on each plate. He can then add the total number of strawberries or compare the plates and declare that his brother has two more strawberries than he has. However, if only the abstract numbers are given him, he may not be able to set up the problem to be solved. The aim of this book is to teach individuals who are, for the most part, concrete (operational) thinkers. These learners need hands-on materials to learn math concepts.

- **Formal operational learning** (usually ages 12 and older) evolves when the child is capable of abstract thought that does not require concrete materials and events to be present when problem solving (Berk, 2001).

What Sets This Book Apart from Other Math Books?

- The early and frequent use of the **calculator**
- The emphasis on relevant, **functional skills**—for example, emphasis on quarters because of their frequent use in vending machines, and much less emphasis on pennies. (Who really wants or needs pennies?)
- Emphasis on problem solving in **real situations** and not getting tied up in the language of word problems. (In our own lives, how often do we have to solve a math problem from a written description in a book?)
- Activities designed to be **successful** with children who have difficulties learning abstract concepts

- Frequent use of games and **hands-on activities**
- An **informal assessment** that can be given as a series of **games**
- Activities appropriate for both **young and older learners**
- Use of **inexpensive, common materials** for the hands-on activities
- Simple, **clear instructions**
- Suggestions for ways these math concepts can be **woven into everyday living**

Who May Teach the Lessons in This Book?

Any interested person can teach the lessons. Parents, educators, volunteers, siblings, or peers can do the activities with the student.

In What Settings?

The "survival math" skills in this book are best taught with a group of two or three children. If the teaching is one-to-one, the instructor will have to play some of the games so the student has a competitor. Different age siblings or peer tutors may also participate. The activities in the book can definitely be taught to a larger group, but the instructor will not be as able to tell what the students' thought processes are. Time should be taken to informally evaluate each individual student's grasp of the concepts on a regular basis.

This book can be valuable for a student who receives math instruction in the general classroom. In other content areas such as science, the general classroom teacher can modify the goals of the instruction so that the student with special needs can participate and learn. In math, however, students with disabilities often need to master some of the earlier-taught concepts before they can understand the math activities of the general classroom. The activities in this book can be prepared and taught by a classroom aide, a volunteer, or an older peer tutor. The teacher just has to evaluate the student's progress and indicate the activities that should be done next. Some of the activities can be set up as a learning center for the entire classroom. Thus, this book can be a resource for appropriate learning for the child with special needs in the general classroom.

In a special education classroom, the groups are frequently smaller, and the lessons in this book can be adapted to the individual child's need. Care should be taken that the pace of learning is not slowed down by the instructor having expectations that are too low or because typical students are not present as models. Students from the older classes may be used to assist. The emphasis on relevant functional skills in this book is certainly helpful for students who are aiming for supported or independent living in the community after schooling.

Family one-to-one instruction can also be very effective. Students may be able to learn from the teacher and children in the regular classroom, but parents (or sometimes a tutor) can make sure that the major concepts are really understood. Family instruction given when your child is very young may help enable him to participate more in the general classroom math instruction. Above all, families can make this instruction fun for the child and for themselves. Too often, both student and parent dread math homework. A special benefit can come from your family's knowledge of what motivates your child and of how to weave number activities into daily living.

Why Is the Subtitle of This Book *Basic Survival Skills*?

Since I originally started working with four young adults who had been out of school for several years, I wanted to teach only those math skills that were necessary for their survival in the community. They had never mastered all the math facts, but they could use the calculator to substitute for this rote memory task. As I worked with them once or twice a week for over two years, I learned that they could be taught math concepts and skills. Why hadn't they learned them while they were in school? Or why had they forgotten them so soon?

Then my goal became to pass on some of the strategies for teaching math that had worked with these young adults. I wanted to make sure that students with Down syndrome or others with cognitive disabilities were taught the essentials of computation (using the calculator) while they were in school and to apply these skills to their daily living, especially in handling of money. Those are what I think of as "survival math" skills.

As I taught and investigated more, I realized that there were really two levels of survival math:

The first level (Basic Survival Math) encompasses those skills that individuals need in order to handle the most common math-related tasks in daily life with the assistance of helping adults. Students at this level will:

1. Have an understanding of what numbers and numerals are about.
2. Be able to add and subtract.
3. Be able to use these computation skills when they are needed. The students may learn the math facts for addition and subtraction, or they may understand when to use addition and subtraction but use the calculator to help with their rote memory problems.
4. Experience some of the practical uses for math such as in measurement and in telling time.
5. Understand the fundamental number concepts that structure our lives.

The student who has mastered these concepts can "survive" as an adult if he has someone to assist in setting up a structure for money handling. He will need family or providers to set up a budgeting system for him and guide him through a routine until he is secure. Family or other adults may need to do some oversight on his banking and his shopping experiences. In reality, however, all of us are dependent on each other in one way or another. I remember setting up a bank account and doing a lot of money counseling on the phone when my older children first started college. "Mom, I never realized that toilet paper and shampoo were so expensive and that I had to pay for them," said my oldest son after a few weeks away at school. And there are some of us who have the ATM card figure out the balances on our checking accounts. Some interdependence is present in all of our lives.

The second level (Advanced Survival Math), progresses to using multiplication and simple division with the calculator for common situations and problems. More emphasis is given to teaching the student how to set up the problems that actually occur in his life. Usually the student will be reasonably proficient at using the calculator but will need guidance and practice in applying his skills. Measurement, time, and fractions are explored in more depth. Heavy emphasis is given on money skills along with the principles of budgeting, banking, and shopping. Some more advanced money skills, such as understanding percent in shopping at stores with sales, will be taught, even if the general area of percent is not thoroughly taught. The student achieving Level 2 will be able use his math in routine situations. Maybe he will not be able to quote the area of rug needed for his living room, but he will be able to measure the width and length. He will let the carpet sales person figure out the area . . . as do most of us.

What Areas of Math Are Included?

BASIC SURVIVAL SKILLS (BOOK ONE)

- Calculator skills
- Prenumber concepts
- Simple comparisons
- Matching
- Simple classification
- Number sense
    - ▾ Number concepts
    - ▾ Counting
    - ▾ Visual spotting
- Numeral recognition
- Using a number line
- Counting large numbers
- Skip counting
- Counting on
- Place value
- Writing of numerals
    - ▾ Drawing lines and circles
    - ▾ Ways of teaching
    - ▾ Alternatives for writing numerals
    - ▾ Words for numbers
    - ▾ Fluency with higher numbers
- Ordinal numbers
- Sequencing numbers
- Comparison words
- Simple graphs (optional)
- Addition
    - ▾ Basic understandings of addition

- ▾ Addition facts (optional)
- ▾ Concrete, simple addition (calculator)
- ▾ Multiple item addition
- ▾ Problem solving
- Subtraction
  - ▾ Basic understandings of subtraction
  - ▾ Take-away subtraction
  - ▾ Subtraction facts (optional)
  - ▾ Concrete, simple subtraction (calculator)
  - ▾ Comparison subtraction
  - ▾ How-much-more subtraction
  - ▾ Figuring change
  - ▾ Problem solving
- Time concepts
- Large blocks of time (days, months, etc.)
- Schedules
- Time telling with clocks
- Measurements
  - ▾ Length
  - ▾ Capacity
  - ▾ Weight
- Temperature
- Shapes
  - ▾ Two dimensional
  - ▾ Three dimensional
- Patterns
- Money
  - ▾ Currency
  - ▾ Coins

ADVANCED SURVIVAL SKILLS (BOOK TWO)

- Calculator principles
- Review addition
- Review subtraction
- Simple fractions (as used in recipes)
- Multiplication
  - ▾ Basic understanding of multiplication
  - ▾ Concrete, simple multiplication (calculator)
  - ▾ Problem solving
  - ▾ Two-step problems
  - ▾ Multiplication of larger numbers (calculator)
- Reading and writing large numbers
- Division
  - ▾ Basic understanding of division
  - ▾ By single digits (calculator)
  - ▾ Practical uses for division
  - ▾ Problem solving

- Recording and interpreting simple data on bar graph
- Banking
  - ▾ Savings
  - ▾ Checking and ATM
  - ▾ Credit concepts
- Budgeting
  - ▾ Essential funds for daily living
  - ▾ Discretionary funds
- More measurement
- Comparison shopping
- Percent (for shopping only)
- Consumer skills

Have fun with this book! It is definitely *not* a workbook. Hopefully, you and your students will enjoy your learning together.

Characteristics of Concrete (Hands-On) Learners:
Especially Those with Down Syndrome

Chapter 2 / Questions to be answered:

1. What are some characteristics of individuals with Down syndrome that pose challenges to math learning?

2. What are some of the strengths of individuals with Down syndrome that can support their math learning?

3. What other students are hands-on (concrete) learners?

4. What about students who are on the autism spectrum?

Students with Down Syndrome

For years, many educators believed that individuals with Down syndrome were not really capable of learning to read and do math computation. And if our expectation was that they were not capable, we didn't give them much of an opportunity to learn these academic skills. In the United States, individuals with Down syndrome were often labeled "trainable" by schools and were excluded from the more academically oriented classes for "educable" students. Of course, there were infrequent examples of exceptional individuals who could read, write, and do some math (Hunt, 1967; Seagoe, 1964). However, until the mid-1970s, individuals with Down syndrome were mostly taught self-help and functional living skills.

Since the advent of what is now called the Individuals with Disabilities Education Act (IDEA), the special education law that opened the doors of schooling to every child

in 1975, students with Down syndrome have been making strides in academic as well as social learning. With higher expectations and more consistent education, achievements for most individuals with Down syndrome have been improving. These academic achievements are higher when the students with Down syndrome are educated with general education students (Bird & Buckley, 2001).

Now that it has become commonplace to teach academics to students with Down syndrome, we are beginning to learn more about how Down syndrome affects learning. Importantly, almost all the research in the United States and Great Britain has shown that their achievements in reading are significantly greater than their achievements in math and number sense (Fredricks, 2001; Irwin, 1989; Buckley, 1985; Shepperdson, 1994). For example, three British researchers studied the academic achievements of 24 children with Down syndrome, ranging from 6 to 14 years, who had been included in general education classrooms with good support (Buckley, Bird & Byrnes, 2001). After two years, their math skills were approximately four years behind the students' chronological age, while reading and spelling were only two years behind.

Similarly, John Rynders and his associate (1997) looked at data from three different studies involving the academic achievement of forty-six school-aged children with Down syndrome. The average reading level was fourth grade; however, the average math achievement was under second grade level. Although some of the authors have theories, no one actually knows why this discrepancy between math and reading achievement occurs.

If you are a parent who is wondering how Down syndrome might affect your own child's math abilities, it is worth remembering that research on the progress of students with Down syndrome in math is very limited. It is also quite probable that present-day adults with Down syndrome have had little systematic instruction in math and thus have not progressed up to their potential. Gillian Bird and Sue Buckley—educators and researchers at the Down Syndrome Educational Trust, UK, who have made it their life's work to help children with DS learn—have stated that in their clinical experience, "There is a wide variation in number ability among individuals with Down syndrome" (2001, p. 8). This variation makes it very difficult to estimate what an individual person with Down syndrome is capable of doing in the math area.

What Characteristics of Individuals with Down Syndrome Pose Challenges?

In the absence of research pinpointing exactly why math is difficult for individuals with Down syndrome, this section offers some of the most common theories. Not all people with Down syndrome have all of these challenges to the same degree, and it is important for anyone working with a particular student to find out exactly which of these problems are stumbling blocks for that individual. In general, however, many children with Down syndrome have at least some of these challenges, and some children may have all of them.

1. Students with Down syndrome frequently have **problems with short-term and working memory.** Short-term memory helps us to keep specific facts or items that we have just heard or observed in mind as we decide what to do with them. For example, you keep a telephone number in memory for a short time until you have used it or have decided to memorize it. Working memory usually contains general processes that you must remember as you work with short-term items. For example, a student needs to keep the steps in division in mind as she plugs in the specific data from the problem she has been given. In math, we often use short-term memory in learning numerals, computation facts, and specific details about the current problem that is to be solved. Working memory underpins the processes of math—addition, subtraction, multiplication, division, and other multi-step processes. Students with Down syndrome need assistance in learning to overcome these possible deficits in memory.

   Of course, if students have difficulties with short-term and working memory, they will not be adept at putting facts into long-term memory storage. When information is not of interest to them (such as math facts) or has little emotional impact, they may seem to remember it one day and forget it the next. This is not willful forgetting on the child's part—instead, it just means that the information was never properly stored in her memory to begin with. However, when items are securely in long-term memory, children with Down syndrome can remember them for a long time—sometimes even longer than their parents.

2. Children with Down syndrome may also have **fine motor delays in their hands and problems with eye-hand coordination.** These delays make it difficult to manipulate objects and make writing numerals difficult and slow. My son says, "I just have fat fingers. I want them to be fast fingers." It may be that children do not get as much experience with exploring objects in their world if they have difficulty manipulating them. Certainly they will have less energy to devote to understanding number relationships if they are struggling with just writing and lining up the numbers in a math problem.

3. Individuals with Down syndrome usually have **significant delays in speech and vocal expressive language**—that is, with communicating their own thoughts in words. Problems

with the oral motor mechanisms of the mouth such as sluggish tongue control, a narrow, high roof of the mouth, and difficulties with lip control can often make them hard to understand. Research has shown that children with Down syndrome usually can understand more that they can speak clearly. Because of their difficulties with expressive speech, others tend to underestimate what they can understand (Miller, Leddy & Leavitt, 1999; Horstmeier, 1985). This underestimation of their abilities could make them lose opportunities for more advanced math learning. They are usually able to learn the meaning of math vocabulary words, though they often have to be taught them directly.

4. Although individuals with Down syndrome usually understand more than they can express verbally, they can also have **difficulties with receptive language**—that is, with understanding other people's spoken messages. Difficulties with receptive language are especially likely to complicate math learning if a concept can be expressed in several different ways in English. Speech-language pathologist Libby Kumin gives a clear example in her book *Classroom Language Skills for Children with Down Syndrome* (2001, p. 130):

"Synonyms can also be a problem when children are learning to sequence numbers. The simplest question is what number comes before or what number comes after, but worksheets to practice sequencing use all of the following:
- Write the missing numbers.
- Write the number that is one less.
- Write the number that comes between the numbers.
- Write the numbers in the correct order."

In addition, students with Down syndrome may need instructions broken down into smaller steps. This is especially evident when a word problem requires two steps. For example:

> Jan has 1 candy bar, Al has 7 candy bars, and Heinz has 4 candy bars. How many candy bars would they each have if they shared them so that each had the same number of candy bars?

If the problem were broken down into parts, the student would be told to count up how many candy bars there were in total. The next step would be to divide the candy bars equally between the three individuals, yielding four each (by physical manipulation or by division).

5. **Processing information given *orally*** can sometimes present another problem. Studies indicate that about 40 percent of individuals with Down syndrome have a mild hearing loss. Ten to 15 percent have a more severe hearing loss (Fowler, 1995). Certainly, if children can't hear verbal instructions, they will have difficulties understanding words and concepts and distinguishing between similar sounding words, such as *forty* and *fourteen*. However, hearing loss does not tell the whole story, since even individuals with Down syndrome who do not have hearing losses usually have receptive language problems.

Although children with Down syndrome can understand much of what they hear, they seem to process speech slowly and tend to miss details and information that is given sequentially, as in directions. Most children with Down syndrome have enough delay in auditory processing of speech that they learn much better through their visual senses or through a combination of the various senses such as tactile (touch) and kinesthetic (movement).

Teachers who teach primarily by talking to the class can be very frustrating to students with Down syndrome. A student may be unable to keep up with processing the speech that she hears and may miss the important points the teacher is trying to make. If the teacher would just show her *real* dollars and cents rather than numbers on a page, she could make a picture in her mind. Sometimes she gets overwhelmed by the flood of speech and just tunes out. She may think, "Someone else in the class will just have to show me how to add those dollars and cents later."

6. Children with Down syndrome may get **insufficient experiences using math** in the real world, unlike typically developing children. My son's behavior in a large crowded grocery store was so difficult to handle that I eventually left him home with his dad and did grocery shopping at the midnight hours. It was so much easier! But he was missing all those naturally occurring experiences of counting the oranges, seeing which breakfast cereal was cheapest, or finding aisle 4 so he could get the ketchup. I didn't always let him explore in the neighborhood and find the third house down where his friend Ray lived, or allow him to experience other number and location concepts. I got more adventurous as he got older, but I still ran along the backyards on our street, watching him, when he first walked down the sidewalk on his own.

At home, parents or siblings may take over for their children in the interest of speeding things up. For instance, when playing a board game, your other children might shout out the number on the dice before your child with Down syndrome gets a chance to count it up, or you might program the phone number of your child's best friend into the phone rather than letting her try to dial the number herself.

7. Children with Down syndrome usually **take longer to progress through the stages of development** when learning how to think. As explained in the previous chapter, Jean Piaget found that typical children go through these stages at particular ages. For instance, at the earliest stage (birth to 2 years for typical children), children learn through their senses and motor activity. At the preoperational level (2 to 7 years), children learn to imitate and to play with toys and others and can use language to describe what they are doing. Schools generally gear their curricula to the developmental ages that they expect typically developing children to have reached at any given grade level. This means that academic tasks are often at a level that the student with Down syndrome has yet to reach.

Remember, many students with Down syndrome are concrete learners. At the concrete operational stage (7 to 12 years for typical children), students are far more effective and capable at problem solving than before. However, their problem solving suffers from one important limitation. They can solve problems in an organized way only when dealing with concrete information that they can see and perceive directly. Concrete operational individuals deal poorly with abstract ideas (Berk, 2001). For example, a child who is at the concrete operational stage may be able to look at a pie that has been divided into sixths and tell you how much of the pie is left when two pieces are taken away. But when confronted with a worksheet that asks her to subtract 2/6 from 1, the problem may be meaningless to her. In other words, children who are concrete (operational) learners can compute with real things that they see, but have little chance of learning when given situations that require picturing the problem in their minds and doing mental math to solve it.

Several authors maintain that many individuals with Down syndrome do not progress much beyond the concrete operational level of cognition (Wolpert, 1996; Batshaw & Perret, 1993; Horstmeier, 1985). If so, this would explain why math skills that are highly abstract (such as using the letters "x" and "y" to stand for two unknown quantities in an algebraic equation) would be difficult or impossible for most people with Down syndrome to master. They have not reached the formal operations stage that would enable them to think abstractly about a situation and figure out possible consequences based on experiences and formal learning.

The concept of concrete learners helps to explain why people with Down syndrome do much better when using manipulatives in math and are motivated by real-life situations even when they are in middle or high school. The real problem solving goes on with concrete materials that they can see.

8. Sometimes the student with Down syndrome has had **so many experiences with frustration that she is not motivated to try** and gives up easily or refuses to participate. She also may not see how the math activity could be important to her. Perhaps one reason that people with Down syndrome are often more motivated to read than to do math is that reading tends to make the world more understandable to them, by allowing them to see words that flit by too quickly for them to process, but math often doesn't make anything clearer to them (at least the way that it is usually taught).

Fortunately, children with Down syndrome will usually respond to interest-catching activities and games and to real-life situations that require the use of math. An enthusiastic parent or teacher is halfway there in the learning process. It is also very important to start by making sure the student experiences success when learning a new concept and to make sure those successes come frequently during the learning.

What Strengths Do Individuals with Down Syndrome Have?

Students with Down syndrome often have strengths that can assist in their math learning. Again, it is difficult to generalize, so it is possible that your student with Down syndrome may not have the strengths listed below. However, many individuals with Down syndrome have many, if not most of these characteristics.

The key is to get to know your student as an individual and use teaching methods and materials that are suited to her strengths.

1. Many individuals with Down syndrome are **eager to please,** especially when young. Establishing rapport is crucial for motivating these students—and also for the enjoyment of their instructors. Children with Down syndrome are often a joy to work with because of their enthusiasm for learning and appreciation of the person doing the teaching.

   Of course, like any children, if they have been affected by frustrating experiences and inept teaching, they may create behavior problems. However, a study by Stephanny F.N. Freeman and Robert Hodapp (2000) indicates that children with Down syndrome have fewer problems with inappropriate behavior compared to children with other types of mental retardation.

2. Many individuals with Down syndrome **learn very well through their visual senses.** Often teachers will find that the student with Down syndrome can learn the concept if they just supplement their verbal explanations with a picture or graphic. Pictures, symbols, and written words are all helpful to understanding for the student with Down syndrome.

3. Even if individuals with Down syndrome have speech that is difficult to understand, they are often **able to communicate** with gestures and can show understanding by pointing or other visual ways of choosing an answer. Teachers who spend time with them can often tell by their expressive faces and imitations of actions what they want to communicate. They may be able to demonstrate the answer even if they cannot write it.

4. Children with Down syndrome seem to **go through the same developmental stages** in learning about numbers as do typical children. They just go through them more slowly. They *do* need to practice and practice important concepts so that they become automatic. They do *not* need endless drills on facts and worksheets of problems to do over and over again. Repetition should be creative and used only on important concepts, not to keep them busy during reading groups.

   Often individuals with Down syndrome enjoy working with "gadgets" such as calculators and computers, and these devices can be used to give the practice that they need to get their math skills securely into long-term memory.

5. Children with Down syndrome usually **enjoy interacting with their peers and often model peer behavior** both in and out of the classroom. Parents and teachers should take advantage of this characteristic and include typical children in play and academic settings. A study of parent and teacher attitudes after inclusion experiences for students with Down syndrome rated peer tutoring one of the most positive factors in the student's success. Teachers of sixth grade and higher reported that peer tutoring often worked better than teacher assistance (Wolpert, 1996).

Other Students Who Are Concrete Thinkers

Piaget's stages of cognitive (intelligence) development do not just apply to children with Down syndrome. Many other children struggle with basic number skills. Some of these students have cognitive disabilities, and some are typically developing in other areas besides math. If they are at the concrete operational stage or below and can work math solutions out with hands-on materials and games, then they will learn best with the "survival math" approach in this book. Certainly if a child's mental age is seven or below, you would want to try step-by-step procedures and concrete materials such as those recommended in this book.

Other students who are concrete thinkers may have specific deficits in learning strategies similar to those experienced by students with Down syndrome. These students will probably have similar experiences with frustration from not being able to learn as easily as others are. They will also benefit from hands-on, visual instruction, motivational strategies, and rapport building. Some students with specific learning disabilities in reading may also have difficulties with math and learn more quickly with the hands-on, game-like approach to teaching math emphasized in this book. If, however, the student is primarily an auditory learner who pays little attention to visual instruction, she will not show as much progress using the activities in this book as the student who learns well from visual supports.

Students with Attention-Deficit/Hyperactivity Disorder (AD/HD) often need their learning sessions to be of shorter duration. However, it is quite possible that students with AD/HD could play the *games* in this book completely through. Russell Barkley, a leading authority in the area of AD/HD, has noted that many children with AD/HD can play video games for long periods of time, probably because the games give immediate feedback that keeps them involved. Barkley concludes that the most important factor in AD/HD is not a deficit in attention but the impulsivity that the child shows and the fact that he is easily bored. The many interesting games and activities in this book could therefore be an addition to traditional math teaching for students with AD/HD.

Students on the autism spectrum are also visual learners, perhaps even more so than most children with Down syndrome. The concrete activities and games in this book could hold interest and involvement for many children with autism. Some students with autism can easily memorize the basic facts and may be able to compute worksheets of number problems with ease. However, they often have difficulty learning how to use the facts appropriately. Teachers of students on the autism spectrum have asked for ways to help their students generalize their computation skills to real situations. The sections in this book on problem solving might prove very valuable to their overall functioning, especially if teachers or parents frequently incorporate math skills into various settings and situations in the student's daily activities.

Teaching Strategies

Chapter 3 / Questions to be answered:

1. What teaching strategies and procedures are successful with students with Down syndrome and other concrete learners?
   - Emphasize visual learning
   - Use hands-on activities
   - Provide structured learning with some flexibility
   - Make learning relevant to the real world
   - Focus the student's attention
   - Provide nondistracting written work
   - Give simple, clear homework
   - Minimize fine motor demands
   - Expect and encourage appropriate behavior
   - Ensure early success in the lesson
   - Consider the use of peer tutors
   - Facilitate short- and long-term memory
   - Use the calculator early and frequently
   - Make your interactions enjoyable
   - Use the computer
   - Break down the task into small steps

2. What adaptations and modifications can be made to general classroom work?

Many of the teaching strategies that are very helpful for children with Down syndrome and other children who are concrete thinkers are simply good teaching techniques that work with most students. If a teacher of general education classes is systematic, creative, and tuned in to the learning styles of all the students in her class, she will probably have the skills that she needs to work with students who are concrete thinkers. Of course, it helps to be a "ham" and a good storyteller and to be enthusiastic about learning, too.

Even though I have been working with students with Down syndrome for years, I still occasionally look at some lists that I have compiled to help me remember good strategies for teaching that just may work with that struggling student. I am including the strategies and procedures here that seem to work best with students who are concrete thinkers. I will also discuss some adaptations and modifications that can be made for these students in the general education classroom.

Teaching Strategies and Procedures

EMPHASIZE VISUAL LEARNING

Students with Down syndrome and other concrete learners are very often visual learners—that is, they learn better by seeing actual objects or pictures of concepts rather than hearing someone talking about those concepts. Time after time, I have seen students' eyes light up when I show a picture of what I am explaining. Most elementary teachers often use visual aids (commonly called visuals) in their teaching. However, when a student goes to middle school or high school, people seem to assume that reading a text should be enough. Visual learning through pictures and graphs are important to all of us as we are learning, regardless of age. In addition, because today's students spend so much time looking at television, playing video games, and using computers, many of them have come to expect visual explanations for learning.

To make learning visual, it is not sufficient to just write numbers on the blackboard or on an overhead projector as you are talking. For younger children, using objects or pictorial representations of activities will be the most effective way of teaching. Once a child is able to read fluently, written numbers or words can supply a lasting explanation that is useful. (Visuals can be looked at repeatedly to help with working memory.) However, even older students may be able to learn more quickly when pictures are included with words or numbers.

Educators working with students with autism spectrum disorders (ASD) have recently developed good innovations in the use of visuals for academic learning, direction following, and social skills. For example, Carol Gray has come up with the concept of "Social Stories"—illustrated stories written by parents, teachers, or speech-language therapists tailored to specific social problems a student is having that can be read and reread to help his understanding. And many students with ASD learn new skills through activity schedules—sequences of photographs or drawings that illustrate the steps involved in the skill. Many of the materials designed for students with ASD can be used as-is or modified for use with other students who are concrete learners. For more information on visual strategies, see the books by Bondy and Frost, Hodgdon, and McClannahan and Krantz in the References.

USE HANDS-ON ACTIVITIES

By definition, students who are concrete learners learn by manipulating objects and working out solutions with hands-on activities. Sometimes materials are left out for the students to discover their properties, but more commonly the parent or teacher demonstrates the actions and the student reproduces the activity with his own materials. These hands-on activities may be more difficult for the parent or teacher to orchestrate, but the student's learning is usually greater and longer lasting.

Think about how you learn. Are you one of those people who just can't make heads or tails out of the instructions in your computer program manual? But if someone shows you and guides in doing the steps yourself, those actions make sense, and then you can do them easily. For me, demonstrations are often not enough. I watch the instructor doing origami and it looks easy. However, when I try to make those folds myself, I need direct help in the folding.

Students who are concrete learners need demonstrations and hands-on activities for almost everything they learn. Math is often a rather abstract process as taught above fourth grade level. Concrete learners need activities that make the process real for them much more than they need pages of written problems. Every time you introduce something new, you should be thinking about how you could help the student to *do* an activity that will help this new idea be understood. Although many activities you may come up with involve fine motor skills such as manipulating beans or counters, it is also important to devise some activities that can be done with large muscles. For example, sorting activities can be done by moving to specific areas of the floor: "All students whose favorite color is red, move to the front door. Now let us count out loud how many people love red."

Another large muscle activity could be used to teach and practice the recognition of numerals: "Put your foot on the numeral 2" shows whether the student recognizes the numeral 2. Even the game of hopscotch can be used for number recognition.

PROVIDE STRUCTURED LEARNING WITH SOME FLEXIBILITY

Many students who are concrete learners are more comfortable with having a schedule and following it faithfully. They would like to have things stay just as they usually do it. As teachers, we need to address their need for structure and also build some flexibility into their learning.

For younger children, we can warn them that in five minutes we will be switching activities. Sometimes this warning is not enough, and we will have to think up a leadership-type activity to help them transition into the next subject. "Tom, I need you to collect the scissors for your group."

Making a classroom schedule with every activity on a separate card (illustrated, of course) and posting it in the front of the room may be useful. I put magnets on the back of large cards so they can be used on the refrigerator or a metal-backed chalkboard. Then if a shift in sequence is necessary, I can make the change as the child watches. For some students, it may be helpful to have their own individual schedules for each day of the week. These schedules can be put in a small pocket chart holder so they can be changed. Parents working at home on math should also have a visual schedule or routine that helps their child know what to expect. Routines are especially important for students on the autism spectrum, who often have much difficulty with change.

Although schedules are useful, it is also important for children to learn to deal with unexpected changes to the schedule or routine because in real life, things don't always go as planned. One teacher in a workshop told me that she had one card with a question mark on it that she used when plans had to change suddenly. Sometimes the card signaled a nice surprise or a treat so the students had a pleasant experience with change.

MAKE LEARNING RELEVANT TO THE REAL WORLD

Just because you have the visual symbol for math at a particular time of the day, it doesn't mean that that is the only time you work on math with the student. It is very important that you weave the skills you are teaching in math into the other parts of the academic day and into real-life settings. Involving them in activities such as measuring sugar for a cake or buying a video with their own money helps them understand why they need to learn something and motivates them to learn.

Parents often have the most opportunities to make math teaching come alive. Grocery shopping, mall shopping, counting calories, using the phone, punching in numbers on the TV remote, going to a restaurant, and many, many other activities can provide opportunities for math learning and practice and motivate your child to use math.

Be careful, however, that the real-world activities are not too complex for your student. Ads and signs often include numbers that can be confusing to students who are learning about money. For example, prices that are given per pound can give the student the idea that the entire piece of meat is only $.99. Or a grocery newspaper ad may offer 3 oranges for $1.00 when the student has not yet learned the process of division.

FOCUS THE STUDENT'S ATTENTION

Some parents and teachers have said that, "I could teach him if I could only get him to sit still long enough." Getting the student's attention may be difficult for several different reasons. First, if he is young, he is at the stage where he *should* be exploring and going from activity to activity. How long does a typical child sit to do activities at the same age? Are you expecting too much?

Another factor may be that you are not matching your teaching to your child's interest level. If the activity is dull or your voice is whiny or monotone, you may have lost him at the first turn of the race. Are your words at his level? Are your sentences fairly short? Are you stating the information clearly? Are you enthusiastic? Is the information concrete enough? Do you have pictures or models that are hands-on?

In addition, you may need attention-getters just to awaken a student's interest. When beginning to teach a new idea, you can do something unexpected such as coming in the room with a ruler balanced on your head but acting as if you don't know it is there. Most students with Down syndrome have a good sense of humor—if the joke is simple and if the joke is not on them.

Most typically developing older students can motivate themselves to do assigned work. Older students with Down syndrome may not make the connection that doing work now will help them get good grades later on. You may have to set up some type of reward system such as putting a sticker on their paper if they started to work in three minutes. The reward must be immediate or part of a token system until they have enough experience to want to do well just for themselves (internal rewards).

Finally, some students with Down syndrome (and autism spectrum disorders) actually satisfy the diagnostic criteria for attention-deficit/hyperactivity disorder (AD/HD). If your student has a dual diagnosis, you may need to read books or attend workshops designed to teach strategies for focusing and keeping children with AD/HD on task. Essentially, the principles behind keeping attention on task are to give almost immediate feedback to the learner and to make sure the tasks are varied and interesting.

PROVIDE NONDISTRACTING WRITTEN WORK

The written material that is given to the student should not distract from the purpose of the activity. Sometimes artists of school materials want to make them more esthetically pleasing, so they use a special color or design to highlight items. These additions may be distractions for the concrete learner.

Sometimes there are just too many pictures in one area. I found that the Richard Scarry books that I had read and looked at with my other children were just too busy for my son with Down syndrome. Watch the student's eyes. If they dart back and forth or if he is unable to locate a prominent feature on the paper, take a look at the materials and see if they have too many distracting elements. One thing you can do to minimize distractions is cut a hole in a sheet of paper, cover the picture, and show him only one part of it at one time.

If you are preparing written work for the student, use your computer or copy machine to make things larger, even if it takes two sheets instead of one. It is better to have fewer math problems on a page and leave more space for the student to write in the answers. Make sure that the print quality is dark, crisp, and legible, so that the student does not have to guess whether a number is a seven or a one, or whether he is looking at a picture of a nickel or a quarter.

A study done in the United Kingdom (Wolpert, 1996) with ninety teachers who had students with Down syndrome in general classrooms found that workbooks were not useful at all. The authors felt that the workbooks were either heavily dependent on language comprehension or had too many distractions or problems on a page, which made it confusing for students with Down syndrome. The teachers felt that the most effective materials for instruction were concrete objects or manipulatives which the student had to use to perform an activity.

Don't give too many directions at the same time when explaining how to do the written work. Processing multi-step directions can defeat a student at the very start. Write the instructions on the work sheet, especially if it is going home. Parents will often help at home, but not if they can't understand what has to be done.

<table>
<tr><td>

MINIMIZE FINE
MOTOR
DEMANDS

</td><td>

Fine motor problems can make it harder and more tiring for children with Down syndrome to hold a pencil and form numbers. When their hands get tired, they can rapidly lose interest in a written assignment. For this reason, you should minimize the amount of copying (from the board or book) you ask the student to do. Whenever possible, it is preferable for an adult to copy down the problems or to use photocopied pages that the student can write on.

</td></tr>
</table>

When it is essential for the student to copy problems himself, be aware that students with Down syndrome often have problems with writing down number problems. The *ones* may be put under the *tens* column, the numbers may not be recognizable, or the decimal points may be lost. Use large graph paper so that the student writes one digit in each square and lines them up. A computer program, *Access to Math* (Mac only) from Don Johnston makes worksheets for you where the numbers are always lined up and shaded areas tell you where the totals should go. See illustration below. (*Access to Math* also prints a worksheet with the right answers for the teacher or parent.)

More information on adaptations for students who have problems physically writing numbers are in Chapter 11.

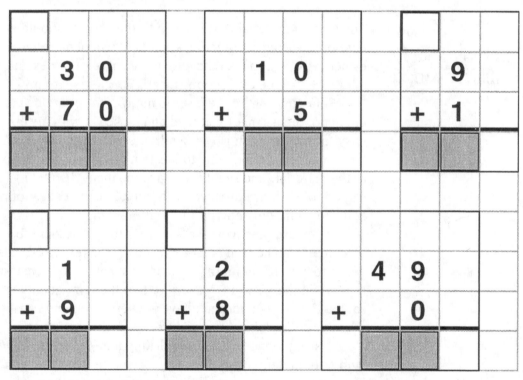

Addition of one and two digit numbers.

<table>
<tr><td>

GIVE SIMPLE,
CLEAR
HOMEWORK

</td><td>

Homework sometimes becomes a source of friction between school and home. The work sent home for math homework should always be something that the student has already learned. Parents should be reinforcing what the student has learned at the school, not teaching him what he didn't pick up in school that day. If the concept has really been learned in class, the student with Down syndrome should be responsible for doing some of each type of problem, but not necessarily the same amount of work given to typical students. Students with fine motor difficulties who have to spend excessive amounts of time writing recognizable numbers should be

</td></tr>
</table>

allowed to do only a representative number of problems, fewer than the rest of the class.

If a student has really worked hard at a subject for twenty or thirty minutes (depending on his age) and doesn't seem to understand the assignment, Mom or Dad should have an agreement with the teacher that he can stop work. They should then send a note explaining that the student has worked hard for twenty or thirty minutes straight and still does not understand. Ask the teacher to explain and demonstrate again to the student what is expected. This will lower the frustration level at home—for student and parents. Parents have to resist the temptation to do the problems for their child. The teacher will not know what areas need to be re-taught if he brings in work he hasn't done himself. (However, it may be acceptable for you to write down your child's answers for him if his hand gets too fatigued.)

Parents can help by having a consistent time for homework that doesn't compete with favorite TV shows or outdoor play. Homework should not be a constant time for conflict between student and parents. If homework is creating such trouble at home, parents, teacher(s), and the student need to talk together and work out some solutions.

> *Rushing out the door, Mrs. Landon said, "I have to go home now. It is Heidi's homework time, and nothing happens if I am not there. I am just getting to hate the time after supper at my house. I don't know how much help to give. Sometimes she says, 'I can do it myself,' and sometimes she says, 'You never help me.'"*

EXPECT AND WORK TOWARD APPROPRIATE BEHAVIOR

Sometimes it is the student's behavior that keeps him from learning. Appropriate behavior is not an area where we can give a few tips that will fit all students who are concrete thinkers. You need to step back, look at the disturbing behavior, and find out what is causing it. That may be something that happened immediately before he screamed and kicked, but you must also look at what has happened further back in time. Also important is to find out what function the screaming and kicking behavior serves for the child. (There is a whole philosophy of looking at behavior that is called positive behavioral support, and one of its chief tools consists of doing a functional behavioral assessment.) Then you have to look to see what happens to the child after his meltdown and see if his behavior is reinforced by the consequences.

For example, Charlie started screaming and kicking today when you closed his book and steered him over to the table for math. Closing the book and steering him over to the table was the immediate trigger for his misbehavior. However, we don't know why he did it. We don't know the function that the meltdown behavior serves for Charlie. Does he get total class attention? Is that what he is trying for? Has he been so frustrated with his last couple math sessions that he wants to get out of the whole situation? Does he get to skip math when he screams? Was he so absorbed in looking at the pictures in the book that he was really upset with having the book closed so abruptly? Did he have enough warning about the coming change? Does he have a schedule to follow? Has everything up to this time been off-schedule and confusing?

You can see that without knowing why Charlie is screaming and what he gets for the behavior, you can't work on his behavior in an effective manner. You need to look at:

1. What happens immediately before the behavior?
2. What happens to Charlie when he behaves in this way?
3. What has Charlie's experience been with the math activity for the last week or so?
4. What function does the behavior serve for Charlie?
   - Does he get attention from the class, parent, or teacher that he enjoys?
   - Does he get out of doing the task he has been given?
   - Does he get to return to a more pleasurable activity?
   - Does his behavior stop a physical sensation he does not like (such as the teacher touching his shoulder)?
   - Especially if he has an autism spectrum disorder, does moving from the floor to the table stop some relaxation movements that he needs to be able to focus?
   - How can we satisfy the need that Charlie is showing with his behavior in a positive way?

Sources for information on Positive Behavioral Support (PBS) are found under "Organizations" in the Resources.

A study was done in the United Kingdom (Wolpert, 1996) which surveyed 90 parent/teacher pairs about the inclusion of students with Down syndrome in regular classrooms. The students had an average age of 9.3 years and a grade level of 3.8. When asked about behavior management strategies used in the classroom, participants said the most successful method was praise from the teacher. Threat of lower grades was not an effective motivator for students with Down syndrome to work harder. Punishment and ignoring inappropriate behavior were also considered ineffective for behavior or instruction. The researchers felt that the children were probably not able to connect their behaviors with the consequences.

The teachers felt that the most effective way to correct behavior was to calmly point out what behavior was not appropriate and the consequences. Consistent follow-through on classroom rules was also essential.

Token systems based on positive actions have been successful for many students with learning difficulties, but may work best if the whole class is on the system. Token systems may also work in a family, where the children get tokens such as stickers for desired behaviors and receive some reward at designated times (such as after 10 stickers). Privileges can often be used as rewards more easily in families than in classrooms because of school principles or rules.

When working one-on-one with a student, I sometimes got a frown, a head down on the table, and a refusal to do any more. I might set a puppet up on a pop bottle and give the instructions to the puppet and laugh and tease it just as if the puppet was a student. Often that is enough to get the student to look up and try. Sometimes I have to say something that is absolutely wrong, and the student can't resist correcting me. My son and his buddies (all young adults) can be kidded about being grouchy. I imitate what they look like (exaggerating, of course), and they usually start giggling and get back to work.

Working with a student at home does not always bring out the best behavior in him. Sometimes children have a difficult time interacting with mother or father as a parent *and* as a teacher. This is especially true if one parent does all the teaching. It does get frustrating when your child can't remember something that you thought he understood perfectly yesterday. It is common for irritation to creep into your voice, although you may not be aware of it. If you find yourself feeling irritated frequently, your child will probably respond better if you bow out and let the other parent do some of the teaching.

Other children in the family can also help for short, directed lessons. You need to monitor their teaching so it is positive and directed toward the proper goals. I recently came upon some notebooks I had written when my son Scott was younger. I had detailed directions for my daughter Heidi to give lessons on sorting and matching to Scott. I remember that those directions were written one summer that I gave my daughter the equivalent of the pay she would have made in a fast food job for babysitting and teaching Scott. She learned teaching skills and got closer to her brother Scott. Scott used to say that he had a mommy and a daddy and a Heidi—which he thought of all in a similar way.

It is possible that your child just will not accept you as a teacher. That is all right. Your most important role must be as a parent. You may be able to find a tutor or an interested neighbor who can teach your child using this book. You also might be able to arrange some individual time with a teacher to use the one-on-one activities given in the book. I usually put on a funny-looking hat when I worked with Scott as a teacher. I told him to call me Mrs. Horstmeier, not Mom, when I was being his teacher. For academics, this seemed to work well. However, when I tried the same approach to teach him to play the piano, it really bombed! Luckily, I found a piano teacher who stepped in successfully.

ENSURE EARLY SUCCESS IN THE LESSON

Success is very important at every level of teaching for students with Down syndrome. The steps in teaching should be very small, and each one should be praised for effort, if not correctness. As the students get older, they often meet with frustration as they try to do what others do. They may give up very soon because it is better *not* to do the activity than to do the activity and fail. Sometimes the students who are higher functioning are more aware of those discrepancies than those who are lower functioning, and, consequently, feel more stress about the situation.

I have tried to include a "success step" before each major learning activity in this book. That is, I recommend a relatively easy activity related to the new skill for the student to complete at the beginning of the lesson. It will only be a success step if the student is able to do it easily. Do not hesitate to change the step to something you know that the student can do well. You may find that some of the activities jump too quickly from one step to another. By observing the student, you can tell whether an intermediate step is needed and can act to preserve the feel of success. Don't hesitate to try your own intermediate step.

Of course, we do not want students so dependent on praise that they can't function without it. In the 1970s, many professionals went overboard on giving praise. "Good talking, good creeping, good eating…" could be heard from many preschool and elementary school classrooms. I felt my son got to be a "junkie" on praise for everything. Some of this praise can actually present a barrier for meaningful communication. If you are saying "Good talking," you are not responding to the content of the student's message in a meaningful way.

As we get older, we are able to see our own accomplishments and get satisfaction from them. We learn that in most work environments, "No news is good news." But even adults need occasional quiet praise for their self-esteem. So, we should sincerely praise our students but also teach them to feel good about their own success. When Scott was younger, I would say to him, "Don't you feel good when you can do that correctly? " Often now, he says quietly to himself, "I did it !" when he has accomplished something.

CONSIDER USING PEER TUTORS

Both parents and teachers in the U.K. study mentioned above felt positive about peer tutors. In fact, the teachers of sixth grade and higher reported that peer intervention worked better than teacher assistance. In the upper grades, students are striving for more independence, and being helped by a friend was perceived as better than being helped by a teacher or aide.

However, peer tutoring should be organized with care. When the students are in first grade or below, they should be just helping each other, not having a peer-tutor relationship. When a peer is actually doing tutoring in an academic subject, the teacher should carefully select the tutor and actually teach him or her some teaching techniques. See if you can enlist a "laid-back" student with a sense of humor and the ability to follow directions. I have the tutor observe a session when I am working directly with the child to model the teaching strategies.

After the first one or two tutoring sessions, the teacher should talk to both students individually about the relationship and the skills learned. The tutor may be puzzled about problems he or she has encountered, and the tutee needs to know that he is expected to study and work with his peer tutor. It is important to look at what goes on in the tutoring session. I have seen sessions where the tutor makes fun of the student he is supposed to be helping, which is exactly the opposite of the effect we are hoping to create.

If you are working at home, it might be helpful to have a sibling for a classmate and even have the sib do a little tutoring. My two oldest children did a good job of tutoring Scott, but his brother just three years older was too caught up in sibling rivalry to create a positive atmosphere. He did, however, enjoy playing math games with Scott.

FACILITATE SHORT- AND LONG-TERM MEMORY

Assist the student to facilitate short- and long-term memory storage by musical or rhythmic associations with the concepts, concrete visualizations, creative practice, and the use of mnemonics.

Music is an excellent way to help students memorize numbers and important concepts. Many children (and adults) can remember the tune and the lyrics to a song that teaches a concept. Think of counting songs like "One Little, Two Little, Three Little Tigers," "Ten Little Monkeys Jumping on the Bed," and "This Old Man." Parents and teachers can make up teaching verses to many common childhood songs. It is important to remember that the tune should be simple and easy to sing so that the emphasis is on learning through the words. See Chapter 7 for suggestions of counting songs.

A chanting rhythm can also be used to help memory storage. For example, Jan Semple, in her book, *Semple Math* (1986), has the students chant, "Numbers together go plus, plus, plus," as they tap their pointer fingers together and make the plus sign.

Concrete visualizations of objects and pictures help students make a visual picture in their minds. We found that many students needed to see the passage of time on a round analog clock even though they could read the time on a digital clock. Likewise, many people picture a cut-up pie or pizza when they think about fractions. Actual manipulation of the materials in problem solving adds the tactile sensation of touching to the visual learning.

Mnemonics, making picture associations with the numbers and concepts, is also a helpful strategy. For example, we easily remember the shape of Italy because we have learned to associate its looks with a boot. Some older school classes share mnemonic strategies that help them remember important items. When reading a word problem that included the word *together,* one student observed, "*Together* starts with *t* and that looks like a + (plus) sign for addition."

Try some of the memory strategies suggested in this book and create ideas tailored to the student's own interests. The student can then choose the strategies that work best for him.

Short reviews at the beginning of each class period will help to make important facts automatic. Practice also should be introduced in a fun way with varied and creative activities. Ideally, each student should learn the addition and subtraction facts 1 to 20 by heart, although this is not an essential skill for survival. That way, simple calculations can be done without paper, pencil, or calculator. Most individuals with Down syndrome will need to practice and practice the simple addition and subtraction facts if they are be useful in this way.

USE THE CALCULATOR EARLY AND FREQUENTLY

When pocket calculators first became widely available, typically developing students weren't usually allowed to use them much before middle school, on the grounds that early calculator use might interfere with learning math facts. However, an analysis of many research studies (Hembree & Dessart, 1986) has concluded that use of a calculator, along with traditional math instruction, improved the average student's ability to do pencil-and-paper calculations and to problem solve. The National Council of Teachers of Mathematics (1989, 2001) has suggested putting less emphasis on paper-and-pencil calculations and to use more technology.

I have noticed that many adults with Down syndrome do not use much mental math in everyday situations, perhaps because of working memory problems. They can, however, be taught to use calculators well. If some individuals with cognitive disabilities, especially those with Down syndrome, are not able to use mental math in a practical way, why not teach them to use the calculator from a young age?

All the activities that specifically use the calculator are indicated by the symbol below. See Chapter 5 for a discussion of the  importance of introducing the calculator early. After Chapter 8, the numeral recognition chapter, you should be having your student(s) use the calculator to check what you are doing with the concrete materials, and checking the calculator answers with concrete materials. Use of the calculator should be automatic for any appropriate math situation.

MAKE YOUR INTERACTIONS ENJOYABLE

Children with Down syndrome usually enjoy social interactions with adults and other children. They are often eager to please. Make your teaching fun and indicate your pleasure in working with them. As they approach school age, they often can be motivated by mild competition. If there are no other children present, challenge the student to compete with you. Of course, you will not always win, and you are *so* surprised that he has learned so much. Use humor as much as you can. Children with Down syndrome often have a broad sense of humor and you can dispel their grouchy mood with gentle teasing.

USE THE COMPUTER

Most computer programs are not designed to teach math but instead provide practice for concepts that have already been learned. The color and graphics in these programs usually get the student's attention immediately. Then the immediate feedback for right or wrong answers can keep him on the learning track. Practice-type programs can usually be taught to the student in one session, and he can work independently from then on. Working with devices such as the calculator and the computer seem to be intrinsically interesting to children with Down syndrome and other concrete learners. They see color and graphics in front of them and they get immediate feedback on their answers.

Other computer programs do some teaching, especially if the student is told the correct answer after one or two tries. The computer is definitely not a substitute for a teacher, and it takes a teacher to set up the situation so that the computer session is productive. However, allowing the computer to do the teaching now and then can be a welcome change for both the teacher and the student, as well as being good motivation for needed practice. Computer software is continually changing, but a few good programs will be listed in the Resources section.

BREAK THE TASK DOWN INTO SMALL STEPS

I have tried to break down the goals and tasks in this book into small steps that can be mastered easily. However, every student will learn in his own way. I'm sure that you will find times when this particular student just can't make the next step in the math goals. You will have to find a way to make the task shorter or less complex or try a completely new activity. Most parents and teachers who know how this student learns best can find a simpler or more effective way to teach the concept. Try it. Breaking down or modifying a task is a lot easier than most people think.

Adaptations and Modifications to General Classroom Work

In the early elementary years, it is possible that some children with Down syndrome may be able to do exactly the same work in math class as the other students. By second or third grade, however, almost all students with Down syndrome or other students who are concrete thinkers will need *adaptations* in the way math is taught or in how the student shows his learning. There will probably need to be some *modifications* in the content of what the student will be learning as he gets to the higher grade levels.

It is beyond the scope of this book to go into great detail about ways to make math work more appropriate for students with disabilities. I do want to stress the importance of determining the most appropriate adaptations for your child and spelling them out in his IEP. With increasing numbers of children with Down syndrome being included in general education, you cannot count on your child's teacher having the special education training to know how to modify classroom demands for your child. There are books dedicated to helping teachers modify the curriculum in the general classroom (Blenk, 1995; Hammekan, 1995, Beninghof, 1998; and Stainback & Stainback, 1992). (See References.) One of the most frequently mentioned programs is explained in the book, *Adapting Curriculum and Instruction in Inclusive Classrooms: A Teacher's Desk Reference* (Ebeling, D.G., Deschenes, C. & Sprague, J., 1994) from the Institute for the Study of Developmental Disabilities, Indiana University. This book and staff development kit categorizes nine types of adaptations:

1. **Size**—reduce the number of items
2. **Time**—extend amount of time for test or assignments
3. **Level of support**—provide more assistance
4. **Input**—modify the way the instruction is given to the student (for example, read the problems aloud to him, or provide manipulatives)
5. **Difficulty**—make the problems easier (for example, by using a calculator or simplifying the rules of a math game)
6. **Output**—adapt how the student reports his learning (for example, using stamps or labels with numbers printed on them, rather than writing them, or having an aide write down the student's answers)

7. **Participation**—the student participates in only part of the task (for example, the student could gather data about favorite ice cream flavors with the other students, but then not figure out what percentage like vanilla best)
8. **Alternate goals (modifications of classroom goals)**—have less complex goals than the rest of the class (for instance, learning single-digit subtraction instead of three-digit subtraction)
9. **Substitute curriculum and goals**—student has different instruction and activities for his specific goals

Because I have found that I often need reminders of each student's special needs, adaptations, and modifications, I have compiled a checklist that can be filled out at the beginning of the year for each student and given to all other teachers involved. I have modified the checklist to be more specific to mathematics education.

Parents can send the checklist to their child's teacher or bring it to the IEP meeting and discuss the most appropriate adaptations to help their child. You have the most accurate, complete knowledge of your child and can be of real assistance to the school.

Student Name: _____ Date: _____

Checklist for Adaptations and Modifications to the General Curriculum

The following adaptations are appropriate and necessary for this student. Check all that apply.

Pacing

___ Extend time requirements
___ Vary activity often
___ Allow more breaks for student
___ Omit timed assignments
___ Work on vocabulary before lesson
___ Pick out only major concepts for learning

Environment

___ Reduce/minimize distractions
___ Provide extra paper and pencils close to student

Presentation of subject matter

___ Teach to student's learning style
    ___ Visual
    ___ Auditory
    ___ Tactile-kinesthetic
    ___ Experiential

Such as:

- Use visual whenever possible
- Use visually colorful computer programs
- Use pictures and mnemonics for memory
- Use chants or songs
- Use sand or Kool Aid in a pan for writing
- Use manipulatives and hands-on activities
- Write with finger on desk when learning
- Wet writing on chalkboard
- Practice with board games

Type of instruction

___ Individual and small group instruction
___ Functional application of academic skills
___ More review
___ Move around the room to gather information
___ Errorless learning

Materials

___ Large print
___ Arrangement of nondistracting material on page
___ Calculator for all math
___ Graph paper
___ Computer (not just as reward)

Assignments

___ Visual daily schedule
___ Calendars and assignment books
___ Use written back-up for oral directions
___ Request parent reinforcement
___ Reduce paper and pencil tasks
___ Shorten assignment
___ Lower difficulty level

Testing and proof of learning

___ Provide thorough reviews before tests
___ Oral testing
___ Correct missed problems for extra credit
___ Test administered by aide or special ed person

Continued on next page . . .

Social interaction support

___ Peer advocacy

___ Shared experiences in school

___ Extracurricular activities

___ Structure activities to foster social interaction

___ Train peer tutors

___ Debrief peer tutors

Motivation and positive climate

___ Offer choice

___ Planned motivating sequence of activities

___ Mostly positive reinforcement

___ Verbal praise

___ Concrete reinforcement, if needed

___ Set up token system

___ Use strengths/interests often

___ Cultivate a general positive attitude

Individual hints for working with this student:

_____

_____

_____

_____

_____

_____

Assessment for Basic Math Survival Skills

Chapter 4 / Questions to be answered:

1. How do you decide where to start a student in this book?

2. What is the Pre- /Post Checklist used for?

3. Why use an Informal Assessment?

4. Do you have to score the Informal Assessment?

5. What skills can be assessed in game or hands-on activity format?

How Do You Decide Where to Start a Student in This Book?

Determining what math activities to give to a student you are just beginning to work with can be done in three ways:
1. Start at the beginning of the book.
2. Use the Pre- /Post Checklists at the beginning of each chapter.
3. Do the Informal Assessment in this chapter.

START AT THE BEGINNING

If your child is young and has not had much training in math concepts, start at Chapter 6, try out the activities and games, and enjoy yourself. You may be able to try these activities for the first time when your child is about two or three, or once she is able to indicate a choice or answer by pointing or some other nonverbal method. If you find that your child already understands one of the skills you are doing, drop it and go on to the next activity. The chapters are mostly hierarchical, with one chapter building on the previous chapter. However, many activities in Chapters 6, 7, and 8 can be done together because their skills are interwoven. You will want to be working on calculator skills along with all the chapters from Chapters 9 through 20.

Some students in the upper elementary grades, middle, and high schools may have had so little exposure to math concepts or have had so much frustration with doing math that you might want to just start from the beginning of the book and do each chapter. If you find that they understand a concept, just skip ahead.

USE THE PRE-/POST CHECKLISTS

If you know the student's skills quite well, just look at the Table of Contents to see the skills that are taught in the book. Estimate where the student needs to start and turn to that chapter. At the beginning of each teaching chapter (6 through 20), there is a list of tasks that the student should be able to do once she has mastered the skills taught in that chapter. For example, Chapter 12, Ordering and Comparing Numbers, asks if the student can:

___ Use ordinal numbers to order objects (first through fifth)
___ Use sequence of numbers to find specific numbers
(i.e., find specific page in a book)
___ Name *one more* or *one less* than any number up to 20

Each one of the items in the checklist describes an objective that will be taught in that chapter. Suppose that the student easily names the ordinal positions in a line of ten people. You would check off that item and not teach the activities in that section. However, you may have noticed that if she opens the book in the middle, she does not know what direction to turn the pages to get to a higher number. She does not know how to use sequence to find a specific number, so you would teach the activities and games about using sequence. If you have worked with the student for some time, you may be able to easily place her in the activities. However, if you are not sure what she can do in that specific area, you can assess her on that one area. Look at the teaching section of the chapter for ideas on how to determine whether she has the skill. Then just continue teaching the skills she has not mastered. In general, the chapters get more advanced as they get higher in number.

USE THE INFORMAL ASSESSMENT

The informal assessment is very useful if you are not sure what the student's skills are. It is called an *informal assessment* because it is given for diagnostic purposes only. Therefore, no age norms or grade levels will be given. The assessment is given in mostly a game format. Some students who have had difficulties with math respond poorly to written tests. Most will enjoy the game format and will be more motivated to succeed without feeling pressure. Some of the young adults I have worked with would *not* take another test because, they said, "I'm out of school now." Younger children can probably attend longer with a game format.

Most of the assessment information will come from observing the student. Each section is quite flexible so that the person doing the assessing does not have to use specific words or follow a specific order of items. Not every area covered in the book is tested in this informal assessment. Only the key areas are assessed. After giving the assessment, look at the chart labeled "Matching Scores to Chapters" at the end of Chapter 4. This chart is a list of chapters to work on aligned with the skills assessed in the Informal Assessment.

Informal Assessment

ADMINISTRATION

It is usually better to split the assessment into short periods over the course of two or three days. The actual board games should be played to completion so the students feel that they are playing real games. The Earn and Pay board game gives the most assessment information of all the games. If you have limited time, play that game first. Each game section has a scoring chart at the end of that section which also indicates what skills have been assessed. You only need to give those parts of the informal assessment that are appropriate for the individual student's skills.

SCORING

You really do not have to score this assessment, especially if you have only one student. If you note the areas where the student has difficulties, it may not be necessary to record any scores. If you work with several students, or if you need numerical scores to show growth, the scoring system is very simple.

TASK	POINTS
Student attempts task but does it incorrectly	1 point
Student does the skill inconsistently or prompted	2 points
Student does the task correctly after training* *Teacher demonstrates skill, gives the same item again (slightly modified by changing a number) and student succeeds. Usually the areas that the student can do with training are the first areas that you target for teaching because they will likely be the most successful.	2T points
Student does the task correctly without assistance	3 points

You may score the student by recording her scores in the boxes that follow each game. If you have several students, you can photocopy the scoring sheets for each student. If you have many students, you may want to use the Summary Sheet at the end of Chapter 4 that puts all the scores together in less space.

Using the "Matching Scores to Chapters" chart (pages 49-50), find the name of the chapter(s) in which the needed skill is taught. Check the student's learned skills on the Pre- /Post Checklist and begin the teaching.

EARN AND PAY BOARD GAME

OBJECTIVE: To display counting skills, sorting, simple money concepts, addition, and subtraction.

MATERIALS:

- Earn and Pay game from Appendix A, pasted onto the center of a file folder (page 302)
- (or Monopoly Junior or Budget Town)
- Pay and Earn cards from Appendix A (pages 304-308), if possible, copied onto cardstock or heavier paper. (There are two sets of Pay and Earn cards—one with higher prices for older students and one with lower prices for younger students)
- Currency: $1, $5, $10, $20 bills - realistic play money
- One die
- Game markers (small buttons, tokens, pennies, etc.)
- Calculator

PROCEDURE:

1. Copy the game board from Appendix A and paste the pages on the inside of a file folder. Color some of the game board, if possible. If you are going to use the board several times, it would be wise to laminate it.

2. Cut out the Pay and Earn cards. Photocopy the Pay cards on one color of paper and the Earn cards on another color, or paste them onto different colored construction paper. You should be able to tell the Pay cards from the Earn cards when they are placed face down. Put the cards face down on the game board as indicated.

3. Give each player: 5 $1's, 2 $5's, 3 $10's, 2 $20's = $85. The adult must play if there is only one student. The adult also serves as the banker.

4. Have the players throw the die, and the highest number starts first.

5. The first person rolls the die and moves his marker that number of spaces. (The adult should not tell the student how many spaces to move or help her move that number of spaces, unless it is clear the student cannot figure this out herself.) The space landed on will be either a Pay space or an Earn space. The player picks up the top card from either the Pay pile or the Earn pile. (If the player has fine motor problems, the adult can pick up the card so the student can see it.) Be sure to read the description of what the player must pay or earn and have the player say what amount of money she must pay out or earn. The player receives (from the banker) or pays out that amount and is given the Pay or Earn card.

6. Sometimes the mixture of the amount of money needed and the description of what is to happen will be funny—e.g., buy ice cream for $40. Comment on the amounts if they are quite improbable. The corner squares involve some kind of direction such as lose a turn or go back 2 spaces. If the player moves up or back

following one of those directions, she does not pay or earn what is on the square she lands on.

7. The first person to reach the finish line is Winner I. She must throw the exact number needed to land on the finish square.

8. Winner II is the person who has the most money left. Have the players sort their currency in piles by denomination. Have each one separately try to count the number of bills in each pile. See if they can count the ones with one-to-one correspondence.

9. If the students are able to *sort* and *count* accurately as in #8 above, have them use the Money Total Slip found in Appendix A (page 312) to figure the total. See if they can count the $5's by *skip counting* (5-10-15 etc.) See if they can skip count the $10's (10, 20, 30, etc.). See if they can get the *total amount of money* for each pile by using the calculator. Help them with adding up the entire amount, either by calculator or regular addition. You will be learning much about their skills as they figure out how much money they have.

10. Each player parades her playing piece around the board in order (according to their finishes) and counts the number of squares on the board.

SKILLS TO BE ASSESSED:

- **One-to-one correspondence**—You want to see how the student counts the squares on the game trail and counts currency such as 1,10, and 20 dollar bills. The student should say only 1 numeral per square or bill.

- **Counting to 20**—Each player should count the number of squares on the board as if on parade. You can see whether the numeral names and sequence are correct.

- **Spotting**—Along with counting, spotting is necessary for the individual to get a visual picture of the gestalt of the number, not just the individual pieces. When you throw dice, you do not count each spot on the die. You see 4, or the "fourness" of the group of dots. See if the student can call out the number on one die without counting the dots.

- **Sorting**—At the end of the game, the students should separate (sort) their own currency into piles of 1, 5, 10, and 20 dollar bills etc. (If you are not sure whether the student can really sort, have her sort knives, forks, and spoons.)

- **Skip counting by 5's and 10's**—With the piles of sorted currency in front of them, students should skip count the $5 and $10 bills in each pile correctly (5-10-15 or 10-20-30-40).

- **Simple money concepts**—Does the student understand the concepts of paying and receiving money?

- **Next highest dollar strategy**—When the student has to pay for something, does she give the next highest dollar or dollars and expect change back?

- **Simple subtraction**—Can the student tell you how much money she should get back when she gives you the next highest dollar? She may use the calculator.

- **Simple addition**—Can the student add two or more amounts to get the total amount of money she has left? She may use the calculator.

Scoring for EARN AND PAY	POINTS
1. One-to-one correspondence	
2. Counting to 20	
3. Spotting	
4. Skip counting by 5's and 10's	
5. Sorting	
6. Simple money concepts (paying and receiving)	
7. Use of the next highest dollar strategy	
8. Use of simple subtraction for figuring out change from bills (calculator can be used)	
9. Use of addition in figuring out total money left (calculator can be used)	
Note here any calculator use:	

TOP THIS GAME

PURPOSE: Recognizing and naming numbers and knowing which number is the largest.

MATERIALS:

- Playing cards (omitting face cards—Jack, Queen, and King) and changing the Ace to a 1.
  OR
- Flashcards (2 sets) of the numerals 1 – 9. (If the flashcards are not in two different colors, you will not be able to do the sorting task.)

PROCEDURES:

1. Divide the deck into the red cards and the black cards. (If the student does the separating, it may give insight on his or her sorting abilities). Deal 6 cards (if possible, of one color) to each player. The game is easiest with 2 players. If there are 1 or 3 players, the tester will need to play.

2. The purpose of the game is to assess numeral naming and the concept of big and small numbers. We will use the word *largest* to refer to numerals with the highest value.
3. To begin, each player's cards should be in a pile turned face-down in front of her. The first player turns over the first card in her pile and says the numeral. The second person turns over her first card and decides which number is largest. The person with the largest number takes both cards.

4. Then the action is reversed as the second player shows her next card and the first player decides which is the largest number. If both cards are the same number, each player keeps her own card.

   The winner is the one with the most cards after all cards are used or after about 15 minutes.

5. If the players successfully named the numerals and determined which number was larger using single-digit numbers, proceed to assessing knowledge of two-digit numbers. For two-digit numbers, the first player turns over one card that will be in the *tens* place (e.g., 4 tens). He then turns over a second card to be in the *ones* place (e.g., 7 ones). Lay the two numerals next to each other to form a two digit number (e.g., 47). The first player should name the two-digit numeral formed.

6. The other player does the same. The second person says which number is larger and the game continues as with the single digits. Only the person laying out the second set of cards should say which is the larger! Keep refilling the players' cards from the pile of red or black cards not used at the beginning of the game.

Scoring for TOP THIS	POINTS
1. **Single digits** named correctly.	
2. **Two-digit numbers** named correctly.	
3. Knows which single-digit number is the **largest**.	
4. Knows which double-digit number is the **largest**.	

Note: *If you are not sure whether the student can recognize numerals in the teens or understands the pattern of naming numbers from 20 to 30, play the Math Bingo game, below.*

MATH BINGO GAME (OPTIONAL)

PURPOSE: Recognizing numbers given orally from 1 to 50.

MATERIALS:
- Metal-trimmed bingo markers (and magic wand, if possible) needed for Time Bingo given later on. (Available for under $4 in discount stores, or various Internet sites sell them under "bingo chips and wands" from $2 to $5. Information available at bingodabber.com, Mr-Bingo.com, info@bingoshop.com, and BingoCart.com)
- Math Bingo cards (page 313)

PROCEDURE:
1. Numbers are called out just like in adult bingo with the letter and then the number. For example, the teacher calls out M-7 and the student goes to the M column and puts a marker on the 7, if she has it. The column M has the numbers

1-10, column A has 11 - 19, T has 20 – 29, and H has 30 - 39. The tester must keep a list of the numbers he or she calls out so the accuracy can be checked. The transparent bingo chips make this step very easy.

2. To win, the student has to cover all the numerals in one column. At first, only the full column is a winner so that you can identify the group of numbers that give the student the most trouble. You can test just the teen numbers or just the 20s, if that is what you want to find out. The winner gets to pick up the bingo chips with the magnetic wand first.

STICK MANIPULATIVE GAMES

PURPOSE: To do *hands-on* single- and double-digit addition, and single- and double-digit subtraction. Also to determine whether student is able to "count on." See explanation below.

MATERIALS:
- Rubber bands
- Popsicle sticks (craft sticks), tongue depressors, plastic knives, unsharpened pencils, or straws. (Give each student 8 single sticks and a bundle of 10 sticks, secured by a rubber band.) Pretzel sticks can also be used for extra motivation.
- Construction paper. (Give each student 3 pieces of construction paper in 3 different colors to use as mats. One mat should always be the answer mat.)

PROCEDURE:
1. **Single-digit addition**—Put 2 sticks on one mat and 5 sticks on the other mat. Ask the student for the total number of sticks. Have her put the 7 sticks on the answer mat. She may count in any manner to give the answer.

$$2 + 5 = 7$$
Repeat with $4 + 2 = 6$

2. **Double-digit addition**—Repeat above with 11 sticks plus 5 sticks. (10 sticks should be bound together as 1 ten.) Take the rubber band off the bundle of ten and count them so the student can see that there are ten sticks in the bundle. Put the rubber band back on. See if the student *counts on* from 10 or if she needs to take the rubber band off and start counting single sticks from the beginning.

$$\begin{array}{r} 11 \\ + 5 \\ \hline 16 \end{array}$$

3. **Single-digit subtraction**—Give the student 7 sticks and ask her to take away 3. Ask her how many are left.

$$7 - 3 = 4 \qquad\qquad (8 - 2 = 6, \text{ if needed})$$

4. **Subtraction with regrouping/place value**—Give the student one bundle of 10 and 2 single sticks (12). Ask her to give you 5 sticks. Give her permission to take the rubber band off. Then ask her how many are left. (Repeat subtracting 3 from the 12 sticks, if needed.)

5. **Multiple items in addition**—Have the student use the sticks to add three numbers: $1 + 2 + 5 = 8$.

$$(4 + 1 + 6 = 11, \text{ if needed.})$$

Scoring for STICK MANIPULATIVE	POINTS
1. Single-digit addition	
2. Counting-on	
3. Double-digit addition	
4. Single-digit subtraction	
5. Subtraction with regrouping	
6. Multiple-digit addition	

CALCULATOR ANTICS

PURPOSE: To see if the student knows how to use a calculator or can be easily taught by demonstration.

MATERIALS:
- Calculator
- Pencil
- Calculator Antics Worksheet from Appendix A (page 316)

PROCEDURE:
1. This game should be used if the student knows what a calculator is for. Say that you have a game to play using a calculator. Demonstrate several two-digit addition and subtraction problems. Then have the student try.
2. Have the student write the answers on the Calculator Antics Worksheet given below.

Note: If you are not giving the calculator assessment, you will need to have the student write the numerals 0-9 on paper so you can check how she writes numerals.

- **Writing of the numerals:** Check to see how the student writes the numerals in the answers. Note which numerals she does not write correctly on the scoring sheet below. The numerals 2 to 9 are used in the answers.

- **Finding the numerals on the calculator easily:** See if the student can find the numerals on the calculator easily. They are arranged differently from the numerals on the phone. The signs of the operations are placed differently on various calculators so do not expect fluency in finding them.

	Problems Correct	Comments
1. Calculator addition		
2. Calculator subtraction		
3. Handwriting fluency		
4. Ease of finding numerals on calculator		

TIME BINGO

PURPOSE: To see if the student can tell time by the hour and quarter hour.

MATERIALS:
- A commercially-made clock with moveable hands, a teaching clock such as the Judy clock, or a cardboard (or paper plate) clock with moveable hands fastened to the clock with brass paper fastener.
- Time Bingo sheets (page 317)
- Bingo chips—If possible, the clear plastic chips ringed with metal and a magnetic wand. Both younger and older students enjoy picking up the markers with the magnetic wand. The clear plastic markers make it easy to tell if the student is choosing accurately. Stores that carry board games may carry the wands and chips. See Math Bingo game above for other sources of bingo chips and wands.

PROCEDURE:
1. Using the clock with the minute and hour hand, ask the student to make the clock say 1:00. See if she can make the clock say 4:30 and then 6:15. If the student seems to understand the hours and minutes to the quarter hour, have her play the following Time Bingo game.
2. Give each student a Time Bingo sheet. You may make additional sheets by rearranging the written times on a bingo sheet.
3. The sheets have fewer numbers than regular bingo sheets because many children with concrete thinking have difficulty scanning groups of numbers. The assessment is intended to show time telling, not scanning abilities.
4. Read the capital letter at the top of the column and then call out one of the times given on the instruction sheet. The players should point to the correct clock on the Bingo sheet. If they are correct, give them a Bingo marker. The

first player to cover one row is the winner. (Continue with the times for the second winner, etc.)

5. The first winner gets to pick up the bingo markers with the magic (magnetic) wand, then the second winner, etc.

6. You are only taking a small sample of the student's time skills. If the student obviously does not know how to read the clock faces, see if she can point to a number on each clock face on her bingo sheet and get a bingo marker to put on the clock face. You do not score the number pointing as a correct score, but she gets a chance to use the magic wand.

Scoring for TIME BINGO	POINTS
12:00 correct	
6:15 correct	
4:30 correct	
Number of correct clock faces on Bingo card	

OBEDIENCE GAME

PURPOSE: To assess knowledge of coins, measurement, comparative terms, and shapes.

MATERIALS:
- Ruler
- Chips or tokens, optional (10+)—You can use chips from Bingo game or pennies, etc.
- Cardstock models of a circle, triangle, square, and a rectangle (page 319)
- Quarter, nickel, dime, and penny (real)
- Things to build with: Lego, large dice, blocks, or empty boxes with lids
- 3 or 4 boxes with different weights of blocks or other materials in them (Do not make the biggest box be the heaviest)
- Scroll with Obedience Master printed on it (page 320)

PROCEDURE:
1. Tell the students that this game will show how obedient they can be. They must *listen* to the Game Master and follow his or her directions exactly. If the student has been working willingly on the assessment, you can just praise her after each task correctly done. If the student needs extra motivation, give her one token for obeying promptly and doing the task (even if the task is done incorrectly). Keep the tokens in a bowl near you so they can be given immediately.
2. Have one student do the game at a time. An alternate number is given in parenthesis if the student needs to be trained. After every instruction, students must bow and say, "Yes, Game Master." You must insist on this so they get into the

spirit of the game. Correct them if necessary. (If the student can't say the words, just have her bow.)

3. Start by having the materials for the whole game on a table about eight feet away from the student. The Game Master says: "(Student's name), touch the ruler." (This first request is to show the student how the game is played and should be something very easy for the student to do.) Student bows and says, "Yes, Game Master" and touches the ruler. The Game Master says, "You have done well," and gives the student a token, if needed.

4. Proceed to the activities in the sections below:

Measurement: Using the ruler for measuring in inches is the most common type of measurement a student will do.

- The Game Master says, "Take the ruler and measure your shoe in inches."
    The student bows, and says, "Yes, Game Master." She then measures her shoe and tells the Game Master the number of inches.
- The Game Master says, "You have done well" (and gives token). (Repeat for length of pencil, if needed.)

Shapes
- Ask the student to bring you the circle. Student bows and says, "Yes, Game Master" and brings you the circle.
- The Game Master says, "You have done well" (gives a token).
- Then ask the student to bring you the triangle. Student bows and says, "Yes, Game Master" and brings the triangle.
- The Game Master says, "You have done well" (gives a token).
- Repeat with the square.

Coin recognition
- In the same manner as with the shapes, ask the student to bring you the quarter and then the dime and then the nickel. Ask which coin she would like to have most. See if she can tell you why.

Comparative words
- Using blocks, etc., you make a small tower of 3-4 blocks. Tell the student to build you a *taller* tower. The student bows and says, "Yes, Game Master."
- Then she comes to the table and builds the tower. Then you make a 5-block tower and ask her to make a *smaller (or shorter)* tower.
- Then you respond with, "You have done very well. Now you may knock them both down."
- In the same manner, ask the student to bring you the *heaviest* thing (box) on the table. Put different weights of blocks or other materials in the boxes so she cannot judge from the size

of the box, but make the weights quite different from each other. See if she picks up the items to judge their weights. Repeat by asking for the *lightest* box on the table.

5. Final Ceremony: All students stand before the Game Master (with their tokens, if used). You may have them each count their tokens. The Game Master bows low in front of each student, (retrieves his or her chips), and says, "You are now an Obedience Master. *I* bow before *you*." The Game Master then gives each person the Obedience Master award (Appendix A).

Scoring for OBEDIENCE GAME	POINTS
1. Measurement to the nearest inch	

2. Shapes
     circle
     triangle
     square	

3. Coin recognition
     quarter
     nickel
     dime	

4. Comparison words
     taller/smaller or shorter
     heavier/lighter	

OBSERVATION/ INTERVIEW QUESTIONS

If you are the child's parent or are well acquainted with her math abilities, answer the following questions. Otherwise, ask the parent or someone who has worked with the student the following questions:

1. Does the student have trouble remembering **math facts?**
   *(Circle operation: **Addition, Subtraction, Multiplication**)*

2. Does the student do some **math problems "in her head"** without writing or counting fingers, etc.?

3. Does the student have **fine motor difficulties** that make using the calculator, a pencil, or manipulatives very slow or awkward?

Student Name: _____ **Date:** _____

Summary of Informal Assessment

A. EARN AND PAY Board Game

___ 1. One-to-one correspondence

___ 2. Rote counting up to 20

___ 3. Spotting (1-6)

___ 4. Skip counting by 5's

___ 5. Skip counting by 10's

___ 6. Sorting

___ 7. Simple money concepts (paying and receiving

___ 8. Next highest dollar strategy

___ 9. Subtraction for change (calc.)

___ 10. Addition for total (calc.)

B. TOP THIS

___ 1. Single digits named correctly

___ 2. Two digits named correctly

___ 3. Knows which number is largest

C. MATH BINGO (TOP THIS Alternative)

___ 1. Numbers 1-10

___ 2. Numbers 11-19

___ 3. Numbers 20-29

___ 4. Numbers 30-39

D. STICK MANIPULATIVE Activities

___ 1. Single-digit addition

___ 2. Counting on

___ 3. Double-digit addition

___ 4. Single-digit subtraction

___ 5. Subtraction with regrouping

___ 6. Place value for tens, ones

___ 7. Multiple items in addition

E. CALCULATOR ANTICS

___ 1. Calculator addition

___ 2. Calculator subtraction

___ 3. Handwriting fluency

___ 4. Ease of finding numerals

F. TIME BINGO

___ 1. 12:00 correct

     6:15

     4:30

___ 2. Number of correct clock faces

G. OBEDIENCE MASTER Game

___ 1. Measurement to nearest inch

___ 2. Shapes

     Circle

     Triangle

     Square

___ 3. Coin recognition

     Quarter

     Nickel

     Dime

___ 4. Comparison Words

     Taller/smaller

     Heavier/lighter

H. INTERVIEW QUESTIONS

1. Trouble remembering math facts?

2. Can do math "in his/her head"?

3. Fine motor difficulties?

Matching Scores to Chapters

GAME   **CHAPTER in Basic Survival Math**

A. EARN AND PAY Board Game

___ 1. One-to-one correspondence .... Number Sense #7

___ 2. Rote counting up to 20 .... Number Sense #7

___ 3. Spotting (1-6) .... Number Sense #7

___ 4. Skip counting by 5's... More Counting Skills #9

___ 5. Skip counting by 10's.. More Counting Skills #9

___ 6. Sorting .... Prenumbers Concepts #6

___ 7. Simple money concepts (paying and receiving) .... Addition #14, Subtraction #16,
Money #20

___ 8. Next highest dollar strategy .... Money #20

___ 9. Subtraction for change (calc.) .... Subtraction #16

___ 10. Addition for total (calc.) .... Addition #13 and #14

B. TOP THIS

___ 1. Single digits named correctly....................................... Recognition of Numerals #8

___ 2. Two digits named correctly .... Recognition of Numerals #8

___ 3. Knows which number is largest .... More Counting Skills #9,
Place Value #10,
Order/Compare #12

C. MATH BINGO (TOP THIS Alternative)

___ 1. Numbers 1-10 .... Recognition of Numerals #8

___ 2. Numbers 11-19 .... Recognition of Numerals #8

___ 3. Numbers 20-29 .... Recognition of Numerals #8

___ 4. Numbers 30-39 .... Recognition of Numerals #8

___

D. STICK MANIPULATIVE Activities

___ 1. Single-digit addition .... Addition #13 and #14

___ 2. Counting on .... Addition #13

___ 3. Double-digit addition .... Addition #13 and #14

___ 4. Single-digit subtraction .... Subtraction #15 and #16

___ 5. Subtraction with regrouping .... Subtraction #15

___ 6. Place value for tens, ones .... Place Value #10

___ 7. Multiple items in addition .... Addition #13 and #14

Continued on next page . . .

	Matching Scores to Chapters

GAME   **CHAPTER in Basic Survival Math**

E. CALCULATOR ANTICS

___ 1. Calculator addition ....Addition #14

___ 2. Calculator subtraction ....Subtraction #15 and #16

___ 3. Handwriting fluency ....Writing of Numerals #11

___ 4. Ease of finding numerals ....Use of the Calculator #5

F. TIME BINGO

___ 1. 12:00 correct ....Time #17
         6:15
         4:30

___ 2. Number of correct clock faces...................................Time #17

G. OBEDIENCE MASTER Game

___ 1. Measurement to nearest inch.....................................Measurement #18

___ 2. Shapes ....Shapes #19
         Circle
         Triangle
         Square

___ 3. Coin recognition ....Money #20
         Quarter
         Nickel
         Dime

___ 4. Comparison Words ....Measurement #18,
         Taller/Smaller   Ordering Numbers #12
         Heavier/lighter

H. INTERVIEW QUESTIONS

1. Trouble remembering math facts? ....Characteristics #2,
                                                         Teaching Strategies #3

2. Can do math "in his/her head"? ....Characteristics #2

3. Fine motor difficulties? ....Characteristics #2

CHAPTER 5

Use of the Calculator

Chapter 5 / Questions to be answered:

1. Why does this book advocate early and frequent use of the calculator?

2. Why should students who are concrete learners use calculators?

3. What type of calculators can be used?

4. What are the basic principles for using calculators?

Why Does this Book Advocate Early and Frequent Calculator Use?

This book strongly suggests the use of the calculator as soon as the student is introduced to the numerals that are the symbols of our number system. Early and frequent use of the calculator can be a real asset to children who have difficulty with short-term memory and rote learning.

I further recommend that children who are concrete learners be systematically *taught* to use the calculator. A student cannot simply be given a calculator and be told, "Just use this if you are having trouble learning your multiplication facts." He needs to be familiar with the keyboard of the calculator, including the position of the numbers and the operation keys, have experience in entering numbers accurately, and learn what keys *not* to push. But even more importantly, he needs to be taught how to set up the problems that can be solved using the calculator.

Parents and teachers are sometimes worried that students will get so dependent on the calculator that they will not be able to compute without it. For students with Down syndrome and other concrete thinkers, I would not be upset if they understood how to set up a problem, but used the calculator instead of pencil and paper to solve it—and then knew whether their calculations were reasonable. Many adults use the calculator in exactly this manner. You should also know that an analysis of many research studies (Hembree & Dessart, 1986) has concluded that use of a calculator, along with traditional math instruction, improved the average student's ability to do pencil-and-paper calculations and to problem solve.

The National Council of Teachers of Mathematics (1989, 2001) has suggested putting less emphasis on paper-and-pencil calculations for *all* math learners, especially with numbers having more than two digits. They also think that math teachers should help students develop the skills necessary to use appropriate technology and then apply the results to problem situations. The NCTM wrote in the first *Curriculum and Evaluation Standards* (1989), "Appropriate calculators should be available to *all* students at *all* times." The analogy is given that calculators simplify work, much like word processing programs help writers (Smith, 1997). Many adults today, including the author, use calculators when adding several items or when working with numerals with more than two digits.

Why Should Students Who Are Concrete Learners Use Calculators?

Students with Down syndrome frequently have difficulties with short-term and working memory, especially if the occasion is not very meaningful to them. For example, have you ever known a child with Down syndrome to forget his Christmas list or forget when you said you would take him to the zoo? Those kinds of things they remember too well. On the other hand, they often have trouble holding abstract numbers in mind and have even more difficulty with using working memory to tell them what they need to do with those numbers, such as add or subtract.

Tests show that children with Down syndrome have short digit span memories, which means that they can't remember as long a string of numbers as other children the same age. In addition, many students with Down syndrome have difficulty processing the things that they hear. When I talk through a problem situation with concrete materials, some of the students say, "Please put those numbers on the board; I just can't keep them in my head." They are visual and tactile learners who derive meaning from seeing the numerals and from touching them on the calculator. Using the calculator capitalizes on their sensory strengths in learning.

Some students have difficulty with fine motor tasks even up into their adult years. When I worked with my son and his young adult friends on math problems, one individual would spend the whole math period writing down the problems from a math book even though he is fluent with solving them with the calculator. It is easier for most people to press a button than to shape numerals on paper.

Students who are concrete learners, by definition, do not do math "in their heads." They need many activities and much practice to learn the important concepts in math, such as numeral order and the sequence of numbers from 20 on. These fundamental skills need to be "overlearned" so that they come automatically and the student only has to think how to apply them. Therefore, it will probably take more time for them to learn the reduced number of important things that they have to memorize. Summer after summer, I worked with my son using flashcards of addition and multiplication facts so he would not forget them before the fall. Since it didn't work, I was essentially wasting time when I could have been helping him learn to solve real math situations.

Lastly, there is a certain intangible feeling of joy to seeing someone who has previously shied away from numbers start to work on a calculator confidently. When I gave my young adult group a written assessment in simple computation, they complained and fussed and found all sorts of reasons to dawdle. After a short while, I said, "Would you like to use your calculators?" "Of course!" they said. They immediately got to work and did the problems like the young adults they are. The difference in their confidence when they used the calculator was amazing!

What Type of Calculators Can Be Used?

Students with Down syndrome and other hands-on learners need explicit instruction on the use of the calculator. Unfortunately, the keyboard is not set up in the same way as a telephone dial. Even if the students recognize the difference, they may have motor and visual difficulty in pressing the correct numbers.

Using a large-keyed calculator (left) and a talking calculator (right).

When I first began teaching students with Down syndrome, I started with the small calculators (3" x 4½") that have an identical keyboard to the overhead calculator that I use (*Calc-U-Vue*). Most of the students had difficulty accurately entering numbers with those calculators. However, I found that the large (8" by 6"), inexpensive calculators that are often given away by companies were very helpful. The numerals are easy to read and widely separated. The answer window shows large numerals and can be tilted so the teacher can observe the answers of several students at a time.

Of course, after the student is proficient on the large calculator, we want him to get a small calculator that can fit in the pocket or purse. Make sure you get a calculator with the numbers from 0-9 arranged in four lines of three buttons each. An on-off button, the operation signs for addition, subtraction, multiplication, and division, and the clear and the equals sign are essential. Some models have a CE (Clear Entry) button that only clears the window you are presently doing if you make a mistake. That will keep you from having to start all over from the beginning if you make a mistake. Some CE buttons do not have this function.

The M buttons and the square root button are not useful for our purposes and can be a distraction for some students. I cover them up with black electrical tape when necessary. Either solar or battery powered calculators are possible or even a combination of both. I do not recommend using a membrane calculator because the students seem to need the definite edges of a button and the slight soft click to make sure they have entered the number. One of my students with fine motor difficulties did his calculations on a Play Cash Register (Learning Resources) because it was easier to see and to push the numbers.

Another calculator that has proved useful is the talking calculator (PCI Educational Publishing, under $20). It repeats the numbers entered and tells the total. Some students seem to need the reinforcement of hearing that they have plugged in the correct number. Even more advanced students may want to earn a talking calculator. When working with a group, you may find hearing all these numerals distracting. However, my students did not seem to mind, especially when everyone was not on the same problem.

For a student who has difficulty writing, you may use a calculator that has a printer. These calculators print the whole problem out on a roll of white paper, something like an old-time cash register would do.

Most personal computers have a calculator on one of their basic programs. You will have to teach the students how to go through several steps to access the calculator on either a PC or a Macintosh computer. With the adaptations that can be made on computers for fine motor and visual problems (adaptable keyboards, touch screens, etc.), the student may be able to do the work on a computer when other solutions do not work.

A special consideration to bear in mind when you are working on math problems involving prices is that most of our calculators are not set to calculate dollars and cents as we visualize them. If your answer is $10.80, the calculator will show 10.8 in the window. Some students have real difficulty with understanding this concept—which is really just a function of the calculator, not of the math itself. PCI Educational Publishing has a brightly colored calculator called Money Calc ($20-25) which has the option of always showing the money amount correctly (to two decimal places). It also has a button for calculating the tax that can be set for your state percentage. Older students may want to use the Texas Instruments 15 Calculator which can be set to always give 2 decimal places. This calculator has quite a few other buttons and functions that could be distracting, however.

What Are the Basic Principles for Using Calculators?

1. **Make it simple.** Cover unnecessary buttons on the calculator. If necessary, put black tape over all but the number buttons, on/off, clear, and the operations

buttons (+ and -, etc.). In all activities you may want to make sure the materials do not have distracting elements. If you are using written problems, put only a few on each page.

2. **Give the student some time to fool around with the calculator** before you have him do work with it. All of us like to fiddle around with a new toy. If you give some unstructured time for playing, the students will be more apt to use it for work later.

3. **Practice frequently using the keyboard of the calculator** before using it to solve problems. Students may find it easier to punch in a number when you show it visually than when you just say it. Teach students to enter numbers *both* ways. Have the students punch in the numerals and then hold the answer up for you to check. It is important to give the students time to train their motor skills in using the calculator as well as their understanding of how to use it.

4. **Use concrete materials for understanding.** It is very important that the student be given concrete materials to work out the concepts that are being taught. Concrete teaching materials should be used often for better understanding. Tally marks can also be used when appropriate.

5. **Use the calculator to verify.** After the initial concept has been taught, have your student use his calculator to verify the concept that has been worked out in a concrete manner. For example, if you are using manipulatives to teach addition, after the student has counted 5 green and 5 red tokens to reach the answer of 10, have him punch in 5 + 5 on the calculator to verify the answer. Sometimes using manipulatives, making concrete drawings, or drawing tally marks to verify the answer on the calculator will be useful.

6. **Use the calculator as soon as possible.** In this book, I begin suggesting calculator activities in Chapter 8, Recognition of Numerals. (Students must be able to recognize the numerals 1-9 and be able to press one key at a time before learning to use the calculator.) If you have a student who is starting to work on the book at a later chapter, you should introduce him to the calculator right away if he has never used one before.

7. **Get in a rhythm when using calculator.** You can even chant the sequence:
    Three (or whatever the number is) as you push the number 3.
    Look (check the number in the window)
    Plus (or whatever the operation is)
    Five (or whatever the second number is)
    Look (check the number in the window)
    Equals (as you press the = sign) to get the answer

It is very important that you have the students enter the data slowly and check at the window every time. You are not looking for speed, just accuracy. It will take them more time if they have to go back and find where they made a mistake because they hurried.

The rhythm in the chant will also help the students put in the operation sign after each number and end with the equals (=) sign.

8. **Ask whether the answer is reasonable.** Students should know whether the calculated answer is reasonable. This concept takes a good deal of time to learn. Students often don't even think about the answer they give. I tease a little to make them think. "Stephen, do you really want to spend $250 for lunch? What are you going to eat for that amount of money? Doesn't $2.50 sound more reasonable for a lunch?"

9. **Start each lesson with review and a success.** Do a few already learned concepts first, including working on accuracy of data entry. Do not encourage speed, just accuracy. It is important that the student feel good about his ability to do math when you are going to introduce something new.

10. **Teach some other math skills at the same time you introduce the calculator.** During the time you are introducing the calculator, you can assess some of the number sense concepts explained in the Informal Assessment and begin teaching some other needed skills.

11. **When teaching a new operation, use easy numbers.** If you are starting subtraction, use simple numbers (9 and 5, not 43 and 14). The student should not have to focus on two difficult concepts at one time. It is a good rule of thumb to use numbers under 20 when you are teaching a new concept.

12. **Use currency (bills) before coins.** Do not use dollars and cents until the concept is learned, and the student has had much practice on the operation. Use dollar bills for money problems at the beginning. Only go to coins and their equivalents after the student is fluent with currency. If you use only currency at first, you will not get mixed up with decimals and the cents sign ($.57 or 57 cents).

13. **Use real situations (not word problems).** Act out or explain authentic situations that could happen in class or at home. Discuss the situations with the students. Get the students to tell you what the operation will be. I have a little slate board that I write the numbers on because after they have figured out that they need to subtract, they have often forgotten what the numbers were. A pad of paper or a dry erase board can be used in the same manner. Be sure to make the numbers large and clear. Don't use possible situations that may come up in the future until the student is in secondary school or able to read and understand word problems.

14. **Consider stipulating in the student's IEP that a calculator is to be used for tests.** The rule of thumb for state testing is that the accommodation (using the calculator) should not be used if the assessment is trying to assess that particular skill. That is, if the test is assessing whether the student has

learned the addition facts, he should not be allowed to use a mechanical aid such as a calculator because that will make it impossible to determine whether he has learned those facts. If the skill being assessed is solving a word problem, he is being judged on his problem solving skill and not on his addition facts, so he should be allowed to use the calculator. The statement in the student's IEP that he may use a calculator when the basic calculating skills are not being assessed will give him a chance to show his basic problem solving skills without being short circuited by his problems with short-term memory. This student should also be using the calculator in daily assessments, not just for large scale testing.

CHAPTER 6

Prenumber Concepts

Pre- /Post Checklist

Can the student:

1. _____ Find the bigger item in comparisons of two items.

2. _____ Identify which group (of 2) has more items (less items).

3. _____ Identify same and different using objects and pictures.

4. _____ Match identical objects and pictures.

5. _____ Sort items by basic colors (red vs. yellow).

6. _____ Sort items by shapes and sizes (round vs. square and small salad forks vs. dinner forks).

7. _____ Sort items by type of item (plates vs. spoons, etc.).

Many people think of math skills as only involving numbers and quantities. However, before you can count, add, measure, or do anything else with numbers, you have to learn certain "prenumber" concepts. For instance, you can't begin to be able to count how many red circles there are until you can recognize both *red* and *circles*. Or you can't tell someone how tall your block tower is unless you know what the word *tall* means.

Children begin to develop some prenumber concepts even before they start counting. They know that some things are heavier or bigger than others, and they may understand the concept of *more*. Many children with Down syndrome learn some math comparison words such as *big* and *little, up* and *down, fast* and *slow, hot* and *cold,* and other simple word pairs from others around them. Others need these concepts to be deliberately demonstrated and taught to them. Sometimes it may be difficult to see these early experiences as forming a base for math, but they do form the cognitive foundation skills that are important for learning math concepts.

Another essential concept is that of sorting or simple classification. If we want to be able to count how many girls are in the family or in the class, we first have to classify the individuals as either girls or boys. Classification is needed to tell us *what* to count. To sort or classify, we also need to pay attention to the details of items and determine whether they are the same or different from each other. Therefore, it is important to learn to distinguish same and different items, and progress to matching, sorting, and classifying them.

The beginning math concepts that will be covered in this chapter are:

- **Simple comparisons**
  - ▾ More or less
  - ▾ Big (a lot) or little (tiny)
  - ▾ Same or different
- **Matching identical items**
- **Simple classification (sorting)**
  - ▾ By color
  - ▾ By size
  - ▾ By other characteristics

Simple Comparison

In the beginning, you do not need to teach your child many comparison words. You just want her to look at a few things and develop an early understanding of quantity. Which one has more? Which one is bigger? The most basic comparison is seeing that one item is bigger than the other is or that one group of things has more than the other. You can begin to talk about the subject when your child is very young. The commonly used game of saying "So...big" while raising the arms up is a possible start. Just talking about *big* things and *little* things with your child in everyday experiences probably teaches the concept best.

You can try some of these simple comparisons when your child is between one and two years of age. If she is not interested, don't force the issue, just continue pointing out comparisons in daily conversation. Or watch a television show such as *Sesame Street,* which shows a lot of colorful comparisons, if your child focuses in on that program.

BIG OR LITTLE

OBJECTIVE: The child will compare two items where one is roughly twice the size of the other and be able to identify which one is *bigger.*

MATERIALS:
- A big box and a small box (if possible, the same color)
- A big book and a little book
- Dad's shoe and child's shoe (if the child could identify them both as shoes)

SUCCESS STEP: Have the child identify both boxes by pointing or naming (Say, "What is this?" or "Show me a box.") Praise her by saying something like, "Right. You did great!"

PROCEDURE:
1. Put the two boxes in front of the child. Ask her to point to the *big* one. If she is correct, praise her. If not, hold the big box closer to her and the smaller box behind it and repeat.
2. Try the same procedure with the big and little books and big and little shoes.

> *Emily looks at her Dad's big shoe and her own little shoe that are placed before her. Her mother asks her which is the big shoe. Emily shakes her head and says, "My shoe." She picks it up and tries to put it on her foot. Her mother realizes that Emily has not responded to the word big but is focused on the possession of her own shoe. Her mother changes the items to a complete Sunday newspaper vs. a half page of the newspaper. Emily then responds to the word big as applied to the newspaper.*

GENERALIZATION INTO DAILY ACTIVITIES: Now it is important to show your child big and little objects in her own world. The items should be quite similar except for size. You might try to show *big* and *little* in helpings of food. At first make comments about things that are *big* or *little*. For instance, "Wow, Dad took a *big* serving of mashed potatoes. Mine is little!" Later you may have your child participate by asking, "Can you point to the *big* helping of mashed potatoes?" You can also give her opportunities to make a choice between big and little. "Do you want a *big* piece of paper or a *little* one? A *big* crayon or a *little* one?"

MORE

OBJECTIVE: The child will compare two groups of items where one group has roughly twice as many items as the other and identify which one has *more*.

Note: *When children first learn to use the word more—especially if they are learning to sign—they use it to request more of something they already have. For example, requesting more food or toys implies a desire for an additional quantity of what the child already has (more banana). She can't have more bananas until she has had some banana. The activity in this section is not focused on this meaning of more, but instead on the concept of comparing two groups to see which group has more items or a larger quantity than the other.*

MATERIALS:
- Blocks of the same size
- Poker chips of one color or pennies
- Dry macaroni (or other small items your child will not try to eat)

PROCEDURE:

1. Build two towers with blocks or with poker chips. One should be much taller than the other. Count the chips or blocks aloud as you make the towers. Ask your child which tower has *more* chips or blocks. If she is correct, let her crash down the bigger tower. If she guesses wrong, say something like, "No, *this* one has more. Look how *big* it is. The other tower is *little*." Repeat as needed. If your child enjoys building, challenge her to make a tower with *more* blocks than yours.

2. Put a few pieces of dry macaroni in one of her hands and put much *more* macaroni in the other hand. Ask her which hand has *more*. Repeat several times. Then see if she can put more macaroni in one of your hands than in the other. This is harder than looking at the two amounts and judging which has more. If she is not able to do it, try it again in a month or two.

COMMERCIAL GAME TO BUY OR TRY

If your child is beyond the stage of putting everything into her mouth, you may want to try playing the commercial game Don't Spill the Beans by Milton Bradley (about $7-9). As each person places a plastic bean on the bean cover, she can say, "Now I have more." The next player says, "No, I have more," until the beans spill over.

GENERALIZATION INTO DAILY ACTIVITIES: Your child will learn far more about the concept of *more* in the course of your regular daily living than can be gained from the structured activities given here.

When serving foods to the class or the family, purposefully give a lot more pretzels or other snacks to one child. If your child does not protest that someone else has more, ask her who has more. If she can't recognize this yet, say, "Whoops! I gave Jason *more* than you!" Equalize the quantity of snacks and say that everyone has to have the same. One child (don't include Mom or Dad) can't have *more* in our class or family. Likewise, when you are handing out craft materials, blocks, dominos, or other items, see if your child notices that another child has more than she has.

Parents, help your child to give Dad or an older child *more* of some food and then to tell Dad or brother that he did. (For example, "Let's give Dad more broccoli than Anna. Dad really loves broccoli!") Talk about who needs more in your family and who needs less. Talk about who has more socks than others when you are putting laundry away or who has more leaves in their pile when you are raking leaves or other similar activities.

Same and Different

For children to start sorting or classifying, they have to be able to look at the details of each object, compare them, and decide if they are the same or different from each other. In teaching about sorting, start with items that are exactly the same (such as three identical shoes) and add another item that is markedly different from those items (such as an orange). Then you can progress to using items that are in the same category but not identical (such as three nonmatching shoes) and again add an item that is markedly different (an orange). The three shoes may differ in style, but they are definitely shoes. The contrasting orange is a long way from being a shoe. You are then actually classifying the shoes as a member of the class *shoes,* which is distinctly different from an orange. That task is more difficult than just finding one different item among other identical items.

INTRODUCING THE CONCEPTS OF SAME AND DIFFERENT

OBJECTIVE: The child will be able to indicate which item is different in a group of four items in which three are the same. Use both objects and pictures.

MATERIALS:

- Several sets of 2 (or 3) identical items and 1 markedly different item that are small enough to be spread on the table in front of the child. Start with two pencils and a piece of paper crushed into a ball.

  Other examples are:
  - ▾ Cars and a book
  - ▾ Bananas and a salt shaker
  - ▾ Forks and a spoon
  - ▾ Pieces of paper and a piece of chalk
  - ▾ Socks and a shoe
  - ▾ Pieces of red paper and a white piece
  - ▾ Same size blocks and an apple
  - ▾ *Pictures* of 3 identical items and one that is very different
  - ▾ Cereal pieces and a marshmallow
  - ▾ Three coats and one boot

SUCCESS STEP: Show the child one familiar item such as a pencil and tell her to touch or point to the pencil. Praise her for success. If she doesn't respond, touch the pencil to her hand and say, "You touched the pencil. Great!"

PROCEDURE:

1. Show the child the two identical items one by one and ask her to touch or point to each one. Hold them all in front of her and tell her that they are the *same.* Repeat at least once. Then show her the crushed paper ball and say, "Is this a

pencil? No! No! This is a ball (or a paper ball). It is *not* the same as the pencils" (showing the pencils).

2. Play catch with the ball with her for a few minutes. Then show her the pencil. "Is this the *same* as the ball? No! No! It is *not* the same. (It is different)."

3. Put the ball behind your back and hold out the two pencils. "Are they the same?" Repeat the activity, if necessary.

4. Put one pencil on the table. Hold out the ball and the pencil in one hand. Ask, "Which one is the same?" using your other hand to point to the pencil on the table. If necessary, hold the pencil up toward her face and the paper ball back farther. "Good, you found the same." Repeat the above activity several times. Later switch to a different set of materials.

5. You will be teaching the concept of same and not same. You may also say the word different, but you are looking for the concept of same and not same at first.

   > **Note:** *If the student has autism or Asperger's syndrome, you should probably use the word* **different** *from the start. Students with autism sometimes have problems processing the word* **not** *and its connection with the following word.*

6. You may need to put a different set of materials out and model touching the different item. Then help the child to do the same thing.

7. It is better to start with tangible objects and then progress to pictures. However, sometimes when you use tangible objects, children want to play with one of the objects and will persist in playing with it without learning the concept of same and different. If so, you should go on to pictures because all four pictures may have about the same play value for the child, and she may be able to concentrate on the activity. If the student has difficulty with 4 items, try using 2 that are the same and 1 that is not. (If you are working with a child who has autism, she may have notable difficulty understanding that a picture can stand for an object, and may need to learn what are called "picture-object correspondence skills." See the book by McClannahan and Krantz in the References for help teaching these skills.)

Teaching with Music

I like to use the song that was used in *Sesame Street* when I am asking a child to show me which thing is different.

One of These Things
Words and Music by Joe Raposo and Jon Stone

One of these things is not like the others.
One of these things just doesn't belong.
Can you guess which thing is not like the others?
By the time I finish my song?

Did you guess which thing was not like the others?
Did you guess which thing just doesn't belong?
If you guessed this one is not like the others,
Then you're absolutely…right.

8. When your child is able to do same and different with pictures, you can use some of the preschool activity and coloring books that have pictures that teach that concept. [If she has trouble holding a pencil or crayon, though, don't expect her to circle or cross out the different picture.

GENERALIZATION INTO DAILY LIFE: Parents have the best chance to help their child learn to use the concepts of *same* and *different.* Your food cupboards are full of items that are the same and different. You just have to point them out. When you go food shopping, you can pick out produce that is the same and different. You can have your child find the different dark sock in the basket of white ones, or one yellow apple among the red ones. You can save fast food wrappers or boxes and have her point out the different one, or, when you are eating at McDonald's, look around the restaurant and see which children got the same Happy Meal toy as she did. You can have her pick out dress pants from a group of jeans. There are many ways to bring this concept into daily living. Just be sure that the *same* items are a lot alike and the *different* item is very distinctly different.

Educators can use things in their environment such as pencils, pens, colored paper, juice boxes or milk cartons, and books to emphasize *same* and *different.* You may try comparing students' clothes, but most pieces of clothing are not exactly alike. If the children understand that different color of pants are still pants (a classification skill), you can compare the children's clothing for *same* and *different.* You can compare girls and boys or men and women if the child has learned that they each fit in a classification.

Matching

By working on *same* and *different* above, you have cued the child to look at the details of the items. She should now be ready to match simple identical items. Matching is the concept of one-to-one correspondence using *like* things. Since it is primarily a visual task, children with Down syndrome usually do well. If your child has a visual problem, you will want to start with concrete objects that can be easily felt. Even if you are using pictures, you can add some different textures such as sand glued to one pictured item as well as to its match for the student with visual problems.

When teaching your child to match, have her move the item to a position *beside* its identical match, or she can point to the matching item and you can move it for her.

MATCHING REAL OBJECTS

OBJECTIVE: The child will be able to match identical objects.

MATERIALS:

- One roll of unopened toilet paper, a cup, a brush, and a spoon (or similar items) on the table

• An open box containing a roll of unopened toilet paper, a brush, a cup, and a spoon

*Note: You may also use some of the items that are mentioned in the materials section of the **same** or **different** activity above. However, it would be wise not to use the same items you used when teaching about **same** and **different**, because you may confuse the student.*

SUCCESS STEP: Have the child name or point to the items in the box. Praise her for correct answers.

PROCEDURE:

1. Lay the toilet paper roll and the brush on a table in front of the student, just out of her reach. Put the box on a chair beside her. Take the roll of toilet paper from the box and put it beside the roll on the table. "See, this roll is the same as that roll. They match. Can you do the same thing (or match them too)?" Give her the roll and prompt her to do the same thing. Praise her and repeat, if needed.

2. Then put the one roll of toilet paper back in the box, and see if she can match the items on the table with the items in the box. When she is successful, add the cup to the items on the table and see if she can match three items. If the objects are distracting her from the learning, go on to using pictures that seem to have less distracting value (next step).

MATCHING PICTURES

OBJECTIVE: The child will be able to match identical pictures.

MATERIALS:

• Pictures from Match a Match Game (page 322)
• A mat so that the pictures won't slip around on the table. The latex mats used for shelf lining work quite well.

SUCCESS STEP: Have the child name or point to several pictures of familiar things. Praise her for correct answers.

PROCEDURE:

1. On a mat on the table, place two different animal pictures in a row, spaced about four inches apart from each other, directly in front of the student. Put the matching pictures to the side or show them to her one at a time. See if she can match the pictures in front of her by putting the correct picture next to its match. Say, "Find the one that's the same," pointing to the animal picture you want her to match. If she puts one on top of the other as she is learning, she can't self-correct as easily as if they are side by side. Repeat, mixing up the pictures.

   Note: If animals are not motivating to the student, try using pictures of toys or cartoon characters that she really likes. You can use black and white line drawings, colored drawings, or computer clip art if that helps motivate the student.

2. Try again, using three and then four pictures to match at the same time.
3. You probably will need to repeat this activity many times with different pictures to make sure the student can really match.

MATCH A BATCH GAME

OBJECTIVE: Same as above.

MATERIALS:

- *Match a Batch* game (constructed as described below)
- A piece of cardboard or poster board that is the same size as nine of the picture cards from the previous activity when they are placed in three rows of three.

PROCEDURE:

1. Cut a piece of cardboard or poster board so it is the same size as nine of the picture cards arranged in three rows of three.
2. Photocopy additional copies of the pictures used in the previous activity so you have nine pairs of pictures.
3. Separate the picture cards so you have two identical sets. One set will be the playing cards and the other set will go on the game board.
4. Begin by placing nine picture cards face up on the game board (in three rows of three). The duplicate cards are shuffled and placed face down in the draw pile in front of the student.
5. Have the children in turn pick a card from the draw pile and try to make a match on the game board. If they are incorrect, they must keep the card. If

COMMERCIAL GAMES TO BUY OR TRY

The commercial game called *Memory* by Milton Bradley uses a little plastic form to hold the cards for the game board. If the student has fine motor problems, she can put her finger in the holes under the frame and push the card out. It also uses thick cardboard items. The commercial game has 12 items to match, but it is a game that families and students can play together with success. At the present time, there are also Winnie the Pooh and Bob the Builder *Memory* games ($8-10), and probably games with other themes.

There are also many simple lotto games that can be bought at discount stores, teacher's stores, and on the Internet. (Lotto games generally include game boards that are preprinted with an array of pictures or photographs of objects, plus individual cards with single pictures of those same objects. Players draw cards and are allowed to place them on their board if they have a match.) For younger children, colorful computer programs such as those by Edmark have matching tasks that give immediate feedback. See the Resources section in the back of the book.

they are successful in the match, they put the draw card on top of or to the side of its match on the game board. The one who makes the most matches wins.

6. For a more difficult and challenging game, turn the cards on the game board face down. The first child turns over the top card on the draw pile. She guesses which card on the game board will match and turns it over. If the card is the same as the card she drew, she puts it on top of its match on the game board. If the card does not match, she turns the game board card over again and keeps the draw pile card. The next player draws a card, turns over a card on the game boards and looks for a match. The idea of the game is to remember where the game cards are located so you can choose the right match. The winner is the one who makes the most matches.

Simple Classification

Classification, the grouping of items that have a property or properties in common, is an important skill for math, reading, and language. Much of the instruction in all content areas consists of making more subtle classifications and giving them names or grouping together items that have characteristics in common and giving the grouping a name. For example, a large body of water may be further classified as a lake, sea, ocean, or river. Dogs, cats, cows, and horses are grouped together as animals. These skills will be taught briefly here, but activities in classifying are expected to be part of reading readiness, cognitive development, and language activities.

Children usually start to classify by size, color, number, or appearance. Jean Piaget describes the development of classification as children learning to form groups of items based on a fixed rule (Copeland, 1984). They may not be able to tell you the rule, but they are using one. Sometimes children are not always able to focus on that one rule through the whole sorting process. These children need to be taught to talk out their rule as they sort.

First, children learn to sort basic items for one characteristic such as color. For example, the child sorts poker chips into a white pile and a red pile. Later, two or more characteristics may be used, such as square red items/round red items and square white items/round white items. Then more difficult distinctions may be required, such as determining the various shades of blues that fit into the category of blue.

SIMPLE SORTING

OBJECTIVE: The child will be able to sort items by different colors, shapes, sizes, and types of items.

MATERIALS:
- Knives, forks, spoons
- A divided silverware tray or 3 separate boxes
- 12 pieces of construction paper (4 pieces each of 3 different colors)
- 3 or 4 different types of small food items that differ in color or size
  (For example, colored miniature marshmallows, raisins and peanuts, Lucky Charms cereal pieces, gummy bears, jellybeans,

chocolate and regular Teddy Grahams, and any other small items of food that the student enjoys.)
OR

- If using food is not wise, use 3 types of small inedible objects such as plastic teddy bear counters that come in 3 or 4 colors, blocks that come in 3 or 4 colors, paper cups differing by size or by color, hair accessories ("scrunchies") of different sizes and colors, plastic combs, socks, plastic utensils in different colors, or cans of food (only 3 kinds).

SUCCESS STEP: Have the child point to a knife, a spoon, and a fork as they are named (when they are laid in front of her).

PROCEDURE:
Sorting by Color
1. Show the child how to sort by color. Say, "Let's put the papers that are the same color together." Then start sorting the papers into piles by color, commenting when you find one that looks "the same."
2. Have the child try sorting colored construction paper into 3 different piles by color. If she makes a mistake, show her that the colors are "not the same" by holding the two mismatched pieces of paper next to each other and saying, "These two are not the same."
3. Later, or if the child is not interested in sorting colored paper, have her sort colored play money, small cars, Lego blocks, or other things she collects by color.

***Note:** The object of this activity is to sort the different colors, not name them, but you can talk about the names of the colors at the same time. Do not mix shades of colors such as light blue, navy, and royal blue at this time. These distinctions are very difficult to make. Expect some students to have difficulty distinguishing black, purple, and navy blue.*

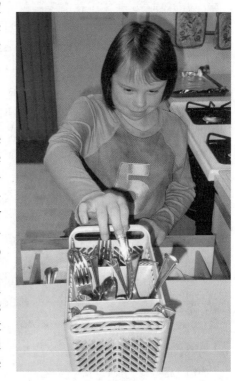

Sorting by Shape and Size
1. After the dishes have been washed or before a meal, show your child how to sort the knives, forks, and spoons into a divided silverware container. You may want to talk yourself through this to show her what to do by picking up a fork and saying, "OK, I'm putting the forks here. Here's another fork, so I'll put it in the same place...."
2. Next, have her sort the knives, forks, and spoons and place them in separate boxes or the divided silverware container. At first, do not present the smaller salad forks or large dishing spoons. When she

is confident about the sorting, you can introduce the different-sized forks and spoons.

3. As an alternate activity for younger children, have them sort their toys into different small bins as part of clean-up (blocks in one bin, dolls in another) or separate different-sized balls for storage.

Sorting Foods by Type of Item

1. Find a sorting task that involves separating two very different food items from each other. Have your child wash her hands.

2. If possible, give your child a reason that you need her help in sorting the food items, so the task will seem meaningful to her. For example, tell her you want to eat some Raisin Bran without the raisins. Then ask her to help you by sorting the raisins from the cereal in a bowl of Raisin Bran.

3. Then she can separate things that are less different, such as potato chips from tortilla chips. ("I don't know how these chips got mixed up together! Can you help me put them back in the right bowls/bags so the potato chips won't start tasting like the tortilla chips?")

4. Then she can go on to a more difficult task of separating food items that are pretty similar, such as the dried apples and dried pineapple in trail mix, etc. Many times children will use the additional clue from slightly different colors of the items, but that is fine because we all use different types of clues for identifi-

Difficulties Sorting by Category

There are many different ways that similar items can differ. If your child is able to do some tasks and not others, help her make a rule to use when making her choices and have her repeat it when choosing. For example, if she is having trouble sorting cans from glasses, you could tell her the rule, "Cans have a closed top; glasses have an open top you can put your finger into"(putting finger into top of the glass). Or you may give her an easier sorting task until you figure out what the problem is.

The underlying problem may be with language as well as cognitive skills. Libby Kumin (2003) explains that as children learn language, they may use *underextension* and *overextension*:

"Underextension occurs when a child uses a word such as "jacket" only to describe the specific jacket in her experience. So, if there is a picture of a blue jacket, and her jacket is red, she will not use the word "jacket" to describe the blue jacket....

"Often, when children are learning new words and concepts, they use *overextension* or *overgeneralization*.... For instance, a child may learn that a dog has four legs and use the word "dog" for any animal with four legs. "

So, for instance, if your child wants to call pretzel sticks and chips "snacks," you may need to teach her the specific words for each type of snack to facilitate more distinction in her classification, but she still can use the word *snacks* for whatever she eats when she gets home from school. You could tell her that *snacks* is the big word that takes in all different kinds of great foods.

cation in daily life. Of course, a part of the lesson will be to have her sample one of each kind of food that she sorts.

Sorting Non-food Objects
1. If the use of food is not wise, mix up some of the household items mentioned in the Materials section and let your child sort them. For example, show her an assortment of paper cups, plastic utensils, and cans of food. Perhaps comment on how messed up your kitchen is and ask her if she can help you get organized by helping you sort these things.
2. It may help if you have a muffin tin or several box lids, etc. to help her sort the various items.

COIN ACTIVITY

OBJECTIVE: The child will be able to sort coins functionally by color, size, weight, or appearance.

MATERIALS:
- Loose change (pennies, nickels, dimes, and quarters)
- 4 clear bottles or containers

SUCCESS STEP: Have your child hand you a penny from two types of coins on a table in front of her. Praise correct choice or help her to make the correct choice.

Note: if you have a student who is ready for more advanced coin sorting activities or is ready to learn the names and values of coins, see Chapter 20.

PROCEDURE:
1. Once your child can successfully sort three colors and the flatware, you can try this very functional activity. Many homes have a big jar or drawer for small change. Sometimes that change will have to be sorted to put in wrappers (especially pennies). Bring out a clear glass or jar for each type of coin you have accumulated. Have the child put the pennies in one jar, the nickels in another jar, etc. She does *not* have to know the values of each coin.
2. Schools may find a time when change has to be sorted from a food sale, a field trip, or other money activity.
3. After your child has sorted the change, show her how you put the coins in wrappers to take to the bank, so she knows the function of her coin sorting task, but don't require her to count the coins. As you are wrapping the coins, show her any that may have ended up in the wrong jar and point out why they are not the same as the others in the jar. ("Whoops. This one is too little and thin to go in this jar. It's not the same as these big silver coins.") If possible, take her to the bank when you exchange the wrapped coins for dollar bills.

GENERALIZATION INTO DAILY ACTIVITIES: There are many ways you can work on sorting during everyday activities, but it will take some planning on your

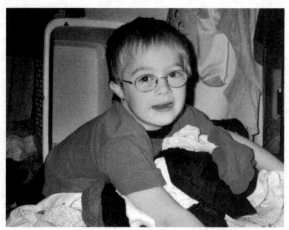

part. Everyday activities usually call for more complex sorting than the simple tasks described in this chapter. For example, it is more difficult to separate the laundry into whites and nonwhites (various colors). Sometimes you will find it difficult to explain the differences between common categories, such as jacket vs. coats. It is also possible for children to make different categories out of the same group of objects than you would, depending on the characteristics they choose. For example, fruits can be classified by similar colors, types of fruit (apples vs. oranges), or similar sizes or weights.

Both home and school daily experiences present numerous opportunities for sorting and classifying. The most common characteristics that are used for classification are:

1. color (white or red, etc.)
2. size (big and little)
3. shape (round or square)
4. weight (heavy or light)
5. appearance (light or dark, bumpy or smooth)
6. temperature (hot or cold)
7. sound (loud or soft)
8. location (up or down) (Smith, 1997)

> *Lanell's family used a laundry sorter that had three pockets. Lanell's mother told her to sort the dirty clothes into white clothes, colored clothes, and dark, colored clothes. About ten minutes later, Lanell called for her mother in frustration. "What do I do with the clothes that have both white and colors in them? Is red a dark color? Where do I put the pink nightgown?"*
>
> *Her mother had not established the rules for sorting or classifying in enough detail for Lanell to be able to sort the clothes easily. Her mother might simplify the task by having her sort the clothes in two piles of white or nonwhite. She could be asked to chant the rule, "White or not white." Her mother might also simplify the task by saying, "All or mostly all white clothes go in the first pocket. All other colors of clothes go in the second packet except blue jeans and black clothes." Again the rule could be chanted. "White here, colored there, except for blue jeans and black."*

To master classification skills, your child will require much repetition and variation in the materials used. Use of mass-market workbooks or early childhood materials will probably be needed. There is also software that has colorful games on sorting and classification (and other math concepts) that even older children like to play. (*Millie's Math House, Carnival Countdown,* and *Zoo Zillions* by Edmark are good choices.) Only the adult working with the child can decide when she has worked long enough on classification.

Learning about matching, sorting and comparing should be fun for both student and teacher. For young children, you can just incorporate learning into daily life. Here are a few ideas:

- If you're playing together with blocks, ask your child to give you all the big ones so you can make a really big garage.
- If you are decorating cookies, ask her to help you find a bunch of yellow M & M's to put on Dad's cookie.
- If you are folding laundry, ask her to find all the socks in the basket of clean clothes for you (and if she can, put all of Dad's socks in one pile, her sister's in another, and hers in another).
- If you're doing a jigsaw puzzle together, search for all the blue sky pieces together or all the brown pieces with fur that are part of the dog.

For older children or students at school:

- Ask her to help you organize your DVD or video storage unit. Put all the kid videos in one place, and the grown-up videos in another.
- Organize the pantry together. Put all the canned goods on one shelf, the cereal on another, etc.
- Ask her for help organizing the supply closet at school. Put the scissors in one container, the markers in another, etc.
- Separate glass, metal, and paper items to be recycled.
- Separate all the pencils that need sharpening from those that don't, or all the markers that are dried out from those that are still good.

This section on sorting and classifying is only intended to scratch the surface of classifying experiences. More experiences will be needed in classifying by two or more characteristics or more difficult distinctions such as white and nonwhite.

---

*(Note: I have used the word **child** or **children** to apply to the learner in this chapter. Starting with Chapter 7, I will use the term **student** so it will apply to older students as well as children.)*

Number Sense

Pre- /Post Checklist

Can the student:

1. _____ Rote count the numerals from 1-10 in correct sequence. Later from 1-30. (He does not have the items to count.)

2. _____ Say the correct numeral for the corresponding item (1-5) in one-to-one correspondence.

3. _____ Count with meaning up to 10 items.

4. _____ Give the last numeral counted when asked for the total number of counted items (cardinality).

5. _____ Use the word zero to show that nothing is there in that place.

6. _____ Count from 11-19 objects, using the correct numeral names.

7. _____ Demonstrate knowledge of the pattern for counting larger numbers by counting from 20-29 correctly.

8. _____ Spot (without counting) the number of dots (up to 5) on one die.

General number sense is defined as the understanding of number concepts and relationships, the ability to compute accurately, and the ability to effectively use numbers in daily life (Reys, 1995). Number sense is not something that a person either has or does not have. Development of number sense is a lifelong process.

The National Council of Teachers of Mathematics has emphasized the importance of development of number sense, especially in elementary school (2000).

Essential for the development of math understanding are the following:

- **Counting/Early number concepts**
- **Rote counting the correct sequence**
- **Early math principles/Beginning counting with meaning (1-5)**
  - ▾ Conservation of number
  - ▾ One-to-one correspondence
  - ▾ Last number counted is the total (cardinality)
  - ▾ The value of *zero*
- **Visual spotting (recognizing small groups as a whole)**
- **Counting larger numbers**
- **Patterns in counting**
  - ▾ Teen numbers
  - ▾ 20 and beyond

Counting/Early Number Concepts

Most children learn how to rote count (say the names of the numerals in sequence) from people in their environment. Family and peers usually count objects for them starting at a very early age. At first we will expect the child to count to 3, then 5, later 10, then to 20, 30, and up to 100. (It may take some time—months or years—for students with Down syndrome to learn the names of the numbers, so don't get discouraged if this skill does not come quickly). In addition to the names of the numerals, he needs to learn the *pattern* that develops when counting the teen numbers and the numbers from 21 to 100. Although we cover these skills in this chapter, if your student is not ready for them yet, come back to this chapter later and try working on other skills in other chapters (such as recognizing written numerals) for now.

ROTE COUNTING (NAMING THE NUMERALS)

OBJECTIVE: The student will rote count to 10 (say the numerals from 1-10 in correct sequence, but without connecting the number words to actual quantities.) Later he will say the numerals from 1-30. (He does not have to have items to count.)

MATERIALS:

- For younger children, counting books that go up to 10 or 20 (See Resources)
- Short songs or cheers that feature counting

SUCCESS STEP: Have the student touch and count his own hands and feet (counting 1, 2) and then praise him. (You say,

"I am going to count your hands— 1...2. Can you count your hands for me?") Just do body parts that he can see directly.

PROCEDURE:

1. Teach a song or rhyme with counting words to 10   (Children under 10 or 11).

For example,	1 - 2 - 3 - 4 - 5	*(put up fingers in order)*
	I caught a bee alive,	*(put pointing finger inside a hive made of the other fist.)*
	6 - 7 - 8 - 9 - 10	*(put up fingers as named*
	I let it go again.	*(both hands open again fast)*
	OW!	*(as if your hand was stung)*

Another variation on the above song is used on the *Barney* show as:

> 1, 2, 3, 4, 5
> Once I caught a fish alive.
>
> 6, 7, 8, 9, 10
> Then I let it go again.

2. Sing the song that used to be called *10 Little Indians* (traditional), with an animal replacing the Indian. For example:

> One little, two little, three little elephants,
> Four little, five little, six little elephants,
> Seven little, eight little, nine little elephants,
> Ten little elephant babies.

3. Another song that is commonly known is *This Old Man* (traditional):

> This old man, he played *one,*
> He played nick-nack on my thumb.

Chorus:
> With a nick-nack, paddy wack, give a dog a bone.
> This old man came rolling home.
>
> This old man, he played *two,*
> He played nick-nack on my shoe...
>
> This old man, he played *three,*
> He played nick-nack on my knee...
>
> This old man, he played *four,*
> He played nick-nack on the floor...
>
> This old man, he played *five,*
> He played nick-nack on my hive...
>
> This old man, he played *six,*
> He played nick-nack on my sticks...

This old man, he played *seven,*
He played nick-nack up to heaven...

This old man, he played *eight,*
He played nick-nack on my plate...

This old man, he played *nine,*
He played nick-nack on my spine...

This old man, he played *ten,*
He played nick-nack over again....

ADAPTATION FOR OLDER LEARNERS:
Use a football cheer instead of a counting song.

1,2,3,4	Who are we rooting for?
5,6,7,8	Who do we appreciate?
	(Name of favorite team)
9,10	Do it over again.

Note: *If the student is not speaking at this point in the instruction, you might go on to recognition of numbers (Chapter 8), so that he can point to the numerals or indicate them on an augmentative communication device. Or you may teach the signs for the numerals so that he can indicate numbers in the songs motorically.*

GENERALIZATION INTO DAILY ACTIVITIES: The purpose of the above activities is more for familiarizing students with the names and sequences of the numbers from 1 to 10. They still need to be able to say the numbers as a memorized sequence, not just in a song. For this reason, it is especially important to help your student(s) generalize rote counting into daily activities.

Much of the learning on rote counting will be accomplished during regular daily living. Most children need to hear their parents and teachers count out loud many, many times before they will begin to memorize the sequence of numbers. Realistically, you should not expect a student to memorize and be able to repeat the whole sequence from 1 to 10 in one fell swoop. He may need to practice counting from 1 to 3 for quite a while before he is ready to try counting to 5. Here are some ways you can naturally expose students to counting throughout the day, and encourage them to rote count themselves when they are ready:

- Throw a ball in the air and see how far you or the student can count before it hits the ground.
- Play Hide and Seek and have the student count to ten (or as high as he can) while others hide.
- You count to 10 when transitioning to a new activity. For example, "I am starting with number 1. When I get to 10, it is time for you to go to speech class (or to get ready for your bath)."

- Bet the student that he cannot get his jacket on by the time you count (slowly) to 10.
- Count to 10 with the referee when watching wrestling or boxing on TV.
- Have the student be the counter for another class member or a younger sibling.
- Some teachers use a rhythmic chant to get their students' attention: "One, two, three … eyes on me!" (clapping on every syllable). Students are expected to reply, "One, two … eyes on you!" (also clapping on every syllable).

Early Math Learning Principles

As you are teaching the names of the numbers in rote counting, you should also be teaching counting with meaning for the numbers from 1-5. Certain principles underlie the process of counting with meaning. Your child does not have to be able to state those principles, but he needs to act with certain understandings about conservation of number, one-to-one correspondence, cardinality, and the meaning of zero. Although I have listed these principles in a sequence, your child might learn them in a different order or learn them almost at the same time. He also may use them inconsistently at first. So we start with counting with meaning for the smaller numbers of 1-5 as we give experiences with these principles of early math learning.

Conservation of Number

Jean Piaget described the phenomenon of the conservation of number as the realization that a given number of items does not vary, no matter how items are arranged (Thornton, Tucker, Dossey & Bazik, 1983). For example, five red blocks can be arranged in a straight line exactly across from five blue blocks, and the child will say the number of red and blue blocks are the same. If, however, the red blocks are arranged in a much longer line than the blue blocks, a child who has not yet mastered conservation of number might say that there are more red blocks than blue blocks. Typical children usually learn this concept by age 4 or 5.

When a child thinks that a number (or substance) can change without anything being added or subtracted, he effectively believes in "magic," not the orderly structure necessary for true understanding of mathematics. Children seem to learn conservation of number slowly, and may sometimes seem as if they understand it one day, but not the next. Continue working on prenumber and number concepts with your student while he is acquiring conservation of number.

INTRODUCING THE CONCEPT OF CONSERVATION

OBJECTIVE: The student will demonstrate by comparison that the amount of items stays the same, even if they are arranged differently.

Children who don't understand conservation will say that there are more chips in the top row as lined up here...

...than here.

MATERIALS:

- 5 blue poker chips or other identical items
- 5 red poker chips or items that are a different color than the above items

SUCCESS STEP: Ask the student to touch a blue chip (making sure he knows the color blue). Praise the correct answer or model touching the chip. Then ask him to touch another blue chip.

PROCEDURE:

1. Put 5 red chips in a straight line. Place the 5 blue chips across from the red chips. Ask the child if there are more red chips than blue chips. (They have the same number.) Move both sets of chips closer so that the red chips are lined up exactly even with the blue chips to show that there are the same number of each color.
2. Then spread the blue chips much farther apart than the red chips and ask the child if there are more blue chips now. (No, they are still the same.) If necessary, show him by lining up the chips across from each other.
3. Spread out the red chips and repeat the question.
4. If necessary, use different objects and repeat, pointing out the conservation of number. A good class demonstration would be to line up students in two lines, facing each other, with the same number of students (4-5) in each line. Then spread out one of the lines and ask which line has the most people. Then have each person in the first line find a partner in the second line to show that the number is the same.

Note: *Jean Piaget felt that children develop conservation of number as they mature, but other researchers believe that exposure to various guided experiences with conservation can speed up the process. If your student(s) can't seem to get this concept right now, go ahead and teach some of the other early math principles such as counting with meaning for small numbers. Return to the activity later.*

One-to-One Correspondence/Beginning Counting

An extension of the principle of conservation of number is the principle of one-to-one correspondence in which one counting word is paired with each item. For example, in counting five apples, we say one number word per apple. A child who does not understand one-to-one correspondence may throw the dice when playing a board game and say, "I get to go 4 spaces." However, as he counts, "1, 2, 3, 4," he skips over 6 spaces on the board. He doesn't understand one-to-one correspondence. Often other children will say that he is cheating. However, he is just not able to match the counting words with each item.

INTRODUCING THE CONCEPT OF ONE-TO-ONE CORRESPONDENCE

OBJECTIVE: The student will be able to say the correct numeral for the corresponding item in one-to-one correspondence for up to 5 items.

MATERIALS:
- Poker chips or other counters
- Items that need to be distributed such as cups, plates, pencils, napkins, etc.

SUCCESS STEP: Have the student hand out cups, pencils, or plates, giving one item to each person present. Say, "Please give **a** cup to everybody." Tell the student that he has been fair. He has given an item to each person present (one-to-one correspondence without counting). If the student is not successful, model the task yourself and then have him repeat it.

PROCEDURE:
1. Have the student hand out some other items (napkins, etc.) one to each person present. Praise his fairness in giving one napkin to each person. (If you are working with your child alone at home, he can pass out items to several stuffed animals or dolls.)
2. Then go on to one-to-one correspondence that includes simple counting (1-5). Count out 5 blue chips, 1, 2, 3, 4, 5, and put them on the table one by one in front of the student as you count them. Give the chips to the student and ask him to do the same thing. If he is not able to count to 5, repeat the activity with 3 chips. He will be saying a numeral and putting the chip on the table in one-to-one correspondence as well as counting with meaning for small numbers.
3. If the student is not successful, draw 3 circles on a piece of paper and tell him to put a red chip on each circle. Have him repeat the task as you count out the numbers in one-to-one correspondence. See if he can do the activity independently.
4. Count other objects (1-5) in the same manner. Do not count higher even if the child knows the names of higher numbers. The emphasis should be on the one-to-one rule while the student is doing a simple counting task with meaning.

MATCH MY DOTS

OBJECTIVE: Given empty cans labeled with 1 to 5 dots, the student will match the correct number of sticks with the dots. (You can also use the game for counting with meaning for small numbers if you have the student count the dots on the cans and also count the sticks as he puts them in the cans.)

MATERIALS:

- Empty soup cans or frozen juice containers (5-9). (They can be painted or wrapped in construction or Contact paper.)
- Round adhesive dots or permanent marker for making dots on the cans
- Tongue depressors or craft sticks (15+)

PROCEDURE:

1. Label one can with 1 dot, another with 2 dots, another with 3 dots, etc.
2. Challenge the student to put one stick in for each dot on the cans. Check when he is done.
3. If he seems secure with the matching, you can have him count the dots and the sticks to check his answer. If you are working with several students, let them take turns filling the cans.

GENERALIZATION INTO DAILY ACTIVITIES: Many daily living tasks can be used for generalizing one-to-one correspondence:

- When making muffins or cup cakes, have the student put the liners in each cup. You may have to separate the liners for him if he has fine motor difficulties.
- Have the student put return addresses or address labels on your correspondence.
- Have the student pass out construction paper in school or pass out straws in the fast food place. Any occasion where one item has to be given out per person will be good practice because the person who does not get the item will immediately let the student know that he or she does not have one.
- Pass out Halloween candy, one per beggar.
- Play *Duck, Duck Goose* where the student has to go around a circle of people, touching each one on the head, saying "Duck…duck" etc. Then, all of a sudden, the player has to touch someone's head and say, "Goose." The goose then tries to catch the player as he races back to an open space.
- Put CDs or DVDs into a case or holder, one per slot.

Most of the above activities can also be used as counting with meaning activities if you use numbers no larger than 5.

Count with Meaning for Amounts Up to 10

The student has already been counting with meaning for small amounts (1-5) when he was learning one-on-one correspondence. When he can rote count to a number higher than 5, you should progress to counting with meaning to that number. This activity is designed to make counting with meaning automatic for numbers through 10 through repeated practice.

INTRODUCING THE CONCEPT OF COUNTING WITH MEANING

OBJECTIVE: The student will count up to 10 items showing one-to-one correspondence.

MATERIALS:

- Varied items such as blocks, pencils, etc. that can be counted, especially objects that the student especially likes or collects
- Container for items

PROCEDURE:

1. Have the student move and count some items such as blocks or pencils and put them in a container. The student says, "1," picks up one pencil and puts it into the container. It sometimes helps if he can hear the object hit the bottom of the container. Then he continues saying the numerals as he picks up other pencils and puts them in the container. By dropping the object into the container, he is less likely to count it twice. (If the student drops more than one item into the container at a time, try handing him one item at a time to count.)
2. Repeat with varied motivating items around home and school. For example, if your student is interested in Pokemon videos, have him count them as he puts them back in the video cabinet. Any item that he collects or has great interest in will help motivate him to count. My son collects "Power Rangers" which he faithfully counts. Likewise, I work with a student with an autism spectrum disorder who would count the cars on the trains that he loves.

Last Number Counted Is the Total (Cardinality)

A student must be able to see that the last number he says when counting items tells how many items there are. A child can count six forks, one by one, as he has seen adults do, and still not understand that his counting is answering the question "how many?" or determining the total number of items. This concept (known as the principle of cardinality) tends to be learned all at once in sort of an "ah ha" moment. Usually, the child can then generalize it easily.

COVER UP GAME

OBJECTIVE: The student will give the last numeral counted when asked for the total number of counted items.

MATERIALS:
- Poker chips or other interesting items to count
- Handkerchief

SUCCESS STEP: Ask the student to name the colors of the chips (if he knows them). Praise the correct answer.

PROCEDURE:
1. Put 3 blue chips down in front of the student, counting 1, 2, 3. Say, "You now have 3 chips in front of you. How many chips do you have?" (3)
2. You then count out 5 chips in front of him, counting 1, 2, 3, 4, 5. Ask, "How many chips do you have now?" See if he understands that the last number counted tells how many chips there are.
3. If he is not successful, try using the numbers from 1-3.
4. Play the game *Cover Up* by covering different numbers of chips with the handkerchief after you have counted them and asking, "How many chips are hidden under the handkerchief?" After the correct answer is given, say, "You peeked."

WHAT'S IN MY BAG? GAME

MATERIALS:
- Poker chips or other small items to count
- Small paper bag (lunch bag size)

PROCEDURE:
1. Count chips or other motivating items in front of the student and drop them in the bag, one by one.
2. Hold the bag closed and say, "Do you know how many chips I have in this bag?" When the child answers with the last number counted, say, "You got me! You saw through the bag."
3. Then take the chips out and count them to be sure. Repeat with different numbers of chips. Each time the student says the right number, he is a winner...and you lose. If the student doesn't understand how to play the game, try again with only 1 or 2 chips.

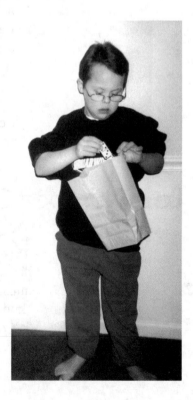

ADAPTATIONS FOR OLDER LEARNERS: Don't use the counters that are used with young children (e.g., teddy bear counters). Use items that are used in daily living such as forks, spoons, poker chips, keys, or coins. Instead of making games out of *Cover Up* and *What's in the Bag,* do the same activities and say firmly, "You are right!" each time the answer is correct.

> *Kyle correctly pairs a numeral with each of the six balls that he drops one by one into a bucket. However, when asked how many balls are now in the bucket, he stammers and guesses that there are four balls. Although he knew how to count each ball, he did not know that the last number he called would give the total number of balls in the bucket.*

GENERALIZATION INTO DAILY ACTIVITIES: Once your student begins to get the hang of counting with meaning, it is important to weave this skill into his daily routine. At first have him count numbers from 1-9. As he learns the counting words for the teens, you can have him count items to 20 and higher.

At first, use items that are very much alike so the student can concentrate on the counting and doesn't have to determine whether something belongs in a particular category or not. For example, ask him to count Legos, not toys. Later, you may want to broaden the category. For instance, use the category of *shoes,* which includes both sneakers, slip-ons, and dress-up shoes. Have other adults or older peers do similar activities to help your student understand that counting is an important activity.

- Count:
  - ▾ Plates on the dinner table
  - ▾ Dirty clothes that go in the hamper
  - ▾ Produce into a bag in the grocery store
  - ▾ Keys on a key ring
  - ▾ Oranges when putting them in the refrigerator
  - ▾ Soap bubbles you or your child blows
  - ▾ The stars as they come out
  - ▾ Small toys like Legos or cars when they are thrown into a basket while cleaning up
  - ▾ Pencils needing sharpening
- Find out how many items are considered one serving of cookies, crackers, or chips. Then count out that number. Then have the student count them out.

- Make a lot of paper airplanes and see how many the student can land in a drawn circle or beyond a certain line. Count them again as they are picked up.
- Have the student guess (estimate) how many Goldfish crackers, small blocks, or clothespins he can pick up and put in one hand. Then count the objects to see how close the estimate was.
- Count the number of ball tosses when throwing back and forth. Begin again when someone misses.
- Play the *Simon Says* game and have the student take 3 steps forward, move back 2 steps, and other movements that involve small numbers.
- Play tic tac toe and try for 3 in a row (using two colors of checkers, poker chips, bingo chips on a grid if the student has trouble writing x's and o's).
- Read the student some of the many counting books that are available.
- Many other similar activities.

Understanding Zero

The concept of *zero* is a basic part of our system of numbering. Remember, the Romans didn't have *zero*, and we are still struggling with quick recognition of Roman numerals today. *Zero* is most commonly used to express that *nothing* is there. In addition, the *zero* is essential as a placeholder for our base ten system. When we add 1 item to 9 items, we place a zero in the ones column and move to the *tens* column and write 1. The *zero* is used to show there are no 1's in the ones column, but one 10 in the *tens* column.

INTRODUCING THE CONCEPT OF ZERO

OBJECTIVE: The student will be able to use the word *zero* to show that nothing is there (at that place).

MATERIALS:
- Small items of food such as jellybeans, pretzels, gummy bears, or strawberries OR
- Nonfood items such as Legos or Matchbox cars

SUCCESS STEP: Ask the student to name some of the items you are going to count. Praise correct answers.

PROCEDURE:
1. Give the student two pieces of food such as jellybeans or pretzels. Tell him that he has two items. Then take one item.

2. Ask him how many he has left.

3. Have him eat the last piece of food and ask, "How many do you have now?" When he answers that he has none, tell him that the name for none is *zero* (and show how the zero looks written).

4. If you want to use nonfood items, make sure that the items you choose have some interest value for the student. Use the same procedures as above. (If you are working with a student with autism, however, it may be better to use low-interest items if it upsets him when you take away a favored item.)

GENERALIZATION INTO DAILY ACTIVITIES: Continue talking about zero with many different types of items.

- Make zero part of your daily counting daily activities by asking questions such as, "How many shoes do I have on? That's right. I have no shoes on. I have *zero* shoes on."
- Make it sort of a sing-songy game when you say, "And how many do we have left now? Zero! That's right, Zero."
- If the student is young, you may want to say, "Zero … Mr. Zero … sad Mr. Zero … he has nothing." Make a zero with your thumbs and forefingers and say, "Zero looks like this."
- If the student is interested in sports, point out when one team has zero points because they have not scored.

Counting Larger Numbers

Learning to count the teen numbers can be very difficult for students. There is a pattern from 14 to 19, involving saying the *ones* first and then the word "teen" (standing for 10). However, this pattern is just opposite from the pattern used in 21 and beyond, naming the *tens* first and then the *ones*. Some students will have difficulties writing down the teen numbers because they hear the digit in the ones place (such as four) before they hear the indicator for the *tens* (teen). Thus, some students write 41 for 14. In addition, 11, 12, and 13 do not fit any pattern. (I have found that most young students do not hear the sound "thir-" in thirteen as indicating 3.) If the student has great difficulty with the teens, move on to recognition of numbers (Chapter 8) so the written numbers can reinforce the memorization.

PATTERN FOR TEEN NUMBERS

OBJECTIVE: The student will first be able to count from 1 to 13, and then from 14 to 19 objects, using the correct numeral names for the teen numbers.

MATERIALS:
- Counters, pennies, or poker chips
- Egg carton, muffin pan
- Pegboard and 13 pegs (optional)

PROCEDURE:

1. The students should be taught the numerals 11, 12, and 13 as separate number names like 6 or 7. Line up 11 people or objects and have the student count them. When the student gets to the last object or person, say, "Whoops! What do we do with this one? We'll call it eleven. Eleven, eleven, eleven—that's a good name. Let's chant it—eleven, eleven, eleven." Set up a rhythmic chant.
2. When the student is successful at counting to 11, move on to introducing the numbers 12 and 13, as above.
3. Use some counting structures that require 12 items to be complete. Have the student put pennies, eggs, and other small items in egg cartons, one item per compartment, naming each one. Use muffin tins for the same purpose. Alternately, cover some of the holes on a pegboard with tape so there are only 12 or 13 holes, and have the student put 12 or 13 pegs in the peg board and count them.
4. Counting from 14 to 19 can be quite difficult, for the reasons discussed above. Once your student can reliably count to 13, explain briefly the pattern in 14, 15, 16, 17, 18, and 19. If the student knows 4, 5, 6, 7, 8, and 9, suggest that he can just make them *teenagers* by saying the word *teen* after those numbers.

GENERALIZATION INTO DAILY ACTIVITIES:

- Count to one of the *teen* numbers when you are warning your child that a play period is almost over or that it's dinner time. Give him plenty of chances to hear you count to the teen numbers.
- Talk about *teenagers* you know and give their ages frequently.
- If he has a collection of toys, CD's, or other items, have him count them, counting into the teens as far as he can.
- Practice counting with the teen numbers frequently with packs of soda pop, other groceries, etc.

Also see the other generalization suggestions given in different sections of this chapter, focusing on the teen numbers.

Pattern for Numbers 20 and Larger

Learning to count to 20 may take a long time for students with concrete thinking. Grasping the pattern for counting and the sheer work of memorization may be very difficult for them. You may find that if you go on and teach recognition of numbers (Chapter 8), the visualization will help them to learn the numerals and patterns. If the student has few fine motor difficulties, writing the numbers (Chapter 9) may give tactile feedback that will assist in memorization.

INTRODUCING THE CONCEPT

OBJECTIVE: The student will demonstrate knowledge of the pattern for counting larger numbers by counting from 20 to 29 correctly.

MATERIALS:
- 40 craft sticks or short pretzels
- Paper plates

SUCCESS STEP: Ask the student to count to 19 as you put down one craft stick (or pretzel) for each number that he counts. Praise him.

COMMERCIAL GAMES TO BUY OR TRY

As your student is introduced to the various skills covered in this chapter, there are a variety of ways you can use commercially available games to make learning fun.

As students begin to understand one-to-one correspondence and counting with meaning, they can play a simple board game where players have to move their marker one space for each dot on the die thrown. Good examples are:

- *Chutes and Ladders (Milton Bradley),*
- *Clue, Jr. (Parker Bro.),*
- *Monopoly Jr. (Parker Bro.).*
- *Trouble (Milton Bradley),*
- *Snakes and Ladders (Fundex),*

If a younger student has difficulty with dice or moving one space at a time, Hi! Ho! Cherry O (Parker Brothers) is a good game to try. Players use a spinner that shows how many plastic cherries to remove from a tree. The student can physically place the cherries he takes off his tree on the cherries shown on the spinner with one-to-one correspondence. Another good game

for students working on early counting skills that does not use dice is Connect Four (Milton Bradley).

Once your student starts to learn about spotting (see below), play a board game with one die. See if he recognizes the number of spots immediately or counts them. Spotting usually comes with fun experiences with games.

Playing dominos can also be a fun way to practice spotting. When you play dominos, point out the numbers on half of the domino. Do not expect the student to spot more than 4 dots. Several excellent activities using dominoes are contained in *Domino Addition and Subtraction* (Learning Resources, around $9).The easy games in the front of the book can be used to teach spotting, and the later games can be used to teach addition and subtraction.

PROCEDURE:

1. Say, "I am going to count some more: 20, 21, 22, 23, 24, 25, 26, 27, 28, 29."
   Put the craft sticks or pretzels on paper plates, 10 to a plate.
   "Let's do that again. Twenty......(what?). Right, 21."
   Continue to ask him to supply the number following 20 all the way up to 29. You can help him by saying, "What number comes after 2? That's right, 3. We have 23."

2. You may write the numbers as you say them, but do not expect the student to recognize them until you have taught Chapter 8, Recognition of Numerals.

3. When you have thoroughly taught 20 to 29 by rote and with objects, see if the student has figured out the pattern. If he has, you may quickly go on to 30. Eventually you will want to have him count to 100 with meaning, but it has been my experience that it is easy for the student to be overwhelmed by so many digits. If you have taught the pattern, you can continue to larger numbers at a later date.

Visual Spotting

Along with counting, *spotting* (also called thinking in groups) is an important part of number sense. Spotting is necessary for the individual to get a visual picture of the gestalt (wholeness) of the number, not just the individual pieces (Reys, 1995; Semple, 1986). When you throw dice, you do not count each spot on the die. You see 4, or the "fourness" of the group of dots. Most people are able to spot up to 6 dots. Students with math learning disabilities or *dyscalculia,* sometimes called *number blindness,* frequently do not have this gestalt and rely on counting and memorization alone (Ranpura, 2000).

FLASHCARD ACTIVITY

OBJECTIVE: The student is able to quickly spot the number of spots (up to 4 or 5) on one die without counting.

MATERIALS NEEDED:
- Flashcards of dots (page 325)
- Dice

SUCCESS STEP: Ask the child to touch the side of the die that has two dots. Praise correct attempt.

PROCEDURE:

1. Show the flashcards of the dots from 1 to 3 quickly. The child should not have time to count the dots. Play a game with him and ask, "How fast can you tell me the number of dots?"

2. Add the flashcard showing 4 dots to the activity. You can try with 5 and 6, but spotting 4 dots is a significant accomplishment.

NUMBER UP GAME

MATERIALS NEEDED:

- One die (If the student is unable to see and count the spots on the regular dice, buy large foam dice or make a square box into a die by putting dots on the sides in the same pattern as on a die)
- Paper and pencil

PROCEDURE:

1. In the first round, a player throws the die and tries to get a 1 (1 dot). If he gets a 1, he gets 1 point. The teacher writes down his score each time. If he does not get a 1, he gets nothing. The next player also tries to get a 1.
2. In the second round, each player tries to roll a 2 in order to get 2 points, etc.
3. After all players have tried each of the rounds 4-5 times, the person with the most points wins.
4. An alternative way of scoring would be to give the players a straight 2 points for every matching throw.

CHAPTER 8

Recognition of Numerals

Pre- /Post Checklist

Can the student:

1. _____ Match the written numerals 1 to 5 with another set of numerals 1 to 5 (Later 1 to 10).

2. _____ Identify written numerals with appropriate groups of items (1 to 10).

3. _____ Recognize the written numerals from 11 to 19.

4. _____ Recognize the written numbers from 20 to 29 and be able to apply the pattern to the numbers 30 to 39.

5. _____ Recognize written numbers 39 to 100.

6. _____ Enter single and double digits correctly on the calculator.

Students who have learned the concepts in Chapter 7, Number Sense, will already understand how to count with meaning from 1 to 20 or more. This chapter will help students to relate the printed symbol of a numeral to the number of items that it represents.

For some students, it may be important to teach recognition of numerals along with Chapter 7, Number Sense. If the student does not have understandable spoken speech, teaching recognition of numerals would allow her to point to written numerals to show understanding of number concepts. In addition, seeing the written numerals can add visual cues to the learning of number concepts.

In some cases, it may make sense to teach the skills in this chapter at the same time you are working on writing the numerals, which is covered in Chapter 11. For a student with good small muscle control, writing the numerals may add tactile and visual cues to aid long-term memory. Research, however, has documented that typical first graders frequently have difficulties with writing numbers, probably because of their immature fine motor control and their limited eye-hand coordination (Payne and Huinker, 1993 as quoted in Rey,1994). Many children with Down syndrome or other disabilities affecting fine motor skills will continue to have difficulty writing numbers beyond the age that typical children can write smoothly. Therefore, they should have frequent experiences with numbers and recognition of numerals before being required to write them.

Important learning concepts about numeral recognition are:
- Matching numerals
- Identifying written numerals with groups of items (1-10)
- Recognizing the written numbers from 11-19 (teen numbers)
- Recognizing the written numbers from 20-39 and their pattern
- Recognizing the written numbers 39-100
- Entering single and double digits correctly on the calculator

Matching Numerals

Before I expect a student to learn the names of numerals, I teach her to match numerals by shape. The student must attend to the important features of the numeral in order to match it with the same numeral that is a different size. Matching also gives the student a successful experience before more difficult tasks are given.

*Note: I suggest writing numerals in the style recommended by Jan Olsen in the **Handwriting Without Tears** method. That is, make a 1 with a simple straight line and an open 4, as well as a 6 in which the back is not curved. Using this method, you can start writing most of the numerals in the upper left-hand corner of a box, which makes it easier for many students with Down syndrome or other disabilities to learn how to write the numerals. (See Chapter 11 for more information on forming numerals.)*

THE PARKING GAME

OBJECTIVE: The student will be able to match the numerals 1 to 5 to another set of numerals 1 to 5.

MATERIALS:
- Five small cars (e.g., Matchbox) with a large numeral written on the top (1 to 5)
- Five individual milk cartons or other small boxes with tops cut off, making a cube with one open side as a garage. Label each garage with a numeral from 1 to 5
  OR
- Paper airplanes labeled 1 to 5
- Five boxes twice as large as the paper airplanes labeled 1 to 5

SUCCESS STEP: Ask the student to push one of the cars across the table to you or to fly the airplane to you. Continue to take turns and praise her for her successful race or flight.

PROCEDURE:

1. Line up the milk carton garages (which have a large numeral on the top) in front of the student. Tell her that the cars need to be put in their own garages. (If you have more than one student, let other students "play" at the same time with their own sets of garages and cars.)
2. Model putting the numeral 1 car in the numeral 1 garage. Pick up the car, point to the numeral on the top and say, "This number is a 1. Let's see if we can find a garage with a 1 on it like the number on the car. Let's find the match."
3. Guide a successful entry of car or plane in the appropriate garage. You may name the numeral as you are teaching, but do not expect her to know or repeat it. You are having her match at first.
4. Have the student put all the cars or planes in the correct garages. See how confidently she can put the cars away.
5. Whoever gets all the cars in the right garages first, wins. You can have many winners.

Note: For elementary-aged students, you may want to give them a few minutes to play with the cars or have a race. Older students may want to make paper airplanes and fly them into labeled boxes.

Identifying Numerals with Items

The next step in learning about numerals is recognizing what numerals stand for. That is, numerals are ways of symbolizing the numbers the students have previously used to rote count and to answer the question "How many?"

INTRODUCING THE CONCEPT

OBJECTIVE: The student will demonstrate that a number of objects can be symbolized by a numeral by matching up groups of dots (1 to 5) with the numerals 1 to 5. Later the objective can be expanded to 1 to 10.

MATERIALS:
- Black marker pen and red marker
- Flashcards with dots (page 325)

SUCCESS STEP: Hold up the cards with one to five dots on them and ask the student how many dots are on each card (assumes the student can spot dots up to 5). Praise correct answers.

PROCEDURE:

1. Using a new set of dot cards 1 to 5 or using the original set which has been laminated, show the student the one-dot card and write the numeral 1 (in a different color than the dots) right below the dot. The dot should look like a round hat on the top of the 1. Say "One dot ... its name is one" as you write the 1 on the card. Have the student repeat orally. Each time you introduce a numeral, point out the dot(s), then have the student say the numeral and count the dot(s). Have her trace the numeral on the card with her finger, starting at the top.

2. Repeat with the number 2 card. Point out the 2 dots. Write the number 2 starting with the first dot and ending with the last dot, as shown in the illustration. Practice as above.

3. Repeat the above procedure with each of the five cards and have frequent, short practices.

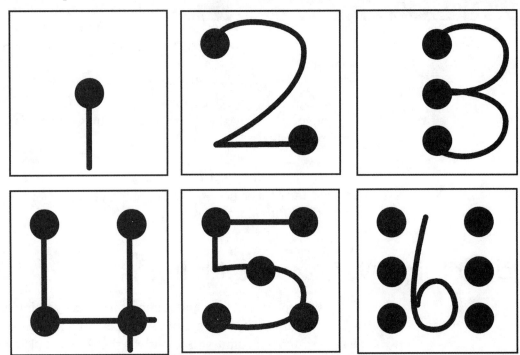

CLIP IT, CLIP IT GAME

MATERIALS:

- Five 3" x 5" index cards, numbered from 1 to 5 in large, black numerals for each student playing the game. If the student has fine motor difficulties, use larger, thicker cards.
- 15 paperclips or clothespins for each player

PROCEDURE:

1. Pick up a card. Model putting on the number of paperclips or clothespins to match the numeral on the card.

2. Let the student practice putting the clips on. If using clothespins (for students with some fine motor difficulty), you may need to paste two index cards together or make the cards out of sturdier cardboard material as from a shipping box. If the student needs assistance, you or a helper can hold the card steady as the paperclips or clothespins are clipped on. If a student doesn't recognize the numerals, add dots to them, as in the previous activity. Fade (remove) the dots as quickly as possible so the student doesn't become dependent on them.

3. To play as a game, give each student one set of cards numbered from 1 to 5 and 15 paperclips or clothespins to match to the numerals. The student with the most correct cards, wins. (They all can win.)

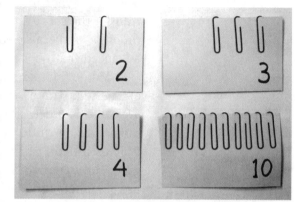

4. When the student does *Clip It, Clip It* confidently, the game can be given as independent work. Later, new larger cards can be made for 1 to 10, and students can compete to finish first accurately. Of course, do not have a competition if one student will be hampered by fine motor difficulties.

HANG IT ON GAME

MATERIALS:

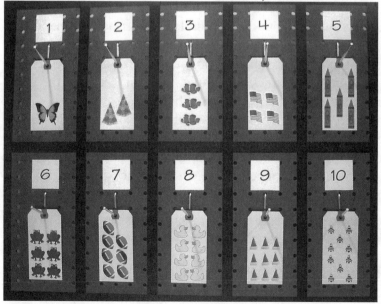

- Pegboard
- "L" hooks (5-10), inserted into the pegboard and labeled from 1 to 5, or 1 to 10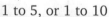
- Index cards with a hole near the top so they fit easily onto the L hooks
  OR
- Picture counting flashcards with a hole punched near the top

PROCEDURE:

1. Draw groups of 1 to 10 items on the index cards or attach 1 to 10 stickers to the cards.

2. Show your student(s) how to hang the cards on a peg beneath the numeral, matching number of items to numeral (Baratta-Lorton, 1972). This activity can become a learning center or a job for independent work.

COMMERCIAL GAME TO BUY OR TRY

A good game to get younger students up and moving while also working on number recognition is *Leaping Frogs* by International Playthings (www.intplay.com). Players bounce beanbag frogs off a mini trampoline and onto numbered lily pads. Play so that players can only keep a frog if they can name the number it landed on.

Remembering the Numerals

Students need to learn to recognize the numerals very thoroughly. Students with Down syndrome and some other concrete learners need creative practice to transfer the short-term learning of numerals to long-term memory storage. Recognition of numerals needs to be automatic to let the student concentrate on more advanced math concepts.

Memory experts have told us that we often remember better when we associate an item with a visual mind picture, especially if the image is funny or unusual. We call this process of using visual or other cues to jog memory *mnemonics.* Mnemonics also includes using chants, songs, and letters to help us remember. Think of Italy as a boot, or the colors of the rainbow as Roy G. Biv (red, orange, yellow, green, blue, indigo, violet). Many of us need to softly sing the ABC song when we are alphabetizing files. We need to use mnemonics more often with students who have difficulties with short-term and working memory.

If the student has trouble remembering what the numerals look like, use mnemonics where possible. You can make up your own that are meaningful to your particular student(s). Or you may want to use a mnemonics system that is commercially available, such as the book *Addition the Fun Way: A Picture Method of Learning the Addition Facts* (1996) by Judy Liautaud. This book has funny rhyming cartoon characters for the numbers (like 3Bee, 4Door, 5Drive, Sick6, 8Gate, and 10Fix-it Men) that may help children to better remember them. The book can also be used later to help memorize the addition facts.

Some students may be able to write the numerals as described in Chapter 11 to help them remember how to form the numerals. Writing the numerals may help by involving their senses of movement (kinesthetic) and touch (tactile). You don't even need to have the student use a pencil and paper. She can just trace the numbers on the desktop or practice with chalk on a chalkboard.

Another aid to memory is creative practice. Although students with Down syndrome do need much repetition to recognize numerals, workbooks and flash cards can be boring and ineffective. Use of games and activities can be fun as well as effective. An example of creative practice, Hop Scotching the Numbers, follows.

HOP SCOTCHING THE NUMBERS

OBJECTIVE: The student will practice numeral recognition while actively involving her whole body.

MATERIALS NEEDED:
- Chalk (for outdoor play)
- Masking tape (for indoor play)

PROCEDURE:

1. Use masking tape to make a hopscotch board with 12 squares on the floor inside or use chalk to make the board outside on the side-walk or playground. Place the numbers from 1 to 12 in order at first. Later put the numbers randomly on the squares. The child hops on the numerals in order from 1 to 12, saying the numeral name. Since this is not intended to be a motor skill game, the player may just walk from one square to another as she calls out the numeral.

2. If the player calls out or steps on the wrong number, another person takes a turn, or if she is alone, she starts over from the beginning.

ADAPTATION FOR OLDER LEARNERS: Instead of *Hop Scotching the Numbers,* older students can use the floor mat of a *Twister* game (Milton Bradley) and tape numerals to the various colored circles. You will need to put the same numerals on the spinner or just use dice instead. You can use simplified rules or invent your own, depending on the age or skill of the players.

COMMERCIAL GAMES TO BUY OR TRY

Once the student can recognize numbers from 1 to 10, she may be able to play many regular children's games such as:
- *Go Fish* (various makers or standard 52 cards)
- *Uno* or *Winnie the Pooh Uno* for younger students (Mattel)
- *Monopoly Junior* (Parker Brothers)
- *Skip Bo* (Mattel)
- *Crazy Eights* (various makers or standard 52 cards)

Many of these games are also available as computer programs such as *Cards for Kids* (Two Lights).

For older learners, find a board or card game that is appropriate for their age that requires recognition of numerals. Examples include: Uno, Sorry, or Racko. Then simplify the rules, if necessary, so they can play it. Use Post-It notes on the board when you need to make changes such as covering over squares on the game board that have directions that are too complex or that prolong the game too much. Since games for older students are often very long, I often just say, "This game takes too long. We are going to make changes so we can play it in 20 minutes. These rules are classroom (family) rules."

Recognizing Numerals from 11 to 19 (Teen Numbers)

As discussed in the previous chapter, the *teen* words often confuse children who are learning about numerals. They hear the *ones* place first so they may think the numeral starts with the number they hear in the *ones* place. For example, they may think 19 is written as 91. Most students will find learning the pattern for 20 and beyond much easier than the teens.

PAPER FOOTBALL

OBJECTIVE: The student will listen to numerals 11 to 19 given orally and match them with the correct written numerals.

MATERIALS:
- 9 index cards with the numbers from 11 to 19 written on both sides using a large marker. To capture interest, cut cards into football, baseball, or other ball shapes. To make the cards easier to throw, you can clip a paper clip or clothespin to each one.
- An opaque bag to hide the index card balls in
- A large cardboard box
- Paper or white board

SUCCESS STEP: Put the index card "balls" in the opaque bag. Have the student guess what is in the bag by squeezing it. Say, "That was a good guess."

PROCEDURE:
1. Take the "balls" out of the bag and throw them, one by one on the floor, as you would do in the sport. Say, "We are going to review some very important rules for this ball game. For you to win this game, you will have to remember the rules for naming the teen numbers." Review the pattern, if necessary. See the section in Chapter 7 on counting larger numbers.
2. Make a game out of calling out a number from 11 to 19 and having the student find it on a "ball" on the floor. If she is correct, have her toss it into a nearby box. Then there will be fewer for her to choose from when you call the next number.
3. If the student is not successful, put only 2 or 3 cards on the floor. Perhaps she will be able to recognize the single digits that are part of the *teen* numbers. You may help her by showing her a written single-digit number and then coach her into recognizing the related *teen* number. Review the patterns for making teen numerals, if necessary.
4. If the student has difficulty recognizing the numerals given orally, write the numbers you call out on a piece of paper or a white board so they she has a matching cue. However, the point of the game is to make sure that she recognizes the written numbers given orally, so you must fade that assist.
5. After she can successfully recognize the teen numbers, throw out all the "balls" every time so she has to choose between all the choices every time.

1 TO 19 BINGO

MATERIALS:
- Math Bingo cards (page 313)
- Metal-trimmed Bingo chips and magnetic wand (See Resources)

PROCEDURE:
1. Photocopy the Bingo cards in Appendix A that only have the numerals from 1 to 19. Laminate the cards if you anticipate using them frequently.
2. Randomly call out the letter above a column and then a numeral that fits in that column—e.g., M – 14. Have students cover up matching numerals on their game boards. Some numerals will be printed twice on a board, and the students may cover both numerals if they recognize that there are two. After the turn is over, they can't go back and cover the second numeral.
3. After each turn, check that the students have covered the correct numeral. If students have difficulty recognizing the numerals given orally, write the numbers you call out on a piece of paper or a white board so the students have a matching cue. However, the point of the game is to make sure that they recognize the written numbers given orally, so you must fade that assist.
4. The winner is the one to first fill in a complete row or a complete column, not crosswise. You can discreetly look at the students' cards and call a number that will enable a frustrated student to win.
5. The winner gets to pick up her chips with the wand first. Then, the others may do the same.

Recognizing Numbers from 20 to 39

Learning the pattern for writing the numbers 20 and larger is usually easier for students than learning to write the teen numbers. The pattern rule for naming the 20s and beyond is consistent and names the digits in the order that most people say them (42 = forty-two). However, if you have thoroughly taught the teen number pattern, it may interfere with applying the pattern for naming the 20s and beyond. If the student mistakenly applies the teen pattern to naming larger numbers, stop and explain both patterns both orally and visually.

BIG 20 AND FRIENDS

OBJECTIVE: The student will be able to recognize the numerals from 20 to 29 and be able to apply the pattern to the numerals from 30 to 39.

MATERIALS:
- The numeral 20 written on an 8" x 11" sheet of paper
- The numeral 30 written on an 8" x 11" sheet of paper

- Half sheets (8" x 5.5") of paper with the numerals from 1 to 9 on them

SUCCESS STEP: Ask the student to hold the paper with the large 20 in front of her chest. Tell her she looks great as the Big 20.

PROCEDURE:

1. Put the paper with the 20 someplace where it will stand up, and the student can see it (against a wall, chalkboard, etc.). Tell her she looked super up there as the Big 20, but she needs a few of her friends.
2. Take the half sheet with the 1 on it and put it over the 0 in the 20. Introduce her to number 21. Repeat the procedure to 25. Then ask her if she knows what friend is going to be up there next. See if she can predict 26 to 29.
3. Show the student the numerals from 20 to 29 again. If you have a group of students, you can have one student bring up the numeral 1, another bring up the numeral 2, and so on.
4. Repeat the procedure with the number 30. You can do the other *tens,* if you want, but the objective is to have the student recognize the pattern and be able to generalize it to another *tens* number.

MATH BINGO GAME PLUS

MATERIALS:

- Math Bingo Plus cards (from 10 to 30), Appendix A
- Bingo chips and magnetic wand (See Resources)

PROCEDURE:

1. Play Math Bingo Plus as was described above in 1 to 19 Bingo, except use the cards with numerals from 10 to 30. If you detect that the student is having trouble with some group of numerals, call these numbers more often. Watch the "teen" numbers closely.
2. Bingo may be played frequently for fun without the students knowing that they are getting good math practice. You can change the numbers on the cards and modify the rules so they do not get bored with the cards provided.

GENERALIZATION INTO DAILY ACTIVITIES: Use everyday life experiences to teach numeral recognition and give practice. For example, have the student:

- Push the numbers on the elevator so they light up.
- Choose TV channels with the remote.
- Weigh herself (or other objects) on a scale.
- Recognize numbers on the calendar.
- Read number books and point to named numbers.
- Learn about clothing sizes, starting with her own sizes.
- Read sports scores in the paper or on the TV screen.
- Use a school schedule (room numbers, sequence of activities or classes).

- Identify page numbers when you are sharing a book.
- Locate the track number of the song she likes on a CD, and then enter it into the CD player.
- Help to find the exit numbers on the highway when you are driving.
- If appropriate, punch in her home number, Dad's cell phone number, etc., on a phone.
- If appropriate, enter the cooking time on a microwave.

- Play games such as writing chalk numbers on floor, then going to called numbers. (Or play a variation on the Cake Walk, where you play music while children walk in a circle around numbers on the floor; when the music stops, they must identify the number they are standing on, or they are out.)

And much more.

Remember to Revisit Activities When Appropriate

Some of the objectives for the activities in this chapter call for you to use one set of small numbers (such as 1 to 5) at first, and a second set that is higher (eventually up to 100) later. Don't forget to go back and systematically teach these higher numbers. The student may not be able learn those higher numbers at the time she learns the smaller numbers, but eventually she will need to recognize the larger numbers to use money and read other identifying numbers.

Recognizing the Numbers on the Calculator

When students can recognize written numbers, they should be introduced to the numbers on the calculator. The numbers on the calculator are not set up like the numbers on the telephone. The calculator starts with 9 on the top row and descends to 1, while the phone starts with 1 and ends with 9. Therefore, individuals who have rather automatic motor skills on the phone may have difficulty entering numbers on the calculator. They also have to remember how to enter the teen numbers and the numbers from 21 to 100.

INTRODUCING THE CALCULATOR

OBJECTIVE: The student will be able to enter single and double digits correctly on the calculator when numbers are given orally (if possible).

MATERIALS:
- Calculator

SUCCESS STEP: Have the student show where the number 1 and the number 9 are on the calculator. Praise correct answer.

PROCEDURE:
1. Call out single-digit numbers and check to see if the students can accurately enter them on their calculators. Have them say the number out loud as they enter it. Next, have them say, "Check" as they look at the window to check that they have entered the correct number. Be sure they know how to clear the window before entering the next entry.
2. Slowly call out double-digit numbers and check the students' calculator windows. If necessary, hold up a visual of the number called. Fade the visual number when possible. Some students will always need a visual image to copy. This is okay, but in daily living people frequently need to enter numbers that they hear given orally.
3. Pair off the students and have one student call out numbers from 1 to 20 while the other student enters the number in the calculator. Then reverse the roles.
4. Practice 5 to 10 minutes each session until students can enter the digits smoothly and accurately (but not swiftly).

CHAPTER 9

More Counting Skills

Pre- /Post Checklist

Can the student:

1. _____ Rote count from 1 to 100.

2. _____ Use a number line.

3. _____ Count forward from any number.

4. _____ Find numbers one more and one less than a named number.

5. _____ Decide which number is larger than another (using a number line).

6. _____ Skip count by 2's (2, 4, 6, etc.).

7. _____ Skip count by 10's (10, 20, 30, etc.) to 100.

8. _____ Skip count by 5's (5, 10, 15 etc.).

9. _____ Count on from the highest number (when combining two numbers).

10. _____ Count backward from 10 and later from 20 (optional).

Counting is not just a simple skill that you learn in a short time. Counting strategies continue to be developed as you have more and more life experiences. Students with Down syndrome may be able to count small numbers accurately but get confused by numbers with several digits. Eventually they will learn the pattern of combining digits to make numerals and be able to use larger numbers in their daily living.

The higher skills for counting this chapter covers are:
- **Counting to 100**
- **Using a number line**
  - ▼ Visualizing the concepts of the number line
  - ▼ Counting forward on the number line starting with any number but 1
  - ▼ One more, one less using the number line
- **Skip counting**
  - ▼ By 2's
  - ▼ By 10's
  - ▼ By 5's
- **Counting backwards (optional)**

Counting to 100

The student should be able to count and use the numbers from 1-40 from previous lessons. Now the larger numbers are introduced so the student can work with the base 10 system for skip counting and place value.

COUNTING TO 100

OBJECTIVE: The student will be able to rote count to 100.

MATERIALS:
- A chalk board or white board
- Chalk or erasable markers

SUCCESS STEP: Have the student rote count to 40 orally. Praise his success. If he is unable to count correctly, you count to 40, having him repeat after every 2 or 3 numbers. Praise his participation.

PROCEDURE:
1. Review rote counting to 39, if you feel the student is not secure in the concept.
2. Write the number 39 on the board. Ask the student what number comes next. He should know that 40 comes next from the review. Write 40 on the board. Then you write 41 on the board and say, "This is 41. What is the number?" and have the student repeat the number 41. Be sure to put commas and some space between the numbers as you write them. Continue introducing 42, 43, and 44 in the same manner.
3. Then ask the student, "What number comes next?" If he does not say 45, point out the pattern in the numbers on the board, pointing out the 0, 1, 2, 3, 4. Then ask again, "What number comes next?"
4. Continue the above procedure with the numbers up to 49.
5. Have the students chant the numbers from 40 to 49 as often as necessary.

6. Repeat the procedure for the numbers from 50 to 100. A good pace would to work on 10 numbers per session. Eventually the student will be able to rote count to 100.
7. Praise the student's efforts. Have him rote count for brothers and sisters, parents, the school secretary, and anyone else you can rope into listening.

WHAT IS MISSING?

OBJECTIVE: The student will fill in the missing numbers on a chart with numbers 50 to 100.

MATERIALS:
- Missing Number Chart (page 328) for each student
- Small Post-It notes (2" x 1½")

SUCCESS STEP: Have the student point to the number 50 and the number 100 on the Missing Numbers Chart. Praise success.

PROCEDURE:
1. Cover 3 of the numbers on the Missing Numbers Chart with Post-It notes. (Cut the Post-It note in half on the longest side. Put the Post-It note over the number and then fold.) Have the student point to each Post-It note and say what the Missing Number hidden beneath it is. Lift up the notes so the student can see if he supplied the correct answer. He needs to *say* the written number, not write it.
2. Cover different numbers on the Missing Numbers Chart, gradually increasing the amount of numbers the student must supply.
3. Continue practicing rote counting to 100 at future sessions to help him maintain the skill.

GENERALIZATION INTO DAILY ACTIVITIES: Counting and recognizing these larger numbers will be more meaningful after students get more experiences with place value in the next chapter. At this stage, try to include numbers into your everyday activities so that the number names are almost overlearned.
- Play hide and seek and count to 100 (or as high as the student can count).
- Have the student help count out small items for a snack or an activity (e.g., give everyone in the family or class 50 mini marshmallows, Goldfish crackers, or craft sticks).
- Count to make sure you still have 52 cards in your deck before playing a card game.
- When sharing a book, occasionally pause and ask the student to read the page number you are on.
- Play Chutes and Ladders by Milton Bradley (the squares on the board are numbered from 1 to 100) and comment on what number you land on, have to go back to, etc.

Using a Number Line

Using a number line is a skill that helps students to visualize the relationships between numbers. In school the number line is usually taped to the desk for reference. Some students can count easily from 1 to 20, but if you ask them to start at any number besides 1, they are not able to do it. A number line can give them a visual picture of the numbers' relationships to each other and help them understand "one more" and "one less." Number lines can also be used to help students visualize what they are doing when adding or subtracting (see Chapter 13). To use a number line, students need to be able to recognize the numerals from 1 to 20.

VISUALIZING THE CONCEPTS OF THE NUMBER LINE

The student needs to have a visual picture of what a number line represents in his mind. That is, that the further you go to the right, the "bigger" the numbers are; the further you go to the left, the "smaller" they are. The first step in using a number line should be to use concrete materials to represent the numbers on the number line.

OBJECTIVE: The student will be able represent the numbers on a number line (1 to 10) with concrete materials.

MATERIALS:

- Poker chips, Bingo chips, small blocks, or other similar items that can be easily stacked
- Number line with numbers 1 to 10. (Cut a strip of light cardboard or cardstock about 15 inches long and 1 inch wide—similar to a ruler. Write the numerals 1 to 10 clearly about 1½ inches apart.)

SUCCESS STEP: Ask the student to make a stack of 1, then 2, then 3 chips or blocks. Check the piles and praise him for the correct numbers.

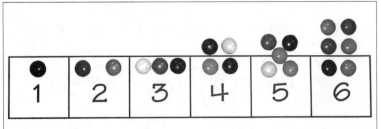

PROCEDURE:

1. Show the number line (1 to 10) to the student, point out the numbers, and have him identify them.
2. See if he can put the right numbers of chips or blocks on the numbers 1, 2, and 3. If he is not correct, model putting the chips on the numbers. Tell him that the chips represent the numbers on the number line.
3. Have the student make piles of 4, 5, and 6 chips and put them on the corresponding numbers. Repeat with 7, 8, 9, and 10 chips.

4. Make a game about pointing to a number on the number line and having the student make a pile of chips that represent the number pointed to.
5. For additional practice, have the student mark dots on the number line itself that show the number of items that the number represents.

COUNTING FORWARD FROM ANY NUMBER

Emily easily counts from 1 to 30, almost on one breath. If you stop her, however, she yells, "Now, I have to start all over again from the beginning." If you say to her, "You were on number 11. Just start from 11." She says, "Oh, I can't! I have to go back to 1 again."

OBJECTIVE: The student will be able to count to 20 starting with any number other than 1, at first using the number line, then without the number line.

MATERIALS:

* Number line with numbers 1 to 20. Use light cardboard or cardstock to make a 20-inch line about 1 inch wide (similar to a ruler), which has the numerals 1-20 written clearly about 1 inches apart. You can copy the number line from page 330 in Appendix B (the 1 to 10 and the 11 to 20 segments) and glue them together onto the cardstock.

PROCEDURE:

1. Using the number line marked from 1 to 20, point to a low number and ask the student to say that number and all the numbers that are higher up on the number line to 20. Say, "Tell me which numbers are larger (higher)." He can just read them off the number line. Practice as necessary. If the student is nonverbal, have him point to the correct number as you say it.
2. Tell him that you are going to play a game to see if he can really count. You know that he can say the numbers from 1 to 20, but can he begin at a different starting number each time? Start from numbers chosen at random, but let him use the number line if he chooses.
3. Then challenge him to count to 20 from any number between 2 and 19 without using the number line.
4. Have the students work in pairs by having one student name any number on the number line except 20. The other student has to count forward while the first student watches the numerals on the number line to make sure he does it correctly.

Note: The skill of counting forward from any number is not easy. The student needs to have a picture in his mind of something similar to the number line in order to start at any number and count higher. Practice will make this skill come automatically if he has the concrete materials to help him visualize the sequence of numbers as he learns.

ONE MORE, ONE LESS (USING A NUMBER LINE)

OBJECTIVE: The student will be able to name numbers that are *one more* or *one less* than called numbers using a number line (1 to 20). Later from 1 to 100 on a hundreds chart, if possible.

MATERIALS:

- The number line used for previous activity
- A large index card or sheet of paper
- Teacher's number line, which can be written on the chalkboard or on an overhead transparency (or make a large number line from cardstock that can be seen by the students)

PROCEDURE:

1. Point to a number (5) on your number line and say, "What number is one more than 5?" (Or any number from 1 to 9). Move your finger over one number and say, "6."
2. Ask the students to do the same thing on their number lines. The students put their fingers first on the 5, and then move one more to the 6 on their number lines. Repeat with numbers chosen randomly.
3. When the students seem to get the pattern, quit modeling the answers immediately and observe the students.

PEEK GAME

4. When the students seem secure with the first step, they can play the game Peek. Cover up the numbers (on the teacher's number line) that are larger than the number you will call. For example, you want to call the number 4. Cover up 5 to 10 and point to the number 4. Then say, "What number is one more than 4?"
5. After the students respond, one student comes up to peek at the next number on the teacher's number line. He announces whether the class was correct and the class receives a point. If they were incorrect, the teacher gets a point, and the number is repeated. Of course the class will win, but the teacher can bemoan the fact that the class is so smart.
6. After the students are secure in knowing one more, change to another activity. In a week or two, use the same activities for one less. This activity is designed to prepare for beginning addition and subtraction.

GENERALIZATION INTO DAILY ACTIVITIES: Deliberately set up situations that will prompt your student to ask for one more. For example, give him one too few items to hand out (cups, napkins, etc.) to the class or family. See if he will ask for one more. Or don't give him enough envelopes for his Valentines or buns for hot dogs and see if he will request one more.

WHICH NUMBER IS LARGER? (USING A NUMBER LINE)

Top This (sometimes called War) as played in the Informal Assessment can be adapted so the number line is used to check each answer. This offers good practice in using a number line to determine which number is larger.

OBJECTIVE: The student will use a number line to determine which number is larger from pairs of numbers under 10 (later from 1 to 40 and then 1 to 100).

MATERIALS:

- Deck of cards with face cards removed; aces representing one
- Number line numbered from 1 to 10

PROCEDURE:

1. Shuffle the cards and deal them to the players face down. (The game is usually played with two players but more can play.)
2. Each player turns over the top card in his pile and compares cards to see who has the largest number.
3. The student with the largest number must show that his number is the largest by pointing at the two numbers on the number line. He then gets to take all the cards in that round. If there is a tie, each player keeps his own cards.
4. The winner is the player with the most cards at the end of the game.

Skip Counting

Skip counting means naming only some of the numbers in a consistent pattern such as 10...20...30...etc. Many children come to school with the ability to skip count by 2's to 10, perhaps from playing childhood games. Counting by 2's helps a student distinguish between odd and even numbers. Counting by 10's is an important skill that helps in understanding our base ten system and in determining place value. After counting by 10's, most texts teach counting by 5's. Skip counting by 5's is very useful in telling time and in adding nickels and five dollar bills. If you have a student with significant memory problems, I would concentrate on teaching him to count by 10's first. Later, you can try introducing him to skip counting by 5's or 2's.

SKIP COUNTING BY TWOS

OBJECTIVE: The student will be able to count by 2's, first to 10, later to 20, understanding the terms *even* and *odd numbers*.

MATERIALS:

- A number line (1 to 20) for each student. You can use the one from the activity Counting Forward from Any Number above.
- Calculator
- One or more small game tokens or other counters small enough to sit completely on one square of the number line
- One die

SUCCESS STEP: Ask the student to repeat or chant after you, "2, 4, 6, 8, 10. Let's do it over again." If he is not successful, have him repeat fewer numbers. "2, 4, 6. Don't do any tricks." Praise him.

PROCEDURE:

1. Using the number line, repeat the chant done in the success step and have the student point to each number on the number line as it is chanted. Repeat as needed.
2. Show the student how you can *hop* or *jump* your marker to every other number on the number line, starting with the number 2. Ask him if he can *hop* the numbers too. You say the correct number as he is making the hop.
3. If he can't get the concept of "every other," highlight the even numbers with a light pencil mark. After some practice with the marked number line, thoroughly erase the pencil marks and see if he can hop to every other number without cues. Have him name his jumps without instructor assistance.
4. Tell the student that the numbers he jumped to are called *even* numbers. When that concept is secure, teach the term *odd* numbers for the other numbers.

JUMPING JACK GAME

OBJECTIVE: The student will practice the concept of odd vs. even numbers.

MATERIALS:

- A 1 to 20 number line for each student
- Small game tokens
- One die

PROCEDURE:

1. Have the players place their markers on the first square of their number line.
2. Players take turns rolling the die. If they roll an odd number (1, 3, and 5), they can't move, and they pass the die to the next person. If they roll an even number (2, 4, 6) they get to jump their token to the next number on the number line. For example, if I roll a 6 on my first roll, I hop to the second space on the number line and give the die to the next person. If I roll a 2 the next time, I hop to the next space on the number line (the third space). (You only move when you roll 2, 4, or 6, but you just move one square at a time.)
3. The person who reaches 20 first is the winner.

EVENS AND ODDS WITH THE CALCULATOR

PROCEDURE:

1. Pair students up. Let them take turns punching a number between 1 and 10 into their calculator and showing it to their partner. The partner must identify it as an even or odd number. If he is wrong, the first player gets a point.
2. Have the student(s) punch the even numbers between 1 and 10 into their calculators (i.e., 246810) and you check his numbers.

GENERALIZATION INTO DAILY ACTIVITIES:

- When cutting a pizza or brownies, say that you want every person there to have two pieces. Then count the people by 2's so you know how many pieces to cut.
- Shoot baskets and give yourself and other players 2 points for each basket.
- Count how many shoes are on in the house or class by counting each person as 2.
- Play the game *I Am Thinking of a Number* (between 1 to 10, then 1 to 20). First announce that you are thinking of an *even* number between 1 and 10. The student has to guess the number. If he guesses the wrong even number, someone else gets a turn (or he gets to guess again, if he is the only player). If, however, the questioner guesses an *odd* number, the other player has won the game and gets to start over with a new number.

SKIP COUNTING BY 10'S

OBJECTIVE: The student will be able to skip count the numbers by 10, first from 10 to 50, then to 100.

MATERIALS:

- 5 bundles (with 10 each) of straws or sticks for each student
- Counting by 10's Chart (1 to 50) from Appendix B with magnified 10's numbers.
- Counting by 10's Chart (1 to 100) from Appendix B

SUCCESS STEP: Have the student take off the rubber band on one bundle and count the straws so he knows that each bundle has 10. Praise correct counting.

PROCEDURE:

1. Give each student 5 bundles of straws (10 in each) and have them chant as they put down each bundle, "10...20...30...40...50." Repeat as necessary.
2. Then the teacher should open all 5 of her own bundles and have the student count the straws from 1 to 50 in rhythm with her. The teacher should then

bundle up her 5 bundles of ten and compare them to the student's bundles. Then have the student chant 10...20...30...40...50 as he counts his bundles.

3. Introduce the Counting by 10's Chart (1 to 50). Have the student count by tens while looking at the chart. Continue until the student is secure with counting by 10's to 50.

4. Next, the teacher should demonstrate counting by 10's with more bundles of ten (her own bundles) until 100 is reached. Repeat the demonstration with the students counting with the teacher.

5. Introduce the Counting by Tens to 100 Chart to the students. Sometimes they will be able to focus on the 10's in the hundreds chart if those numbers are larger. You may want to outline the 10's in red to help the students focus. Have them count by 10's, pointing to each one on the hundred's chart.

6. At another session, have the students work in pairs and put their 5 bundles with the other person's 5 bundles so they both can count to 100 by 10's. If the students have much difficulty with the numbers from 50 to 100, go back and review skip counting with only the numbers from 10 to 50. When the large numbers become more familiar to the student, he may be able to pick up the skip count to 100 much quicker.

GENERALIZATION INTO DAILY ACTIVITIES:

- Play the game *Spud*. Assign each player one of the 10's (for example, "Josh, you're number 20; Lauren, you're number 30.") One player yells "Spud," throws up a ball, and calls out the number given to another player. The person whose number has been called must catch the ball before it bounces. The Spud thrower must know the 10's to make a good call.
- Count your pennies by making piles of 10. Count off the piles up to 50 to put in penny roll wrappers.

SKIP COUNTING BY 5'S

OBJECTIVE: The student will be able to skip count by 5's from 5 to 50. Later to 100.

MATERIALS:

- Small paper cups
- Small items like raisins or macaroni
- 5 five dollar bills (play money) for each student plus extra for the teacher
- Counting by Fives Chart (page 332)

SUCCESS STEP: Have the student show you how to put 5 items in the paper cup. Make sure he is successful and praise him.

PROCEDURE:

1. Place 5 paper cups on the table. Lay out a line of 25 small items in front of the student on the table.

2. Count out all the long string of items from 1-25.
3. Then have the student count out five items to put into each paper cup. (Younger students may enjoy the activity more if some of the cups are placed in front of stuffed animals.)
4. The teacher says, "I have a faster way to count all these small items." Chant, "5...10...15...20...25," touching each cup as you count, thus getting the total number of items. "Is that the same number we had when we counted them one by one?" (It should be the same.) "See, that was faster! Would you like to learn the faster way?"
5. Then direct the students (together) to count the items in the same way, chanting or singing the 5's. Ask if that is faster than counting each item separately. Give each student a chance to skip count the items in the cups by himself.
6. Use the Counting by Fives Chart (Appendix B) that has the 5's magnified to help them learn counting by 5's. They can read off the 5's numbers until they have memorized the numbers. Point out that every other number ends in 5.
7. If young students are having a lot of trouble memorizing the sequence, you can make up a song to help them remember. For example, to the tune of the traditional "10 Little Indians," you could sing "5... 10... 15... 20/ 25...30...35...40/ 45... 50... 55... 60..., I can count by 5's."

Do not be concerned if the student's skip counting is not consistently correct. Repetition is the key to memorizing the numbers in skip counting. When the student works with money, counting by 5's and 10's will probably become a more functional skill. If the student is older, you may want to go to Chapter 20 (Money) for more explanation and practice.

Nathan knew how to count his $5 and $10 bills so he could figure out how much money he had. He easily said, "5, 10, 15, 20." He could also skip count $10 bills up to 100. However, when he was asked to skip count by 2's, he was unable to remember how. "I did that once" he said. He had many occasions to use his skip counting by 5's and 10's, but very little occasion to skip count by 2's.

GENERALIZATION INTO DAILY ACTIVITIES:
- Play games where you score 5 points at a time such as darts or another game where you can make up the scoring.
- Count how many fingers there are in your family or in a small group in your class. Touch each finger as it is counted. Then count the number of fingers by 5's. Point out how much faster counting by 5's is.
- Play hide and seek where the seeker closes his eyes and counts by 5's to 100. You can use skip counting by 10's or 2's in the same way.

Review skip counting until the students can count the 5's and the 10's without using the number lines or charts. A workbook on skip counting, *Hopping Good Cents: A New Method for Teaching the Counting of Money* (Pro-Ed, 1999), teaches skip counting with different types of number lines and tokens (e.g., knight in armor) to capture a student's interest.

Counting On

When students learn the strategy of *counting on,* they become more efficient in counting two groups of items. When the student is combining two groups of items, and knows how many are in each group, he can start with the total of the largest group and *count on.* For example, when we combine 9 and 4, we do not have to count each one of the items starting with 1. We can start with the number of the largest group (9), then count 10, 11, 12, and 13 for the 4 additional items in the second group to get the total. Students must be able to *rote count forward* as explained in Chapter 7 to *count on* with meaning.

Research with typically developing children shows that they do not just "catch on" to *counting on* and use the strategy from then on. Sometimes they use it and sometimes they do not for a period of time. Eventually it becomes a consistent part of their math strategies. So, if you are working with a child with Down syndrome or another hands-on learner, just continue to remind him gently about *counting on* as he does other math problems and don't expect a quick change in strategies.

> *Jake had 6 Sunday newspapers at his feet. His brother handed him 5 more. Then his brother yelled, "How many papers do you have now?" Jake started counting the whole pile of newspapers at his feet. "1, 2, 3, " up to 11. Jake got the correct answer, but it would have been much faster to count on: " 6, 7, 8, 9, 10, and 11."*

WHAT'S IN THE BAG?

OBJECTIVE: When combining 2 groups, the student will *count on* from the total number of the largest group to get a final answer.

MATERIALS:
- Several varieties of items that are alike (pencils, poker chips, pennies, etc.)
- Paper bag

SUCCESS STEP: Have the student count 3 of the items. Praise him.

PROCEDURE:
1. Put the three items already counted in a paper bag. Say, "I put in 3."

2. Pick up 1 more item and say, "And this is 4" and put it in the bag.
3. Pick up another item and ask, "What number is this?" (5) Put it in the bag.
4. Then dump all the items out of the bag and count them to be sure there were 5 there.
5. Point out how much faster it was to *count on* from the number that we knew was in the bag compared to counting each one. Repeat with different items.
6. If the student is nonverbal, have him raise his fingers to show the number of items in the bag or point to the numbers on the number line.
7. Pair off students and have one put the items into the bag, as done above, and the other check the total by counting all the items.
8. Repeat with a variety of items or counters.

COUNT-ON GAME

OBJECTIVE: The student will combine two groups by saying the largest number and counting on with the second group to get the total.

MATERIALS:
- Two dice
- Paper and pencil

PROCEDURE:
1. Each player in turn rolls two dice. He then must say the number of dots on one die and count on to get the total of both dice. The teacher writes the total number under the student's name on the paper.
2. If the player counts *all* the dots on the dice rather than counting on, he does not receive a score for that turn. If he counts incorrectly, he does not receive a score for that turn.
3. Set a time limit for the game such as 10 or 15 minutes. Then the teacher totals each student's score. High score wins.

(Of course, you should give the students some time to learn the game without keeping score. This game also assesses spotting skills as described in Chapter 7, Number Sense.)

GENERALIZATION INTO DAILY ACTIVITIES: Any time the student is counting two groups, you can emphasize how much faster it is to *count on* instead of starting all over again from the beginning. Games using two dice are good examples of the efficiency of *counting on*. Have the student look at one die and spot the number of dots there. Then have the student *count on* with the dots on the second die. You can always have him check the answer by counting each of the individual dots. (More advanced students can try Yahtzee by Milton Bradley and count up the total of five dice.)

When you are getting supplies that come in boxes or multi-packs, you can have your child count on to get the total count. For example, have him figure out how many cans of juice, eggs, or any food item there are when the total of one group is already known. Then both of you can count on to get the total amount. For instance, if you have two six-packs of juice, point to the first six-pack and say "six," then count on to find out how many cans you have in all. Or at school, if you have already taken attendance and know there are 21 students in the room and then 1 more student walks in late, let the students count on to help you find the total.

Backwards Counting from 10 (Optional)

Backwards counting is much harder than forward counting. It requires the reversal of a well-known process. Counting backwards is not an essential survival skill. Counting backward can be useful, however, for understanding a number line and for one way of doing beginning subtraction. For example, "You have 9 pencils and I take away 3 of them. Tell me how many you have now?" The student could count backwards, "8...7....6. However, if the student knows how to use a number line, he can count backwards with the help of that aid, so it is not absolutely essential to remember the numbers in backwards sequence.

BACKWARDS COUNTING FROM 10

OBJECTIVE: The student will be able to count backwards from 10, using a number line if necessary.

MATERIALS:
- Songs that incorporate counting backwards (such as *Ten Little Monkeys)* where monkeys, frogs, or jumping children keep being eliminated one by one
- A picture or a model of a rocket
- A number line

SUCCESS STEP: Have the student clap and sing, "3, 2, 1, 3, 2, 1" to the tune of the first two lines of *Three Blind Mice*. Praise him for correct responses.

PROCEDURE:
1. Teach a backward counting rhyme such as *Ten Little Monkeys* (elementary students only).

> Ten little monkeys jumping on the bed.
> One fell off and bumped his head.
> Mama called the doctor and the doctor said,
> "No more monkeys jumping on the bed."

> Nine little monkeys jumping on the bed.
> One fell off and bumped his head.
> Mama called the doctor and the doctor said,
> "No more monkeys jumping on the bed." etc.

Or, *Ten in the Bed:*
There were ten in the bed,
And the little one said, "Roll over, roll over!"
So they all rolled over and one fell out,
There were nine in the bed,
And the little one said, "Roll over, roll over!" etc.

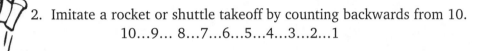

2. Imitate a rocket or shuttle takeoff by counting backwards from 10.
10...9... 8...7...6...5...4...3...2...1

3. If the student already knows how to use a number line, he can just practice reading the numbers from 10 back to 1. (He can also use the number line to keep track of what number he is on when singing or chanting one of the backwards counting songs.)

ADAPTATIONS FOR OLDER LEARNERS: Use items for counting that adults use such as poker chips, bingo markers, pennies, and pretzel sticks. Do not use the singing games or finger plays that are commonly used by younger children. If possible, use the number line to teach counting backwards. You may teach the names of the numbers backward from 10 by making them into a chant or rap song.

If you can stand to hear the song, have the students sing the song *100 Bottles of Pop on the Wall* (a version of *100 Bottles of Beer on the Wall)*. You can start with any number of bottles of pop on the wall, depending on what numbers you want them to be counting back from.

CHAPTER 10

Place Value

Pre- /Post Checklist

Can the student:

1. _____ Demonstrate with sticks or straws how to make the numbers 40 and below using tens and ones (units).

2. _____ Build named numbers (under 40) showing tens and ones with the Clothespin Box described in this chapter.

3. _____ Place two- and three-digit numbers into ones, tens, and hundreds columns on a place value mat.

4. _____ Read two- and three-digit numbers correctly.

5. _____ Have a visual concept of what 100 items looks like and distinguish between 40 and 100 items.

Moira is reading out numbers for Rowan to type into the computer. Rowan does well with numerals up to 13. For 14, however, she types in 41.

This is an understandable error since she hears the words "four-teen" with the four spoken first. However, if Rowan understands something about place value, she can be taught this irregularity in the English counting sequence.

Our system of numeration has evolved from a need to record quantities and a desire to convey the amounts of these quantities to others. Our system is a base-ten model with one to nine digits in the first column. When one more is added, there is an exchange of 10 *ones* for 1 *ten,* which is then placed in the second column. This regrouping allows us to record both small and very large numbers with a rule-driven system. The *value* of any digit is determined by the *place* that the digit holds in the given number. For example, in the number 582, the digit 2 is in the *ones* place, so there are 2 *ones.* The digit 8 is in the *tens* place, so there are 8 *tens.* The digit 5 is in the *hundreds* place, so there are 5 *hundreds.* You could not give the correct value for the digit 5 unless you knew that it was in the *hundreds* place.

We have actually been working with place value when we worked with two-digit numbers, even if the students were not aware of it. However, we are now going to have the students get a visual, concrete image of the place value of numbers.

This may seem so elementary to you that it goes without saying. However, it cannot go without saying for young students. They have to be taught what place value means and have a mental picture of how the numbers are made in their minds. That learning is really not so elementary. The Romans struggled with a system that required letters and specific placements to record quantities. Every time I look for the production date of an older movie, I remember that those Roman numerals do not give me instant recognition as our Arabic numerals do . . . and they string out much longer.

Place value has its roots in counting with meaning. If your student can count to 30, understanding the patterns, she is probably ready to learn about place value. Essential steps in understanding place value are:

- **Understanding that single digits are *ones***
- **Grouping and counting items by *tens***
- **Making numbers showing place value**
- **Reading two-digit numbers**
- **Breaking numbers down into *ones, tens,* and *hundreds***
- **Having a mental concept of 100 items**
- **Reading three-digit numbers**

Ones and Tens

If you have used sticks and straws to give concrete meaning to numerals, most students will have the mental image of the numeral 1 as being *one* concrete item. You may teach them the name *units* or *ones* for the single digits depending on the name preferred in your school. If you have done the lesson with skip counting by 10's from Chapter 9, the student will already understand that the sticks or straws can be bundled up in a group of ten which is called *tens.* If the student has not been given that lesson, see if she understands about groups of *tens* by having her count 4 bundles of ten. If not, go back to Chapter 9 and teach her the concept of skip counting by tens.

OBJECTIVE: The student will be able to represent single-digit numbers concretely on a *ones* mat.

MATERIALS:
- Craft sticks or straws
- *Ones Mat* made of construction paper. Cut the paper so it is only wide enough to hold 9 of the craft sticks or straws. Put the title *Ones Mat* at the top of the paper.
- Construction paper and a marker or pen

SUCCESS STEP: Have the student count out 10 sticks or straws. Praise correct counting.

PROCEDURE:
1. Have the student count out 9 sticks or straws and put them on the *Ones Mat*. Point out the written title on the mat and demonstrate that only 9 sticks can fit on the *Ones Mat*.
2. Repeat the process by picking up the sticks, giving them to the student and having her put down 4, then 2, then 8 sticks until you think that she has a visual picture in her mind of single digits on the *Ones Mat*. End with her counting 9 sticks onto the mat, laying them side by side so the mat is completely covered.
3. Give the student two more sticks and ask her where they should go on the mat. Tell her the rules are that you can't put one on top of the others or put the stick over the title at the top of the mat.
4. Suggest that you make a new mat for the *Tens*. Take out another colored sheet of paper and write *Tens Mat* at the top. You must then make sure that she does not just put the two single sticks on the *Tens Mat*. Say, "That mat *says tens* on it."
5. Bundle up 10 of the sticks with a rubber band and show her the bundle as 1 bunch of ten. Then put the bundle on the *Tens Mat*. Say, "When you have 10 ones, you can put them all together and make 1 ten."
6. Ask her how many *ones* are left on the *ones* mat now. Say, "Yes, we have 1 bundle of 10 and 2 ones sticks." Place the 2 ones on the *Ones Mat* and help her count the total. Say, "One bundle of 10 makes 10 (as you touch the tens bundle), and here we have 2 ones.... so that makes 11, 12."
7. Take the rubber band off and see if she can repeat what you have done with the 12 sticks.

Grouping and Counting Items in *Tens*

One purpose of these activities is to give the students a mental image of numbers from 10 to 40. Then they will learn how to represent numbers (40 and under) on a chart showing the *ones* and *tens* places. When they were skip counting bundles of ten previously, they were just naming bundles. Now we want them to be able to lay out the single digits and bundle the tens independently. This ability will show that they understand the meaning of place value. After additional practice, they should be ready to extend the concept to *hundreds* and *thousands*.

USING THE *ONES* AND *TENS* MAT INDEPENDENTLY

OBJECTIVE: The student will demonstrate how to use single straws and bundles of 10 straws to make the numbers from 10 to 40.

MATERIALS:
- 40 straws or craft sticks and 4 rubber bands for each student
- Two pieces of colored paper in contrasting colors taped together for mats, one labeled *Ones Mat* and the other *Tens Mat,* as done in previous activity

SUCCESS STEP: Ask the student to tell you which mat is for the *ones* and which mat is for the *tens.* Praise her if she is correct. If she is not correct, tell her which color is the *Ones Mat* and let her tell you which is the *Tens Mat.*

PROCEDURE:
1. Ask the student to count out 10 straws/sticks and put the rubber band on the bundle herself.
2. If the student is unable to put the rubber band on or has difficulty picking up the straws/sticks, have her count them as you put each one in her hand. Then you or someone else can band her straws/sticks.
3. Have the student band all 40 straws/sticks into bundles of *ten.*
4. Have the student skip count the bundles to 40 (10, 20, 30, 40). See Chapter 9, More Counting Skills, for direction on skip counting.
5. Put the *Ones Mat* and the *Tens Mat* in front of the student. Open one of her bundles so she has 10 separate sticks and 3 bundles of ten. See if she can put 11 on the mats—1 bundle of ten on the *Tens Mat* and 1 single stick on the *Ones Mat.* If not, you model putting 11 on the mats. Have her repeat making 11 as you have done.
6. Try some other two-digit numbers (under 40) with you modeling and the student repeating until she can make the numbers on her own.
7. Write one numeral at a time (under 40) on a paper or a slate and show it to the student. Tell her what the number is and ask her to make that number using the straws. She should put the *tens* on the *Tens Mat* and the *ones* on the *Ones Mat.* Check and explain after each number. Repeat as often as necessary.

CLOTHESPIN BOX

Some students will have difficulty picking up the flimsy straws or the flat sticks used in the previous activity. They may get frustrated at their lack of control of these items. A better activity to help them understand place value may be the Clothespin Box. Some of students can squeeze open clothespins and clamp them on a cardboard box edge. Others do better with the kind of clothespin that has no moving parts, but slides onto the box edge. I have found that students usually enjoy working with the brightly colored clothespins and the shoebox as described below.

Clothespin Boxes are easier to store if you cut the two short sides that are not labeled with ONE and TEN. Then you can fold the short sides in and fold the whole structure flat. If the cardboard is strong enough, the box will stand up well when you pull the sides out part way.

MATERIALS:

- 50 colored plastic clothespins per student
- Several plain wooden clothespins or wooden clothespins painted black for each student
- 1 shoebox per student with **TENS** printed on one half of the long side of the box and **ONES** on the other half of the box
- The rectangular cardboard holders that the clothespins came on, cut to hold only 10 clothespins. (If no holders are available, cut cardboard strips about 1½" wide and long enough so that they will only hold 10 clothespins.)
- A larger box for the teacher to demonstrate on (optional)

SUCCESS STEP: Have the student put 2 clothespins on the ONES section of the box. Then ask her to put on one more. Praise her.

PROCEDURE:

1. Demonstrate to the student how you can clip 9 clothespins to the ONES section and no more. (Use marker to delineate the area where the clothespins can go if there is room for more than 9 clothespins.)
2. Then take one of the long strips of ten clothespins attached to a cardboard strip and hang it on the TENS side. I use a plain or black-colored wooden clothespin to hang the strip of 10 on the box. (Black color or plain wood keeps it from being counted as one of the strip.) Give her a chance to try doing the same.
3. Have the student make all the numbers from 1 to 9 with the clothespins on the ONES side of the box.
4. Write the numerals from 21 to 29 on paper, one at a time, and have the student try to make each with the pins using two bundles of *tens* on the TENS part of the box. Repeat over a period of days.
5. Now have her make the numerals from 11 to 20 on the clothespin box. The *teen* numerals are more difficult because the student does not hear the predictable pattern of *twenty-one, twenty-two, etc.* However, if you show her the written numeral, she will usually be able to reproduce it.
6. Make numerals to 40. If you need more space to hang ten strips, glue or staple a strip of cardboard to the left side of the box.

Clothespin Colors

The clothespins I use come in four bright colors. At first, I was afraid of confusing the students, so I only used one color (yellow) for the lesson. Later the students tried to replicate the lesson, and some of them mixed the colors of the clothespins. I asked them to tell me which was the easiest way to work with the clothespins. One boy said, "If the pins are the same color, I can't count them from here. If you mix up the colors, they are easier to count." It seems that the yellow clothespins meld together and are hard to count when on the box. The group was able to disregard the difference in the colors in order to count more easily.

Place Value of Numbers Up to 100

If the student has learned to accurately make the numbers from 1 to 40 using the Clothespin Box, she should be ready to make the numbers from 41-100. However, you should make sure that she can count all the way from 41-100, understands the rules for making these higher numbers, and can recognize these higher numbers when they are written and given orally. It would be helpful if she could count on from the highest number, but not absolutely necessary. Refer to Chapter 8, Recognition of Numerals, and Chapter 9, More Counting Skills for review of these preliminary skills. Then she should be introduced to *hundreds*.

HANGING NUMBERS

OBJECTIVE: The student will be able to place any two-digit numbers into *ones* and *tens* columns and read them correctly.

MATERIALS:
- Clothespins
- Clothespin Box used in previous activity

SUCCESS STEP: Have the student make a single-digit number on the Clothespin Box. Praise her if correct. Model making the number for her and have her repeat, if she is not successful.

PROCEDURE:
1. Using the Clothespin Boxes, show the students the numbers 27 and 19. Then write the numerals on paper or a board so the student can relate the written number to concrete items.
2. Using clothespins, make some of the numbers from 21 to 40 on the Clothespin Box and see if the students can figure out what the numbers are. They do not have to read all these numbers correctly. If you feel that they are still shaky on recognizing the larger two-digit numbers, replay the MATH Bingo game from the Informal Assessment using the double-digit numbers. You may change the numbers on the bingo cards so they teach only the numbers from 40 to 99.

ANOTHER WAY
TO VISUALIZE
PLACE VALUE
(OPTIONAL)

For students who are having difficulty with the concept of place value, you may want to introduce them to a simplification of a mnemonic developed by Jan Semple (1986). In this illustration called *Whole Number Street,* the numbers in the ones place are visualized as Kids, those in the tens place are thought of as Teenagers, and those in the hundreds (and higher) place are Grown-ups.

KIDS, TEENS AND GROWN-UPS

OBJECTIVE: The student will be able to visualize and explain the relationship between *ones/units, tens,* and *hundreds* (place value) by comparing it with the relationship between Kids, Teenagers, and Grown-ups and their allowances.

MATERIALS:
- Place-Value-People chart showing *ones, tens,* and *hundreds* from page 334. (Before teaching this lesson, copy this onto the chalkboard or make a laminated poster that can be referred to later)
- Teens and Kids worksheet from Appendix B (page 335)
- Pencil, colored pencils, or crayons

PROCEDURE:
1. Ask your student(s) if they would like an easy way to remember place value. Show them the positions of the *Kids, the Teenagers,* and the *Grown-ups* on the chalkboard or on the teacher's Place-Value-People poster. The *Kids* get allowances in one dollar bills. Explain that the *Kids* are closest to home, which is shown by the wall (which is a wall representing the decimal point, used later on.) The *tens* column is for *Teenagers* who get allowances in ten dollar bills. The *hundreds* column is for *Grown-ups* who get their money in hundred dollar bills. (Later we will have more categories of *Grown-ups.)*
2. Talk about various one- and two-digit numbers and write them in the proper places on the teacher's Place-Value-People chart. Be sure to talk about the *Kids* and *Teenagers.* Remind them that *Kids* get dollar bills for allowance and *Teenagers* get 10 dollar bills for allowance. If students don't understand what an allowance is, just say they "get paid" in one-dollar or ten dollar bills.
3. Have students do the Teens and Kids worksheet from Appendix B. Have them circle or scribble with red crayon or marker on the Tens (Teens) of the two-digit numbers shown on the page. Also have them circle or scribble with blue crayon or marker on the Ones (Kids).

FAT FORTY GAME

MATERIALS:
- Fat Mats (place value charts) for each student (page 336)
- All the students' plastic clothespins or craft sticks. (If using clothespins, the teacher needs the cardboard *tens* strips. For craft sticks, the teacher needs rubber bands for bundles of 10.)
- One die

PROCEDURE:

1. Give each player a Fat Mat copied from Appendix B. On each Fat Mat (place value chart), you will have written in large numbers, 4 in the *tens* column and 0 in the *ones* column. The object of the game is to end up with exactly 4 *tens* and no *ones* on the Fat Mat.

2. Tell the students that you are going to throw a die and see who can be the first one to hit "fat forty." The first player throws the die and calls out the number thrown. The teacher gives her one clothespin or stick for each of the units in the number. The student puts the clothespins or sticks in the *ones* column of her fat mat. The next student throws the die, etc.

3. As soon as a player has more than 9 clothespins in the *ones* column on her fat mat, she must clip them on the cardboard *tens* strip (or band 10 sticks together) and put the bundle in the *tens* column. She continues adding sticks or clothespins to her Fat Mat. She must bundle or clip the 10's together as soon as she gets them.

4. To finish, players must throw the exact number that will make 4 *tens* with 0 in the *ones* column. If a player does not throw the exact number, she stays put and the other players continue. When a player throws the exact number needed to win, she yells, "Fat forty" and she is declared the winner.

5. If you feel that 40 items are too many for the student to handle, use 30 items and call the game *Dirty Thirty*.

The Concept of 100

Rote counting to 100 was introduced in Chapter 9, More Counting Skills. Many students need to have a concrete image of what 100 means. Have them collect 100 of any item to get that mental picture. You can use pennies, empty drink cans, leaves, or any small objects that can be collected fairly quickly. In a classroom, the students can all bring a specified number of objects which, when added together, will equal 100. Students can be collecting the 100 items while you are teaching them the place value of the smaller numbers. Teachers can also relate the collection of 100 items into teaching units such as rocks and minerals, plants, etc.

UNDERSTANDING HUNDREDS

OBJECTIVES: 1) The student will be able to distinguish a collection of 100 items from a collection of 40 to 60 items without counting. 2) The student will be able to read aloud numbers including hundreds.

MATERIALS:

- Small items such as coins and stones that students can easily collect in large quantities
- Place value mats with ones, tens, and hundreds

SUCCESS STEP: Have the student decide what items she is going to collect to make her collection of 100. Praise a reasonable choice or assist the student to choose a reasonable item to collect.

PROCEDURE:

1. Tell your student(s) that they each need to make a collection of 100 things. Suggest small, inexpensive items that she may enjoy collecting if she has trouble deciding (acorns, sports cards, erasers, etc.).

2. Make collecting 100 items a fun activity for the student. Have her count the items she has collected every day. Arrange it so that she doesn't collect all 100 items on one day and there is a little suspense building up to when she finally has 100 items.

3. Make her feel special when she gets 100 items. Give her a plaque, sing her a song, or have others stand and applaud to show that she has accomplished something important. Ask her how she collected the items. See if she recognizes that 100 is a large number from her reply.

4. Display a collection of 100 items next to a collection of 40 or 60 items and see if she can immediately tell which collection has more items. Be sure that she understands that it is not the biggest or tallest pile, but the pile with the most items, even though they are small. Have her count the items in each collection if she can't tell which collection has 100 just by visually comparing them.

5. Write some three-digit numbers on a place value mat with places for *ones, tens,* and *hundreds.* Read them aloud. Referring back to the Place-Value-People chart introduced above, talk about how you can think of hundreds as Grown-ups. Grown-ups are sort of snotty, and they always want people to say their last names, so you must say the number followed by the last name *Hundred.* For 426, you say 4 Hundred, 26. *Kids* and *Teenagers* don't need you to say their last names. Have the student read the three-digit numbers that you have written there.

6. Practice having them read three-digit numbers, first using the place value mats and then just the numbers themselves. Do not expect the students to be able to read three-digit numbers correctly all the time. Practice in real-life settings will help them get more consistent.

GENERALIZATION INTO DAILY ACTIVITIES:

- Teachers often celebrate the 100th day of school to convey an idea of what 100 means. If you search the Internet for "100th Day Celebration" you can get a variety of ideas for classroom activities.
- Parents can often weave the concept of 100 into daily living such as by counting 100 disposable diapers, cans, or books, or by putting 100 pennies into a savings bank or penny rolls.
- Do a 100-piece jigsaw puzzle. Count the pieces first to see if there really are 100 pieces.
- Have a contest. Tell everyone to take 100 steps forward and see where everyone ends up. Or see who can clap or bounce a ball 100 times first.

- Tape 4 pieces of notebook paper together and number the lines from 1 to 100. Write down every book that class members (or family members) read and when you get to 100, do something special. Or, every time one of your children or students does something she's supposed to (e.g., puts her clothes in the hamper without being told, pushes in her chair when she leaves for the day) write her name on the list, and when you get to 100, do something special or have a prize.
- Read counting books that go up to 100. For example: *From One to One Hundred,* by Teri Sloat; *The Very Kind Rich Lady and Her One Hundred Dogs,* by Chinlun Lee; *One Watermelon Seed,* by Celia Lottridge; *Count to 100 with the NBA,* by Erin Soderberg. (See Resources.)

CHAPTER 11

Writing Numerals

Pre- /Post Checklist

Can the student:

1. _____ Draw straight lines and circles (or semi circles).

2. _____ Write the numerals 1 to 5 and 7 each on a 4" x 6" card starting in the upper left corner.

3. _____ Write the numerals that do not use the above pattern (8 and 6 start in the upper middle, 9 starts in upper right-hand corner).

(If the student has fine motor problems, he can choose from numeral cards that are already written correctly.)

4. _____ Demonstrate understanding of number problems by choosing correct answers from an array of already written numerals.

5. _____ Read aloud correctly 4- and 5-digit numbers.

As was related in previous chapters, young children typically have difficulty writing numerals, even when they can recognize numbers and do simple addition. This is mainly due to the limited development of the muscles necessary to write and the lack of mature eye-hand coordination. Some authorities suggest that students would learn to write quicker (numerals and letters) if writing was introduced in second, rather than first grade (or even in kindergarten), as is normally done (Reys, Suydam & Lindquist, 1995).

Many children with Down syndrome or low muscle tone have additional difficulties with fine motor skills (Bruni, 1998). Too early insistence on writing numbers may bring frustration that has little to do with number concepts. This chapter will discuss different ways to teach the writing of numerals and will also explain ways that students can indicate the correct number without writing. For example, by using numeral cards, a student can show that he knows the answer to the problem even though he can't write it.

The areas covered are:
- **Drawing lines and circles**
- **Ways to teach numeral writing**
- **Cues for remembering**
- **Alternatives for recording numerals**
- **Fluency in reading higher numbers**

Drawing Lines and Circles

Writing numerals is not a simple task. The student must have a mental picture of the numeral and then must duplicate this picture with motor actions. Children who are just scribbling back and forth on paper are probably not ready to write numbers. First, they must be able to draw a straight line and stop where desired. They also must be able to draw controlled curved lines. From plain scribbling, children usually progress to making circles, perhaps in representation of a face. When a child has enough control to make the curved line of a circle, he may be ready to try very simple writing of numbers.

INTRODUCING THE CONCEPT

MATERIALS:
- Large, unlined paper
- Large crayons or markers
- Music (for encouraging drawing large strokes)

OBJECTIVE: The student will be able to draw straight lines and stop on command and draw controlled circles or semicircles.

SUCCESS STEP: Have the student pick out his favorite crayon or marker.

PROCEDURE:
1. Demonstrate making large circles on chalkboard or large paper. Play some music or sing a song that has long phrases while saying a chant like "A-round, a-round, a-round" while you are drawing. Have the student do the same. You can try slow movements of classical music such as waltzes by Johann Strauss or children's songs such as "Found a Peanut" or "Ring Around the Rosy."
2. Check to see if the students are drawing circles.
3. Turn off the music. Repeat the activity but tell them that you are going to play a game. You are going to yell "STOP," and they have to stop drawing and put down their crayon or marker immediately. Practice this activity until they are doing

semicircles with control. You might want to try playing or singing "Pop Goes the Weasel" during this activity, having the children stop drawing at the word *pop*.

4. Practice drawing lines and stopping them. For younger students you can tell them to draw railroad tracks and then pretend to have an engine (a line down the middle) race down the tracks until you say "STOP."

5. If the student is unable to control drawing lines and circles, wait a while before teaching numeral writing. You really can't hurry physical maturity very much.

Ways to Teach Numeral Writing

Some children with Down syndrome can learn to write numerals and letters using the same method as the other children in the class use. However, many benefit from slower, more systematic approaches that give them the time and instructional support to both visualize and practice the necessary movements.

There are several programs that teach handwriting of numbers along with the writing of letters. See the Resource Guide for publication/ordering information.

- *Handwriting without Tears* is an excellent program that moves developmentally and emphasizes learning in multi-sensory ways. The program teaches simplified but completely legible number and letter shapes (without any extra curlicues) and uses paper with fewer guide lines than usual for beginning writers. Jan Olsen, the author, has programs for each grade, Kindergarten through Grade 4 (which can also be used by older students who still need help with printing or cursive writing).

- In *Semple Math,* Jan Semple explains how to progress from using the spotting dots (explained in Chapter 7) to writing the numerals. Her program focuses only on teaching how to write the numerals, not the letters. She also uses the students' fists as cues to help them remember the direction of writing, and mnemonics to create visual pictures of the numerals and what they mean.

- *Handwriting '03* by Zaner-Bloser teaches numeral writing together with letter writing. This program is used in many schools in the United States, but is not necessarily the one that will work best for students with Down syndrome or other disabilities.

Most parents and teachers teach the writing of numerals along with the writing of letters and words. It is possible, however, that a student could learn to write the more limited amount of numerals *before* he tackles the entire alphabet, including words and sentences. The primary principles are to:

- Make sure the students are able to draw straight and curved lines before beginning to teach numeral writing.

- Make your models of numerals large. Then have the students write their numbers no smaller than their fist.

- Give students a starting point for the numerals. Visualize a 4" by 6" index card. For numerals 1 to 5 and 7, the starting point is the upper left-hand corner, 8 and 6 start in the middle, and 9 starts at the upper right-hand corner.
- Give students some way to visualize the numeral and to memorize the sequence of strokes necessary to write the numerals.
- Vary your materials and methods of teaching.
- Gradually decrease the size of the numerals.

Using *Handwriting without Tears* to Teach Numerals

For parents who are working on numeral and letter writing at home, I recommend using *Handwriting without Tears* (Olsen, 2000). The method has been successfully used to teach many children with Down syndrome how to write their letters and numbers without too much frustration. If you are a teacher, you may be expected to use another handwriting method with your students in the general education classroom. However, if you have a student with fine motor difficulties due to Down syndrome or another disability who is not progressing satisfactorily, you might want to have a trial of *Handwriting without Tears* written into your student's IEP.

The *Handwriting without Tears* method has the student begin learning to write numerals on a small slate. The teacher first writes the numeral with chalk on the slate board, making it as large as the entire slate. (The numeral should be drawn close to the left side of the slate.) The student wets her finger on a wet sponge. She traces the numeral with her wet index finger and wipes out the teacher's chalk numeral. She may then wipe the numeral dry by tracing over it with a small piece of paper or a dry sponge. Essentially the student is tracing the numeral two times, but it is so much more exciting to use water on the board and then dry it than it is to trace it on a piece of paper. Then the student may try to write the numeral herself with the chalk. Jan Olsen also recommends  giving writing cues such as saying, "2 starts in the starting corner, 2 makes a big curve. 2 stops in the corner. 2 walks away on the bottom."

Each numeral is learned with a similar format. Olsen suggests that the students make up a story for each numeral to help them remember. A sample given is a story for the numeral 5. "Mr. Five is bald. He goes *down* the street on his way to work. He feels raindrops on his *head* and goes *back home* for his umbrella" (Olsen, p. 40, 1998). Demonstrate one numeral at a time. First, the student should trace the numeral, and then the student should try to copy the numeral from your model. Eventually the student should be able to write the numeral without a model to copy.

The *Handwriting without Tears* program emphasizes that for numerals 1 to 7, the starting point is the upper left-hand corner, while 8 starts in the middle, and 9 starts at the upper right-hand corner. (Other teachers feel that the numeral 6 begins in the middle, just like the numeral 8.) This change can easily be incorporated into the *Handwriting without Tears* program, as I have suggested earlier in this chapter.

EARLY WRITING ACTIVITIES

OBJECTIVE: The student will write the numerals 1 to 9 on a small slate or a 4" by 6" card.

MATERIALS:

- Markers and paper
- Small slate and chalk
- A small wet sponge and a small dry sponge or paper towel. (The slate that is part of the *Handwriting without Tears* program has a wooden border around it that gives a tactile cue for keeping the numeral inside the slate. If you have a slate board without a border, you can use several layers of duct tape to make a tactile frame around the slate.)
- A dry erase board with a frame and markers can be used instead of the slate, chalk, and sponges
- Numerals to Trace, page 337
- Textured wallpaper or another slightly rough surface can be used underneath the page for more tactile cues
- 9" by 11" cake pan
- Play sand OR bright colored sugar-sweetened Kool-Aid or Crystal Light drink mix
- Cutout numerals that have a slightly rough surface (e.g., cut from sandpaper) to trace with the finger
- Cutout numerals for the overhead projector (for small groups)
- Yarn
- Small items such as macaroni, cereal, and popcorn to glue on paper to make numerals

SUCCESS STEP: Have the student make a short vertical line with a marker on paper. Praise him and tell him he has just learned his first numeral—the numeral 1.

PROCEDURE:

1. Have the student repeat drawing the numeral 1 on paper. See if he can draw straight lines and stop them when told to.
2. Make some curved lines by demonstrating a large curve and two small curves (as are used in parts of 2 and 3). See if the student can imitate them. If he needs more practice, switch to the chalkboard and have him draw BIG curves and straight lines. You may need to have him do lines and curves in finger paint if he needs that tactile experience. Later, graduate to an individual slate.
3. Students often need experience with feeling the numerals to help them get a visual picture of their shapes. You may write the numeral on paper, put it on the bottom of a shoebox lid, and cover the numeral with fine play sand. The student then traces the numeral with his finger, pushing aside the sand. The texture of the sand makes the activity both a visual and a tactile (touch) experience.

4. Others use sandpaper numerals and have the student trace them. My son wouldn't touch the sandpaper letters (due to tactile defensiveness). We found a substitute that worked every time. I spread sugar-sweetened red Kool-Aid on a rectangular cake pan. He had to trace the numeral several times, and if he did it, he could lick his finger. He loved this activity, but the red color stayed on his finger for a while. At first I wrote the numeral on a piece of cardboard and buried it in the Kool-Aid. Very quickly he could write the numeral independently without tracing. You can also make a softer tactile feel by putting a piece of textured wallpaper underneath the paper with the numeral the student is tracing.

5. If you are teaching a small group, you can take advantage of the overhead projector. Put cutout numerals on the overhead projector. One student can trace the numeral on the chalkboard or screen. The others trace the numeral in the air or on their desk. Students can also clap out the number (4 = clap, clap, clap, clap) to link the meaning with the numeral. Again, multiple senses come into play.

6. Another way to build on the tactile feeling of the numerals is to glue pieces of yarn in the shape of numerals on pieces of cardstock or cardboard. If you make numerals with double lines, the student can glue things such as popcorn, cereal, or macaroni on the outlines and have a variety of textures to feel.

7. Use a song, rhyme, or cues to help students remember how to write the numerals. See the box on page 137 for some number rhymes to try.

8. Eventually, you should have your student progress from making large numerals to smaller numerals and from using a marker to using a crayon or fat pencil. Large graph paper can be used to help align the numbers correctly. Or, if your child is squirming during a religious service or concert, you can even draw rectangles on the back of the bulletin or program and have your child put a numeral in each one. This process may take some time, and you can just go on to other lessons about numbers while practicing numeral writing and gradually providing models of smaller numerals.

A variety of teaching strategies have been discussed here because the students need to be motivated to learn a difficult skill. You can think up other ideas that will be interesting to the specific students you teach. Be creative and find some way to keep their interest. For example, you may have a puppet that is learning to write numerals too.

GENERALIZATION INTO DAILY ACTIVITIES: Wait until the student is comfortable with writing numerals before asking him to generalize the skill into real life. He should be able to write the numerals somewhat automatically before you ask

Number Rhymes

There are a variety of rhymes that can help children remember how to form the numerals. One poem that has surfaced in many early childhood programs is *Writing Numbers*. I found this version in the book *Bucket Math* (no copyright date given).

A straight line one is fun. __1__

Around and back on a railroad track - two-two two. __2__

Around a tree and around a tree is three. __3__

Down and over, then down some more. That's four. __4__

Fat old five goes down and around.
Put a flag on top and see what you've found. __5__

Down to a loop, a six rolls a hoop. __6__

Across the sky and down from heaven.
That is how we make a seven. __7__

We make an S, but do not wait. *(not useful if child doesn't know that letter)*
We climb back up to make an eight. __8__

A loop and a line, make nine. __9__

It's easy to make a one and a 0.
Ten is all your fingers, you know. __10__

The following is another anonymous rhyme accessed from the Internet. Some of these directions would only be useful for a child who already knows his letters, but the instructions for 2 and 5, for instance, might work for any child.

0 Round and round just like an "O"
Now you've made the number zero.

1 Start at the top and down you run
That's the way you make a one.

2 Make a candy cane and give it a shoe
That's the way you make a two.

3 Around and around just like a "B"
That's the way you make a three.
(Or: Around a tree and around a tree
That is how you make a three.)

4 Down and over and down some more
That's the way you make a four.
(Or: Down and across and slice through the door.
That is how you make a four.)

5 Short neck, belly fat
Mr. Five wears a hat.

6 Make a "C," then in you go
Now you've made a six you know.

7 Across the sky and down from heaven
That's the way you make a seven.

8 Make an "S" and then don't wait
Go back up and make an eight.

9 Make a circle, then a line
That's the way you make a nine.

him to write numerals during daily activities. Both school and home have many activities where it is natural to write down numerals. A few are:

- Write down the number of students present/absent.
- Lunch count—record how many students are buying lunch. ·
  Count and record the number in various groups (such as when taking a vote on several options).
- Write friends' and relatives' phone numbers and addresses.
- Be the scorekeeper for sports or for card games or board games.
- Write down channels of favorite TV shows.
- Make temperature predictions or record other data for science class (such as the number of tadpoles or butterflies that have hatched).
- Number your paper (as for a spelling test).

Alternatives for Recording Numerals

Students who do not yet have the fine motor skills to write numerals can still express mathematical understandings. They may be able to combine small items into sets for addition or put numbered items in the correct sequence. They may be able to indicate small quantities by showing the appropriate number of fingers. In addition, they may be able to name the numerals orally. Still, there are times when you will want to have a permanent product to illustrate a student's understanding. Several alternatives can be used:

- Choosing answers from already formed numerals;
- Using number stamps and other options;
- Using assistive technology such as a computer or a printing calculator.

CHOOSING ANSWERS FROM ALREADY FORMED NUMERALS

Here are some options for students who can orally identify numerals but who are not quite ready to write the numerals themselves. You can use these methods to enable everyone in a class to respond to a question at the same time or as a lead-in to the slightly more advanced ways of indicating responses described in the next section. Use only those materials that are appropriate for the individual student.

1. **Number Line.** Make a large number line drawn with chalk or tape on the floor. (It is also possible to write the numbers on white shelf paper or an old shower curtain.) Using the number line that you have drawn on the floor, have the student go to the number you have named and stand on it. Choose the numerals at random from 1 to 10 or from 1 to 20, if you have room. Practice until the student goes to each number without hesitation. You are checking that he can recognize the numerals as given orally.

2. **Numeral Cards.** Cut 3 to 4 squares of paper or cardboard for each numeral and write numerals on the squares with marker. Store the squares in separate compartments of an egg carton or muffin tin. (It is easy to make cards with the numerals up to 30 by cutting up an old calendar. Gluing some heavy backing on will make it easier for students to pick them up.) Then make an answer mat by pasting or taping different colors of construction paper (squares of at least 3" by 3") together (in any shape). Ask the student(s) to pick up a 2 card and put it on a certain color on the answer mat. Then tell him to pick up the 7 card and put it on different color on the answer mat. (Or, ask him to add 7 plus 2 and put the answer on red, etc.) You can check the student's work later by matching the numbers with the colors you chose.

3. **Magnetic Numerals.** Your student(s) can also use the magnetic numerals that are sometimes included with sets of magnetic letters instead of writing them out. That way your refrigerator or most chalkboards can be a large math field. You can also give students cookie sheets or other small metal baking trays (not aluminum), use marker to draw rectangles on them, and ask students to indicate the correct answers by putting magnetic numerals in the rectangles.

4. Some of the activities in Chapter 8, Recognition of Numerals, would also be appropriate here.

USING NUMBER STAMPS AND OTHER OPTIONS

For students who were successful with the methods described above, have slightly better fine motor skills, or are ready to work more independently on math activities, here are some more ideas for indicating responses without physically writing numerals.

1. **Number Stamps.** You can have one stamp made for each of the numbers from 0 to 9. They must be clearly labeled and easily accessible for the student to be able to use them accurately.

2. **Racko.** You can also put the stamps or numeral cards on a small rack that is used for the game Racko (Milton Bradley, under $10). Racko includes 4 cardholder racks and 60 cards numbered sequentially that can be used for teaching math as well as playing the game (age 8 and above).

3. **Number Labels.** If the student has the ability to peel labels off a contact sheet, you could type numbers, one to a label, and let him use the stickers to complete math worksheets.

4. **Multiple Choice.** List the answers to math worksheets as multiple choice options. The student can then just mark the correct answer. Have him circle the correct answer so his decision can't be mistaken for a random pencil slash.

ASSISTIVE TECHNOLOGY

The Individuals with Disabilities Education Act (IDEA) defines assistive technology as "any tool or item that increases, maintains, or improves functional capabilities of individuals with disabilities." So, the adaptations described in the sections above would technically be considered low-tech assistive technology. However, often when people talk about assistive technology, they are thinking about computers or other high-tech gadgets that can improve someone's functioning. In the United States, IEP teams are required to consider a student's need for assistive technology, both low-tech and high-tech options. Here are some high-tech options to consider writing into your student's IEP:

1. **Printing Calculator.** A student may be able to use a calculator with a printer. If the numbers on the calculator are big enough for him to be accurate, the printer can produce a written product that can be corrected later by the teacher.

2. **Software.** The computer can be used to solve math problems. For example, the computer program *Access to Math* by Don Johnson lets the teacher program a certain kind of math problem, and the student just fills in the answer by computer. Other computer software such as Edmark's *Carnival Countdown* and *Zoo Zillions* includes computer games that allow the student to choose the right answer using a mouse, keyboard, or touch screen. These computer games are self-checking so the student learns the correct answer. Computer keyboards can be adapted to the student's individual needs so that a small keyboard is not a barrier to use. (Adapted keyboards such as IntelliKeys are available from Intellitools and others). A touch screen that registers the answer when the student touches the screen in the right place would also qualify as assistive technology.

Fluency with Larger Numbers

Being able to read numbers with four or more digits is just an extension of the skill learned in Chapter 10, Place Value. However, it is introduced and extended at this time in hopes that the student can deal with more digits than previously. Students need more proficiency in reading larger numbers than in writing them. However, both skills may be taught together to strengthen their storage in long-term memory.

FLUENCY WITH LARGER NUMBERS

OBJECTIVE: The student will read four-digit numbers correctly by labeling the thousands, hundreds, tens, and ones. (If the student is nonverbal, have him point to the numbers as they are called.)

MATERIAL:
- Place Value People Chart (page 340)
- Place Value Worksheet (page 341)
- Small items such as pennies, pretzel sticks, acorns, bottle caps, etc. that can easily be collected in large quantities

SUCCESS STEP: Ask the student to tell you some *very* big numbers. He will probably say millions or billions. Praise him.

PROCEDURE:

1. Just as we had the student collect one *hundred* of some kind of object in Chapter 10, we probably need to give him some experience with one *thousand* of something now. This time, use family members or class members to help make the collection. If possible, have 10 people collect 100 objects each so the student can visualize that 1000 is much bigger than 100. If you have not previously collected 100 objects, it would be very helpful to collect both one hundred and then one thousand objects. Then see if the student can visually distinguish between a pile of 1000 of an item and a pile of 100 of an item.

2. Have a place value mat filled out with 4-digit numbers. Tell the students that they are going to learn how to say some really big numbers, but they have to do it right. Show them the place value mat but cover up all but the first number with a blank sheet of paper. Repeat the instructions from Chapter 10, Place Value, on how to read numbers:

3. Taking a cue from Jan Semple's (1986) explanation of *Whole Number Street,* tell the students that the ones column is for *Kids. Kids* get allowances in one dollar bills. Explain that the *Kids* are closest to home, which is shown by the wall. The *tens* column is for *Teen-agers,* who get allowances in ten dollar bills. The *hundreds* column is for *Grown-ups,* who get their money in hundred dollar bills. There is another group of Grown-ups who get even more money, and their last name is T*housands.* Tell them that *Grown-ups* are sort of snotty, and they want people to say their last names, so you must say the number followed by the last name *Hundred* or the last name *Thousand* (Semple, 1986). For 426, you say "4 Hundred, 26." *Kids* and *Teen-agers* don't need you to say their last names. For 6,582 you say "6 Thousand, 5 Hundred, Eighty-two (82)."

4. In school, you can have four children stand in line facing the others, holding cards showing the individual numbers. (For example, four students hold the cards 2, 5, 6, 3.) A student facing them reads off the number as "two thousand, five hundred, sixty-three." If he is correct, the four children put up another number card. If he is not correct, he must trade places with one of the four children. You can have some fun by having the people playing the Thousands and Hundreds act insulted if the student doesn't say their last name. At home, you can have stuffed animals or siblings hold the number cards. Discourage the students from using the word *and* when reading off the numbers. We want to reserve the word *and* for the decimal point, which will be taught later.

GENERALIZATION INTO DAILY ACTIVITIES: Reading larger numbers needs to be practiced frequently so that it becomes almost second nature. You and the student can scan the newspapers for numbers with four or more digits that you can practice reading. Stay away from prices, though, because we have not introduced the decimal point yet. Other ideas:

- Read mileages on signs or the car's odometer when traveling.
- Look at how many calories are in food when you are shopping or preparing meals.

- Find numbers with four or more digits while watching TV.
- Read the high scores for video games or arcade-like computer games.
- Read off how many "hits" you get when using a search engine on the Internet.

CHAPTER 12

Ordering and Comparing Numbers

Pre- /Post Checklist

Can the student:

1. _____ Use ordinal numbers to order objects (first through fifth).

2. _____ Use sequence of numbers to find specific numbers (find specific page in a book, etc.).

3. _____ Find rooms in a hallway having two- and three-digit numbers.

4. _____ Name *one more* or *one less,* given any number up to 20.

5. _____ Represent simple data in an object, picture, or simple bar graph (Optional).

In the previous chapters, students have been learning about regular or *cardinal* numbers that answer the question, "How many?" Another important use of numbers is telling the location of the item or person in relationship to others. This use of numbers emphasizes the sequence or order that the numbers show, so numbers that indicate order are called *ordinal* numbers. Many children know the meaning of a few ordinal numbers such as *first* or *second* when they come to school.

Ordinal numbers can be used to give the sequence of items in time (first you do x, second you do y, third you do z) or in space. This chapter will focus on helping students understand how an ordinal number can give the *location* of each item in space by using the words *first, second, third, fourth, fifth, sixth, seventh, eighth, ninth, tenth,* and more.

In addition to learning about ordinal numbers, it is also important for students to learn how to order numbers so they can follow a sequence of numbers either forward or backward to find a specific number. It is as if we had a long number line in our heads, and, starting from one spot on the line, we need to go forward or backward to our special number. We have to know in which direction the numbers get bigger or smaller and proceed in the correct direction. The second step is to remember the sequence of the numbers that will come before we get to our specific number. The task becomes more and more difficult as the numbers get longer.

Yet another use of numbers is to compare two or more quantities. In the early sections of the book, the comparisons of *more/less* and *big/little* were taught. The purpose in this chapter is to convey a more comprehensive look at *one more* and *one less* as they relate to number sequencing. This knowledge will be needed shortly when working on beginning addition and subtraction. As part of ordering and comparing numbers, it is also practical to look at the use of graphs to represent comparisons. While graphing may not seem like an essential survival skill, it can help hands-on learners get a visual picture of how counting is used and why the numbers are important. Although this section is optional, the graphs are very simply made and are about things in the student's life.

The topics covered in this chapter are:

- **Ordinal numbers**
  - ▾ 1st, 2nd, 3rd
  - ▾ 4th, 5th (including pattern)
  - ▾ 6th, 7th, 8th, 9th, 10th
  - ▾ last/first
- **Sequencing numbers**
  - ▾ Finding pages in a book
  - ▾ Finding room numbers
- **Comparison words (math vocabulary)**
  - ▾ One more/one less
- **Simple graphs (optional)**
  - ▾ Objects or persons
  - ▾ Written

Ordinal Numbers

Ordering numbers is important to help the student organize her world and form a foundation for later, more complex, number understanding. Many students who are concrete learners do have some understanding about what it is to be *first* in line. Building on this concept of position, we can teach the student the ordinal order through 10.

INTRODUCING THE CONCEPT

OBJECTIVE: The student will be able to use ordinal numbers to order objects (first, 1 to 5, and later 1 to 10).

MATERIALS:
- Other students or family members willing to stand in line
- Dolls, stuffed animals, action figures, etc. that can sit or stand in a line

SUCCESS STEP: Ask the student what the objects are. (Or ask her to point to the named objects.) Praise her.

PROCEDURE:
1. Set up four objects or toys in a straight line in front of the student so that she can see each individual object or toy. Or, ask four students or family members to line up in front of her.
2. Starting at the left, ask the student to touch the toy or person that is *first* in line. If she does not know, you touch the toy as a model or put her hand on the first toy. Praise her. Repeat the step several times.
3. Repeat step one and then ask her to touch the *second toy*. Model or physically prompt if necessary. Repeat with *second* several times. Then go back and ask for the first toy and then the second toy. When teaching ordinal numbers, it is important to show the second location in relation to the other toys in the line. Practice first and second several times. If possible, set up a second line of different toys and repeat the questions to see if generalization has occurred.
4. Continue the sequence with first, second, and third until the student seems secure in the knowledge.
5. Then line up two more toys or persons to teach fourth and fifth. You can explain the pattern of adding the *th* sound to the regular (cardinal) number to form the "order" number (ordinal). However, fifth is not pronounced *five+th* but is changed to *fifth*. Tell the student that our tongues got twisted up trying to say *fivth* so we call it *fifth* because it is easier to say. Use the procedure given in step one to work on fourth and fifth, alone and then together. When the student is secure, you can go back and review first, second, and third, and add fourth and fifth.
6. If the student is young, do the finger play of *Five Little Pumpkins:*
   Five little pumpkins, sitting on a gate. *[hold up five fingers]*
   The *first* one said, "Oh, my! It's getting late."
      [point to wrist as if looking at a watch]
   The *second* one said, "There are witches in the air."
      [fly hand through the air like a witch on a broom]
   The *third* one said, "But we don't care!"
      [shake finger back and forth signaling "No"]
   The *fourth* one said, "Let's run and run and run"
      [move arms in a running motion]
   The *fifth* one said, "It's lots of fun." *[wiggle body]*

Then, "Whoo," went the wind and out went the lights.
[blow, moving head]
And five little pumpkins rolled out of sight. *[roll hands one over the other]*

7. Explain the pattern for making order numbers from sixth through tenth. Write the numbers on paper to show the students. Model saying the ordinal numbers with the student chanting along with you. When she seems secure on the pattern of forming the numbers, have her show you the sixth through tenth toys in the line, as was done in step one. If you are having trouble teaching sixth through tenth at this time, drop it and try again later. Many people only use the first five ordinal numbers with the addition of the word *last.*

8. Teach the meaning of *last* as you see the occasion in the student's daily routine. For instance, when the student is looking at a line of students, comment that, "Peter is last. He is at the end of the line. We don't need to count his place. He is last." Repeat enough times during the daily routine until the student shows understanding of *last* in line.

> *Scott, who has Down syndrome, looks at the teacher with bewilderment when she asks him to touch the first toy. The teacher gently takes his finger and puts it on the first toy [physical prompt]. Scott smiles and repeats the touch when asked to touch the second toy. However, when the teacher goes to help Kala, who is somewhere along the autism spectrum, she shrinks back and pulls her hand away. The teacher then gets Kala's attention and models touching the toy. After a minute of silence, Kala touches the first toy herself.*
>
> *Although we have been told to use a hierarchy of prompts from physical to verbal, it is important to know the individual child's preferences and learning styles when deciding what assistance to give.*

ORDER, ORDER GAME

MATERIALS:
- 5 baskets or tubs
- Beanbags or tightly rolled-up socks

PROCEDURE:
1. Line up 5 baskets or tubs in front of the students. Explain to the students, "This is the first basket," and point to the first basket on the left. See if the students can supply the ordinal numbers for the other 4 baskets.
2. Give the students chances to throw a beanbag or tightly rolled socks into the basket that you name by ordinal number. Let them get close so the throwing is not difficult. You are teaching the ordinal numbers, not throwing skills.
3. Later, you could make them stand back further and give 1 point if they can identify the correct basket you name and 2 points if they can identify the basket *and* throw the bag in it.

FIND ME GAME

MATERIALS:
- 5 opaque cups
- Small object that will easily fit in the cup

PROCEDURE:
1. Work in pairs if possible. Have both students face the same direction.
2. One student (or the teacher) lines up the cups upside down, one behind the other. She then hides the object under one of the cups. The other student must ask for the cup to be turned over by its ordinal position (first, etc.). When the object is discovered, they change roles.
3. After some practice, the guessing person must cover her eyes as the object is being hidden, making the task more difficult. If you really want to score the game, count up the number of tries that it takes to find the object for each of 10 rounds. The lowest number wins.

GENERALIZATION INTO DAILY ACTIVITIES:
- The real use for ordinal numbers comes when the student has to form a line with classmates or family. The student has to be able to recognize the ordinal number that is being called and accurately count to find her place in the line. School offers many occasions to teach ordinal position in lines. Parents may have to create some lines so their child can practice.
- Point out when you are using ordinal numbers in following directions. For example, "Now we need to go to the *third* traffic light and the *fourth* house on the right."
- When playing or watching football games, point out the downs that are described with ordinal numbers, such as third down.
- When doing schoolwork or homework, ask the student to "do the second, fourth, and fifth problems," or follow instructions such as, "Start at the third line."
- Talk about being in grade levels such as second grade, third grade, etc.

Sequencing Numbers

Just because a student can rote count to high numbers, it does not mean that she can use the order of numbers to find a specific number. Even if she can tell which number is bigger or smaller than another number, she may not know the entire sequence of numbers mentally. Understanding the sequence of numbers is essential to being able to do addition, subtraction, time telling, money handling, and other skills.

Katri could recite the numbers up to 100. One day in music class, the teacher told the children to turn to page 22 in the songbook and find out what animal the song was about. Katri opened the songbook to page 50, but did not know if she had to go forward or backward in the book to find page 22.

SEQUENCING BOOK PAGES

OBJECTIVE: The student will use the sequence of numbers to find specific page numbers in a book.

MATERIALS:
- 3 children's books with page numbers visible on each page
  - ▾ One book with 6 or fewer pages
  - ▾ One book with 10-19 pages
  - ▾ One book with 20-30 pages

SUCCESS STEP: Have the student read or point to three page numbers in a book of less than 30 pages. Praise her.

PROCEDURE:
1. Using a book with few pages (perhaps a board book), point to the pictures on each page and show the student the page numbers on each page. If the book does not have visible page numbers, write them in yourself. Together, leaf through the pages of the book, saying the page numbers.
2. Open the book in the middle. Ask the student, "Where is page 1?" (or page 2 if 1 is not numbered). Help the student turn the pages, if necessary. As you leaf through the pages looking for page 1, call out the page numbers as you go. Explain to the student that just like you count, 1, 2, 3, 4, etc., the pages are in order 1, 2, 3, 4, etc. See if the student can find page 6 and page 3.
3. Call out some other page numbers and have the student find them. If she starts too far ahead of the called number, help her count backwards. Counting backwards is a difficult skill for some students. You may need to use a number line to help her count backwards for this activity.
4. Next, do the same steps with the book with 10-19 pages.
5. After the student is secure with the 10-19 page book, try the larger book. If the student is not able to do the larger numbers, try again in a month or two.

PAGE CHASE

MATERIALS:
- One or more books that you used in the activity above (later, any book)
- Paper and pencil

PROCEDURE:

1. Prior to beginning the activity, find a "magic word" in the book that can be made by writing down the first letter on specific pages. For example, on page 5, the first letter might be C, on page 8, A, and on page 13, T. Write down those page numbers in sequence (5, 8, 13).

2. If the student can read, have her turn to a specific page (such as page 3) and write down the first letter on that page. Then send her to other specific pages to write down first letters until she has the "magic word."

3. For a variation, have the student copy the first or second words on specific pages until she has found a complete sentence.

This activity may be quite difficult for younger students, but can be a fun challenge for older students, especially if they are familiar with books and know the letters of the alphabet thoroughly.

Making Page Turning Easier

If the student has difficulty turning pages, put your finger under one page and hold it up so she can get just one page. If she still can't turn the pages, use a board book with thick pages or make a book with heavy poster board and notebook rings. You can also glue small pieces of sponges to the backs of the pages to separate them, if it is a book that she uses often.

GENERALIZATION INTO DAILY ACTIVITIES: The skill of finding specific pages in a book needs to be reinforced by everyday activities with books. At first, use short books that have little text on each page. Progress to longer books as the student has contact with books having more pages. As you are reading to her, occasionally ask her, "I'm on page 31—I need to find page 22. Do I go this way (right) or the other way (left) to find it?" If you use a songbook for church or other occasions involving sitting still for long periods, you can make a little game to keep young children occupied by challenging them to find certain page numbers.

Teachers frequently ask students to "turn to page 7 in your science book, etc." Sometimes teachers do not realize that the student who doesn't get to work quickly has not been able to find the page by looking at the numbers. She is looking for the page with the pictures like her neighbor's. Pairing two students together may assist with that learning.

FINDING ROOM NUMBERS

OBJECTIVE: The student will be able to find rooms in a hallway where the rooms are sequentially labeled with two- or three-digit numbers.

MATERIALS:

- A small hallway with numbers on the doors (You can use the rooms in your house if you put up signs to label each room.)
- Paper and marker

SUCCESS STEP: Go through the hallway and have the student point out the room numbers. If you are labeling the rooms in your house or school, take the student with you and let her put the signs up.

PROCEDURE:

1. Pretend that the student is a messenger, and you are sending her out with important messages. Give her a piece of paper folded like an envelope with the room number marked on it. Give her the messages one at a time and have her slip them under the door at each room (if possible). If necessary, you model finding the room numbers.

2. It would be nice to surprise her with a small reward at one of the doors.

3. When she is secure with the initial teaching situation, find a hallway in an office building, hotel, or motel that is new to her and that uses small numbers so she can really practice this skill.

4. Then find a hallway using three-digit room numbers (the first number being the floor level). Explain the numbering system to her, model finding a room, and have her pretend to be a messenger taking a message to each room chosen in random order. (If the child has autism and has trouble pretending, you can give her a Post-It note with the number on it, and have her stick it to the correct door.)

GENERALIZATION INTO DAILY ACTIVITIES: After the initial explanation of the numbering system, the only way this sequencing skill can be learned is by being in a real situation.

- If your child is young, read counting books to her. See if she notices if you skip a page, such as jumping from the page with the number 4 to the page with the number 6, skipping 5. This will work best if the book is fairly new to her. If not, she may have memorized the picture order or the rhymes and will not be responding to the number sequence.

- When driving in the car, challenge your child(ren) to look at signs and find all the numbers from 1 to 10 (or higher) in order.

- Help her use the TV remote systematically to get to a higher number channel rather than just guessing whether to use the "up" arrow or the "down" arrow.

- Likewise, if you have a television where the volume is indicated on screen by a series of increasing or decreasing numbers, ask her to turn the volume down to 15 or up to 20, etc.

- As you are looking for room numbers yourself, perhaps in a medical building or motel, say your thinking out loud, "No, I am looking for numbers that get larger. These numbers are getting smaller. I have to go in the other direction." Eventually this skill must be enlarged to finding house and street numbers in a new area. (These skills will be covered in the second volume of *Teaching Math*.)

- When you are grocery shopping, talk about the aisle that you are in (aisle 5) and tell your child you need an item that is in aisle 10. Does she know what direction to turn? Can she self-correct if she is wrong? Can she follow the sequence of numbers for aisles in a fairly large store?
- Help her understand how books are numbered in the library. Say, "I am looking for 567. Let's go look on the shelf that has a sign saying 500 to 600. It should be somewhere around here." Do not call attention to any decimals in the call number for now.

More or Less, Revisited

In Chapter 9, Recognition of Numerals, the concept of one more or one less was introduced when working with the number line. Now it is time to expand on the student's understanding of this concept, to prepare for beginning addition (and subtraction).

Before beginning work on this section, the student should already understand the concept of quantity. She should also understand the concept of *more* when looking at two quantities. She probably needs to learn the word we use for the category of *not more*, which is *less*.

ONE MORE/ONE LESS

Check to see if the student has the concept of *more* as explained in Chapter 6, Prenumber Concepts. If you haven't used the word *less* for the concept of *not more*, you need to introduce it. Use the number line introduced in Chapter 9 to explore *one more* than any number.

OBJECTIVE: The student will be able to name one more and one less, given any number up to 20.

MATERIALS:
- Number line numbered from 1 to 20
- A small figurine or a game piece that will fit on one square of the number line

SUCCESS STEP: Have the student move a marker one more than the number 1. Praise her.

PROCEDURE:
1. Review moving the game piece *one more* than numbers on the number line under 20.
2. Tell the student that she is going to learn the opposite of *one more*, which is *one less*. Explore *one less* with various numbers on the number line. *One less* is more

difficult than *one more* because the student is used to counting forward. Counting backwards requires more conscious thought, even one number backwards. The student is so used to counting forward in sequence that the next number comes almost automatically. Counting backwards requires the student to hold the stated number in mind and figure out what number would come before that number if she were rote counting.

3. If the student has trouble remembering which way is less vs. more, you can modify the number line to help her and then fade the modifications. For example, if she can read, you can write LESS on the left end of the number line and MORE on the right end. Or, if she can't read, make a picture showing just a few of something on the left end, and a picture showing a lot of it on the right end. You can also color the first number on the left a pale color (for *less*) and the last number on the right a bright shade of the same color to symbolize *more*.

4. If the student needs extra practice, you can tell a story about a brother who had a sister one year younger (less) than his age. When the big brother is 9, his sister will be only 8, etc. No matter what age the brother grows up to be, his sister will always be one year less. Give the brother's age and ask the student what the sister's age will be.

MORE OR LESS CARD GAME

OBJECTIVE: The student will practice finding numbers that are one more or one less than a given number, 1 to 10.

MATERIALS:
- A deck of cards with the face cards removed

PROCEDURE:
1. Deal the deck of cards (minus the face cards) to each of two or three players. Make sure they all receive the same number of cards. (You keep any extra cards.) Each player puts down four cards, face up, in front of her and the rest of the cards face down in a pile.
2. Next, each player takes the first card from her facedown pile and puts it, face up, in the center of the table.
3. The first player tries to build up one more or one less on the two or three cards in the center. If one card in the center is a five, the player can put either a six or a four from her face-up cards on top of the center card. That player can keep on putting down cards as long as she has the right cards. When the first player cannot play any more cards, she takes cards from her facedown stockpile to replace the ones she got rid of (so she again has four cards face up in front of her). The players should always have four face-up cards in front of them when they begin their turn—unless they do not have any cards in their stockpile.
4. The second player now tries to play her face-up cards on the center cards. When neither player can put down *one more* or *one less* on the two (or three) center cards, the next player puts another card in the center of the table to start a new pile.

5. They play until one player runs out of cards and becomes the winner. If that takes too much time, set a time limit and the person with the least cards left wins.

6. When you first play the game, you may help the players find the cards in front of them that are one less and one more. Next, tell the player that she has some cards she can still play, but do not tell her which ones. A common error occurs when a player thinks she only has one card that can be played. After she plays that card, it opens up the opportunity for another one of her cards to be played, but she doesn't recognize it. Students of a variety of ages and abilities can play this game together if a peer or adult helps the less able student see the possible matches.

Simple Graphs (Optional)

Many people think of graphs as part of research findings, and so may consider them too difficult for young children and students who are focusing on survival math skills. However, the National Council for Teachers of Mathematics (NCTM) has emphasized that collection and analysis of data have their beginnings in pre-kindergarten and early elementary years (1989, 2000). The NCTM and many states (e.g., the Ohio Academic Content Standards, 2002) have set standards calling for students to collect and represent data in the form of floor, picture, and bar graphs, starting as early as grades one and two.

For individuals with Down syndrome, as well as other visual learners, graphs can give more meaning to information. Graphs can make abstractions such as fractions or percentages more concrete and easier to visualize (as in pie charts). They can also make it easier to compare quantities (as in bar graphs).

MAKING A FLOOR GRAPH

OBJECTIVE: The student will represent simple data by making a graph with people arranged on the floor.

MATERIALS:
- Five or more people or dolls/action figures, if five people are not available.
- Two equal columns of squares marked off on the floor with tape or floor tiles outlined in chalk.

SUCCESS STEP: Choose the physical characteristic that you want to show in your graph. Choose a characteristic that will only result in two variations. For example, light vs. dark hair, boys vs. girls, tie shoes vs. shoes that don't tie. Have the students decide whether the color of hair of each class member or each family member is light (blond) or dark. Praise their efforts.

PROCEDURE:
1. Have all the people with dark hair sit down together and all the people with light hair stand up together (a sorting or classifying task). Put all the people with dark

hair, seated or standing, one in front of the other, in one of the columns indicated on the floor and the people with light hair in the other column.

2. Tell the students that they have made a people graph. Discuss which line or column is longer (bigger). Have one student stand up on a chair to look at the lines from above. Have her tell the group which line is longer (bigger).

3. Try another people graph such as boys vs. girls, all people wearing jeans vs. those not wearing jeans, people who have some red in their clothing vs. those with no red, etc.

MAKING A PICTURE GRAPH

OBJECTIVE: The student will represent simple data with a picture graph.

MATERIALS:
- 6-8 same-sized pictures of ice cream cones (page 342)
- Brown, pink, and off-white or yellow crayons, markers, or colored pencils
- 3 paper or cardboard labels that say "chocolate," "vanilla," and "strawberry"
- Masking or scotch tape
- Scissors

PROCEDURE:
1. Have the students find out the favorite flavors of ice cream (out of vanilla, chocolate, and strawberry) from their family members (and friends) or their class members.
2. Give each student a sheet of ice cream cone outlines from Appendix B. Ask them to color one cone to indicate their favorite flavor (pink for strawberry, brown for chocolate, etc.). Have them also color cones to show which flavors their friends and/or family members said they prefer. Have them cut the cones out (or you can cut the cones out ahead of time).
3. On a table, wall, blackboard, etc. tape the labels with the ice cream flavors in a row, about 2 to 3 inches apart. Have the students tape their colored ice cream

cones above or under the appropriate label. Have the students tell you which lines are longer and see if they can tell which flavor was most popular. Tell them this is a picture graph.

MAKING A BAR GRAPH

OBJECTIVE: The student will represent simple data with a bar graph.

MATERIALS:
- Two colors of 3" x 5" index cards (10 each)
- Masking or clear tape

PROCEDURE:
1. Give the boys one color of index card and the girls another.
2. Have the two groups line up by color.
3. One person from each group should tape the index cards from his or her group end to end on the wall or the chalkboard. (Make sure the second group's first card is taped directly above or below the first group's first card.) It is also possible to hand the tape down the line and have each student tape her card to her neighbor's. This is the beginning of a simple bar graph showing the number of boys versus girls in a class.
4. If you are working at home with your student, you could count kids vs. adults, or add pets, action figures, and dolls (assuming someone knows what gender they are!) in with your family so you will have enough to make a clear bar graph.
5. Have the students figure out what to title the graph. Tell them this is called a bar graph.

GENERALIZATION INTO DAILY ACTIVITIES: Point out the graphs in the newspaper and explain what they are trying to show. Find other graphs and talk about what they mean. *USA Today* almost always has a picture graph on its first page illustrating interesting facts. Since we are working with concrete thinkers, making and using simple graphs may be a way to make the abstract numbers more visual and meaningful.

If your children or students are trying to reach a goal, make a graph to help them see their progress toward that goal. For example:
- If everybody is trying to read 10 books by summer, let them put an index card with the book title on the wall or bulletin board above their name every time they finish a book.
- If your children are going to get a reward when they have each walked the dog 10 times or everyone has walked around the mall 10 times, make a graph of that.
- Keep track of the number of teeth elementary school children have lost using a graph.
- Have your students extend a bar graph for each time the entire class gets all their homework in on time (for intermediate and secondary students).

- If students have personal fitness goals (such as walking, running, or swimming a certain number of laps per week) give them one index card per lap so they can graph their progress toward their goal.

CHAPTER 13

Beginning Whole Number Addition

Pre- /Post Checklist

Can the student:

1. _____ Combine two groups by *counting on* from the highest number.

2. _____ Indicate that addition is needed when two or more groups are put together.

3. _____ Demonstrate that the order of two numbers does not matter when adding.

4. _____ Tell total number of items of two groups whose sums are 12 or under.

5. _____ Demonstrate place value of *ones* and *tens* with concrete objects when adding two-digit numbers (sums under 50).

6. _____ Demonstrate skip counting (repeated addition) by 5's and 10's with the calculator.

Addition Facts (optional)

7. _____ State some beginning addition facts.

8. _____ Add doubles.

9. _____ State addition facts adding up to ten (complements).

10. _____ Demonstrate patterns in addition facts.

11. _____ State difficult facts that follow no pattern.

If you have done some of the previous activities in this book, you have probably already introduced addition to your student(s). While working with small numbers, we do addition by counting. Working with hands-on materials, it is easy to see that 2 straws added to 3 straws makes a total of 5 straws. However, when working with larger quantities, it becomes tiresome to count all those straws, even if you know how to "count on" from the highest number. Addition is a process that gives us a system for joining two or more quantities in an efficient way.

The focus of this chapter is first to understand *when* to use addition. By using hands-on materials and pictures, the student should be able to *see* the situation in his mind, realize that items are being put together, and understand that means we need to use addition.

Much experience needs to be given in combining small groups (sums 10 and under). With experience, many students will just naturally learn the addition facts of groups whose sums are 10 or less. First, they count to find the answer. Later, they may visually remember those small groupings and come up with the answer without counting.

However, the premise of this book is that the student does not have to learn the addition facts if he knows how to set up the problem on the calculator. Some students will always rely on the calculator. Still, if your student(s) can memorize some addition facts, they are very useful for doing mental math or estimating when you don't need an exact answer. The last half of the chapter therefore covers strategies for learning the addition facts. For most concrete thinkers, especially those with problems with rote memory, this will be an *optional* section. When I think of all the time I wasted trying to get my son to learn the math facts, I really would like to go back and do it over.

For some students, including those who are higher functioning on the autism spectrum, memorization of the math facts will not be difficult. The emphasis for these students will need to be on how to *use* the math facts. Try having your student(s) memorize some of the addition facts, but be willing to drop the teaching if he is inconsistent in learning or is showing signs of real frustration.

Addition will be addressed in the following ways:
- **Basic addition concepts**
  - ▾ Counting on
  - ▾ Addition is used when items are put together
  - ▾ Commutative property (order of items not important)
  - ▾ Addition vocabulary
- **Addition of numbers using manipulatives**
  - ▾ With sums of 12 and under
  - ▾ Place value in addition
  - ▾ Addition of single-digit numbers
- **Addition facts (optional)**
  - ▾ Beginning addition facts
  - ▾ Doubles
  - ▾ Addition facts adding up to ten
  - ▾ Patterns in addition facts
  - ▾ Difficult facts

Should Addition and Subtraction Be Taught Together?

Most schools teach subtraction along with addition in order to emphasize that the addition facts are related to the subtraction facts. That is, they teach "fact families" such as 2+3=5, 3+2=5, 5-2=3, 5-3=2. This approach may or may not work for students with Down syndrome and other concrete learners. If the student is included in general classes for math and is doing well, it is probably best to go along with the math textbook used in the student's school and have him try to learn the two processes simultaneously. Watch for signs of confusion or frustration, however.

Students who have difficulty learning the two processes together will profit by learning addition thoroughly before starting on subtraction. Worksheets giving both types of problems are often difficult for typical children as well as students who are concrete thinkers, because they mechanically get in one gear such as addition and have difficulty switching.

Hopefully, thoroughly learning to use each process in real and simulated situations, as is done here, will help students think about the process to be used before doing the mechanical operation. Using the calculator forces them to make a decision as to what operation is needed from the very beginning.

Basic Addition Concepts

Before beginning work on these activities, students need to understand the process of counting to find an answer. Learning to add is much more efficient if the students know the process of *counting on*. The concept of *counting on* was first introduced in Chapter 9. Another basic understanding is that addition is needed when groups are put *together*. Whether there are two groups being put together or many more groups being put together, the answer is found by addition. The last basic understanding related to addition is that the numbers that are to be added do not have to be in any special order (4+3=7 and 3+4=7). It does not matter which number or group is written first (*commutative property*). The answer is the same.

COUNTING ON

You can teach the student to be more efficient in counting two groups of items by using the strategy of *counting on*. Students may *count on* from either number and be mathematically correct. In this chapter, we are going to emphasize *counting on* from the largest number because it is the most efficient way to reach the total.

When the student is combining two groups of items, and knows how many are in each group, he should start with the number of the largest group and *count on*. For example, when we combine 9 and 4, we do not have to count each one of the items starting with 1. We can start with the number of the largest group (9), then count 10, 11, 12, and 13 for the 4 additional items in the second group to get the total. Check to see whether the student counts on from the highest number when he is counting the numbers on two dice or is adding two groups of sticks or straws. If he is unable to *count on* in these situations, review the counting on section in Chapter Nine, More Counting Skills.

REVIEW OBJECTIVE: The student will combine two groups by saying the largest number and counting on with the second group to get the total (sums under 20). (Repeat objective from Chapter Nine, More Counting Skills, if needed.)

REVIEW ACTIVITY: Play the *Top This* game from Chapter 9 to make sure the students understand which number is the largest from a choice of two. You can use the number line made previously to check the *Top This* answers if the student needs a visual picture of the value of numbers. If he needs practice with spotting the number of dots instead of the numerals, have him pull dominos out of a bag and compare.

GENERALIZATION INTO DAILY ACTIVITIES:

- Any time the student is counting two groups, you can emphasize how much faster it is to *count on* instead of starting all over again from the beginning. Games using two dice provide good examples of the efficiency of *counting on*. Have the student look at one die and spot the number of dots there. Then have him *count on* with the dots on the second die. You can always have him check the answer by counting each of the individual dots.

- If the student is already counting dollar bills, you can start him with a five or ten dollar bill and count on with any additional dollar bills. He does not have the individual bills to count when he has the five or ten dollar bill to begin with. Thus, he must say "10" for the ten dollar bill and count on each single bill as 11... 12... 13....
- At mealtimes or snack times, if your child asks, "Can I have one more?" ask him how many he already had (hot dogs, cookies, etc.). Then say, "If I give you one more, how many will that be altogether?" Later, use higher numbers of smaller items such as raisins and marshmallows that you can give in larger amounts than one. "If I give you two more raisins, how many will you have had altogether?"

ADDITION NEEDED TO PUT GROUPS TOGETHER

OBJECTIVE: The student will indicate that addition is needed when two or more groups are put together.

MATERIALS:

- Various groups of small identical items that can be grouped together, such as craft sticks, rocks, straws, counters, buttons, large cereal pieces, raisins, and similar toys
- Two 4" x 6" index cards, one with a big plus sign and the other with an outline of a stop sign.

SUCCESS STEP: Show the student the plus sign and the stop sign and ask him to show you the stop sign.

PROCEDURE:

1. Show the student the plus sign. Tell him that it is used for addition or putting groups together. You may tell him that it is two little straight lines that cross each other, and then make a plus sign with your index fingers. "This is called the plus sign." Ask him, "What is this sign called?" (the plus sign). Show him both the stop sign and the plus sign and ask him to point to the stop sign, then the plus sign.

2. Make up some stories about two small numbers that must be combined that will appeal to the students. For example: two boys cleaned out their jacket pockets. They both found some pennies in their pockets. One boy said, "Let's see if we have enough pennies to buy some gum. Let us see how many pennies we have together."

3. Give the students copies of the plus sign and the stop sign. The students should listen to the stories and indicate the correct sign that is needed. They do not have to add the numbers together at this time. They just need to indicate whether the plus or stop sign is indicated. Of course, the students will choose the plus sign for addition because the stop sign is not relevant to the situation. Jan Semple (1986) has the students chant, "Numbers together are plus, plus, plus." She has the students cross their fingers into a plus sign three times.

4. Repeat the above procedure, making simple stories about some of the following items. If the students do not already know the word "addition," make sure you use it often when discussing these activities. For example, say things like, "Let's do some more addition"... Or, "Who knows which sign we should use for this addition problem?"
   - Two groups of blocks
   - Two colors of poker chips
   - Two students combining pencils
   - Two groups of sticks
   - Two groups of pennies
   - Two groups of shells, rocks, or leaves
   - Two groups of balls

- Two groups of pipe cleaners
- Two groups of toothpicks
- Two groups of spoons
- Two groups of trading cards, beanbag animals, Barbies, or anything else highly motivating to your students

5. To make sure that your student(s) can distinguish the plus sign from the stop sign, you might slip in a problem that can use the stop sign, such as when the car is coming up to the dog in the road, what sign do you use?

ADDING REGARDLESS OF THE ORDER OF THE NUMBERS

Students need to recognize that they can *add* numbers in any order. Especially when doing addition with the calculator, the numbers can be entered in any order, as contrasted with subtraction, where the largest number must be entered first.

OBJECTIVE: The student will be able to demonstrate that the order of two numbers does not matter when adding.

MATERIAL:

- Two paper or plastic dinner plates of differing colors
- Small craft sticks, pretzels, unsharpened pencils, counters, or straws
- Post-It notes and marker
- Paper and pencil
- Teacher's calculator (for a group, it is useful to use an overhead projector and calculator such as Calc-U-Vue, available from Learning Resources)

SUCCESS STEP: Place the two plates about a hand's width apart. Ask the student to put 4 sticks on one plate and 2 sticks on the other plate. Praise the student for correct actions.

PROCEDURE:

1. Review the number of items on each plate done in the success step and the position of each plate. Move the plates close together. Count the total number of sticks (6). Then move the plates back to their original positions.

2. Pretend that you are a magician and move the plates to opposite the original positions. Ask, "Do we have the same number of sticks?" Move the plates together and count the total. "The total number of sticks is the same, even when I move the groups around." Explain that "total" means how many there are altogether, if necessary

3. Write the appropriate numerals (4 and 2) on Post-It notes and fasten them to the appropriate plates. Say, "See I have written the number on each plate which matches the number of sticks. Now if I move these plates around, are the numbers the same? Is the total the same?" Repeat as necessary.

4. Have the student repeat the above with 3 objects on one plate and 5 on the other. If he can write the numbers on the Post-It, have him do it. Otherwise, you write the numbers on the notes and have the student stick them on the plates.

5. Have the student act like a magician and move the plates around and call out the total.

6. Write the same numbers on a piece of paper as addition problems: 3 + 5 = __, 5 + 3 = ___ . Point out the plus (+) sign that you have previously introduced. Point out the equals sign and explain that it means that the answer number is coming next. The sign is called the *equals* sign. Have the student write in the total for each problem. To reinforce vocabulary, say, "That's right. The **total** is 8. After the *equals* sign comes the number that is the *total*."

7. Make up 5 different problems with sums less than 10 and draw them as sticks or tally marks on a paper to illustrate: III + IIII = IIIIIII. Two of the problems should be the reverse of two other problems. See if the student can answer the problems correctly by counting. See if he can point out the problems that are really the same (2 tally marks + 4 tally marks = 6 tally marks and 4 tally marks + 2 tally marks = 6 tally marks). Repeat if necessary. Then write the appropriate numeral beside each group of tally marks and have the student repeat the numerals that stand for the tally marks. Teach the rule that in addition, the order of the numerals does not matter.

8. Make a worksheet with 3 problems with sums less than 10. As in Step 7, use sticks or tally marks instead of numerals and write the problems in the form: III + I = _____. Do not make any problems that are the reverse of the others. Have the students solve the problems by counting and write the answers (numerals) in the blanks on the paper (someone else may write the numbers for them, if needed). Now ask the students to change the order of the first two numbers in the problems (showing them with tally marks) and again count them up and write the answer in numbers.

CALCULATOR ACTIVITIES:

- When you introduce the plus and equals sign, show the students where those signs are on the calculator. Ask them to touch the plus or equals sign when you name it.
- After you have shown them how to write addition problems on paper, as in step 6, show them how you can punch in the numbers and symbols (for the operation) that they have written down, and that the calculator will "magically" give them the answer once they put in the equals sign.
- Model doing simple addition problems (numbers under 10) on the calculator. Do some problems that are the reverse of others. Show your student(s) that the answers are the same regardless of the order. Write some of the problems you have modeled on paper and let the students try to solve them with the calculator.

Practice with Addition of Numbers (Sums of 12 and Under)

Concrete learners need to have many experiences with small numbers so they get a visual picture of what addition of these numbers means. It is important to use simple numbers so the student can concentrate on the process of addition. If plenty of concrete experiences are given, the student may learn the addition facts with sums under ten without being drilled on them.

Families sometimes ask if they should discourage their child from counting on his fingers. My answer is no, at least not initially. Fingers are always with us. Having five fingers on each hand is probably the reason for our base ten system. Almost everyone counts on their fingers at one time or another. However, if the students are older when they are learning to count and add, use of the fingers could be considered "babyish." Instead, you could suggest that they tap on their desks, one finger at a time. If the motion is very slight, others will probably not notice or will think that it is just a mannerism. Or, you could teach them to just move the fingers on the open hand slightly, and it won't be considered inappropriate. Counting on fingers is inconvenient for larger numbers regardless of the system used, so students should be encouraged to use the calculator for large numbers.

PRACTICE, PRACTICE, PRACTICE

OBJECTIVE: The student will say or indicate (point, etc.) the total number of items in two groups whose sums are 10 or under.

MATERIALS:
- Various groups of small identical items that can be grouped together, such as sticks, rocks, straws, counters, buttons, large cereal pieces, raisins, and similar toys
- Calculators for teacher and each student
- Two paper or plastic plates
- Post-It Notes

SUCCESS STEP: Have the student put some of the items on each plate. Praise him.

PROCEDURE:
1. Using some of the small items suggested in the Materials section, put a few on each plate and have the student indicate what process or sign (addition) is needed to find the total. You may want to use the + and the stop signs from the previous activity and have him hold up the right sign when you assemble the two groups of items to be added. Then find the totals for the items by counting on. Use as many groups of items as are needed for the student to become confident in visualizing the groups being combined.

2. Reinforce the visual sense by writing the numbers of items on Post-It notes and putting them on the appropriate plates. Then write the addition problem on paper or on a slate so the student sees the concrete items and the numerals. When writing the problems, make a number sentence by writing the numbers horizontally, 4 + 5 = 9.

3. Give the students as much experience as possible with combining concrete items, labeling the groups with numbers, and finding the total.

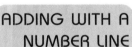

4. Next, demonstrate checking each problem by **calculator.** Practice doing the procedure explaining each step. Tell the students to punch in a number, look at the number in the calculator window to make sure it is correct, then put in the + sign. Next, punch in the next number, look at the window to check, and end by putting in the = sign. Check Chapter 5, Use of the Calculator, for more details on calculator use. Practice doing problems with sums less than 12 on the calculator. Soon you may see that the student can indicate the correct total by memory from practicing on the calculator.

ADDING WITH A NUMBER LINE

If your student is included in a class that is learning to use a number line for addition, it would be appropriate for him to learn that skill too.

On the number line, the student will touch the largest number that is to be added. He will then count forward on the number line for the amount of the other number to be added. The last number that he touches will be the sum or total of the two numbers. An important concept for use of the number line concerns how the students actually count. They are not to count the number that they start on. Usually the teacher explains that they are counting the number of hops that are taken, not how many numbers are there.

If the student is making mistakes in counting (as illustrated in the box) because he counts the first and last number, give him a green button (or similar marker) and tell him this is his frog. Put the frog on the numeral representing the largest number and ask him to count the jumps the frog makes (which represents the second number to be added).

You can give him additional practice by counting bunny hops or hurdles jumped over by a runner or anything that emphasizes the hops rather than counting the numerals.

Mark never seemed to get the correct numbers when he used his number line. The volunteer who worked with him asked him to show her how he counted, explaining what he did out loud. Mark put his finger on the first little slash mark that was labeled 2. He then counted each slash as another number in the counting sequence. Thus 2+3=4.

The volunteer said, "You are counting each slash mark. We are really counting jumps or giant steps. Here is a pretend frog. Put him on the number 2. He needs to jump 3 times. If you count his jumps instead of the slash marks, you will have the right answer." Mark did, and came up with the correct answer of 5.

IN A LINE GAME

MATERIALS:
- Two dice
- Game board number line for each student (page 343)
- Bingo tokens or pennies (12 per student)

PROCEDURE:

1. Each student should have a game board number line with squares for the numerals 1 to 12. Each player gets a game token or a penny to be put on the #1 square.

2. The first player shakes the two dice and calls out the number on each die. He then must add those two numbers to get a total. For example, one die shows 3 dots and the other die has 5 dots. The player says, "This die has 3 and the other die has 5 dots. 3+5=8." (He may use counting-on or the calculator.)

3. The player puts a marker on the square of the game board that matches the total (e.g., on the number 8 of the game board). An adult or a peer who thoroughly knows his facts should be there to make sure the answer is right. Then the next player takes a turn shaking the dice and covering a square on his own game board.

4. At first, let the students use the **calculator** if they are not sure of the answer or if they give a wrong answer. If some of the students are not able to learn these simple addition facts, they should be allowed to use their calculators all the time. They must get the correct answer the first time they work the problem on the calculator or they do not get to move their game token

5. If a player does not say the problem (e.g., "three plus five equals eight"), he loses his turn. Only enforce this rule after the students have had time to be prompted and understand the consequences. Players must say the problem and do the addition even if they can see that the answer is a number they already have covered.

6. If a number has already been covered on a player's game board, the player cannot cover any more numbers and the next player takes a turn.

7. The game is finished when one player has covered all his numbers. If time is limited, the player with the most numbers covered after the specified time is up is the winner. When the game gets to the point where all but one square is covered, the player will probably be throwing the dice many times until he gets the right combination. At this time he does not have to say the problem and do the addition each time. He just continues throwing the dice until he gets the right combination of dots.

Understanding Place Value in Addition

Since this book advocates teaching children to use a calculator earlier than is customary, it is important to make sure they are not just blindly punching numbers in, without understanding why. For instance, when using calculators, students will find little difference between the addition of one-digit numbers and the addition of two-digit numbers. That is, the process of entering the numerals in the calculator is the same as long as they understand the place values of the numbers. It is important that they do know the place value for each number they enter in the calculator, however. When they are putting in the number 21, the 2 represents 2 *tens* and the 1 represents 1 *unit* (ones).

There are several reasons why understanding the concept of place value is important. First, we are emphasizing the *meaning* behind the use of addition. Mechanically operating the calculator is not useful if the individual does not know how to use the skill in a functional way. Second, understanding place value helps students to have a sense that the answer they get is reasonable, and they may be able to represent a visual picture in their minds of *tens* and *hundreds* (perhaps as bundles of straws or sticks from your hands-on instruction.)

INTRODUCING THE CONCEPT

OBJECTIVE: The student will be able to demonstrate the place value of *ones* and *tens* with concrete objects while adding two-digit numbers whose sums are under 50.

MATERIALS:

See the materials used in Chapter 10, Place Value:

- Clothespin Box (1 shoebox per student marked **TENS** on one half of the long side of the box and **ONES** on the other half of the box)
- 40 or more colored plastic clothespins
- The cardboard holders that the clothespins came on, cut to hold only 9 clothespins. (If no holders are available, cut cardboard strips about 1" wide and cut them long enough so that they will only hold 9 clothespins.)

SUCCESS STEP: Have the student put 22 clothespins on the place value box (two groups of 10 pins and 2 single clothespins). Praise him. Remove the 22 pins and have him then put 13 clothespins on the box. If he has difficulty, go back to Chapter 10, Place Value, for review. Praise his success.

PROCEDURE:

1. Ask the student if he can put the group of 22 together with the group of 13. Can he add them? Assist the student to see that now he has 3 groups of 10 clothespins and 5 single clothespins. How many all together? Check the answer with the calculator.
2. Repeat with groups of 21 + 24 and other two-digit numbers as needed and check with the calculator. (At this stage, be sure not to have the student add two numbers that require regrouping, such as 29 + 13.)
3. You may want to have the students do some worksheets with single- and double-digit addition problems. First have the students use the clothespin box to illustrate the addition. Use only numbers under 30 so that the students can easily see the addition. Check each problem with the calculator. When the student does

several problems accurately, you can have him use the calculator only. You can make the problems up yourself or use worksheets from school textbooks or commercial addition workbooks, often found in discount stores. If books are used, you will have to teach the student how to do problems written vertically. It will be easier to use worksheets where the student only has to write in the answer, not write out the whole problem.

Skip Counting Review

 Now that your students have a beginning understanding of place value, it may be a good time to revisit the skip counting by 5's and 10's introduced in Chapter 9. See if your students are able to remember how to count by 5's and 10's. Then show them how skip counting is actually adding the same number over and over again.

1. Have the students count by 10's on their calculators several times. Start them out putting in the number 10, then press + and put in 10 again and say, "10 more is 20," looking at the answer on the display. Pair up students and have them take turns counting by 10's on the calculator, with their partner checking the display for the right answer.
2. Begin the next few sessions by challenging the students to count by 10's with the calculators while you watch them.
3. Next, have the students count by 5's on the calculator several times. Start by putting in the number 5, then press + and put in 5 again and say, "5 more is 10," looking at the answer on the display. Pair up students and have them take turns counting by 5's on the calculator with their partner checking the display for the right answer.
4. Give the students plenty of practice on the 5's. They should be able to see the pattern of the ending digit being 0…5…0…5 from the number lines or the 50 or 100 chart.

Addition Facts (Optional)

With the approach used in this book, the student does not have to learn the addition facts if he knows how to set up the problem on the calculator. Some students will always rely on the calculator. However, the addition facts are very useful for doing mental math or estimating when you don't need an exact answer. Some students will learn some combinations just from the repetition involved in learning about addition. Some strategies for memorizing the facts will also be given below, but learning them is not a necessity for doing addition. Traditional math textbooks often require students to know the facts before going on to learn uses of addition. In this book, however, students can be learning the addition facts at the same time they are using addition in practical situations.

The optional addition facts will be addressed in the following areas:
- Beginning addition facts

- Addition facts adding up to ten
- Patterns in addition facts
- Doubles
- Difficult facts

BEGINNING ADDITION FACTS (OPTIONAL)

OBJECTIVE: The student will memorize the addition facts with sums up to 5 (later up to 10). (Do only as much of this objective as you see the student can handle. It is a rote memorization task that may be difficult or almost impossible for some learners.)

MATERIALS:
- Addition flashcards or cards you have made with the addition facts on them
- Paper plates
- Craft sticks or straws
- Marker
- Post-It notes

SUCCESS STEP: See if the student can tell you what 1 + 1 is when you illustrate with your fingers.

PROCEDURE:
1. Using flash cards or your written problems, find out what facts with sums up to 5 the student really knows. Students often know simple facts such as 1+1=2 and 2+2=4 from their daily experiences. You may already know what facts are known from doing the previous activities.
2. Using the concrete activities with craft sticks and straws that have been used for previous activities on addition, have the student work out the problems using the numbers from 1-5 (1+1, 1+2, 1+3, 1+4, 2+2, 2+3). For example, have him put 2 sticks on one plate and 3 on the other, then count or add on to tell you the total.
3. After the student has successfully put the concrete groups together, bring out another plate to serve as the answer plate. The answer plate will not have sticks or straws on it, but you will have written the answer or sum on it in large numerals. A Post-It note can also be used here.
4. The student will now see two plates with sticks or straws on them showing the numbers being added. He will also see another plate with the number representing the sum written prominently on its surface. You may also make a card with the equals sign (=) so you can show the entire number sentence as the student will see later (3*** + 4 ****= 7).
5. After you have shown the student all the combinations using the numbers 5 and under, you can make 5 answer plates (numbered 1-5) for him to choose from, so he can place the correct answer plate down in the number sentences.
6. You can transition to writing numerals in the number sentences by gradually replacing the sticks with a Post-It containing the appropriate numeral. For ex-

ample, the student has one plate with 2 sticks and one plate with 1 stick. He can tell you that that equals 3. You then take away the one stick and put down a Post-It note with a 1 on it instead and ask, "Now how much is it?" See if he can remember that 2 sticks plus the number 1 equals 3. If he can, try putting down a Post-It note for the 2 sticks too and see if he can remember that 2+1 equals 3.

7. Using flashcards, see if the student has learned any of the addition facts from the previous concrete activities. Repeat the concrete activities with sticks or straws for those facts that are missed.

8. Once the student can remember addition facts with sums up to 5, work on the facts with sums up to 10 in the same manner.

DOUBLES IN ADDITION (OPTIONAL)

As the name implies, doubles are math facts in which you add two of the same number (e.g., 2+2, 8+8). Learning the doubles of up to 9 + 9 can be helpful. Students seem to have an easier time learning the sum of two numbers that are the same than other fact combinations. Some theorists say that it is because the student doesn't have to remember three different numbers, since two of the numbers are the same.

OBJECTIVE: The student will be able to name the answer to the doubles facts (1-9), or as many as possible.

MATERIALS:
- A number line
- Straws or flashcards
- Dice
- Dominos

SUCCESS STEP: Have the student throw two dice until he gets doubles. Praise him. Say, "You got doubles! See, you got two of the same number."

PROCEDURE:
1. Continue to have the student throw the dice until he gets doubles. Count up the dots on the dice. Write the numerals on paper or a chalkboard close to the student. Say, "You threw a 3 and another 3. They are doubles. How many dots in all?" Then write the answer on the board or paper. Continue as long as the student is interested.

2. To make sure that the student understands what doubles are in written numerals, write several number facts, mostly doubles but with a few that are not. Have him cross out the problems that are *not* doubles. (For instance, write 2 + 2, 3 + 1, 4 + 4, 5 + 5, 3 + 6, 3 + 3, on the board or paper. See if he can cross out 3 + 1, 3 + 6.)

3. Introduce mnemonics that will help your particular student(s) remember doubles facts. For instance, you may know the song *Inchworm* from the movie, *Hans Christian Andersen.*

Inch worm, inchworm
Measuring the marigolds
You and your arithmetic
You'll probably go far.

Two and two are four,
Four and four are eight,
Eight and eight are sixteen,
Sixteen and sixteen are thirty-two.

The lyrics could be changed to:
Two and two are four,
Three and three are six
Four and four are eight
Five and five are ten.

4. Other mnemonics can be used (and created) to help learn the doubles. For example:
   - A car has 2 wheels on one side and 2 wheels on the other, which makes 4 wheels altogether. Have the student look at a car or picture that shows all 4 wheels of a car so he has a visual picture of that common combination of numbers.
   - Introduce pictures of insects (such as grasshoppers) that have 3 legs on each side for a total of 6, or spiders that have 4 legs on each side for a total of 8.
   - Of course, the student should be able to picture 5 fingers on 2 hands which equal 10 fingers total.
   - You can use an egg carton to show $6 + 6 = 12$.
   - If you use the 16-crayon boxes, you can show that there are 2 rows of 8 crayons each, so $8+8=16$. Or you can have the students remember the phrase, "I ate (8) and ate (8) until I was sick – teen (16)."
   - For $9 + 9$, you could sketch 9 boys and 9 girls on the "A team" (eighteen).

   The above clues should be made very visual so the student can see the accompanying picture in his mind (see sample on the next page).

5. If the students are able to pick up dominoes easily, spread out dominoes in front of them and challenge them to see how many doubles they can pick up from the group. Pick the dominoes up, shake them, and throw them out a second time to repeat the challenge. After the students are familiar with spotting the doubles, have them state the problem and the answer before they get credit for spotting the doubles. For example, have them point to each side of a domino and say, "4 and $4 = 8$."

   If you have two students of relatively equal abilities, you can set a time limit such as two minutes and have them compete against each other to see who can find the most doubles. However, be careful that the time competition is not frustrating and self-defeating for the students. This activity tests spotting ability as well as doubles.

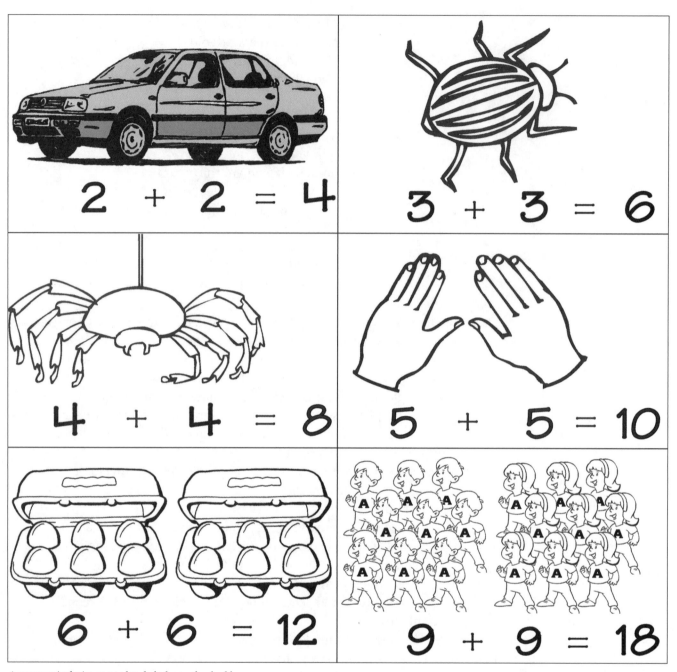

A mnemonic device created to help learn the doubles.

USING DOUBLES TO FIND ONE MORE, ONE LESS

If a student has learned the doubles facts well, he can sometimes use them as stepping-stones to other facts. He may be able to find *one more, one less* using those doubles. For example, if he knows that 3+3=6, he may be able to look at the combination 3+ 4 and think, "If 3+3=6 and this problem has a number 1 more than 3, then the answer will be 1 more than 6, which is 7." To do this, the student needs to be able to visualize two equal groups plus one more.

OBJECTIVE: The student will learn to visualize two equal groups plus one more.

MATERIALS:
- Poker chips
- Calculator

PROCEDURE:
1. Give the student an even number of poker chips (4 to 20).
2. Have him make two groups of chips with the same number in each group. Ask him to tell you the total if he knows the doubles fact, or to find the total by counting or by using the **calculator** to add the two groups.
3. Then add one more chip to one of the two groups of chips and ask what the total is now. If the student is correct, do many more concrete illustrations with the chips. If the student does not understand what number is one more than the total he had originally counted, go to Chapter 9 and review *one more* using the number line.

This strategy requires more mental math than is easy for most concrete thinkers. However, if the student is really secure with the doubles, he may be able to use this strategy. You can call the numbers on both sides of a number its *neighbors*. Using the doubles as bases, the student can figure out what the sum would be if the numbers were doubles (e.g., the problem is 5 + 6, so the student figures out that 5 + 5 = 10). The student could then add 1 more to that sum to account for the *neighbor* (6) that is one more than 5. If the student is successful with using the *one more* strategy for doubles, he may be able to use the *one less* strategy (e.g., thinking of 5 + 6 as being one less than 6 + 6). That seems to present a more difficult memory problem for most people with Down syndrome, however.

Heidi seemed to be learning the addition facts under 20 from flashcards very well. She could rattle off the answers almost as fast as the teacher could flash the cards. However, she made quite a few mistakes when she wrote the answers on a worksheet. Her teacher tried to analyze the errors: 3 + 7= 4, 8 + 7=9, 2 + 7 =3. The errors on the worksheet all contained the number 7, but she did the flashcards of the 7's correctly. The teacher suspected a vision or a visual perception problem. The problems would have all been correct if you substituted the number 1 for the 7. By teaching her to look for the "hat" on top of the 7, she was able to distinguish the 7 from the 1.

Addition Facts Adding Up to Ten (Optional)

Many adults do not realize that they use the pairs of numbers adding up to ten (complements) when they are doing mental math. Think of the numbers 4 and 6. Perhaps they are easy for you to add mentally because they add up to 10. Some people also use the complements and add one more or one less to mentally add numbers such as 4 + 7. That is, they think, "3 + 7 is 10, so 1 more is 11." This activity is designed to help students learn the pairs of numbers that add up to ten, although they can also play by counting instead of remembering addition facts.

GOTTA BE TEN GAME

OBJECTIVE: The student will be able to tell the pairs of numbers that add up to ten (complements).

MATERIALS:

- An egg carton that has the top two pockets cut off so that there are ten pockets left (You may want to outline the top of each pocket with a black marker to make the individual pockets stand out)
- 20 poker chips, 10 each of two different colors
- Dice

PROCEDURE:

1. Set out the egg carton that has 10 pockets and the 2 colors of poker chips.
2. Have the first player throw the die and call out the number. The teacher should put that many of the same color chips in the pockets of the egg carton. Put the chips in adjacent pockets, not scattered apart, to make a more graphic visual picture and make counting easier for the players.

3. Say, "How many more chips do you need to make 10?" Have the player count how many empty pockets are left. That will be the number of chips that are needed to make ten. Have him put in the correct number of chips in a different color. For many students, using one color for the first number and another color for the complement will assist the learning.
4. Let the other players, if any, roll the dice and count how many more chips they need to make 10.
5. After the combinations have been counted out several times, some of the students will be able to say, "I got a 2. The other number will be 8," without having to count the empty pockets. They are learning the combinations that add up to ten. At this point, let the student make one guess before counting how many more chips he needs. If he is incorrect, have him count the empty pockets by touching each one. If you wish to keep score, you can give a point each time the student gets the other number of the combination right, no matter how he gets the answer. You might want to eventually give two points if the student gets the number right without counting.

6. Some students with Down syndrome will have difficulty in remembering these combinations because of their problems with short-term and working memory. Let them feel as if it is perfectly correct to count the empty pockets each time. They will usually try to memorize the combinations because it makes the game go much faster.

7. The combinations will be easier to learn if they play the *Gotta Be Ten* game for a few minutes each day. If students do not make progress over a week or two, it is probably better to go to the calculator and not worry about learning the complements at this time.

Patterns in Addition (Optional)

At the same time you are working with the concrete addition activities, you can be working to help students memorize the addition facts that follow a pattern. I call these **Short Cuts to Addition.** When students learn the pattern, they have many facts learned quickly. The patterns used most commonly are:

- *Any number plus 0 equals that number.* (9 + 0 = 9)

  Discuss the principle that if you add nothing to any number, it remains the same number. Do the page on *Short Cuts to Addition Facts* in Appendix B several times to make sure the student has the principle securely.

- *Any number plus 1 is just one number higher on the number line or in the rote counting sequence.* (5 + 1 more = 6 or 1, 2, 3, 4, 5 + 1 more = 6)

  Discuss the principle as an example of *one more* which has been learned earlier. Use the number line and the rote counting sequence to go through adding 1 to numbers from 1 to 12. Do the bottom section of the *Short Cuts to Addition Fact* sheet from the Appendix as many times as needed. The student may write the answers or give the information orally.

- *Any number plus 10 just needs a 1 (tens) in front of the other number.* (For 6 + 10, just put a 1 in front of the 6.)

- *Any number plus 9 will result in a sum in which the last number is one less than the original number.* (e.g., for 9 + 7, you know the last number will be one less than 7, or 6. The entire answer is 16). Using a number line, you might ask the student to put a finger on the number that is not 9 (e.g., for 9 + 5, put your finger on 5). Then ask what is *one less* than that number. The student writes down the number one less in the *ones* place and then writes a one in the tens place to get the answer (14). This is quite a difficult concept so you may have to re-teach it after the student has learned other facts. It may not be worth the effort to teach the shortcut to add nines if rote memory is a problem because each answer requires two steps, making the task more difficult.

If the student has learned how to add 10 to any number, he may be able to figure what 1 less will be when adding with 9.

COMMERCIAL GAMES TO BUY OR TRY

Sum Swamp (Learning Resources) is a game that children of all ages may enjoy once they can add by counting on or by using mental math. You throw the two numbered dice and an operations die (with a plus or minus sign) and add (or subtract, if players know the operation) two numbers and move your game piece (a swamp creature) along the board, trying to avoid obstacles and land on shortcuts.

Math Mat Challenge™ (also by Learning Resources) combines gross motor activity (stomping) with mental math. The game consists of a large vinyl mat with numbers around the edge like a clock. You can set it so the voice calls out one-digit addition problems (or problems involving other operations). The player must step on the correct number on the mat, earning a satisfying "ding." A wrong answer receives an irritating buzz. When the player has answered a certain number of problems correctly, the mat cheers like a crowd.

Learning Difficult Facts (Optional)

If your student(s) succeeded in learning the addition facts in the previous sections, you can proceed to teaching the difficult addition facts that don't fall into the above categories.

Assuming that they are visual learners, try thinking up and drawing some pictures to illustrate the difficult addition facts. It doesn't matter if you are not much of an artist—sometimes the more dreadful your art is, the more memorable it is. If this approach works, you can introduce one new fact every couple of days, allowing you time to come up with new stories and pictures.

For example:

- Make the 8 into a snowman and the 5 into a skater. They both are on the ice, and they lose control and pile right into a light pole (the numeral 1). They hit so hard that the 5 falls down and the 8 is sliced right in half, making it a 3. So the only thing that is left standing is the light pole (1) and half of a sliced 8 (3), making $8 + 5 = 13$.

- Or, draw the 2 so it looks like a swan. It was out swimming when it ran into the 6, which looks like a tadpole. What did the swan (2) do to the tadpole (6)? It ate (8) it!

If you have a student who really enjoys these kinds of stories, you might want to invest in a copy of the book *Addition the Fun Way* by Judy Liautaud, which associates each of the numbers with a specific picture (for instance, the 3 is always shown as the "3-bee") and teaches all the addition facts with stories. However, many of the stories are quite long and involved and may be difficult for children with Down syndrome or similar disabilities to remember.

Making the difficult facts into picture stories may assist in your students' learning. Just give it a try.

Another way to help your student(s) remember facts is to appeal to their sense of humor. For example, you could make a joke about the fact (even if it is not a good joke) that 8 and 7 are fif(hiccup)teen. You say, "8 and 7 are 15 but you hiccup between the *fif* and the *teen* and be silly about it." Likewise, you could burp between the syllables of 17 to impress the answer for 9 + 8." Being silly can often help the student remember the fact. (Use your judgment. If you think students will get *too* silly with these kinds of antics, don't encourage them!) Some parents have also used references to already known dates such as family members' birthdays to teach difficult combinations. For example, perhaps a cousin turned 18 on June 12th (6/12) so they point out that 6 + 12 = 18.

Eventually you will have to use flashcards of the difficult facts, and the student will have to memorize the ones he does not know. Even if he is unable to learn some of the harder addition facts, the ones he does know may help him in informal situations.

Math Software

At any time while you are working on the activities to learn addition facts (and later, subtraction facts), you can use computer games for practice and to make the learning more interesting. The games usually do not *teach* the facts; they are used for practice and cementing the facts into long-term storage. Many of the games are made so that you can select the level to match the students' skills. Some useful games include:

The Quarter Mile (published by Barnum Software, 5191 Morgan Territory Road, Clayton, CA 94517; 800-553-9155; www.barnumsoftware.com):

> This software drills students on addition, subtraction, multiplication, and division facts. It can be set to drill a very specific set of facts (such as any number plus 1, or addition facts up to 5 + 5, or doubles, or doubles plus one). The student can choose to be either a racecar or a horse, and answers a set of math facts at his own pace during an on-screen car race or horse race. Once he has completed a set of math facts, in subsequent races he tries to beat his own previous best time. To play, students must be able to find the correct number on the keyboard and type it in. Because the level of difficulty can be adjusted very incrementally and the player has no time constraints (other than trying to beat his own best time), this software is ideal for beginners as well as people who are frustrated by time limits.

Gold Medal Math (published by EdVenture Software; 203-299-0291 (fax); www.edven.com; available commercially from sources such as Amazon.com):

> This software also drills students on addition, subtraction, multiplication, and division facts. Players begin by choosing what Olympic sport they want to participate in and what country they want to represent. They then answer math facts in either a practice mode (ten facts, untimed) or performance mode (as many facts as they can answer in one minute). They are then rewarded with a short animated clip of a male or female figure doing a routine in their chosen sport, and are notified if they won a medal in the sport afterwards (depending on their performance in answering math facts). To play, players must be able to use a mouse to choose from four multiple-choice answers. Players can choose a level of difficulty and an operation to practice, but it is not possible to choose the facts to be

drilled as precisely as in *The Quarter Mile.* In addition, even Level 1 addition asks problems with sums up to 20, so this software cannot be used until a student is fairly advanced.

Math Blaster (published by Knowledge Adventure in various levels of difficulty; available commercially):

Math Blaster software provides arcade-style practice of math facts. For instance, players must click on the right answers to addition problems to avoid having their space station destroyed by meteors. This software is most appropriate for students who can recall facts fairly quickly and are adept at using a computer mouse to click on moving targets (e.g., the correct answers drifting down the screen).

JumpStart (Published by Knowledge Adventure for various grade levels such as first grade or third grade; available commercially):

Titles in the JumpStart series typically include several activities for each academic area (math, reading, science, etc.), with adjust-

Some Commercially Available Methods

There are some commercially available methods that are sometimes used to teach addition and addition facts to students with Down syndrome or other disabilities:

Many concrete learners have used *Touch Math* (Innovative Learning Concepts, Inc.) success-fully, especially for number recognition and small sum addition. In *Touch Math* materials, each of the numerals has a number of dots superimposed on the numeral shape, corresponding with the number itself. For example, the numeral 3 is depicted with 3 dots in a certain configuration, the numeral 5 has 5 dots, etc. Students are taught to touch each of the dots on the numerals and count them when adding. For example, to add 5 + 3, students are taught to say "1, 2, 3, 4, 5" while touching the 5 dots on the 5 and then to continue "6, 7, 8" when touching the 3 dots on the 3. Although *Touch Math* can be useful in helping some concrete learners learn to add small quantities, I have not found it as successful with more complex computations.

Another promising method called *Numicon* is being researched in Great Britain by Sue Buckley (2001) and others of the Down Syndrome Educational Trust. *Numicon* materials consist of plastic templates for each numeral. Each numeral's template is a different color and has the number of holes that correspond to that numeral (e.g., the template for the number 5 is red and has 5 holes; 3 is yellow and has 3 holes). Through repeated practice placing the templates on a pegboard-like base, children learn to recognize what shape the template for a particular number has, and to visualize how different numbers look when their templates are joined together (added). I do not have any experience using the method for teaching, but have been impressed with the materials used. Combining numbers could be easier due to the way the materials are constructed to fit to-gether. I am not aware of the materials being sold in the U.S.A. at present, although you can order them online from the Down Syndrome Educational Trust (www.downsed.org) in Great Britain.

able levels of difficulty. After players complete educational activities (such as answering addition problems correctly) they receive an on-screen reward such as a game piece needed to do the final activity. May be appropriate for students who don't like racing against a time limit.

Generalization into Daily Activities

It is vitally important for children with Down syndrome and other hands-on learners to use addition early and often in daily activities in order to understand its practical use. Chapter 14, Using Whole Number Addition, focuses on practice doing addition with the calculator and knowing when to use addition. Generalization activities are included as part of this chapter (see pages 185 and 195).

Using Whole Number Addition

Pre- /Post Checklist

Can the student:

1. _____ Add 2- and 3-digit numbers with a calculator.

2. _____ Add multiple items with a calculator.

3. _____ Add 3- and 4-digit numbers with a calculator.

4. _____ Solve addition story problems with already made pictures.

5. _____ Draw pictures of simple addition story problems.

6. _____ Make a number sentence out of a simple story problem.

7. _____ Use tally marks to illustrate a story problem.

8. _____ Do simulations of possible story problem situations.

9. _____ Use addition in real-life situations.

If this were a traditional math textbook, the emphasis in this chapter would probably be on learning to do paper and pencil addition of larger numbers than in the previous chapter. Typically, after students learn to add single-digit numbers, they progress to adding double- and triple-digit numbers, with regrouping (what used to be known as "carrying").

However, because this book emphasizes teaching math skills in a way that is meaningful and useful to students with Down syndrome and other concrete learners, this chapter will have a different focus. It will focus primarily on two areas:

1. on using the calculator to add two- to four-digit numbers, and
2. on developing a better understanding of how and why addition is used in the real world.

Students need to get a great deal of practice using the calculator for addition. The mechanical process should be almost automatic so the student can concentrate on problem solving. Some worksheets for calculator practice are included in this book. However, students will probably need more practice adding with the calculator than can be given here. There are some excellent mass-market workbooks that give practice with addition, such as *The Complete Book of Math* by McGraw Hill Education. Most also provide the answers. You will find these workbooks labeled for kindergarten to grade three. If your student is beyond those grades, you may need to cover up the words that show the younger grade label. I usually use address labels.

The process of learning to regroup (*carrying* when the sum is over 10) is usually a major step in beginning addition. If your student is progressing satisfactorily in general classroom math, you may want to see if she can understand the concept of regrouping. Use the materials introduced in Chapter 10, Place Value, for showing concretely how to make 10 *ones* become 1 *ten* to be added to the existing *tens*. However, most concrete thinkers will do better using the calculator for adding numbers beyond 9. With the calculator it does not make any difference if the addition involves regrouping (*carrying*) or not. For these students, you should give more attention to helping them learn to enter the numbers accurately and understanding when to use addition.

The divisions of calculator practice are:
- **Two- and three-digit addition**
- **Multiple item addition**
- **Larger numbers**

The sections on addition use in actual or story problems cover:
- **Using objects or already made pictures of an addition story**
- **Picturing an addition story**
  - ▼ Semi-concrete representations
  - ▼ Number sentences
- **Doing simulations of possible situations**
- **Actually doing the situation (if possible)**

A Word about Worksheets and Written Work

Once students reach this point in their mathematics learning, they will increasingly be called upon to solve written math problems. It is worth putting some thought into how the problems are presented on the page, as well as the amount of writing that is expected of children with Down syndrome, autism, or other disabilities.

Most students with Down syndrome and some students with autism spectrum disorders or other disabilities have low muscle tone. Especially when they are young, their writing hands tire quite quickly. They may also have problems just forming the numbers correctly. If they are asked to copy down problems before solving them, it often takes a lot of time and is physically tiring. When students are learning the process of addition, it is wise to have them concentrate on that learning and not on the copying process. Using preprinted worksheets or having the practice work photocopied onto the students' papers will help them focus on the math skills they need to learn. Consider adding this accommodation to your student's Individualized Education Program (IEP) at school so she can focus on math, rather than fine motor skills, when completing written work.

When students are first learning to solve addition problems written vertically rather than horizontally, I suggest printing the problems on graph paper with large squares, one numeral per square. (See the illustration in Chapter 3, page 24. Tell the students that it is easier to add the *ones* with the *ones* and the *tens* with the *tens* when the numbers are written underneath each other, lining up the similar units.

TWO- AND THREE-DIGIT ADDITION

OBJECTIVE: The student will be able to accurately add 2- and 3-digit numbers with the calculator.

MATERIALS:
- Copies of math worksheets (Addition with 2- and 3-Digit Numbers) from Appendix B (page 347)
- Pencil
- Calculator

SUCCESS STEP: Give the students the first problem on the worksheet and go through the steps with them so that they are successful. Guide them to:

Get in a rhythm when using a calculator. You can even chant the sequence:
  Forty-eight or (whatever the number is) as you push the number 48.
  Look (check the number in the window)
  Plus (or whatever the operation is)

  Eighty-eight (or whatever the number is)
  Look (check the number in the window)
  Equals (as you press the = sign)

It is very important that you have the students enter the data slowly and check at the window every time. You are not looking for speed, just accuracy. It will take them more time if they have to go back and find where they made a mistake because they hurried.

PROCEDURE:

1. Ask the student(s) to try the next problems alone. Make sure they are not racing through the problems on the worksheet. Accuracy is much more impor-

tant than speed! Be sure that they follow the steps taught in Chapter 5, Use of the Calculator.

2. Bear in mind that when adding multiple-digit problems, some students may have to touch each number on the paper as they enter it in the calculator. Other students will need an index card or straight edge to hide the other distracting numbers on the page. You might also need to highlight (or have the student highlight) all of the units (ones) with one color, the *tens* with another color, etc. The highlighting is done before the student starts to enter the problem in the calculator and is faded when the student seems to have internalized the place value concepts. Try some of these adaptations if you notice a student is having difficulty knowing which number to enter next or loses her place in the worksheet frequently.

3. Have students check the accuracy of each answer by redoing the calculation. If possible, ask them to put the numbers in the calculator in the opposite order from their original entry. You will be able to see if they can apply the principle of commutative property (order of items not important).

4. You can give each worksheet several times. You can also change one number of each pair to make different worksheets with different answers.

Modifying Worksheets

The way in which worksheets are designed can make a lot of difference in the performance of concrete thinkers. At first, 6 problems to an 8 x 11 sheet of paper will be optimum for most students. The problems should be spaced far apart, on wide graph paper or in marked columns with little distracting instructions or pictures. Teachers can just enlarge part of the regular worksheet or math textbook page on a photocopy machine. Parents may have to rewrite the addition problems from the textbook with larger numbers on large-sized graph paper.

Once the student becomes proficient in doing math with the calculator, you can probably increase the number of problems to 12 on a page. This one accommodation in the size and clarity of written math work may help the student with learning a variety of math concepts taught in school.

MULTIPLE ITEM ADDITION

Adding up several items to get a total is a more difficult task than adding just two numbers—even with a calculator. There are more chances of making an error with multiple numbers, and students often have trouble keeping their place in the list. For students with Down syndrome, who are more apt to have short-term memory problems, this type of addition can be especially frustrating.

OBJECTIVE: The student will be able to accurately add multiple one- and two-digit numbers with the calculator.

MATERIALS:
- Addition with three single- and double-digit number worksheets from Appendix B (page 345)
- Pencil
- Index cards

SUCCESS STEP: Ask the student to show you the addition and equals sign on her calculator. Praise her.

PROCEDURE:
1. Have the students go through the first problem on the Multiple Item Addition worksheet with you. Use an index card to cover up all the numbers that are not being entered into the calculator at this time.
2. Teach the students to start with the top number. Slide down the index card to uncover one number at a time.
3. Recheck the answer by adding the numbers in reverse order.
4. Redo the worksheets at a different time. Make other worksheets with three or more numbers to add if more practice is needed.

GENERALIZATION INTO DAILY ACTIVITIES: Adding multiple items is a very useful skill that can be used in many ways in everyday life:
- Shopping for several items can be an excellent way to generalize this skill. However, you should have the student add multiple items in dollars, not in cents. Adding dollars and cents will be covered later in Chapter 20, Money. If the price is given in dollars and cents in the store or in the ad, you change the prices to the next highest dollar, write the prices down, and give the paper to the student. You can also write the simplified prices on Post-It notes and put them on the ads over the dollars-and-cents prices. Have the student do the addition with the calculator herself. The practice will be even more beneficial if she is motivated to really buy the items.
- There are also chances to do small number multiple item addition when adding scores for games such as Scrabble, Hearts, or darts where you get points for every round.
- Miniature or regular golf requires the addition of small numbers for each hole. My son Scott liked to ride (or drive) in his dad's golf cart and keep score.
- Sometimes students with Down syndrome or other disabilities are made "managers" of the middle or high school baseball, volleyball, football, or soccer teams. These managers can also be taught to keep score as a backup for the team. What a wonderful opportunity for students to use their math and calculator skills!

Kyle had learned to add single digits in his head without writing anything down. However, when he had a shopping list and several items to buy, he was not able to add accurately.

Adding several numbers, even if they are small, is more difficult than adding two numbers. The first two numbers can be added easily, but when adding a third number, the student must remember the first total and add the third number to that total—two different numbers to remember plus the pertinent addition facts.

Writing down the numbers can usually address this issue. Kyle had progressed to using a small calculator, and he used it to keep track in multi-item addition.

LARGER NUMBER ADDITION

When students can accurately add two- and three-digit numbers, they need some practice in adding even larger numbers with the calculator accurately. They should learn to accurately add larger numbers so that they are able to learn the addition of dollars and cents that will be important in shopping, banking, and budgeting needed for daily living in the future.

They may have to be reminded to look in the calculator window after they have entered each number that has several digits.

OBJECTIVE: The student will be able to add three-and four-digit numbers accurately using a calculator.

MATERIALS:
- Addition of 3- and 4-Digit Numbers (page 349)
- Other workbooks on addition, especially those written for home use that can be purchased at discount stores. Try to find books that have interesting pictures and situations.

SUCCESS STEP: Have the student enter a problem in the calculator that is very easy for her. Praise correct answer.

PROCEDURE:
1. Have the student practice doing addition with the numbers from the Large Number Addition worksheet in Appendix. Give her some practice time at the beginning of each lesson for several weeks. You can give her a clean copy of the page that you used the previous time. Familiarity may make the operation more accurate.
2. Tell the student to check each sum by adding the same numbers in the opposite order. If you are adding 4381 + 3269 = 7650, adding backwards will give 3269 + 4381 = 7650. If the numbers do not match, she should do the original prob-

lem again. If the numbers do not match this time, she should signal an adult to check for errors.

3. For additional practice, make your own worksheets (and figure out the answers). You can find workbooks for early math in the coloring book section of most grocery or discount stores. Although this text can't supply all the examples and exercises that are needed to teach, you can judge what types of workbooks are appropriate for your student by looking at the samples in Appendix B.

You may be able to find Internet sites that have sample worksheets or freeware on addition. For example, www.funbrain.com has a variety of games using math such as Number Cracker, Tic-Tac-Toe Squares, Math Baseball, Line Jumper, and Mathcar Racing. Also, www.kidsdomain.com has download sites for addition and subtraction, as does www.learningplanet.com (e.g., Spacey Math Game).

Addition from Concrete Representations to Story Problems

While students are learning fluency in using the calculator, we want to make sure that they understand when to use the addition process. In this section, we will therefore teach a process in problem solving. We will progress from using concrete objects to semi-concrete representations to abstract numbers. Students will learn to draw math problems—first, with pictures, and later, with stamps, tally marks, and numbers. Then, in a teaching situation, some simulations of a possible real-life situation will be made that will emphasize the uses of addition. Using several problems with a similar theme can help the students realize the uses of addition with less distraction from various new situations. A scenario about the planning of a birthday party will be used.

USING OBJECTS OR ALREADY MADE PICTURES TO SOLVE ADDITION STORIES

The easiest way to solve a word problem is to use the actual objects that are to be added together. After the student has manipulated the actual objects that are to be added, she may be able to see the parallel in counting pictured objects on a page. Some students (including those on the autism spectrum) may have difficulty understanding that a picture stands for an object. You may have to continue using objects as manipulatives while you teach the transition from objects to picture representations. (See the box below on teaching picture-to-object correspondence.)

The objects pictured should be exactly the same at first. Later, progress to using pictures with slight differences, such as one sheep looking the opposite way from the rest of the group, or people who are wearing different colored hats, etc.

OBJECTIVE: The student will read simple story problems that include pictures and use the pictures to assist in addition.

MATERIALS:

- Illustrated addition stories from:
  - ▼ Appendix B
  - ▼ Mass market workbooks (such as *The Complete Book of Math,* McGraw-Hill Children's Publishing)
  - ▼ Websites—If you are teaching several students, you may want to use the material on www.mathstories.com. This site has some free math materials, but requires payment for the story problems. The advantage is that they supply the pictures for beginning story problems, use fairly large print, and explain the problem situation very clearly. Or try the free worksheets with story problems at www.schoolexpress.com/#worksheets.
- Pencil

PROCEDURE:

1. Find math word problems that have few words and clear pictures. For example:

Bob has 3 flashlights.

Ann has 3 flashlights.

How many flashlights do they have altogether? _____
(or, total number of flashlights: _____)

Teaching Picture-to-Object Correspondence

For children who cannot understand that a picture can stand for a real object, autism experts Lynn McClannahan and Patricia Krantz recommend the following steps in their book *Activity Schedules for Children with Autism* (Woodbine House, 1999):

1. Take pictures of five familiar objects (with no other distracting objects in the background). Mount the photos, one to a page, on pieces of construction paper and put them in a binder to make a book.
2. Assemble the five objects that you photographed on a table.
3. Look at the book with your child. Point to the first photo, and ask your child to "find" the matching object. Guide her hand to the proper object, if necessary.
4. As soon as your child finds the matching object, praise her, give her a special hug or tickle, etc.
5. Continue with the other four objects in the "book."
6. Practice with this book until your child can accurately find all five matching objects without your guidance. Then make a new book with pictures of five different objects.

This type of addition story problem requires that you understand that putting items together requires addition. You will also be using the word *total* for the phrase "how many do you have altogether?" as an alternative. Use as many of the already illustrated math stories as are needed to make the transition from concrete objects to pictures. Encourage your student(s) to count the pictures if she does not know the appropriate addition fact.

DRAWING PICTURES OF A MATH STORY

You can make a transition from using already illustrated math problems to having the student draw pictures of the items that are to be added. You can have her draw very simple pictures such as balls or cats. However, sometimes the time needed to do the drawing distracts from the math learning. Using a simple stamp or a bingo marker saves time and usually makes the task more fun for the student. For this activity, we will therefore have students make semi-concrete representations (drawing or stamping).

OBJECTIVE: The student will be able to represent (draw or stamp) items in simple addition story problems and solve for the total.

MATERIALS:

- Story Problems from Appendix B (page 356) and those made up *by the teacher or parent*
- Washable markers
  OR
- Washable ink stamps made for children and washable ink stamp pads (Crayola)
  OR
- Colored Bingo markers (for older students)
  OR
- Stickers
- Paper

SUCCESS STEP: Have the student show you how she can make a circle or mark with the markers or stamps on paper.

PROCEDURE:

1. Go through the first story problem orally (without pictures) and make sure the students understand what is wanted. Repeat the numerals and write them on the chalkboard or on a tablet of paper that they can see.
2. Have the students illustrate the first story problem by making a drawing or stamp for each one of the items in the story problems. Have them make the marks in a straight line across the paper with a space between the groups of objects to be counted (e.g., make 4 butterfly stamps, space, and then the next 3 butterfly stamps). Make sure that they do not start making other marks or drawing other objects. It may be wise to give them a blank sheet of paper to experiment on with the stamps or markers before you start with the math problem.

3. Ask the students what operation (process) they need to use when they are putting items together or finding a total. Have them put the operation sign between the two groups of stamps on each problem. Then let them count the marks or stamps to find the total. Then they must check the answer with the calculator and write the answer on the paper.

4. Write or type another of the suggested addition story problems on the top of a piece of paper. See if the students can make the stamp marks, count them, and check the answer with the calculator independently. Continue giving them the simple addition story problems from Appendix B, as well as ones that you make up until you feel that they are able to do the process carefully and well. (They will probably be more motivated to solve your problems if you use their names in some of them.)

5. If the student has a great deal of difficulty visualizing the concepts, continue short sessions over a long period of time. Vary the materials that you use as suggested in the Materials section to keep her interest. If you still have little success, try again 6 months later. The ability to move from concrete to semi-concrete representations improves as a student gets older.

6. For students who learn best with visual teaching, you may want to set up a structure for solving an addition story problem. Use a graphic organizer such as connected boxes to show the addition story problem. For example:

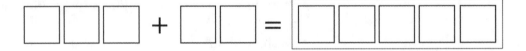

   If this graphic organizer is already on the paper, the student only has to put a stamp or drawing in each box to solve the problem. The graphic organizer is just a teaching device that can be dropped when the student is more competent in doing story problems.

WRITING SIMPLE NUMBER SENTENCES

OBJECTIVE: The student will write one-digit number sentences for word problems.

MATERIALS:
- Pencil
- Word problems (including some problems previously done in above two activities)

PROCEDURE:

1. If you have taught the addition skills in Chapter 13, you introduced adding single digits with the problems arranged horizontally in what we call a number sentence. Check to see if the students know the label *number sentence* for problems such as 6 + 9 = 15. Model making *number sentences* for the students using some of the story problems with already made pictures you used previously. Say,

Wording Your Word Problems

Be careful that you do not make up questions that change the normal word order of the sentence or use terms the students may not know. We are not testing their language comprehension.

At first, use simple declarative sentences that do not change the order of the sentence as "Wh" words do. For example, "He *had ___ boxes*" is easier to understand than "How *many boxes did he have?*" Many times students would be able to do the math required in a story problem, but the word order and the language of the problem are the barriers that impede success. The ability to understand the change in word order when making "Wh" questions comes developmentally late in a child's language learning.

Here is an example of a word problem that is written well for a child who has language delays:

Bob and Allison went looking for marbles in their backyard.

Bob found __3__ marbles.

Allison found __6__ marbles.

They had __9__ marbles altogether.

"I write the 3 here to stand for Ted's 3 flashlights. I write the 2 here to stand for Alice's 2 flashlights. If we want to know how many flashlights are here altogether, we have to add (as you draw a plus sign). The total (write the equals sign) is 5. That is a number sentence."

2. Have the students make up number sentences for other problems. Begin by using some of the problems they already worked out with pictures in the activities above. That way, they can count the objects to be added and write down the appropriate numbers. You may want to give them a form for a model such as:

___ + ___ = ___

If you are working with several students, have each one make up simple problems to give the others to make as number sentences.

3. Repeat the above process until you are confident the students understand what to do to make a number sentence from the very simple one-step story problems. Later have them make number problems from any real situation or story problem.

Making number sentences is not an easy concept. You may not get complete understanding at this time. However, as you teach them about the use of addition for solving problems, keep reminding them, "Let's make a number sentence out of this before we solve it with the calculator."

TALLY MARKS

It may be helpful for some students to learn to make tally marks to represent the objects in an addition word problem (instead of, or in addition to using stamps, stickers, etc. as above). Some students may see this as a more grown-up way to figure out a problem. In addition, using tally marks provides practice in counting by 5's, which is an essential skill for telling time and counting money.

OBJECTIVE: The student will learn to use single tally marks and groups of five when counting objects.

MATERIALS:
- Markers
- Paper
- Craft sticks
- Simple word problems

PROCEDURE:
1. Use simple story problems as in the previous activity. Instead of making stamps to represent each item in a story, show the students how you can make a tally mark for each item. You may demonstrate with craft sticks how you put down four sticks and then put the fifth stick across the other sticks.
2. Have them practice with markers on paper at first, putting large spaces between the groups of five. Review how to skip count by fives to find the total. Practice making the groups of five carefully and have them write the number sentence for the problem after the tally.

$$||| \quad + \quad \cancel{||||}| \quad = \quad \cancel{||||}\,|||| \quad \text{(Tally marks)}$$

$$\mathbf{3} \quad + \quad \mathbf{6} \quad\quad = \quad \mathbf{9} \quad \text{(Number sentence)}$$

3. Give the students practice in making tally marks for every number up to 20.

GENERALIZATION INTO DAILY ACTIVITIES:
- Do a survey of likes and dislikes in your family using tally marks (for example, who likes chocolate chip cookies with nuts and who likes them without; which of 5 possible board games would each family member agree to play after dinner).
- Have an election at school that requires a tally of responses.
- Have the students count off for a game and then make tally marks to make sure the teams are even.
- Tally responses to how many students are bringing lunch versus those buying lunch.
- Tally responses to a choice of songs to sing in assembly.

- Tally times that various family members have fed or walked the dog in a week, set the table, emptied the dishwasher, or done other chores that are shared among family members.
- Tally how many times your family goes to the pool, goes to the health club or YMCA, visits the local zoo, etc. (to see if it's worth spending your money on an annual membership, etc.)

SIMULATION OF ADDITION SITUATIONS

OBJECTIVE: The student will be able to use addition to solve problems in a simulated situation using the calculator.

MATERIALS:
- Paper and pencil
- Any props as suggested by the scenario (optional)

SUCCESS STEP: Have the student describe her own birthday party or one that she attended as a guest. Praise good descriptions.

PROCEDURE:
1. Tell the student that the two (or more) of you are going to pretend to plan a surprise birthday for someone. For instance, say, "We are going to plan a pretend surprise birthday party for our young cousin, Dan."

2. Explain, act out, draw, or find concrete items as you talk about each situation. Use paper, white board, or a slate to write the numbers on so the students can refer back to them, but do not have the students read the specific numbers as if it was just another story problem.
3. Talk the students through the questions below, in order to find out how many people might come to the party, how much supplies will cost, and what will actually happen at the party.

Who Comes to the Party?
1. How many people should we invite to the party? Dan's mother told us that she would like one child for every year Dan is old. Dan is eight. How many of Dan's friends can we invite to the party? _____
2. Of course, the relatives are going to be invited too. Dan has four aunts and three uncles. How many relatives should be invited? (Draw or make tally marks to illustrate the situation.) _____

3. With both Dan's friends and his relatives coming, how many invitations should we send? (Draw or make tally marks for his friends and relatives. Check with the **calculator.**) _____

4. Of course, you and I will be at the party, and so will Dan's mother and father. We do not need invitations because we know all about the party. How many people will be there who do not need invitations? (Use tally marks.) _____

5. How many people could come to Dan's party altogether? Make a number sentence. _____

When the students have worked out the invitation problems as a class, give the students new numbers to do the same problems.

Buying Supplies for Dan's Party

1. We decide to have pizza at the party. We will buy two large pizzas. One pizza costs $10 and another pizza costs $8. How much will the two pizzas cost together? Illustrate the problem with pictures and add. _____

2. We decide to have lemonade for the party. The lemons will cost $2. The sugar will cost $1. The water is free. How much will the lemonade cost all together? Write a number sentence (multiple item addition) for the situation (include the water) and solve. _____

3. We want to have special decorated paper plates and cups for Dan's party. The plates cost $3, and the cups cost $2. (Put in a theme that the students would like to be reflected in the plates and cups such as Batman or balloons.) How much will the plates and cups cost together? Make a number sentence and add. _____

4. We are going to decorate the room with streamers. The crepe paper streamers cost $1 for each roll of one color. We want both blue and yellow streamers. How much will all the streamers cost? Make a picture of the rolls and add. _____

5. When you have all the totals from questions 1-4, add all the costs (multiple item addition) and find the total amount needed to buy supplies.

At the Party

1. At Dan's birthday party, his mother and father give him 2 presents. His friends and relatives give him 10 presents. How many presents will Dan open at his party? Use tally marks to figure the total. _____

2. All the people invited to Dan's party come early and hide in the living room. When Dan comes home from soccer practice, he opens the door and looks in. The guests jump up and yell, "Surprise!" Dan is very surprised. He sees 7 adults and 8 of his friends in the room. How many people were able to come to Dan's party? Don't forget to count Dan. _____

Go over each problem orally with the students. Draw or model any of the situations as need be. Correct any mistakes and record the answers on a piece of paper. That way, you can refer back to any of the answers needed for a new problem.

You may do the situation in several parts at different sessions, especially with younger students. Older students may be able to plan the whole party at one sitting.

At another session go through the exact same problems giving the students less assistance. Sometime later, repeat the scenario using different numbers. If students are really interested in the scenario, add new questions (for instance, ask how many whacks it took to break open the piñata, or how many tubs of ice cream (vanilla and chocolate chip) were eaten. You may change the instructions about drawing or making a number sentence or using tally marks so the students can find their favorite method for picturing story problems.

If possible, plan a real party for your class or family.

GENERALIZATION INTO DAILY ACTIVITIES: The entire idea for this chapter is to assure that, faced with actual situations requiring addition, students can make visual pictures to illustrate them, set up addition problems, and solve them accurately with the calculator. Parents, you have the best chance to make sure that the students can generalize these skills into daily living tasks. Teachers will have to look at possible ways to use addition during the school day.

- When grocery shopping and buying packs of items such as hamburger buns, hot dogs, gum, pencils, bagels, cartons of yogurt, juice boxes, or cartons of pop in cans, add to see how many total items you are getting.
- When baking cookies, cupcakes, or muffins, keep track of how many you've made each time you take a pan out of the oven. For example, the first pan had 10 cookies; the second pan had 12 cookies on it. How many total cookies did you bake?
- Play darts, toss a beanbag at a target, or play some other game where you can earn different point scores. Add up your score as you go along.
- Count how many items (sports cards, Barbies, seashells, etc.) you have in a collection and write down the total. Each time you add a few items to the collection, add that number to the total instead of counting each item.
- Play games that require two dice. Purchase or make dice (such as from Learning Resources) that have the numerals imprinted on them instead of dots, so players must add the two numbers rather than count dots to get their total.
- At school, if the class is working toward a reward by earning a certain number of points or tokens for accomplishments, you can add the number of points earned to the previous total to see how many you have now. You can do the same at home if your child has a reward chart or is saving her allowance.

CHAPTER 15

Whole Number Subtraction

Pre- /Post Checklist

Can the student:

1. _____ Demonstrate subtraction with a small number in a "take away" situation.

2. _____ Demonstrate with concrete materials how subtraction is the reverse of addition with 3 fact families.

3. _____ Write or recognize the correct way to write a subtraction problem when the numbers are given orally (largest number on the top or entered first into the calculator).

4. _____ Unbind a *tens* group of sticks (yielding single-digit sticks) in order to have like units to subtract from like units.

5. _____ Demonstrate several two-digit take-away subtraction problems with concrete materials

Subtraction facts (optional)

6. _____ Solve one- and two-digit take-away subtraction problems using the calculator

Most mathematics texts teach subtraction along with addition so that the students learn subtraction facts that are in the same *fact family* as the addition facts that are first learned. In this book, however, we recommend teaching the two operations at different times so that students who are concrete thinkers can thoroughly learn the addition process before moving on to sub-

traction. As was mentioned in Chapter 13, you may want or need to follow your school district's sequence for introducing addition and subtraction if your student is included in the general classroom for math. You might have to do the addition problems with answers under 12 and then skip to the subtraction problems that are part of those fact families. Use both the addition and the subtraction chapters in a similar way to help the student stay with his class in math. If the student is older or his classmates have already finished addition and subtraction, though, you can do each process separately.

If your student has learned most of the addition facts for numbers under 10, you may be able to help him learn the related subtraction facts. However, most concrete thinkers will need many activities and experiences to understand the concept of subtraction. Learning the facts is not as crucial as long as students can accurately use the calculator. Bear in mind, too, that regrouping ("borrowing") when subtracting larger numbers is more difficult than adding large numbers, so the actual computation of two- or more digit numbers will usually need to be done by calculator.

The following areas of subtraction will be covered:
- **Basic Understandings of Subtraction**
  - ▼ What is subtraction?
  - ▼ Addition and subtraction are related
  - ▼ Largest number first
  - ▼ Subtract only like units
- **Take-away Subtraction**
  - ▼ Concrete
  - ▼ Symbolic
- **Subtraction Facts (Optional)**
- **Subtraction with the Calculator**
  - ▼ Take-away subtraction
  - ▼ One and two digits

Basic Principles of Subtraction

Children are usually aware of the process of subtraction without knowing that it is labeled *subtraction*. For example, they know that if they have four cookies and someone takes away two cookies, they have fewer cookies than they started with. Children are also usually familiar with the common term *take-away* used for the type of subtraction most often encountered in daily life. Parents and teachers should start saying the word *subtract* for take-away situations to ready the student for this math process.

Subtraction is really the inverse of addition. If you know that 3 + 5 = 8, you also know that 8 - 3 = 5. Essentially, addition is bringing two smaller numbers together to form a larger number. Starting with that larger number and subtracting one of the smaller numbers will yield the other smaller number. The relationships between those three numbers are what math books often call a "fact family."

Although some activities for learning subtraction facts will be presented here, remember that students learning these survival math skills do not have to rely on their short-term memory to do either addition or subtraction if they are able to use the calculator. Subtraction becomes more difficult when regrouping into different units or borrowing is involved, but the student can jump that hurdle by using the calculator.

WHAT IS SUBTRACTION?

The student has probably already been doing simple subtraction activities in his everyday life such as commenting, "Mom, Jason took 2 of my Legos! Now I don't have enough for a bridge. I had 10 Legos and now I have only 8." You just need him to be aware of the process he is already using in small ways and to learn to express the process mathematically.

OBJECTIVE: The student will be able to write a number sentence for simple problems (10 or fewer) which use subtraction.

MATERIALS:

- 10 pennies
- Small slate or white board
- Chalk or whiteboard markers

SUCCESS STEP: Give the student 3 pennies and ask him how many pennies he has. Praise a correct answer.

PROCEDURE:

1. Take away 1 penny from the 3 you gave the student and ask him how many pennies he has now. He will say 2. Then write on the slate board the number sentence that has been made. Say,
    "You had 3 pennies" (and write the number 3 on the board).
    "What did I do next?" (took away 1 penny)
    "I am writing a minus sign (-) to show that I took it away
        (or subtracted it)."
    "Then I write the 1 penny after the minus sign to show how much
        I took away."
    "Then I write an equal sign (=)" (already known).
    "And how many did you have left?" (2)
    "Yes, I write the 2 after the equal sign to show what you have left."

$$3 - 1 = 2$$

The student should understand what an addition number sentence is if he has completed Chapter 14. Tell him that this is a "take-away" or subtraction number sentence. Read the whole thing out loud for him. "Three minus one equals 2."

2. Repeat the demonstration with 5 pennies and take away 1 or 2 and see if the student can write part of the number sentence. Progress to doing simple "take-away" problems with some of the 10 pennies.

3. At a later session, see if the student can make subtraction number sentences for all of the facts using 10 pennies. If he is unable to write the numbers, have him tell you which numbers to write. You can also write the numbers from 1 to 10 on index cards and have him point to them or arrange them into a number sentence.

4. Spend several sessions doing simple concrete subtraction problems with 10 or fewer items and writing their number sentences. You may want to pair two students and have them take turns "taking away" objects from each other. (It can be done in a "funny" way. For example, give one student a number of objects he doesn't especially want, such as worksheets to do, and then have him invite another student to take some away or pretend that the objects are cookies and have one student take some—sneakily.)

Take-Away Subtraction

Unlike addition, subtraction is used for more than one situation. The most common use for subtraction is the type students usually call "take-away." Take-away occurs when some of these items are taken away from a larger group of items $(9 - 5 = 4)$. Most of the problems that students will encounter in daily living are take-away situations. The other kinds of problems using subtraction will be covered in Chapter Sixteen when the students have learned to be accurate with subtraction on the calculator.

SOCK EATER GAME

OBJECTIVE: Same as above.

MATERIALS:
- 9 different colored socks—none of them pairs
- A small box with one side cut out (can be a large shoe box)
- Index cards with $9 - 1 = 8$, $9 - 2 = 7$ and all the other 9-based subtraction facts

PROCEDURE:
1. Tell the story of the Sock Eater. Mom has Ellen wash some of her own clothes in the washer and dry them in the dryer. Somehow, Ellen never seems to get as many socks out the dryer as she puts. When she told her mother, her mother said, "You must have a Sock Eater stealing away your socks" and she laughed. Ellen laughed with her mother at the joke. However, later she thought, " What if there is a Sock Eater in our laundry room ?" She counted the socks that she put in the dryer and she counted the number of socks that came out of the dryer. Here is what she saw:

- The first day she put 9 socks in the dryer and she only got 8 socks out of the dryer. The teacher acts out the story with the socks going in the box (dryer). He shows the one sock that was stolen, and then the teacher and class count out the number left. (The teacher may pretend to gobble up the one sock or put it behind his back while the students count the remaining socks in the box.) The teacher writes the problem $9 - 1 = 8$ on a piece of paper or chalkboard so the students can see what the number sentence looks like.
- The teacher then takes all the socks out, shakes them, and repeats the story for the second day as he puts them back in the box. The second day the teacher (Sock Eater) takes another sock out, so now two socks are missing. He writes the number sentence $9 - 2 = 7$ and shows the students.
- The teacher continues eating socks until there are no socks left in the dryer or whenever the students get bored—whichever comes first. You can "ham" up the story to grab the students' attention and even put a small black mask around your eyes to better play the part of the Sock Eater.

LARGEST NUMBER FIRST

In addition, it does not matter which number comes first, but in subtraction the largest number needs to be given first. Whether you are putting the problem horizontally or in columns vertically, the largest number must come first or at the top of the problem.

OBJECTIVE: The student will be able to write or recognize the correct way to write a subtraction problem when the numbers are given orally.

MATERIALS:
- Paper and pencil or small chalkboard and chalk for teacher and student
- Paper plate
- Craft sticks or pencils

SUCCESS STEP: Show the student a simple take-away subtraction problem using sticks and paper plates. Put 5 sticks on a paper plate and then take some away. Ask him which is the largest number—the number you started with (5) or the number that is left after you have taken some sticks away. Praise the correct answer. Repeat if the first answer is not correct.

PROCEDURE:
1. Call out some simple subtraction problems, and ask the student(s) to write them. If a student cannot write, have a set of index cards with the problems pre-written on them so he can choose. The simple subtraction problems should be written horizontally.

2. After practice with simple problems, show the student how the problems can be written vertically. Give him practice with solving problems written vertically. Remember to give the student graph paper if he has difficulty lining numbers up.

3. If the student is having difficulty writing a problem, ask him which is the largest number of the numbers you called out. When he correctly identifies the largest number, tell him that is the number he needs to start with. If he has trouble understanding this, demonstrate with objects why you can't take away more than you have.

TAKE AWAY GAME

OBJECTIVE: The student will be able to demonstrate at least 5 one- and two-digit take-away subtraction problems (without regrouping) with concrete materials.

MATERIALS:
- 19 craft sticks or straws for each student
- Large paper plates
- A slate, whiteboard, or piece of paper for the teacher

SUCCESS STEP: Ask one student to put 11 sticks on his plate. Praise him for doing it correctly.

PROCEDURE:

1. Divide the group into pairs—either pairs of students or the student and the teacher as a pair. Have one student hold the large plate with 11 sticks. Have the other student (or teacher) be the grabber. The grabber takes away the number of sticks that the teacher calls out. For example, the teacher says, "Take away 1." The grabber takes away the 1 single craft stick, saying, "I am taking away 1." The teacher asks the other student how many sticks are left. The student says, "I have 10 left."

2. The teacher then writes the number sentence of 11 − 1 = 10 on paper or a slate so the students can visually see the symbols that represent that situation.

3. Then the teacher says, "There are 10 sticks left. Take away 4 sticks." The grabber takes 4 sticks leaving 6 sticks with the first student.

4. The teacher then asks the students what she (or he) should write for the number sentence on the paper. Help them if they are not sure how to write it.

5. Reverse the pair of students and have the other person be the grabber. Make it a little like a game of take-away. Make sure the students do the dialogue as given in step 1. It will help them to learn the steps in subtraction with this creative practice.

6. Make up one- and two-digit subtraction take-away problems with and without regrouping. Give the students as much practice as necessary to visualize the take-away problems.

7. At this point, students should be ready to learn to subtract on the calculator. See "Subtraction with the Calculator" below." Have the student check the take-away subtraction problems with the calculator.

SUBTRACT ONLY LIKE UNITS (REGROUPING)

The important concept is for the student to understand that *ones* can only be subtracted from *ones, tens* from *tens, hundreds* from *hundreds,* etc.

OBJECTIVE: The student will unbind a group of *tens* in order to have like units (ones) to subtract from like units.

MATERIALS:
- The Clothespin Box labeled ONES and TENS from Chapter 9
- 9 individual clothespins and 20 additional clothespins grouped in *tens* on cardboard strips
  OR
- 9 individual craft sticks and 20 additional sticks bound together as two groups of tens

SUCCESS STEP: Have the student point to the groups of *tens* and to several single clothespins or sticks. Praise correct identifications.

PROCEDURE:
1. Put the number 14 on the place value box using one strip of tens and 4 single ones (or lay out one group of 10 craft sticks and 4 single sticks). Tell the student that you need to take away 6 single clothespins right now. Say, "There are only 4 single clothespins on the box. What should I do?"
2. Encourage the student to come to his own conclusion that he needs to take apart the group of 10. You may want to tell him that breaking down one ten into ten ones is called *regrouping,* if he will need to know that word in the math curriculum in the general classroom.
3. Take away the 6 single clothespins (or sticks) and thank him for solving your problem. Ask him how many single clothespins or sticks are left on the table (8). Then write the problem in numbers so he can see what it looks like.
4. Emphasize that you can only subtract *ones* from *ones.* If the student has more than 9 clothespins for the *ones* column (on the box), put the extra ones on the table in front of the *ones* space. Ask the student what should happen next. Encourage him to bundle 10 together and pin the loose (ones) pins to the box .
5. Repeat this sequence with a few different numbers until the student feels secure.

Subtraction Facts (Optional)

Subtraction facts are usually taught when the retrieval of addition facts is almost automatic. Many students can learn the subtraction facts under 9 if the related addition facts are secure. However, some students have difficulty seeing the relationship between the fact families such as $2 + 4 = 6$ and $6 - 2 = 4$.

Students with Down syndrome may also have difficulty with the rote memorization involved in this task. Other concrete thinkers (often those with autism spectrum disorders) may learn the facts easily.

Even if your student(s) does not know many addition facts, you can teach some of the easier subtraction facts, such as that any number minus 0 equals that number. "If you take away nothing from a number, it will still be the same number." You may also be able to teach that any number minus 1 is the same as *one less,* which your student(s) may already know how to figure out. However, the authorities say that it is much harder for a child to count backwards than forward, so do not press the issue with a student who does not seem to grasp how to do this.

Some students can use a number line to count backwards for subtraction. One value of the number line is that it is visual (if abstract), and, with frequent use, the student may learn the related subtraction fact.

LINKING KNOWN ADDITION FACTS TO SUBTRACTION

OBJECTIVE: Using the addition facts the student already knows, he will learn the related subtraction facts.

MATERIALS:
- 2 to 3 paper plates and whatever counters you have used before (Pretzels, straws, craft sticks, etc.)
- Index cards and red and black marker
- Small chalkboard or pad of paper and pencil

PROCEDURE:
1. Make a list of all the addition facts that the student knows.
2. Using the list, make up subtraction fact families for each known addition fact. Write the known addition fact in red on an index card. Write each related subtraction fact on a card with black marker. For example, write the addition facts $3 + 4 = 7$ (as well as $4 + 3 = 7$) in black. Write the related subtraction facts, $7 - 4 = 3$ and $7 - 3 = 4$, in black.
3. Have the student show with the plates and counters the subtraction facts that are related to the known addition fact(s). For example, if you know he knows $4 + 3 = 7$, say, "Show me $7 - 3$ with your counters."
4. When the student has shown the facts concretely with the materials, show him the addition card in red and the two subtraction cards that make up the fact family. Tell him it is a "fact family," if that will make it seem more interesting to him.
5. Practice with the index cards to learn the subtraction facts. Let him draw a circle or a house shape around the fact families when he learns them.
6. If this concept of fact families seems difficult for the student, try again several months later. Some students can learn and use some addition facts but are unable to learn the more complicated subtraction fact families. That is okay—we do have calculators! In the meantime, have the student do the single-digit subtraction problems on

the index cards using a number line (made in Chapter 9). Practice single-digit subtraction as frequently as possible. Even if the student has difficulty with larger numbers, the single-digit facts will be useful for mental math and estimating.

Subtraction with the Calculator

Your student(s) needs plenty of practice in doing the mechanical process of subtraction with the calculator. This process should be practiced until it is almost automatic. If the student feels secure in subtracting on the calculator, he will be able to give his attention to the more difficult task of deciding when the operation of subtraction is needed.

Regrouping (borrowing) in subtraction has always been difficult for some typical students in general classrooms. However, when students use the calculator, the regrouping is done for them. It is still important that they understand the concepts in regrouping and place value so they can understand real-life subtraction problems. Once the concept of regrouping has been introduced, I suggest that teachers and parents review simple take-away problems involving regrouping with the place value box and clothespins for about 5 minutes before each math session in this chapter.

SUBTRACTION WITH THE CALCULATOR

OBJECTIVE: The student will be able to accurately subtract one- and two-digit numbers with the calculator. Later, he will solve three- and four-digit problems with the calculator.

MATERIALS:
- Subtraction practice sheet from Appendix B (page 357)
- Pencils
- Calculator

SUCCESS STEP: Work out the first problem on the worksheet for the student, talking as you solve it. Ask the student to do the same problem. Praise his success.

PROCEDURE:

1. It may be a good time to reinforce the ritual of using the calculators described in Chapter Five.

   Get in a rhythm when using calculator. You can even chant the sequence:
   - **Five** (or whatever the number is) as you push the number 5.
   - **Look** (check the number in the window)
   - **Minus** (or whatever the operation is)

   - **Three** (or whatever the number is)
   - **Look** (check the number in the window)
   - **Equals** (as you press the = sign)

It is very important that you have the students enter the data slowly and check at the window every time.

2. By now, the students should be very familiar with writing subtraction problems horizontally. Point out the way the problems are written vertically on the worksheet. Just as when the numbers are written horizontally, you enter the largest number first. Explain that the top number is entered into the calculator first, then the minus (-) sign , followed by the second number. Have them practice putting some of the problems in the worksheet into the calculator and check the calculator windows.

3. Then have the students do the problems on the subtraction worksheet from Appendix B.

4. You will probably have to give them many more problems to solve on the calculator before they can use the calculator smoothly.

   This book cannot give you enough practice materials to teach the skills that take years to learn in school, but once you have introduced the concepts, it will be easy to make up or buy materials to practice subtraction. This would probably be a good time to use some of the mass market workbooks for primary level math that you can often find in discount stores such as *The Complete Book of Math* (2001) by McGraw-Hill Children's Publishing or *Jumpstart: Second Grade Math* (2000) by Scholastic Trade. Some of the websites listed in the Resources section could supply interesting subtraction practice (either worksheets or interactive games to play on the computer).

5. Gradually increase the size of the numbers that are used. Using the calculator, the student should be able to work with numbers in the hundreds or more.

SUPER BOWL SUB GAME

OBJECTIVE: Same as the previous objective.

MATERIALS:
- The Super Bowl Sub football field from page 359 (mounted on cardstock or inside a file folder and laminated, if used often)
- Football cards from Appendix B mounted on cardstock, both subtraction problem cards and play cards with instructions
- Two game tokens
- Calculator

PROCEDURE:
1. Only two players can play *Super Bowl Sub* at a time. If you have more students, several people can form a team and use one game marker, taking turns solving the subtraction problems. Players put their markers on the opposite 10 yard lines. Have a coin toss to see who goes first.

2. Shuffle the subtraction problem cards and the play cards together, so they form one stack. Place the cards face down in a stack in the middle of the table.

3. The first player takes a card. If it is a subtraction card, he does the problem with the calculator and announces his results. The teacher checks the answer. The

other team can be checking the answer with the calculator if it is not too distracting. If the student is correct, he advances 10 yards. If he draws an instruction card, he follows the instructions, if possible. If the penalty is more than he has advanced, he moves back to his own 10 yard line.

4. Play then switches to the second player, and they alternate back and forth unless the play instruction cards say otherwise.

5. When a player reaches the opponent's goal, he gets 6 points. He then turns around and goes back toward the opposite goal. (It is all right if he ends up going in the same direction as his opponent for a short time.) Set a time limit, and the player with the highest score wins. If you want a short game, the winner can be the first one who gets to the opposite goal.

GENERALIZATION INTO DAILY ACTIVITIES: Students with Down syndrome and other hands-on learners need to use subtraction frequently in daily activities in order to help them understand its purposes and practical uses. Generalization activities are listed in the next chapter, on pages 221-22.

CHAPTER 16

Using Whole Number Subtraction

Pre- /Post Checklist

Can the student:

1. _____ Compare two sets of items and say which set has more items and how many more.

2. _____ Use subtraction to see if she has enough money to buy something, and, if not, how much more is needed.

3. _____ Tell how much change she should get back when she pays more than the cost of the item.

4. _____ Be able to determine which operation (+ or -) is needed for a problem situation (including type of subtraction).

5. _____ In a real or simulated situation, determine the operation needed and do the calculations.

6. _____ Do subtraction problems with up to four digits using a calculator.

Take-away subtraction, the most common use for subtraction, was covered in Chapter 15. Subtraction is also frequently used for comparisons of two groups where nothing is taken away from either group but the difference is calculated. For instance, two uses for subtraction that are often encountered in shopping situations are, "How much more is needed?" and, "What change should be given back?" Students with Down syndrome and other hands-on learners usually have more difficulty with these

types of subtraction than they do with take-away subtraction. Word problems in particular can be very difficult for them.

Although the two types of situations above are often covered at the same time as other types of subtraction, this book treats them as separate situations which students should immediately recognize as requiring subtraction. More about these money situations will be given in Chapter 20, Money.

The major areas covered in this chapter are:

- **Types of Subtraction**
    - ▾ Comparison subtraction
    - ▾ How-much-more subtraction
    - ▾ Figuring change (currency only)
- **Subtraction in (Almost) Real Situations**
    - ▾ Determine type of problem
    - ▾ Do a simulation of a problem
    - ▾ Make a number sentence out of the problem
    - ▾ Use subtraction in real situations

Rowan was able to do take-away subtraction problems accurately, including checking with the calculator. However, when she was asked how many more tokens she had compared to her partner, she didn't know what operation to use. When her teacher suggested that she use subtraction, she indignantly said, "No, no! I can't take away her tokens." To Rowan, subtraction could only be used if someone was "taking away" something from someone else. She needed to experience other uses of subtraction.

Comparison Subtraction

Aside from take-away subtraction, the most frequently used type of subtraction is comparison subtraction. Comparison occurs when two groups of items are brought together and matched one-on-one to see which group is the largest (or smallest) and by how much. In this situation, nothing is taken away, but the two groups are matched to compare them. For example, if Peter has 8 baseball trading cards and Nelson has 6 baseball cards, who has the most baseball trading cards and by how many more? The match-up shows that Peter has 2 more cards. Students usually need practice in seeing comparison situations as requiring subtraction.

WHO'S GOT MORE?

OBJECTIVE: The student will compare two sets of items and be able to say which set has more items and how many more.

MATERIALS:

- 5 cups and saucers
- 5 empty jars or bottles with lids
- Poker chips or checkers (6 of one color and 9 of another)

SUCCESS STEP: Ask the student to count the number of items in the two sets, jars and lids. Praise her for counting correctly.

PROCEDURE:

1. Give the student 4 jars, and show her 3 lids. Ask her if every jar has a lid. Then put your 3 lids on the matching jars. She will probably say, "One does not have a lid" or something similar. Ask her, "Are there more lids or jars?" (jars). How many lids do I need?" (one). Remove the lids from the jars.
2. Have the student line up the jars on the table. You put one lid next to each jar. Ask, "Which poor jar does not have a lid?" The student should point to that jar. Bring out the hidden lid and say, "I need one more lid," and put that lid by the empty jar.
3. Repeat the procedure with the cups and saucers, varying the number of items, ending with 6 saucers and 4 cups.

4. Then, have her get out the calculator. Tell her to enter the number of saucers (6). Have her push the operation (subtraction), then put in the number of cups (4), and then push equals (=). The answer should be the same as when she lined up the cups and saucers to compare. Tell her that she can use subtraction when she **compares** things. The answer will be the difference between the two groups of items or how much more one group has than the other does.
5. Now give the student 6 poker chips or checkers that are the same color. You line up 9 chips or checkers in a contrasting color on the table. Ask her who has the

most chips. The student should lay her chips by each of your chips in one-to-one correspondence. (If she doesn't, line up a few to show her how.) Then ask, "How many more chips do I have compared to your chips?" (3). Have I taken away any chips from you?" (no). Tell her again that even though we are not taking away any chips, we use subtraction to get the answer when we **compare** amounts.

6. If the student is not motivated to figure out the difference between two groups of checkers or poker chips, try giving her 2 or 3 fewer pretzels (or stickers, if you don't want to give food) than you give yourself or a classmate. Ask her if both people got the same amount of pretzels (or stickers). When she says no, compare the two groups. If she is able to do it correctly, give her the extra items so the groups are equal.

7. Redo the previous problems with the calculator. Remind the students about using the minus sign and putting the larger number first. Using the poker chips (or more desirable items), make up a few simple comparison situations and have the students compare with each other or with the instructor. Then redo the problems with the calculator.

8. Repeat doing real situations for several days, using different items and stressing that when we compare groups, we use subtraction. Continue giving a few comparison situations a day until you feel she is secure in using subtraction for comparisons.

The major idea here is to have the students recognize that both take-away and comparison situations require subtraction. Discuss the vocabulary words used, such as *compare, minus, subtraction,* and *difference.*

Note: *Use sets that fit together, such as the jars and lids or cups and saucers when first teaching comparison subtraction. Other examples include: pencils and eraser caps, CDs and clear plastic cases, envelopes and mailing labels, drinking glasses and straws, shoes and laces, dolls and hats. Matching those pairs up is usually easier than just comparing like items.*

How Much More Is Needed?

Some authorities include the how-much-more category with the comparison type of subtraction. Strictly speaking, there are differences, though. In comparison subtraction, we can line up two sets to see which is larger and by how much. In the category of how-much-more, we know the final number and one of its parts, but have to imagine the other part. The most frequent occasion for using the how-much-more type of subtraction comes when we need to know if we have enough money to buy something, and, if not, how much more money we need. For example, "I have saved $4, but the action figure or Barbie costs $10. Do I have enough money?" (no) If not, how much more money do I have to save before I have enough money to buy it? Since this application is a vital life skill, it is introduced now in the first volume of *Teaching Math,* and will be discussed more extensively in the second volume.

WHAT CAN I BUY?

OBJECTIVE: The student will be able to use subtraction to determine if she has enough money to buy an article and, if not, how much more money is needed.

MATERIALS:

- Dollar bills (simulated or real) for student and teacher
- Pictures of desired items from newspaper ads or catalogs (glued to index cards, if that will make them easier to handle)
- Post-It notes with prices in whole dollars (currency) only

SUCCESS STEP: Have the student look at 10 or more pictures of desirable items and decide on her 3 favorite items. Praise her selection.

PROCEDURE:

1. Give the student 12 single dollars. Put a Post-It note with a currency price that is higher than $12 on the pictures of the 3 most desired items. Start with prices that are just a little too high, such as $13, $14, and $15. Ask the student if she has enough money to buy any of these three items. Discuss how much money is still needed to buy the item. Have the student hold out the $12 and put it next to the picture and price of the desired item. Ask the student to guess how much more money is needed. Then put down one dollar (from your money) at a time, asking if there is enough money now. The student should count every time.

2. When the student does have enough money to buy the item, ask her how many dollars you had to give her. This answer is in the how-many-more category of subtraction. Point out that if you take the price and subtract 12 from it, you will get the amount of money you need to have enough to buy it. Show the same problem on the calculator.

3. Repeat the procedure with different amounts of dollar bills and different desired items. Make the practice fun by adding some silly items and some ridiculous prices. Use the calculator to check each answer. Make sure that the student is entering the largest number first and pressing the minus sign to subtract. Repeat as needed.

4. For motivation, it will be important to have pictures or ads of things that the student would really like to have. (See photo for examples of pictures of ads from Learning Resources. Images used by permission of Learning Resources,

Measuring Monkeys™
Measurement Game

$18

M-Gears Roadster™
$15

Pretend & Play®
Dish Set

$13

Inc.) Individualize the items according to her age and likes. The student may want to count on or use a number line to find out how much more is needed. That is fine. There isn't only one way to do it, but using a subtraction problem is the most efficient. More practice on this concept will be given in Chapter 20, Money, and again in the next volume.

Figuring Change (Currency Only)

The other vital life situation that requires subtraction occurs when we pay for an item with more money (larger bill) than needed and require change back. Many individuals give the next highest dollar and receive change back. I seldom count the change I receive back. For the many small purchases I make, I trust the cashier to give me the right change. For larger purchases I do check the change, often with the calculator. Students need to know how to figure the amount of change they should get back, even if they do not check their change every time.

EARN AND PAY GAME

OBJECTIVE: The student will be able to accurately tell how much change she should get back when she pays an amount over the price of the item.

MATERIALS:
- *Earn and Pay Game* from the Informal Assessment in Chapter Four (page 302)
- Realistic looking currency

SUCCESS STEP: Give each student 3 ten dollar bills and 4 twenty dollar bills. Ask the student how much money she has in ten-dollar bills. Praise success. If she has forgotten, show her how to count the currency by tens and have her repeat the same counting exercise.

PROCEDURE:
1. Set up the Earn and Pay game as described in Chapter 4. A condensed version of the instructions are given below:
2. The first person rolls the die and moves his or her marker that number of spaces. The space landed on will be either a pay space or an earn space. The player picks up the top card from either the pay pile or the earn pile. Be sure the player reads the description of what she must pay or earn and have her say what amount of money she must pay out or earn. The player receives or pays out that amount and receives the pay or earn card.
3. The purpose of playing the game at this time is to have the students use big bills to pay for items, and then figure out the amount of change that they need to get back. As the banker, you can give out single and five dollar bills in change, but the students have only bigger bills (at first) that require change when making a purchase.

4. As the teacher/banker, you ask, "How much money do you owe me?" The student says the amount of money written on the pay card. The teacher asks, "How much money did you give me? Wow, that's a lot! Do I have to give you money back?"

5. Help the student to enter into the calculator the largest number (the amount she gave) first. Then have her subtract the amount that she really owes the bank. The difference will be how much change she needs to get back.

6. The first player to cross the finish line is Winner I and the player with the most money left is Winner II.

Using subtraction for making change is not an easy concept even when we are using only currency. It becomes more complex when we use both dollars and cents. Dollars and cents subtraction will be covered in more detail in volume two.

Subtraction in (Almost) Real Situations

Teaching Math places more emphasis on students understanding when to use subtraction than on the mechanics of subtracting or on learning the subtraction facts. Subtraction facts are useless if you don't know when to use them in a real-life situation—which I have found is often the case, even for young adults with Down syndrome or other disabilities. Students need to learn to recognize that subtraction is needed when we compare things or when things are taken away, as well as when we see if we have enough money to buy something we want or to make change. They should be able to decide what needs to be done in a real situation or to listen to a description of a situation, determine what operation is needed, and then do the calculation on the calculator.

DETERMINING THE TYPE OF PROBLEM

OBJECTIVE: The student will be able to determine which operation (+ or -) is needed for a problem situation, including those that require take-away, comparison, how-much-more, and figuring change (currency only).

MATERIALS:
- Situations needing various types of subtraction
- Craft sticks or pencils
- Plate

SUCCESS STEP: Put 6 sticks on the plate and ask the student to subtract 2.

PROCEDURE:
1. Do a few concrete subtraction problems with sticks or pencils to see if the student remembers take-away subtraction. For example, put 8 sticks on a plate, and have her grab 3 sticks away to illustrate 8 – 3. Then ask her how many are left.

2. If necessary, review the other types of subtraction with the student using concrete materials.

> **Comparison**—Two groups of items compared one-to-one.
> **How-much-more**—Total compared with smaller amount of money (student's) to find how much more money is needed.
> **Figuring change**—Total amount given is larger than amount needed (price) so amount of change can be found by subtraction.

3. Discuss some simple math problems orally and illustrate with concrete items. Ask what kind of subtraction is needed.

> 6 cars in the parking lot (Take-away)
> 2 cars leave
> How many left?

> Alice had 8 library books. (Comparison)
> Nell had 6 library books.
> Who has more books and how many more?

> Sam wants a CD sung by Faith Hill that costs $17.
> Sam has $8.
> Does he have enough money to buy it?
> If not, how much more money is needed?

> Todd wants to buy a $13 baseball cap. (Figuring change)
> He gives the clerk $15.
> How much change should he get back?

> Tina buys a cake for $8. (Figuring change)
> She gives the clerk a ten dollar bill.
> How much change should she get back?

> Alex has 6 trees in his back yard (Take-away)
> His father cuts down 2 of them.
> How many trees are left?

> Mark has 18 model cars in his bedroom. (Comparison)
> Chuck has 7 cars.
> Which boy has the most cars and how many more?

> Jennie has 13 CDs. (Comparison)
> Ruth has 8 CDs.
> Which girl has more CDs and how many more?

> Addie wants shoes that cost $22.
> She has saved $17. (How-much-more)
> Has she saved enough?
> If not, how much more money should she save?

4. At first, you do not have the student solve the above problems. Ask her what type of subtraction is needed. Have index cards available for each type of subtraction so she can point to the appropriate card. It is not really necessary for her to know the names of the types. All the practice will give her samples of the types. After many examples, the "light bulb" may turn on and she will get the pattern.

Note: *If the students need more of a challenge in naming the operation needed, mix in some addition examples. Jan has $3. Kathy has $5. Jill has $4. How much money do all the girls have together?*

DO A SIMULATION OF A SUBTRACTION PROBLEM

MATERIALS:
- Washable ink stamps for children or Bingo daubers
- Paper

PROCEDURE:
1. After you have talked through the problems above and the students can identify what kind of subtraction is needed, have them use a washable ink stamp and illustrate the problems, as was discussed in Chapter 15, Whole Number Subtraction.
2. Have the students cross out the correct number of stamps for the take-away problems, show comparisons of items for the comparison problems, and use the comparison format for illustrating the how-much-more problems.

WRITE NUMBER SENTENCES OF PROBLEMS

MATERIALS:
- Pencil, chalk, dry erase markers
- Paper, chalkboard, or white board

PROCEDURE:
1. Later work out the above problems on the chalkboard or paper with the students participating in the discussion. You model writing a number sentence for each problem.

Cake problem: $10 - $8 = $2 change needed

2. Have the students check your answer with their calculators.
3. Ask the students which way they like to work out the problems best—using the stamps or writing the number sentence. Let them use whichever method they like for the rest of the problems.

Use Subtraction in Life (or Life-Like) Situations

Some authorities say that a student needs to get more involved in problem solving than to just be given a short two-line scenario with some children's names, as in simple traditional story problems. The following situation is designed to be more life-like than traditional problems and the problems are connected to one another. To get the most benefit out of this situation, you need to tailor the events and items so they are relevant to the student or students. You can change the items listed and the amounts of money (but keep them only as currency) or change the description of the occasion. You can also do only a few problems at one time; however, you must review the previous situation at the beginning of each new session to get the benefit of the connected, more life-like story.

THE BIRTHDAY GIFT

OBJECTIVE: The student will be able to listen to a real or simulated situation being described, determine what operation needs to be done, and then do the problem correctly on the calculator.

MATERIALS:
- Paper and pencil
- $50 in $10 bills (realistic play money) for each student
- Different colored pieces of construction paper for each student
- Props suggested by scenario (optional)
- Calculator

SUCCESS STEP: Ask the student(s) if anyone has ever given them a lot of money. Ask them if they have ever bought a big present for themselves. Praise participants.

PROCEDURE:
1. Read this story to your student(s):

> *Ann's grandma had been sick for a few weeks. She was not able to come to Ann's birthday party. Grandma did, however, send a birthday card with $50 for Ann. She wrote, "Dear Ann, You can use this money to buy yourself a big birthday present or several smaller presents. Let me know what you buy. Love, Grandma."*
>
> *Ann was very excited to have the money to spend. Her mother sat down with her to discuss the ways that she could spend the money.*

2. Now tell your student(s) that they are going to pretend to be Ann and figure out how she can spend her $50. Have them put the 5 $10 bills on a piece of construction paper so that they can see each bill. For each problem, have them start with the total amount and then "take away" the amounts suggested. By looking at the paper, they can tell how much money is left. Then have each student do the

problem with the calculator to check. They learn the routine of putting in the largest number first, then "taking away" (subtracting) the smaller number and pushing the equals (=) sign.

3. Continue with the story: At first Ann wanted to buy a boom box radio. The one she likes costs $99. Does she have enough of Grandma's gift money to buy the boom box radio? When the student says that there is not enough money, say, "No, that will not work!" Take back the money and say, "We will have to start all over again." Give her the money as if you are just giving it to her for the first time and say, "You need to pick a gift that costs less money."

4. Then Ann thought about getting a small present. She could buy a CD that she really liked for $10. Does she have enough money to buy the CD?

5. If Ann buys the CD, how much money will she have left from Grandma's gift? Do the problem with the currency and determine how much will be left. Check the problem with the calculator. Comment that Ann has quite a bit of money left over.

6. Seeing the amount of money left, Ann decided there was another gift that she would like better. (Pick up the money and say that Ann can't make up her mind and we will start over.) She could sign up for a class in kickboxing at the recreation center. The course costs $40. Does she have enough money?

7. If Ann decides to pay for a kickboxing class, how much money will she have left? Do the comparison with the currency and then check the answer with the calculator.

(This is probably enough problem solving for the first day. At the next session, review Ann's decisions from the previous day.)

8. The next day Ann's mother suggests that instead of spending all the money on a class, Ann could buy a nice present for herself and a small gift for Grandma. Ann thought that sounded like a good idea. She knew that her grandma liked a little bear figurine that she had seen in a shop window. Her mother said that figurine cost $10. If Ann bought the bear figurine, how much money would she have left for her own present? Do the problem with the currency and repeat with the calculator.

9. Ann saw an advertisement in the newspaper for a two-volume CD that she wanted even more than the $10 CD she had originally picked. The two-volume CD, however, was $30. How much more would the $30 CD be than the $10 CD?

The next day Ann just couldn't make up her mind what to buy. (You can make fun of her a little.)

10. All of a sudden, Ann's brother Bob stuck his head in the door and said, "Great, now that you have some money you can pay back the $10 you borrowed from me last week. Come on, pay up!" Ann reluctantly gave her brother $10 from Grandma's gift. How much money is left in Grandma's gift after Bob took away his $10? (Take away the $10 from Ann's $50.)

11. Ann said, "Now I have to start all over again. I only have $40 to spend." Her mother said, "Okay, do you really want that two-volume CD, the one that costs $30?" Ann said that she was sure that she wanted that two-volume CD. Her

mom said, "You will spend $30 out of your $40 gift. How much money will you have left?" (Take away $30.)

12. Ann said, "If I have $10 left now, I should have enough money to buy Grandma the bear figurine for $10. How much will I have left if I buy the figurine?" (nothing)

13. Her mother said, "If you *had* a little bit of money left, what would you do with it?" Ann said, "I *should* save it." (Ask the student, "What would *you* do?") Ann decided that she would buy ice cream with it. Is she going to have money left over?

14. Redo the previous scenario, giving the student $50 (4 ten dollar bills and 2 five dollar bills). Change the numbers so they either end in 10 or 5. Using tens or fives is more difficult than just tens. Repeat as needed.

15. Redo the scenario, giving out one dollar, five dollar, and ten dollar bills. Then make the amounts any possible number. Repeat varying parts of the scenario frequently.

16. If the student has difficulty with the subtraction situations (story problems) here, you may want her to keep practicing subtraction on the calculator for the time being and return to these more life-like situations after you have finished the chapter on money.

Word problems using subtraction are more difficult than word problems using addition. In addition, the student just has to add all relevant numbers and get a total. In subtraction, the student has to decide whether subtraction is the appropriate operation for "take away," or comparison, or how-much-more, or change situations. Then she needs to determine which number is the largest and subtract the smaller number from it. Students need much more experience in the various types of subtraction before it becomes useful for them. We do not mix addition and subtraction problems in this chapter unless the students need an occasional challenge.

SUPER BOWL SUB GAME

This game can also be played in the previous chapter on subtraction, using easier subtraction problems.

OBJECTIVE: The student will be able to do up to four-digit subtraction problems with the calculator.

MATERIALS:
- The Super Bowl Sub football field from page 359, mounted on cardstock or inside a file folder and laminated (if used often)
- Football cards from page 360 mounted on cardstock paper, both the subtraction problem cards and the play cards with instructions. If the student has played the Super Bowl Sub game before, you might want to make new subtraction problems that are more difficult than those used in the original game.
- Two game tokens

SUCCESS STEP: Have the students set up the football field and the cards in the places indicated. (Model the set-up the first time you play the game.) Praise the students' set-up.

PROCEDURE:

1. Use the instructions given with the game at the end of Chapter 15.

GENERALIZATION INTO DAILY ACTIVITIES: It is crucial to learning for you to find daily situations that are motivating for your student and that involve subtraction. Identify the different types of subtraction as you encounter them, but do not require the student to know those names. If your child/student hasn't learned subtraction facts, be prepared to whip out a calculator so she can get the practice and satisfaction of figuring out real-life situations with a calculator

- Playing simple bowling games with plastic pins or pop cans can be a subtraction exercise. You can put up 10 cans and have the student roll a ball into them. You say, "You had 10 pins up, and you knocked down 5. How many are left standing? Let's count to see if you are correct." You can make the task more or less difficult by varying the number of cans you set up. You may tell the student how many pins she knocked down because it is the subtraction operation that is important, not counting the fallen pins.
- Perhaps if you bring in flowers from the garden or receive flowers, you can count the fallen or withered flowers to see how many are still standing.
- Play games that use two dice and alter the rules so players can either add or subtract the numbers—whichever is to their advantage. For instance, it may be better to subtract and land on a "good" space than add and land on a "bad" space. Or, play Sum Swamp™ or Math Mat Challenge™, recommended in Chapter 13.
- As the student saves money for some desired item, you can have her count her money frequently and subtract to get the answer to how-much-more she needs.
- If your child asks if she can have more of something at dinner such as chicken or corn-on-the-cob, say, "I'm not sure there is any more left (assuming the food is out of sight).There were 6 pieces, and we ate 4. Are there any left? How many?"
- If you use an illustrated chart to record daily activities toward a goal, ask her how many more stars are needed to reach her goal.
- If the student enjoys watching sports, discuss final scores and ask her how many points her favorite team won or lost by.
- Deliberately give her less food or play materials than a peer or sibling. When she asks for more, have her tell you how many more you need to give her to make the amounts equal.
- Have her figure out how many pages she has read (for instance, if she started on page 15 and is now on page 30) or

how many more pages she needs to read to finish the book (for instance, if she is on page 48 and there are 64 pages).

- Talk about how many pictures she has left to take on her camera. If her camera has a counter that starts at 1 and counts up to 24, you can subtract the number of shots she's taken from 24 to see how many she has left.

- If she is selling items for a school, scouting, church, or other fundraiser and will get a prize if she reaches a certain level, help her subtract to find out how many more items she needs to sell (for example, if she has sold 18 candy bars and will get a prize if she sells 20).

CHAPTER 17

Time

Pre- /Post Checklist

Can the student:

1. _____ Name the days of the week in proper sequence.

2. _____ Use the calendar appropriately.

3. _____ Tell the months, major holidays, and the seasons.

4. _____ Use a daily schedule.

5. _____ Tell time by the hour.

6. _____ Tell time by the half (quarter) hour (e.g., 6:30) on an analog clock.

7. _____ Tell time by the quarter hour on analog and digital clocks.

Time does not just involve being able to read the hours and minutes on a clock. Time as a larger concept includes an inner awareness that time is passing and a rough concept of the duration that certain activities take. Time also includes the sequence in which these activities occur. Jean Piaget (Berk, 2001) asserted that children grow and develop in their sense of time. Sometimes children confuse physical size with age. In childhood, a person grows taller as he or she grows older. From adolescence on, this correlation does not work—which can be confusing to young children and concrete thinkers. Grandmother may be smaller than mother, but she is really older in age. Children also may have difficulty understanding that they can't catch up with an older brother or sister in age. Ben will always be three years older than his younger brother, Ted, no matter how old or big Ted gets.

Understanding time concepts is often difficult for concrete thinkers. Time is abstract; you can't really see what you are measuring. On top of that, the measurement of time does not proceed in an orderly fashion by tens or twenties. With 60 minutes in an hour, 24 hours in a day, 7 days in a week, and 4 or more weeks in a month, is it any wonder that these and other measures may seem to have no numerical relationship to each other in the minds of concrete thinkers? An individual not only needs to understand the names of these time periods, but also needs to acquire an intuitive feeling for their size or duration.

Not all aspects of time will be covered in this book. Some more complex time concepts will be covered in the next volume. In addition, there are some simpler concepts that will be touched on only briefly here since most families and teachers already do a good job of teaching about them. For example, almost every primary level teacher begins the school day with a discussion of the day, the month, the season, and any special events that are occurring. Families also reinforce this teaching, especially with the holidays. This chapter will focus mainly on the concepts that may prove troublesome to the student and his teachers.

Concepts covered include:

- **Large blocks of time**
  - ▼ Days of the week
  - ▼ Calendars, months, and seasons
- **Schedules**
  - ▼ Class schedules
  - ▼ Individual schedules
  - ▼ Time judgments
  - ▼ The language of time
- **Time telling with clocks**
  - ▼ Analog vs. digital
  - ▼ Telling the hours
  - ▼ Telling time to the half hour and quarter hour

Large Blocks of Time

As mentioned above, most families and teachers emphasize the days of the week, the months, the seasons, and the holidays in their everyday rituals. A specific teaching procedure will not be given here except to point out that students should work on learning about these large blocks of time over a long period of time. Students should learn about the following concepts:

THE NAMES AND SEQUENCE OF THE DAYS OF THE WEEK

Parents can start by giving their children experiences with the idea that days follow one another in sequence. Perhaps you could have a fun, page-per-day calendar and let your child tear off one page per day. You can talk about a new **day** coming at sunrise and at nighttime talk about the **day** being over.

Teachers often work with the calendar each morning to accomplish this task. You can teach the days of the week to the tune of "Clementine" as done on the *Barney* TV show:

There are 7 days, there are 7 days, there are 7 days in a week.

There are 7 days, there are 7 days, there are 7 days in a week.
Sunday, Monday, Tuesday, Wednesday, Thursday, Friday, Saturday.
Sunday, Monday, Tuesday, Wednesday, Thursday, Friday, Saturday.

It may be important for the students to be able to read the names of the days of the week, even if they have to be taught as sight words. Make pictures that go with the days of the week such as a smiling sun face for Sunday or the number 2 for Tuesday. It will be easier to remember the words for the days of the week if visual pictures accompany the word.

THE NAMES OF THE MONTHS, SEASONS, AND HOLIDAYS

Again, daily discussion of the calendar with accompanying pictures and decorations for the holidays should be the major way your child learns about these topics. If the school is not providing this training, parents should discuss daily and weekly events using a calendar, and specifically teach the vocabulary and time concepts to their child. Here are some things you can do at home:

LEARNING THE MONTHS IN ORDER
* You can use a song. To the tune of *10 Little Indians:*
  January, February, March, and April
  May, June, July, and August
  September, October, November, December.
  Twelve months in a year!
* Let your child pick out a calendar that he likes with a separate page for every month. On the first day of each new month, remind him that it is time to change the calendar so you can see the new month. "Yesterday was the last day of June. Time to change the calendar to July." Once your child flips the page, you can preview any special events that month with him. "Look, it's almost the Fourth of July. Let's make sure Uncle Jim is coming to see the fireworks with us."

WAITING FOR AN UPCOMING EVENT
* Mark special events on the calendar with pictures or stickers. Let your child cross off each day as you get closer to that special event.
* Another way to help your child "see" how much longer he needs to wait for an event is to make a paper chain with one link for every day until the event and then let him rip off one link every day. For example, put 30 links on the chain if it is a month until your child's birthday. You could also put 30 marbles, tokens, etc. in a jar and have your child take one out every day.
* Use an advent calendar before Christmas and open one door each day.

LEARNING ABOUT THE SEASONS
* When looking at family photos or videos, you can comment on when they occurred. "Brrrr. I get cold just looking at these

pictures from winter time." In some areas of the country the seasons are not clearly distinguished by nature. Your child still needs to know what months are fall months, even if the leaves do not turn colors and fall from the trees. You might say, "Oh, that was last fall. See, you were carrying your new backpack. I think it was in September."

- You can make a big deal about packing away summer clothes and getting out winter clothes, or putting away winter jackets and getting out spring jackets. "Sorry, you can't wear your sandals now. I'll get them out again in the spring, but it's winter now!" Or, "You'll be too hot in your winter coat. It's spring now!"

- Of course, you will want to comment about the changes in season that are typical of where you live. "Oh, look at the frost on the windshield. Now I know that winter is really here." Or, "The pool is finally open again. That means it will be summer any day now."

- Sometimes children need to get a picture in their mind of the months related to the seasons. Do you picture the months of the year as a circle from January to December? But January *and* December are both winter months. A graphic can be shown of the months in a circle, surrounded with another circle delineating the four seasons. This visual image can be used with calendar study to make the relationship of months to seasons more clear.

The Language of Time

> When young, Allie often confused the words yesterday *and* tomorrow *when speaking. She would say things like, "Yesterday we are going to Grandma's house" or "Tomorrow I went to the pool." She clearly understood that* yesterday *and* tomorrow *were time words, but didn't know how to use them correctly.*

Think of the time words *yesterday, today,* and *tomorrow.* A day passes and what was tomorrow becomes today and what was today becomes yesterday and you have an entirely new tomorrow. How do you explain those terms to someone who does not understand? Most children with Down syndrome and some other concrete thinkers have delays in general language learning. Abstract language terms for time concepts will probably need to be introduced and repeated long before children are taught to tell time.

Some teachers use their morning calendar routine to teach *yesterday, today,* and *tomorrow.* They use a little frame made of poster board with three windows labeled yesterday, today, and tomorrow. The frame is put on the days of the week on the calendar, with the dates showing. "This is *today*—Tuesday, October 22. Let's see, what was *yesterday?* Monday, October 21. And what is *tomorrow?* Wednesday, October 22." The next day the teacher moves the frame to show the new *yesterday,*

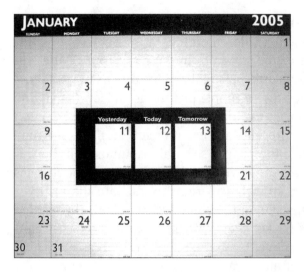

today, and *tomorrow.* Just showing the student the time words will not teach him the real meaning behind them, however. You need to relate the words to the student's life.

Parents can weave those time words into their child's world. Make a point of telling your child that *tomorrow* he is going to the zoo. When he wakes up on the day of the event, remind him that he is going to the zoo *today.* On the day after, have a conversation about what you did at the zoo *yesterday.* If he wants to do the same activity, day after day, comment that, "We read this book *yesterday.* Do you want to read it *today* too?" Many events can be discussed in this manner. Teachers can talk about special activities that happen occasionally such as a field trip or an assembly as happening *tomorrow, today,* or *yesterday.*

Some people with Down syndrome have problems using tenses correctly (for instance, always speaking in the present tense or leaving off some verb endings such as "-ed"). For instance, Amanda has generally good speech and language skills, but seldom uses anything other than present tense. When she is recounting what she did on the weekend, for example, she'll say, "Well, it's my mom's birthday, so I eat dinner at a restaurant with her." For students who have difficulty expressing tenses, it is especially important to learn to use the words yesterday, today, and tomorrow correctly. That way listeners can figure out when something happened regardless of verb endings.

If your child is having difficulty with these words and he is in elementary school or older, make sure his IEP includes goals to work on these concepts in speech-language therapy or in language arts class. In speech therapy, it might help him to express verb tenses in the same way as deaf people who sign in English word order. That is, to express past tense with signs, you flip the palm of your hand back over the shoulder. To express future tense, you put your open right hand up with the palm facing left, close to the right temple. Move it in a forward-upward arc. Ideally, the signs would only be used as a teaching device while the regular past tense ending (-ed) and the irregular past tenses (*are* becomes *were*) are being taught. However, the signs would provide visual cues for past and future.

Schedules

> *A classroom teacher told me that she has the class schedule on a pocket chart so the cards with activities can be moved around. Since changes may have to be made, she has a laminated card with a symbol and the words **"Something Different"** written on it. She makes sure that the **Something Different** is sometimes a treat, free time, or a favorite activity so that the card is not always the signal for an unwelcome change.*

A picture chart of the daily classroom schedule should be present in all elementary school classes. Because some activities such as P.E. happen only once or twice a week on Tuesdays and Fridays, the teacher also needs to have a weekly

| pledge |
| desk time |
| computer |
| calendar time |
| desk time |

chart or a monthly calendar where the weekly events are highlighted. Having a visual schedule is very important to some children on the autism spectrum or others who need the concrete evidence of the structure in the classroom. These students will often need an individual schedule personalized for them.

For young students, most teachers use a simple picture or an icon (small line drawing) from a software program such as Boardmaker™ (see Resource section under Mayer-Johnson Company) to represent each event or subject area. The time may also be written on the pictures. If the picture schedule is laminated, the student can check off each time on the schedule with washable marker as he finishes the activity. Pictures can be arranged from left to right to indicate the order of activities, or from top to bottom (especially if the child has trouble distinguishing left from right). Some teachers use a pocket chart where the student moves a card from one pocket to another when he moves to another subject or area.

As students get older, they can often use a time and word schedule for daily events and a calendar or planner for the weekly and month events. If the teacher puts a class schedule on the board and the students have their own individual schedules, they can feel more secure in the school surrounding. Typical middle and high school students may all have an individual planner required by their school that can be adapted with pictures to help concrete thinkers.

Since a classroom will not always be able to stay on the schedule, teachers should have some kind of symbol to alert children with Down syndrome, autism spectrum disorders, or related disabilities to the fact that it is okay to have things change. For example, for young children, they might use a question mark or a symbol of a present being opened to indicate a surprise change.

Schedules can be helpful in teaching about the passage of time and controlling impulsiveness, as well as in teaching the sequence of activities. For example, the teacher can point at the schedule and tell the student that he can get a drink as soon as it is time for math. Parents can also use schedules at home for similar purposes. A parent can stifle some of the whininess of a child who has to wait for dinnertime by showing him the clock and the time on the family schedule for eating.

Developing a Sense of Time and Its Passage

> *Emily never seemed to be ready when the family wanted to go some place. Her mother would call, "Emily, you need to get your shoes and coat on now. You will be late for your 9:00 doctor appointment."*
>
> *Emily would reply, "No, I won't. It isn't 9:00 yet."*
>
> *Emily didn't really get ready until the time she was supposed to get there. (You may know of some adults like that.) She needs to be taught a structure in which a getting-ready-time (8:10-8:30am) and a travel-time (8:30-8:45am) are part of her going some place.*

Long before children are expected to learn to tell time, they are exposed to the units we use to measure time. In addition to the larger units discussed above (days, months, years), they constantly hear about seconds, minutes, hours. If they ask their parents to do something for them, they may hear, "Wait just a second" or, "In a minute." On a car trip, they may hear that it will take two more hours to get to Grandma's house.

For children who can't tell time, these words are usually not that informative. To add to the confusion, sometimes time may seem to go faster than other times. For example, when doing a favorite activity, the time may go very fast, but the opposite occurs with a dreaded activity. "Isn't it time to go home now?" usually indicates that time is dragging for the child.

If words such as *minute* or *hour* are still basically meaningless to a child, you may want to describe time in other terms that make sense to him. This can reduce frustration or anxiety if he really wants to know how long it will be before something will happen or how long something will go on. I have been successful with using the TV schedule as a reference for when time has passed and for how long activities take to accomplish. For instance, you can say, "We will eat dinner as soon as Nickelodeon is finished," or some other TV program that comes on near dinnertime. You can also use other frames of references, such as "right after Dad gets home" or "after we take the dog for a walk."

Eventually, of course, children need to develop a feel for the length of a second, minute, and hour. Parents can help their children understand these terms in much the same way as described above for yesterday, today, and tomorrow. For example, talk about how you are going to go to the mall in an *hour,* or how you are going to stay there for an *hour,* or how you can't have a snack right now because you had one an *hour* ago at the mall. You can talk about how many *minutes* it takes the cake to bake in the oven, especially if you are using a timer with a dial or hand that moves with each minute.

It also helps if parents can give their children a sense of how long things they routinely do take so they can pace themselves. For instance, it may be difficult for a child to learn how long it takes for him to get dressed or get his coat and boots on. The adult can watch the child doing the activity and time it. Then when the child is dawdling, the adult can say, "It takes you 15 minutes to dress when your clothes are already laid out for you. You need to start now." Likewise, you could tell your child it takes 15 minutes to do his spelling homework or to get ready for bed.

To further help students understand what 15 minutes (or some other length of time) means, you can use a kitchen timer that has a dial that keeps turning until the bell rings. My favorite timer is called the Time Timer (see Resources section) which has a red ring around the dial that shows visually how much time is left (the less red that is visible, the less time is left). The student can easily see the passage of time and get an idea of when "time will be up." This Time Timer does not have a bell signaling that the time is up. Some students dislike buzzer sounds, so this timer would be appropriate for them.

Some ways to use a timer during daily activities include:
- Ask your child to set the timer for X minutes when you begin cooking or baking something, or when you begin playing a game that you want to stop after a set period of time.
- Use the timer to signal him when his time on the computer, phone, TV, etc. is up. Say, "I'm setting the timer for 20 min-

utes" as you are setting it, and then inform him, "Your 20 minutes is up" when the timer goes off.

On Time!

- Challenge your child or student to "beat the timer" when he is doing routine activities such as getting ready for bed, writing his spelling words, sorting silverware into the kitchen drawer. Make it easy for him to beat the timer and say, "Wow! You did that in less than 10 minutes!"

COMMERCIAL GAMES TO BUY OR TRY

There are many games commercially available that involve "racing against the clock." These games typically come with a sand timer or a mechanical timer that runs down in a minute. Playing these games can help children learn how long a minute really is. Some good choices include:

- *Cranium Cadoo (Cranium): Players have one minute (measured by a sand timer) to act out, draw, or sculpt out of clay a word or phrase for other players to guess*
- *Eyecatcher (Game Development Group): Players have one minute (measured by sand timer) to match the patterns on colored tiles with matching spaces on a board (or, in Eyecatcher Jr., to match tiles with animals to matching spaces on the board)*
- *Outburst Jr. (Hasbro): Players have one minute (measured by sand timer) to name all the words in a particular category (e.g., flavors of ice cream) that they can*
- *Perfection (Milton Bradley): Players set a mechanical timer for a minute and try to place 25 plastic shapes in their matching spaces on the toy*
- *Pictionary Jr. (Milton Bradley): Players have one minute (measured by a sand timer) to draw a picture in a certain category well enough for their teammate(s) to guess what it is*

Students who become very anxious when being timed in a game, can watch as other people play the games, or they can be the designated time keeper and announce that time is up when all the sand has run out of the timer. You can also extend the time that players have to complete activities by using a kitchen timer or visual timer and setting it for five minutes or so. Just make sure you tell the players how long they have so they can develop a feel for that length of time.

Time Telling with Clocks

When digital watches and clocks became widely available, I thought that the problem of telling time was solved for students with cognitive disabilities. I was wrong.

Although students could be taught to read the digital clocks by hour and minute fairly easily, this was not a substitute for telling time with a round-faced analog clock. A major reason is that students did not get a concept of the movement of time by reciting a digital number. Something about seeing the minute and hour hand move on an analog clock must give a better visual picture of the movement of time. It is much harder to figure out how much time until an event occurs if the student only sees a digital number such as 11:50. With an analog clock, the student can see that the hour and minute hands have only a little distance to go before it becomes 12:00. In addition, we do not have digital clocks everywhere and students have to be able to read the time in many different places.

One thing that I did learn from digital time telling was the efficiency of having a consistent way to describe the minutes. Naming the hour and then giving the minutes after the hour is the most understandable way to express time for young children and concrete thinkers. Expressions such as "quarter to 9" or "half past 8" or even "10 to 9" are difficult for students to remember or for teachers to teach at the beginning. At this level of *Teaching Math,* we do not talk about these more colloquial phrases used for time telling. When the student has thoroughly learned time telling, we will acquaint him with these phrases. It may be important for him to recognize what these phrases mean, but at this stage, he should consistently express times with the hour and then minutes after.

At this level, we teach the hour and 15-minute increments after the hour. The student should say the hour and then 15, 30, or 45 minutes after.

TELLING TIME BY THE HOUR

Clocks are made with many different shapes of hands, placements of the numbers (or sometimes no numbers), colors, and markings for minutes. It helps to use only one clock when beginning to teach about time, and to use a simplified clock at that. At first, use a clock or a model of a clock that has all the numbers in the standard positions, but only has the hour hand.

OBJECTIVE: The student will be able to tell what the hours are on a clock with only an hour hand.

MATERIALS:

- A large model of a clock for the teacher with only the hour hand (can be made of cardboard or a plain paper plate with the hour hand fastened on with a paper fastener)

- Student clocks with the numbers and hour hand (a commercial teaching clock with hour hand only, or a clock made from a paper plate with a cardboard hour hand colored black and fastened in the center with a paper fastener)

SUCCESS STEP: Ask the student(s) to point to a clock or clocks in the room. Praise correct answers.

PROCEDURE:
1. Demonstrate how the hour hand sweeps to each number on the large clock. Talk about the hour hand and how it moves slowly for each hour.
2. Have students move the hands on their own clocks to each hour. If a paper fastener attaches the hour hand, adjust it so that the hour hand moves freely. At first tell them to move the hand to the number, "Put the hour hand on the 5." Later you may change your wording and say, "Make the hour hand show 5 o'clock."
3. Relate the different hours to your daily schedule. "When the hour hand is on the number 12, we go to lunch."
4. At random, give the hours orally (6 o'clock, 3 o'clock) to the students and have them move the hour hand to that hour.
5. Teach the students how to read the hours, saying "one o'clock, two o'clock, etc." Set the hour hand on your large clock to different hours and ask the students, "What time is it?"
6. On a real clock, the hour hand will move slowly toward the next number. If the hour hand is half past a number, tell the students that if doesn't count as the next hour until the hour hand is right on the next number.

SPINNER GAME

MATERIALS:
- A clock made from a paper plate and paper fastener (as above) with just an hour hand. The hole for the paper fastener may need to be enlarged so the clock hand can spin like a game spinner.
- Any of your own board games where players advance one space at a time.

PROCEDURE:
1. Lay the clock down flat and use the clock face as a spinner for your board game. Check to see that the spinner moves freely. Have players spin to see who goes first (highest number first).
2. To begin the game, the first player spins and moves the number of spaces the hour hand indicates. If the hour hand lands between numbers, you take the lower number of spaces. If the spinner lands between the 9 and the 8, you move only 8 spaces ahead because the time is still the eighth hour (as they have learned with the clock). If the player does not spin correctly or hard enough, he loses that turn.
3. The first one to reach the finish line wins. You must spin the exact number to cross the finish line.

READING THE MINUTE HAND BY QUARTER HOURS

Learning to read the minute hand can be tricky for any child, but can be especially difficult for students with cognitive disabilities. When the hour hand is on the 3, you say "three," which is relatively easy to understand. But when the *minute* hand is on the 3, you say "fifteen." Even if a student is able to understand *why* you say fifteen (for instance, you count off the minutes on the clock leading up to the 3 and show him there are fifteen), it can still be very difficult to remember how we count off these 15-minute increments.

OBJECTIVE: The student will be able to tell the correct hour and the minutes by 15-minute intervals on a teaching clock.

MATERIALS:

- A large cardboard teaching clock with both the hour and minute hand. (Add a black minute hand to the teaching clock used in previous activities. Make sure the minute hand is considerably longer than the hour hand. Also add an outer ring to the clock indicating the minutes by 15-minute intervals. The outer circle should have: :00 above the 12, :15 near the 3, :30 below the 6, and :45 near the 9. Write the minutes in a different color than the hours. The colons should be shown so that the student will be familiar with how the minutes are written.)
- A paper plate copy of the teaching clock for each student

SUCCESS STEP: Ask the student to read the numbers (15, 30, and 45) on the outer ring of the teaching clock. Praise him or model the correct numbers if he is incorrect.

PROCEDURE:

1. Tell the students that we sometimes want to know more than just the hour. Point how slowly the hour hand moves toward the next hour. We can tell if it is a little after the hour or almost to the next hour by looking at the hour hand. We can tell even better with the long hand on the clock that we call the minute hand.
2. Let the students move the minute hand around the clock for a little while to get them used to how it moves.
3. Explain why the numbers are written on the outer ring of the clock. Show them the number 3 on the regular clock face. Then explain that the number 15 on the outer ring means that it is 15 minutes after the hour if the minute hand is on the 3.
4. Put dots to represent minutes between the numbers on the clock. Tell the student that the dots stand for minutes. Have the student count the dots between

the 12 and the 3. (Make sure you have placed the right number of dots!) It should be 15, just like the number on the outer ring.

5. Add more minute dots between the 3 and the 6. See if the student can guess how many minutes (dots) there are between the 12 and 6. Then have him count the dots.

6. Repeat the procedures with the 9 (45 minutes). Next, explain that you read the number :00, above the 12 as *o'clock*.

7. Practice showing times that are hours and 15-minute intervals on your teaching clock. See if the student can correctly read the times that you show.

If your student(s) can learn to identify the quarter hours quickly and easily, he will probably be able to function quite well in his environment. The next volume will cover reading the clock to the minute. For now, if the student recognizes that it is "almost" 15, 30, or 45 when the minute hand is not exactly on the quarter hour, that will be precise enough.

PRACTICE WITH CLOCKS

OBJECTIVE: The student will be able to read the hours and the minutes by the quarter hour on a teaching clock (without the outer ring) and on a working clock (all numbers visible).

MATERIALS:
- Student teaching clocks with hour and minute hands (homemade as above, or plastic teaching clocks available from Learning Resources or teacher supply catalogs)
- Drawings of clock faces without hands from page 365
- Index cards or slate

SUCCESS STEP: Ask the student to point to several hours.

PROCEDURE:

1. Write some times (hours and 15-minute intervals) on index cards or display them one by one on your slate with chalk. Have the students make the times on their individual clocks.

2. Students may have problems when the minute and the hour hand both point to the same number (at 3:15, 6:30, 9:45, and 12:00). It can be difficult to tell that both hands are at the same spot. Explicitly show your student(s) these times and tell them that the hands are trying to play a joke on them. They are both hiding in the same spot. Show students now how those times look on the teaching clock where the hands are more clearly different, and, later, show them how those times look on real clocks.

3. You can use the page in Appendix B with clock faces (without hands) to see if students can draw the hour and minute hands on the clock to show the numerical times you give them. (Make copies of the page so students can practice for several sessions.) Give a review of clock faces at the beginning of each session until the students are secure in the learning.

Software to Consider

A computer program called *MatchTime: Practice Telling Time* (Attainment Company) covers beginning time telling skills to time telling at 5-minute intervals. The CD (MacWin) is available through many teachers' stores and online at www.AttainmentCompany.com. The cost is around $100. It begins with simple matching of the hour hand and progresses in small steps to regular time telling. Schools or resource libraries may have the program available to lend.

TIME BINGO GAME

OBJECTIVE: Same as in previous activity.

MATERIALS:
- *Time Bingo* cards from Appendix A (page 317)
- Index cards: 12 showing the time on a clock and 12 showing the same time written with numerals (Cut out clock faces and times from pages 363-64 and glue to index cards)
- Magnetic wand and chips

PROCEDURE:
1. Give each player a bingo sheet from the Appendix A labeled TIME, a magnetic bingo wand, and about 12 chips.
2. Show the clock face cards that match possible numbers on the Bingo sheets, saying the letter above the column, e.g., M. Players look at the M column on their bingo sheet to see if they have a written time that matches the card clock face being shown. (Call the letter column first so they do not have to search the whole card for the possible answer, which can be overwhelming to a struggling student.)
3. Players put a bingo chip on the time that matches the clock face. The winner is the first one to fill all one row or all one column. The winner also gets to pick up his bingo chips with the magnetic wand first.
4. For an easier variation, use the cards with the times written in numerals. Call out the times without saying the letters above the columns.

GENERALIZATION INTO DAILY LIVING: At this point, students need to get plenty of practice reading the time on different clocks and watches. Do not use clocks or watches that do not have all the numbers on them for this practice. See if students notice time on digital clocks and relate it to time on analog clocks. We are not specifically teaching how to tell the time from digital clocks at this point, because we can't simplify the time-telling procedure as we do with analog clocks. The next volume will explain how to teach students to relate the time on analog clocks to digital clocks.
- Parents, you may want to give your child an analog watch of his own at this time. Look at the watch carefully before you buy it.

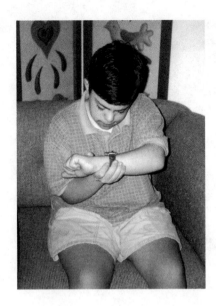

The numerals should be large and clear. Cartoons or pictures should not obscure the hands or numbers. Don't get a watch with many functions that would confuse your child at this early time-telling stage. Also, don't pay a lot for the watch because he may lose it. A few watches designed for beginners have the minutes on an outer ring much like the one on the teaching clock, above. I would recommend buying a watch *without* this feature first and buy a special one only if your child really struggles for several months with the typical watch.

- At home, give your child many occasions to need to tell time:
  - ▾ Remind him what time his favorite TV program comes on and have him look at a clock or watch so he knows when to turn it on.
  - ▾ Ask him to remind you when something cooking or baking should be ready. ("Come and get me at 4:00.")
  - ▾ Tell him he can phone his friend at a specific time.
  - ▾ Tell him he can leave for the park, his friend's house, the movies, a fast food place, etc. at a specific time.
  - ▾ Instead of telling him you will do something he asks "in a minute" or "soon," give him a specific time that you will do it and ask him to remind you then.
  - ▾ If your child is an adolescent or adult, let him assume some of the responsibility for remembering when to take a medication or test his blood sugar if he has diabetes. For instance, write down the times that he needs to take a medication and let him check off the times.
- Praise your child when he comes home at the correct time or is dressed and ready at the right time for school or other occasions. Sometimes children are only taught about time when they are late or in some other situation when the parents are angry. The phrase "Catch them doing something good" certainly applies to time learning.
- If your older child is learning to take public transportation, begin showing him how bus schedules work. See if he can assume some responsibility for looking at a clock and knowing when to walk out the door to catch the bus.

CHAPTER 18

Measurement

Pre- /Post Checklist

Can the student:

1. _____ Order objects by length and use comparison terms such as big, bigger, and biggest.

2. _____ Compare lengths by using personal referents such as her thumb.

3. _____ Measure objects with a ruler marked in inches or centimeters (whole inches or centimeters only).

4. _____ Demonstrate that the capacity (liquid volume) of a certain amount remains the same despite being put in different-shaped containers.

5. _____ Compare relationships among units of capacity such as cups, pints, and quarts.

6. _____ Estimate which of two objects is heavier and check with a balance or scale.

7. _____ Read the temperature on a thermometer.

If we consider the nonacademic uses of mathematics, it becomes clear that concepts involving money are the most useful in our daily lives. However, the concepts of measurement come in a close second. Time is usually considered a part of measurement, but it is covered separately in this book because of its importance.

Before you introduce the activities in this chapter, it may be necessary to review the concepts of comparison. If the quick review provided in this chapter is not enough, students may have to return to Chapters 6 or 11 and the activities given there.

Jean Piaget's (Copeland, 1984) concept of conservation is as important in learning about measurements as it was in the concept of early numbers. (See Chapter 6, Early Number Sense.) The student needs to understand that however we cut up, arrange, or move an item, its total quantity is the same as before (if nothing is added or removed). If we divide a broom into 4 parts, the sum of the 4 lengths is the same as the total length of the undivided broom. If we measure the 4 sides of a rectangle individually, the total length of the sides should be the same as when we bend a measuring tape around to measure all four sides at once. Students do not have to be able to describe conservation as a formal rule, but it should be a basic assumption behind their measuring.

Vocabulary is an important part of measurement. We use different terms for similar concepts, such as *bigger* and *larger* or *small* and *little*. Students have to be able to *recognize* these terms even if they don't use them in their own speech.

You should probably not try to teach everything in this chapter at one time. There are too many concepts to grasp and remember in a short period. In addition, you need to take the time to teach measurement with actual hands-on experiences to show its practicality. Many of the concepts can be taught with science lessons at school or at home when cooking, when shopping for food, or when dealing with weather or even with a fever.

This chapter will cover the following categories:
- **Length**
  - ▾ Comparison terms
  - ▾ Using self-measurements
  - ▾ Standard units of length
  - ▾ Conversion of one unit of length to another
- **Capacity**
  - ▾ Concepts of capacity
  - ▾ Conversion of one unit of capacity to another
- **Weight**
  - ▾ Concepts of weight
  - ▾ Standard units
- **Temperature** (simple concepts)

Length

In this book, we are not using the word *length* in its narrowest sense—that is, we are not just talking about the greatest of the dimensions of an object (in contrast to its width or height). Instead, we are using length to mean the distance that anything extends in any direction. We are exploring ways to give students an understanding of linear measurement with commonly used units of linear measurement (inches, feet, centimeters), as well as ways to use self-measurement.

USING COMPARISON WORDS

Length is one of the most noticeable attributes of an object or item. One issue that often confuses all students, but especially those with language delays, is the vocabulary used in talking about length. There are many different words that convey length, such as *height, width,* and *depth, big, tall, long,* and *wide,* as well as their opposites such as *short, narrow,* etc. They all mean something slightly different, depending on the context in which they are used. Therefore, teachers must give hands-on experiences with measuring length and labeling with the word that is most often used in that setting. The comparison forms of the words such as *tall, taller, tallest* must also be learned.

OBJECTIVE: The student will be able to order groups of three different persons or objects by size and use comparison words such as big, bigger, and biggest (at least four different sets of words). Sample words could be tall, long, wide, deep, high, low, short, small, little, etc.

MATERIALS:
- Class members or members of the family who are three different heights
- Shoes of three different lengths
- Wash cloth, hand towel, and bath towel that are similar, three sizes of balls, three different lengths of chalk, or a set of three other everyday items that are three different sizes

SUCCESS STEP: Ask the student which one of you has the bigger hand. Compare hands. Praise correct answer.

PROCEDURE:
1. Have the class or family members stand up and compare their heights. Ask the student to put them in order from small to large. You label them with comparison terms such as big, bigger, and biggest. Then mix them up and have the student put them back in order and point out the big, bigger, and biggest. You can also try another term such as tall, taller, tallest.
2. Ask everyone in the family or class to take off one shoe. Then have the student line the shoes up as big, bigger, and biggest.
3. Find many things in the environment that can be described with three comparison words. Get as much variety as possible. Model the variety of comparison words that can be used so the student can recognize what the words mean. See the objective above for suggestions. After you've labeled a few sets of items for the student, show her a novel set of items and see if she can generate the comparison words herself. For example, give her a soup spoon, a tablespoon, and a ladle, and say, "This one (soup spoon) is *large.* How about these two?"

You do not have to formally teach the student that we add "-er" and "-est" to make the comparison words. She should be able to figure out that rule herself

from the variety of examples that you give her. If that does not occur, ask the speech-language therapist for help in teaching these concepts. If the student clearly understands how to put objects in order of size, but doesn't use "–er" or "–est" words in speech, it could also be that she is having trouble hearing word endings (a common problem for students with Down syndrome). If she can read simple words, you can emphasize the proper comparative endings by writing the words on strips of paper with the endings in a bright color so she can see the difference.

GENERALIZATION INTO DAILY ACTIVITIES:

- Play a game like Jenga and talk about building your stack of blocks taller. What is your family record for tallest stack?
- At the beach, see who can make the longest sandcastle. Can you make it even longer?
- When it snows, make a big snowball, then a bigger one. Should you put the biggest snowball at the top or the bottom of your snowman? Where is the snow deep, deeper, and deepest?
- When you're using clay or play dough, make a thin snake. Can you make it thinner? Whose snake is thinnest?
- If your child is going to get a haircut, talk about how short she wants her hair—shorter than Mom's? The shortest ever? Longer than her friend's?
- Draw with chalk or crayons and talk about making thick vs. thin, wide vs. narrow lines. Ask for the markers that make the thin lines.

USING SELF-MEASUREMENTS

When learning to measure length, the student should start with self-measurements so that she can see the need for standard measurements. The system used in the United States comes from self-measures such as the foot. Even if the students are going to use the metric system, it can be useful to know how to use self-measurements when estimating or when measuring tools are not available.

OBJECTIVE: The student will be able to compare lengths by using two different types of personal referents such as thumb, foot, face-to-arm span, arm, hand span, palm, etc.

MATERIALS:
- Things on the floor to measure
- Book
- Cardboard, cardstock paper, or poster board to trace foot
- Marker
- Chalk

PROCEDURE:

1. Have the student measure off the length of a rug or a piece of furniture that touches the floor using his toe-to-heel foot measurement. It may be easier if another person marks each foot-length with chalk on the floor. Have the teacher or a partner record how many of the student's foot-lengths it takes to equal the length (width) of the rug or refrigerator. Then have the partner or teacher do the same thing and record how many of their foot-lengths equal the length (width) of the rug or refrigerator. Quite probably, the number will not be the same. If the number of foot-lengths do not come out even, have the student say, "a little bit more than 4" or "almost 5" (rather than 4½, etc.).

2. Repeat the procedure with a different piece of furniture, pacing off the number of feet by walking alongside furniture that is off the floor such as a table or a desk.

3. Ask the students why the number of foot-lengths was not the same for each partner. Look for the answer that the feet are not the same length. (This answer will lead up to the need for standard measurements.)

4. Have the student take off one shoe and stand on a piece of cardboard while the teacher or partner traces her foot on it. Do the same with the teacher's or partner's foot.

5. Using a straight edge, have the student draw a straight line from the back of the heel to the farthest-forward part of the toe. Cut the cardboard so that it is the same length as the straight line and approximately 2 inches wide. Use the cardboard like a ruler to measure some of the same lengths again. Compare the measurements with the previous measurements. They will probably not be the same.

6. Have the students use some other personal referents to measure smaller objects such as a book. Younger children can probably use their entire thumb to measure, while older students can use the tip of the thumb to the joint to measure something similar to what they will learn later is an inch. Stretching their fingers apart can give them a hand span length that is convenient to use. The width of a finger can also be used to approximate a centimeter. They also can learn to measure fabric using the nose-to-arm-stretch method similar to the measurement of a yard. Let the students think of some other parts of their body or things they always keep with them that could be used as personal referents for measuring.

GENERALIZATION INTO DAILY ACTIVITIES:
- Play bocce ball or lawn bowling. Each player throws two balls towards a special target ball. Only the team whose ball comes closest to the target ball scores, and you often have to use self-

referents such as a foot or hand span to decide which ball is closest to the target.

- Horseshoes and ring toss games also provide opportunities to use self-referents.
- If you are playing miniature golf and you pick up your ball to get it out of an opponent's way, use self-measurement to put it back where it was.
- Plant bulbs or seeds and use a hand span or other self-measurement to space them evenly.

Using Standard Units of Length

Teaching Math will focus on inches, feet, and yards as units of measurements. Activities using these units can be adapted to the metric system, including centimeters and meters.

Note: Students can get confused by the very small markings or slash marks on a regular ruler. Use a simple ruler with only the whole inches or centimeters showing at first. After practice with the simple ruler, you may be able to introduce a regular ruler without confusion. You may want to draw a colored line with a marker on the whole inches or centimeters so the student can easily pick them out.

LEARNING ABOUT INCHES (CENTIMETERS)

OBJECTIVE: The student will be able to measure 5 common objects less than a foot (30 centimeters) long using a ruler marked at one-inch (or one-centimeter) intervals.

MATERIALS:
- Cardboard or poster board rulers marked by hatch marks from 0 to 10 inches or 0-25 centimeters (The students will write in the numbers on the rulers)
- Various items in the environment under 10 inches (25 centimeters) in length
- A standard ruler for each student

SUCCESS STEP: Have the students write the numbers from 1-10 on the marked cardboard rulers. Students who have difficulty writing can point to the already written numbers as they are named. Praise correct responses.

PROCEDURE:
1. Review with the students why using the length of different people's feet wasn't a very good way of comparing things. Have them look at the foot-length cardboards they used as rulers in the previous session. Compare the pieces of cardboard and ask the students if they are the same. Then tell them that now they are going to learn about a measurement of the foot that is exactly the same every time.

2. Demonstrate how to measure a small item with the cardboard ruler. Point out that you line up the left edge of the ruler with one edge of the item you're measuring.

3. Have the student(s) measure a pencil, a paper clip, the width of a sheet of paper, a book, and other objects *under 10 inches*. (This way, they do not have to mentally add several measurements to get the length of something that is longer than a foot.) If possible, have the students pair up to check each other with their measurements. Practice in measuring small objects as part of daily activities can be fun.

4. Introduce a simple regular ruler. You may want to draw colored lines marking the whole inches on the ruler itself so the student can transition from the cardboard ruler more easily. Then use the regular ruler to measure some of the same things you measured with the cardboard ruler. If the measurement falls between the inch marks, have the student go to the next higher number. Some students will have had a lot of experience with fractions and may be able to read the ruler by half inches.

ROAD RACE GAME

MATERIALS:

- *Road Race* game board (from page 366) mounted on a file folder
- *Road Race* game cards (page 368)
- Game tokens (Matchbox cars or paper cars made with pattern on page 372)
- Simple poster board rulers, 5 inches (or 12 centimeters) long, marked off by inches (or centimeters)

PROCEDURE:

1. Photocopy the Road Race game board found in Appendix B. (Gluing the game to the inside of a file folder makes it possible to use the game many times.) Decide what kind of cars you want the players to use to drive past the buildings of the town on the game board. You may make the cars from the pattern and instructions given in Appendix B. You may also use Matchbox-type cars that really roll around the raceway. The Matchbox-type cars are fun and real for the students, but they can also roll away or be used for play that has nothing to do with the math game. The poster board cars are not as real but they move just like regular game tokens. You decide which are appropriate for the students you are teaching.

2. Cut out the small game cards, turn them face down, and mix them up on the board. Give each player a poster board ruler that is 5 inches long, marked off by each inch.

3. Players follow the instructions given on the game card, such as "Go three inches forward," or "Go one inch backwards." Players must use the ruler to measure three inches and place the front of the car at that exact point. Players can challenge each other's measurements or where a player places her token by measuring themselves.

4. If players have trouble measuring around the turns of the track, start the race using just one side of the track. Put a paper finish sign at the end. Later, progress to using

the whole race track as they get more proficient at measuring. You can also give them a little demonstration and practice time on measuring around the corners.

5. The first car to cross the finish line is the winner. Be sure to supervise the first few road race games to make sure that all the students follow the rules and measure correctly.

6. You can change the rules so that several students become a team for one car if you have more than two students who want to play.

LEARNING ABOUT FEET

OBJECTIVE: The student will learn to measure common objects that are over one foot long (American units only).

MATERIALS:

- A standard ruler and a piece of chalk for each student
- Objects approximately 13 to 19 inches long (e.g., long file folders, manila envelopes, shoe boxes)
- A yardstick (for American units only)
- A small tape measure (optional)

PROCEDURE:

1. Have the students take off their shoes and measure their feet now using the regular 12-inch rulers. Compare measurements. (If you are doing the activity at home, compare several family members' measurements.) Explain that even if their feet are smaller than 12 inches, the standard measurement we call "one foot" is always 12 inches.

2. Then have the students measure the length of an object that is larger than 12 inches (between 13 and 17 inches would be the simplest). Explain that you lightly mark the object with chalk at the far edge of the ruler (by the 12). Leaving your finger at the chalk mark, move the near edge of the ruler to that mark and count the number of additional inches. Show the students how to add the 12 inches to the second number of inches to get the total number of inches. Show them how you can count on by saying 12 and then counting up. (Have them round any fractions of an inch up to the next highest inch.)

3. Give the student some objects that are between 13 and 19 inches long to measure in the above manner. If she has a lot of difficulty using a small ruler and turning it over, use a yardstick or tape several poster board rulers together to measure longer objects.

4. Find larger items in the school or house that are not over 3 feet in length. Have the students measure them and compare answers. If possible, have them go outdoors to find additional things to measure.

5. After the students are secure in measuring feet with rulers, tell them that they are going to learn to measure more accurately. Explain how we read to the largest number of feet and then count by inches. For example, the chair is over 2 feet tall but not 3 feet tall. We say that it is 2 feet and (counting the inches) 6 inches tall. Have the students redo the measurements for the things in their environment, being more accurate in feet and inches. Practice as needed.

6. Tell the students that 3 feet equal one yard. To help them remember, ask them how many feet they have. When they say two, ask them, "What if you had three feet? Wouldn't you look funny if you had three feet? If you had *three feet,* I would send you out in the *yard.*" You could have the student draw a cartoon illustrating that conceptual picture so that she has both visual and tactile input.

7. Some students may easily make the transition to using a tape measure. A small tape measure that has a push button to rewind the tape may have great appeal for some students. Using this interest, the student can be taught to measure both short and long lengths.

Yards vs. Feet

Do not worry about the student learning to read yards at this level. Most of the household length measurements are expressed in just feet and inches. The yardstick is introduced because it is easier to use for items larger than 1 foot.

GENERALIZATION INTO DAILY ACTIVITIES: Measuring length can easily be included in home and school activities.

- Both at home and at school, heights can be measured on a height chart or on an interior door. Families should be sure to date the height marks of each child every time they are measured. At school, heights can be made into a bar graph or other visual record.

- Sometimes students get the visual image of length being only a tall, thin attribute. You can use a string to measure your child's waist and then measure the string, giving an expanded picture of what length is. You can also use a fabric tape measure in the same way.

- Measuring length can be integrated into shopping excursions. Fabric can be measured for home furnishing and clothes. Or you can measure a photo or picture at home that needs framing and then shop for a frame that will fit.

- When shopping for new jeans, measure the inseam on an old pair that fits well and show your child how to look for jeans with the right inseam.

- If your child is going to get a new rug or a new bed or other large piece of furniture, teach her how to measure the space in her room and then measure prospective rugs, beds, and furniture to be sure of the correct fit.

- If your child is a sports fan, help her understand the measurements used to talk about the game. For instance, talk about how many feet a baseball player hits the ball when he hits it over the fence, or help her understand what football expressions such as "first and ten" mean in relation to yards.

Capacity

The term *capacity* is used here for liquid volume such as water and sand. (Cubic volume is considered in the next volume.) Students often have use for the concepts of cups, pints, and quarts (or liters) in daily life before they understand what they are.

Children are often fooled by appearances when it comes to capacity, according to Piaget (Copeland, 1984). They often think that a tall, thin quart bottle holds more than a short, squat quart bottle, for instance. Developmentally, typical children acquire conservation of capacity/volume in stages from ages 7 through 11 years of age. That is, they understand that if you pour the contents of one container into another container, you still have the same amount, regardless of the shapes or sizes of the containers. Students who have not reached that developmental level will therefore have difficulty understanding this concept. They still can learn to use liquid volume in many practical ways throughout the day, however.

Again, we are going to work with the units of measurement used in the United States for these activities. If your area uses the metric system, you should use those units instead. Then you can explain the beauty of conversion of the metric measures based on 10, while we spend much more time memorizing the relationships of our units to each other.

INTRODUCING CONCEPTS OF CAPACITY

OBJECTIVE: The student will demonstrate understanding that the liquid volume of water stays the same despite being put in different-shaped containers (conservation of capacity).

Note: This objective may not be developmentally appropriate for students who are young or are not at the developmental level of a seven-year-old.

MATERIALS:
- Glass measuring cup
- Clear bottles of different shapes
- Food coloring
- Water
- Funnel (optional)

SUCCESS STEP: Ask the student to point to the cup. Praise correct identification.

PROCEDURE:
1. Put food coloring in a cup of water. Choose two clear bottles that are different in shape. If possible, have the student pour the cup of colored water into the tallest container. Use a funnel if that will help. Then have her pour the same water into the short bottle. Point out that the same amount of water looked different in the different bottles.
2. Put a different food color in another cup of water. Pour that cup of water into the tall bottle. Compare the two bottles. Emphasize that the amount of water in

both bottles is the same even if they look different. Pour the water back into measuring cups to show that the amount of water is the same. Try again with different-sized bottles.

1 cup   1 cup

3. Have the students fill jars and bottles to show a cup (or a liter) of water in as many different-shaped containers as possible. If a student does not seem to understand the concept after several good tries, drop the teaching and do it again 6 months later.

> *Jake enjoyed working with Play Doh. He usually rolled it into balls and rolled them around on the table. One day when he had rolled two balls that were approximately the same size, his friend taught him how to roll a ball into a snake. "Oh, look!" he called, "I made a real big ball." When the teacher talked to him, she realized that he thought he had made one ball bigger by stretching it out into a long snake. The teacher asked him to make the snake back into a ball. Jake did, but he still thought the snake had more Play Doh than the ball. Jake was not developmentally ready to understand that the amount does not change even if the shape does—the concept of conservation.*

STANDARD UNITS OF CAPACITY

The student will now learn how to measure with cups, pints, and quarts. Even if she does not completely understand the concept of conservation of capacity, she can learn to use cups, pints, and quarts in play or in meal preparation.

OBJECTIVE: The student will be able to compare the relationships among units of capacity measurement such as cups, pints, and quarts.

MATERIALS:
- Standard measuring cups
- Pint and quart (or liter) canning jars or clear plastic pint and quart storage bottles

- A quart jar or more of uncooked rice
- A sheet cake pan (rectangular) for each student
- Colored water
- Clear jars or glasses

SUCCESS STEP: Model the names of the standard measures as you hold them in front of the student, saying cup, pint, and quart. You may want to have the names labeled clearly on the measures. Then ask the student to point to the cup and then the pint. Praise correct recognition or put the student's hand on the correct item and praise her.

PROCEDURE:

1. Cover the floor under the table or desks with newspapers or a drop cloth. Give each student a rectangular cake pan or cut-down cardboard box and measuring utensils. Explain that the rice must stay in the cake pan or box at all times. Good luck! Give each student a container of rice. Let the students feel the rice and move it around.

2. Model filling and dumping with the measuring utensils. Ask them how many cups of rice will fit in the pint jar? Then have them try to put that many cups in. Let them spill the rice into the cake pan as they pour and tell them that the measurements will not be perfect. Dump the rice out of the pint jar and have them see how many cups will fit in the quart jar. Let them practice making the comparisons as long as they are filling the cup up completely each time and counting the cups that are needed.

3. See if the students can tell you how many cups make a pint and how many make a quart. Write the numbers on a chalkboard or paper so the students can see them visually: 2 cups = 1 pint, 4 cups = 1 quart. If the student is not verbal, have her point to the correct number out of 3 or 4 numbers written before her.

4. Do not introduce the comparison of pints to quarts at the early sessions. When the student is secure in the number of cups in a pint and quart, you can see if she has figured out by herself how many pints are in a quart. If not, you can teach that concept in a separate session where you practice with pints and quarts, pouring water or rice back and forth.

5. You want your student(s) to generalize these units to anything that flows so also do these activities with sand or very small pieces of macaroni, if possible.

6. Have the students make their own measurement devices with clear bottles or empty two-liter pop containers. Pour water in the cups and have the student mark the bottle with a permanent marker at each cup level. Try to find a use for these pop bottle measurers such as watering plants. You may also have the students bring in sealed food containers that are labeled in cups, pints, or quarts and have them open and pour the contents into their pop bottle measurers to see if the labels are correct.

7. Give the students many opportunities to measure capacity in everyday activities. They will usually enjoy the hands-on activities and they will need many repetitions in different settings to maintain the skills.

GENERALIZATION INTO DAILY ACTIVITIES:

- Of course, the best generalization activity would be in cooking. However, most recipes use fractions that have not been introduced yet. Making Kool-Aid or Jell-O or a simple recipe such as for trail mix using only whole cups would be most appropriate.
- When shopping, ask your child to get a quart of milk or a pint of whipping cream or half-and-half and point out the different sized containers for dairy products.
- When eating foods that can be easily measured in cups such as popcorn or breakfast cereal, measure out a cup to show how much it is. This would be especially useful for older students who are learning about serving sizes as part of eating a healthy diet.
- When preparing to mop the floor or wash the windows, let your child help measure the cups of cleaning solution needed. Likewise, let her help measure out laundry detergent, if appropriate.

Weight

When children are first learning about weight, they need to be able to lift two objects to compare their weight. When the objects are very different, the student will be able to perceptually feel that one is heavier than the other is. When the objects are similar in weight, you can help her understand that some standard type of measurement is needed to show differences. Children also need to realize that appearances can be deceiving. Some big objects may weigh very little. Only the unit pounds (kilograms) will be discussed in this volume of *Teaching Math*.

THE BALANCE GAME

OBJECTIVE: The student will be able to estimate which of two objects is heavier and test her predictions with a pan balance.

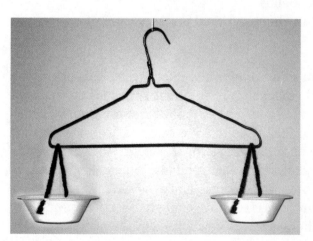

MATERIALS:
- A commercially built pan balance or a pan balance made with a coat hanger, wire, or string and two paper or Styrofoam soup bowls
- Objects of different weights that will fit in the soup bowls

SUCCESS STEP: Hold up two items, one of which is definitely heavier than the other. Ask the student which one is heavier. If she is correct, praise her. If not, model the correct answer and have her try again. Tell her that we are going to find a way to measure which object is heavier.

PROCEDURE:

1. Demonstrate how the scale works. Balance one object in one bowl on the left side of the balance and the other in the right bowl. The heavier object will pull that side of the balance down. Therefore, that object is heavier. Let the student do the same thing.

2. Have the students form two teams or pit the teacher against one student. You hold up two objects, and one student or team must guess which object is the heaviest without touching.

3. After guessing, the student puts the items on the balance and sees if she is correct. She gets one point if she is correct, and the other team or the teacher gets one point if she is incorrect. The game is more fun if some of the objects do not look as light or heavy as they are. Possible "foolers" would be heavy brass or pewter objects, a small box full of light packing materials, a box of Splenda (a sugar substitute), glass vs. plastic drinking "glasses" or utensils, or a baseball vs. a tennis ball.

4. You can also play the game so the students do not see the items until after the guess is made. Have one student close her eyes (or blindfold her) while another puts an object in each of her hands. She then must tell which is heavier from just holding them. Depending on the items used, holding the items should be a more accurate way of judging weight than looking at them.

5. Reinforce weight-related vocabulary, if necessary, while playing the game. For example, say, "Yes, that one is *lighter* than this one. You can tell it *weighs less* because the bowl didn't go down as far."

USING A CONVENTIONAL SCALE

OBJECTIVE: The students will learn what a pound is and how it is used as a unit of measurement.

MATERIALS:
- A spring-type bathroom scale
- A pound of butter, rice, or other food
- A watermelon, pumpkin, box of books, jug of water, or other items weighing several pounds
- Chalkboard and chalk or whiteboard and markers

PROCEDURE:

1. Show the students the bathroom scale. Draw a spring connected to a pointer on paper or on a chalkboard. Explain that you cannot see the spring inside this bathroom scale, but when you stand on it, your weight pushes the spring down, which moves the pointer to a number on the scale that we call your weight. Someone who is lighter than you does not push the spring down as much, so the point goes to a lower number. The number shows how many pounds (kilograms) you weigh.

2. Show the students the pound of butter (or rice, sugar, etc.). Tell them this is what one pound looks like. If your scale is sensitive enough to register one pound, put the butter on the scale to show that the scale will say 1.

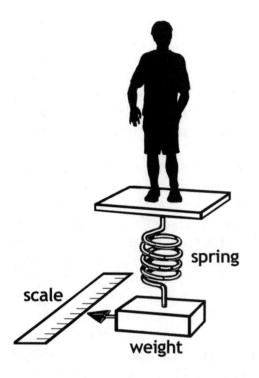

scale

spring

weight

3. Let the students weigh the other objects you have collected for this purpose and call out the weight for each object. Record the weights (in whole numbers) on a chalkboard, whiteboard, etc. After you have weighed several objects, ask the students if they can tell which object is heaviest by looking at the weights you have written down. If they don't figure out for themselves that higher numbers correspond to higher weights, explain this to them. "The pumpkin weighed 10 pounds and the telephone book weighed only 2 pounds. Which number is bigger, 10 or 2? Right, so the pumpkin weighs more pounds than the telephone book. It's *heavier*." Let them pick up a heavy object followed by a lighter object and see for themselves that pounds increase the heavier an object is.

4. Let the students weigh themselves. Be sensitive to their age and feelings as to whether others get to see their weight. Small children may shout the number out, while older students will not want other people close enough to read their weight.

5. Let them weigh themselves again, holding a heavy object such as a pumpkin so they can see how their weight increases when they add pounds.

6. If the students are older, you may want to show them how the word *pound* is written, and the crazy abbreviation for pound, which is *lb*. Point out that the abbreviation is commonly used in store displays and ads. A chant could go:

> A pound's a pound,
> The world around.
> I tell you no fib,
> Why write it as lb.?

GENERALIZATION INTO DAILY ACTIVITIES:

- When grocery shopping, let your child weigh the produce: tell her you want two pounds of bananas or three pounds of tomatoes, and let her add or subtract items from the scale to approximate that weight.

- Ask your child to get you a five-pound bag of potatoes or a two-pound bag of sugar when shopping. Show her where to read the weight on the package.

- Older students who go to a gym to work out can keep track of how many pounds they are able to lift on different kinds of equipment. Over time, they could make a graph showing their improvement.

- Older students who are making recipes that call for meat can note how many pounds total of ground beef, chicken, etc. they need to buy at the store.

Temperature

Most children come to school with some understanding of temperature. They probably know the meanings of hot, cold, and warm in general terms. Students living in zones where the temperature changes substantially with the seasons are constantly being bombarded with temperatures as part of the weather news on TV and as a common topic of conversation.

In the United States, students mostly hear about Fahrenheit units of temperature. Since Fahrenheit has 32 degrees as the freezing temperature of water and 212 degrees as the boiling point, students need some kind of benchmarks to determine what type of clothing to put on and what activities are appropriate, given the temperature. (This may also be necessary for the Celsius scale. Even though the freezing and boiling temperatures are easier to remember, the degrees are almost twice as large as Fahrenheit degrees. There is less numerical difference between temperatures that are cool and cold and warm and hot.) As a child growing up in Wisconsin, I benchmarked 60 degrees as when I didn't have to wear my heavy jacket and could use a sweater. My family also had a water temperature where it was okay to swim in Lake Michigan. (I shiver just to think of it now.) Families and teachers may want to talk about temperatures when discussing the daily weather and indicate appropriate temperature benchmarks.

In this volume of *Teaching Math,* I will just *introduce* the topic of measuring temperature. Here we are just striving for an awareness of temperature and a beginning ability to measure it. Volume 2 will cover the topic in more depth.

USING A THERMOMETER

OBJECTIVE: The student will demonstrate understanding of the measurement of temperature by correctly moving the temperature band up and down on a simulated thermometer for various temperatures given by the teacher. The student will also be able to read the temperature on a dial or red alcohol thermometer.

MATERIALS:

- A thermometer with a moveable red band, made commercially or by the teacher. (Draw a thermometer on poster board, numbered from one to one hundred or just spanning the temperature range common in your area. Cut an opening at the top and the bottom of the thermometer and thread a long paper strip partly colored with red in those openings that can be slid up and down.)
- Sources of temperature news, such as newspapers or radio and TV broadcasts
- Real thermometers that are large enough to read clearly (dial, red alcohol, etc.)

SUCCESS STEP: Show the student some ice cubes and a bowl of very warm water. Ask the student to point to the water that is cold. If the student does not recognize ice as very cold water, explain it to her. Show how water is already melting off the ice.

PROCEDURE:

1. Show the student the large, moveable band thermometer. Tell her that it is a *thermometer* and that it tells you how cold or hot the air is. Also tell her that the red band goes higher when it's hot and lower when it's cold.

2. Using the large moveable band thermometer, ask where she thinks the red band will be if it is that cold out (pointing to the ice cubes). If she points anywhere below the middle of the scale, praise her and move the band around to show winter temperatures. If not, say that the upper part of the red band shows when it is warm out like the water in the bowl. Move the red band around to show what it would be if it were hot or just warm outside.

3. If you are a teacher working on temperature at school, put a big paper thermometer on the bulletin board so you and the students can demonstrate what the temperature is each day. Some TV weather stations have temperature gauges in schools where their temperatures are reported as part of the weather news. If your school does not already have such a gauge, consider hanging a thermometer outside a large window (or check the current temperature on the Internet if you have a computer in the classroom). Every day, ask one or more students to mark the temperature on the paper thermometer and tell you whether that temperature feels cold, cool, hot, or warm to them.

4. If you are a parent working on temperature at home, hang a large dial thermometer outside a window. Ask your child to read the temperature on a daily basis. Talk about how warm or cool that is and what kind of clothing or outerwear would be best to wear.

Taking Your Child's Temperature

Young children tend to have bad associations with thermometers used during illness. Both mouth and rectal thermometers can be uncomfortable. Fortunately, other choices are available. Thermometers used to measure body temperature often are difficult to read. In this volume, we are not going to introduce that use of thermometers. When you do take your child's temperature, you should point out that you are using a *thermometer*, but do not expect her to read it or use it as a teaching tool now.

GENERALIZATION INTO DAILY ACTIVITIES:

- For young children, use *Miss Weather Colorforms Play Set* to talk about appropriate clothing for different temperatures. Children can dress Miss Weather in a swimsuit, coat, etc. depending on the weather. If your child has a doll with many outfits, she could also dress it for the weather.

- Make a game of seeing if you can guess the temperature when you step outside. Over time, give your child clues she can use herself. For example, you could comment: "I can see my breath. That means it's probably below freezing" or "It feels a lot warmer than in the house. I'll bet it's in the 80s."
- One family has a thermometer in their car that measures the outdoor temperature. In the mornings when they walk from the house to the car, they try to guess what the temperature is. The adults guess first and let the children guess some numbers above or below their estimates.
- For students who are allowed to use the Internet, show them one or two websites where they can find out the local weather. If you are planning an outing or event where the weather matters, sometimes ask your child to go to a weather site and tell you what the temperature is going to be on a certain day.
- If your home thermostat is not a complicated computerized one, show your older child how you can use it to tell what the temperature is inside and how you can make it warmer or cooler in your house. This is probably not a good idea for school classrooms, however.
- If your family has a hot tub or swimming pool, your child can be assigned the duty to check the water temperature each day. She needs to know what a comfortable temperature is for people to enjoy the water. Likewise, she could help monitor the temperature in a home aquarium.

CHAPTER 19

Shapes and Patterns

Pre- /Post Checklist

Can the student:

1. _____ Recognize a circle, triangle, square, and rectangle.

2. _____ Recognize circles, triangles, squares, and rectangles in everyday shapes in the environment.

3. _____ Identify a ball (sphere), a box (cube), and a tube (cylinder).

4. _____ Identify balls (spheres), boxes (cubes), and tubes (cylinder) in the environment.

5. _____ Recognize a repeating pattern with two or more different numbers.

6. _____ Create a repeating pattern using two or more numerals.

Most parents and teachers acknowledge that learning about number sense and basic computation is valuable now and in the future for children. The National Council of Teachers of Mathematics (1989, 2000), however, has broadened the scope of early math learning by emphasizing the importance of teaching about geometry (shapes) and pattern finding.

Learning the characteristics of two- and three-dimensional objects can help students to discriminate between items. So many things in the environment have shapes that can be recognized by a student and then described using names that communicate to others. However, some teachers teach the names of many plane figures such as trapezoid and rhombus in the early elementary years. Of what use are these names to a first or second grader? I found that more than half of the elementary school teachers for whom I do professional development didn't know what a rhombus was. "Why should I?" said one teacher. "I haven't had any use for the word in my entire life."

Students can reap all the advantages of being able to discriminate shapes if they are taught using the more common shapes of circle, triangle, square, and rectangle—the plane figures we all use in daily life. This is survival math and we don't teach "so what" concepts—or at least try not to!

Finding patterns, the second major area addressed in this chapter, is a fundamental problem-solving skill. Much of mathematics is based on finding patterns and quantifying relationships. Sorting, classifying, and ordering of items as given in Chapter 6, Prenumber Concepts, are early skills related to finding patterns. This chapter will focus on a few more early pattern-determining skills.

The concepts that will be covered in this chapter are:

- **Two-dimensional Shapes**
  - ▾ Matching
  - ▾ Recognizing (and describing)
  - ▾ Drawing
- **Three-dimensional Shapes (some)**
  - ▾ Matching
  - ▾ Recognizing
- **Patterns**
  - ▾ Repeating
  - ▾ Growing

Two-Dimensional Shapes

Children are often introduced to plane (two-dimensional) figures via various shape sorters and puzzles. Most hands-on learners can tell when two flat pieces are the same or different if they can touch and compare them. They may not be able to describe what makes a circle or a triangle, but they do see the difference. The teacher's job is to teach them the names of these simple figures and help them understand what makes them different or similar. Some students may say that a large square and a small square are not the same because of their size. However, size is not the important attribute when we are considering whether shapes are square. Instead, we need to determine whether they have exactly four sides that are each the same length.

The most important use of teaching shapes is for students to be able to identify objects in their environment that are similar to the shapes they know and to be able to describe them using the shape names.

CIRCLES, TRIANGLES, SQUARES, AND RECTANGLES

OBJECTIVE: The student will be able to recognize a circle, triangle, square, and rectangle when he sees them as simple concrete shapes or when drawn before him.

MATERIALS:

- One large set of shapes (square, circle, triangle, rectangle) for the teacher and another set of smaller figures for each student. (You may use the figures from a shape sorter toy or you can cut out figures from heavy cardboard or several layers of card stock)
- One copy of the worksheet on shapes from Appendix B for each student (page 373)
- Crayons or markers

SUCCESS STEP: Hold up the teacher's large circle and ask the student if he can find something like it in his own set. If he is incorrect, put the small circle on the teacher's circle and tell them that they are both circles.

PROCEDURE:

1. Once the students have matched their circle with yours in the Success Step, ask how they know the two shapes are similar. Some may know the name of the circle. If not, teach them the name circle and see if they can explain what a circle is.

2. If they can't explain why the shapes are similar, hold up your circle and run your finger around the outer rim and say, "Look, I am making a circle. I am going around the circle. I start and stop at the same place. A circle is like a sun or a happy face." Have the students run their fingers around their circles several times. Teach both the label of *circle* and the word *round* if you can.

3. Draw a circle and several triangles on paper or the chalkboard. "Which one of these is like my circle?" Hold the cardboard circle near the one that you drew so they can see the similarities.

4. Repeat the same steps with the square. Have the students run a finger around the four sides of their squares several times. Tell them that this box is called a *square* because it has four straight lines making up four sides that are the same size or length. Using a string, measure one side and cut the string that size. Then take the string and hold it up to each of the four sides. The four sides must be the same length to call the shape a square.

5. Do not teach all the shapes in one lesson. Do the triangle and the rectangle at later lessons after reviewing the circle and square. Have the students feel the shape with their fingers and name it out loud. Use as many senses as possible to teach the concepts. The triangle can be described as a shape with three sides—and not one side more. Chant the words, "Count the sides, 1,2, 3—and not one more!" Make a chant out of those words and repeat every time the student encounters a triangle.

6. Seeing the difference between the square and the rectangle is the most difficult discrimination. Make sure that the students are secure on the other shapes before you teach the rectangle. Show the student some cardboard squares and some cardboard rectangles. Let them touch the sides of the figures. Softly label the squares as *squares* and rectangles as *rectangles*. Give each student a cardboard square and a cardboard rectangle that are similar in size. Tell them, "You have two shapes. One is a square. Show me which one is the square. Tell me how you know that it is a square." Get them to recall that a square has four sides that are the same length.

Tell them to look at the other shape and ask if all four sides are the same. Cut a string the same length (size) as the longer side. Have the student measure the short side with the string and acknowledge that the sides are not the same. Cut a string the length of the short side. Continue to measure the other long and short side with the two strings. See if you can get the students to discover that the two long sides are the same length, as are the short sides. This is not the complete definition of a rectangle, but they do not have to know that the corners are right angles at this time. See if the students can come up with their own definition of a rectangle. If not, tell them slowly and clearly.

7. Continue to discuss the simple shapes with your other lessons. You should point out the attributes that distinguish them from each other.

8. Using several students' sets of shapes, have each do a sorting activity for those simple shapes, putting the circles with the circles, the triangles with the triangles, etc.

9. Using copies of the shape worksheet from Appendix B, cut apart the shapes. Have the students color the circles red, the triangles blue, etc. Have them show you their colored shapes and name them, if possible. This activity can be repeated as often as desired.

THE THINKING GAME

MATERIALS:
- A set of cardboard shapes (circle, square, triangle, rectangle) for each student (page 373). You will need to paste the worksheet shapes onto cardboard and cut them out or cut the shapes out of heavier paper using the worksheet for the patterns, if you have not already done so. The students need to have a sturdy model that they can feel.

PROCEDURE:
1. Have the students lay their cardboard shapes in front of them on the table or desk.

2. The teacher should say, "Hold up the circle." The students should all hold up their circle. Repeat with the other shapes until the student matches the model most of the time.

3. Then in a mysterious voice say, "I am thinking of a shape. It has four sides. The sides are the same length. Do you know what I am thinking?"

4. The students should hold up the appropriate shape. Praise them saying, "You are a great thinker." If the students are verbal, ask them to tell you the name of the shape you are thinking of.

5. Repeat in random order for the other shapes. Recognizing the attributes of a shape from a verbal explanation is much more difficult than just recognizing shapes visually. The student must make a mental picture from the teacher's description. If they are unable to use the clues to recognize the shape, go back to steps 1 and 2.

Paul was able to recognize the two-dimensional shapes of circle, rectangle, and triangle when they were drawn on paper or displayed on the chalkboard. However, when he was asked to find similar shapes in the room, he looked at the shapes and said, "Nothing looks like this circle." He was looking for something exactly like the line drawing of the circle.

The teacher went around the room showing him items that had the basic shape of a circle. His face still looked puzzled. Finally she had him draw a circle with his finger on objects that might be circles. The light suddenly went on in his face. "Yeah, I got it!" he said. He went to the next room and identified circles without having to trace them with his finger.

MESSY SHAPES ACTIVITY

MATERIALS:
- One copy of worksheet on shapes from Appendix B backed with cardboard or cardstock and 3 plain paper copies of the same sheet for each student
- Glitter glue or white glue with sand, glitter, or colored sugar

PROCEDURE:
1. Give each student a copy of the worksheet on shapes that has been backed with cardboard or is on cardstock.
2. Cover the working area with paper.
3. Have each student outline each shape with the glitter glue (found in craft and school supply stores). Let it dry thoroughly before moving the paper.
4. If you do not have glitter glue, use white glue from a squeeze bottle and have the student trace a steady stream of glue on the shape outlines. Then have him pour small amounts of sand, glitter, or colored sugar from baking supplies on the glue. Let it dry thoroughly before you brush off the extra sand or sugar. (This is where it can get messy. Have some volunteers ready to sweep or vacuum the floor, if necessary.)
5. When the outlines are completely dry, let the student feel the shapes. Have him say the name of the shape softly each time he traces it with his fingers.
6. See if some students can figure out the shapes when blindfolded. Children with Down syndrome often have difficulty identifying things by touch, so do not spend much time on the activity if they seem frustrated.

SNACK SHAPES ACTIVITY

MATERIALS:
- 1 piece of lunchmeat shaped like a circle for each student
- 1 piece of cheese or lunchmeat shaped like a square or a rectangle for each student

- Two pieces of bread (rectangular or square) for each student
- Plastic knives for each student
- Butter, mustard, or mayonnaise (optional)
- Paper plates

PROCEDURE:

1. Give each student 1 round piece (circle) of lunchmeat or cheese and 1 square or rectangle of meat or cheese. Give them each two pieces of bread and a plastic knife.
2. Have the students show you the circle (or the round piece, if you have taught that label) of meat or cheese and do likewise with the square or rectangle. Then ask them if they have a triangle. See if someone will volunteer that he can make a triangle by cutting the bread. If no one does, show them how to do it with your own piece of bread. Discuss the two triangles made.
3. Then let the students make sandwiches. Let them add butter, mayonnaise, or mustard, if desired.

RECOGNIZING SHAPES IN THE ENVIRONMENT

OBJECTIVE: The student will be able to recognize two items in the environment that resemble a circle, a square, and a triangle.

MATERIALS:

- 1 set of cardboard shapes for each student

PROCEDURE:

1. Have the student hold the cardboard circle in hand while he searches the room for things that are like the circle. The clock, circles on pictures or in cartoons, CDs, round lids, etc. can be seen as circles.
2. Repeat the search with just the rectangle (box). It is usually easier to focus in on one shape at first.
3. Repeat the activity in several different rooms. There are often distracting pictures or letters on environmental objects that make this task difficult. If the students find a triangle, make a special fuss or clap because triangle shapes are usually not as common as the others.
4. On another occasion, have the student find all the simple shapes in one room. You may be able to point out when two shapes are combined.
5. This activity may be extended into a scavenger hunt. Give students a list telling them how many of each shape they need to find and have them bring back objects with the correct shapes or draw pictures of the shapes they found.
6. Many students will be able to draw the shapes, especially if they have a model to look at. Most students who do not have major fine motor difficulties can draw a circle and a line at an early age. Those skills can often be shaped into drawing the simple shapes. For students who have a lot of trouble drawing shapes, you can give them stencils of shapes to use. Tape the stencil down to the paper and let them color in the whole cutout shape, rather than trying to outline it.

COMMERCIAL GAMES TO BUY OR TRY

- For the youngest children, wooden shape puzzles with knobs to make picking up the pieces easier, or simple shape sorters (cover some of the holes at first to make matching easier; circles are usually easiest to fit in the holes)

  - *Shapes & Colors* (Ravensburger) (three boards with pictures to complete by filling in the game pieces with the correct shape and color)
  - *Basic Shapes Colorforms Kit* (reusable vinyl stickers and coated cardboard play boards)
  - *FeltKids Numbers & Shapes* (Play System) (flannel board with colorful felt pieces in basic shapes of different sizes, plus numerals)

- For older students, try playing a barrier game. Put an opened file folder between two players to serve as a screen and give them each the same number and sizes of colored shapes (make your own or use the Colorforms). One player arranges his shapes and tells the other player what he's doing ("I'm putting the red triangle above the blue square") while the other tries to do the same thing, asking questions for clarification. ("You mean the big red triangle or the little one?"). At the end, you remove the barrier and see if the two players made the same pattern.

Three-Dimensional Shapes

Students usually have contact with many three-dimensional objects even before they come to school. We all handle various boxes, balls, and cans on a daily basis. Students do not need to know that a ball is a sphere to have a concept of its roundness and shape. We want them to be able to tell the difference between a ball (sphere), a box (cube), and a tube (cylinder), but the technical geometric terms are not really necessary. However, if the rest of the class is learning the technical names, the student with Down syndrome can learn them to be part of the group—not because he (or any student, for that matter) will use them frequently.

SPHERES, CUBES, AND TUBES

OBJECTIVE: The student will be able to point to or identify a ball (sphere), a box (cube), and a tube (cylinder) and identify at least one item in the environment that is like the three-dimensional objects.

MATERIALS:

- Two balls (not the same size)
- Two tubes (not the same size). You can use the tubes from the center of toilet paper or paper towel rolls
- Two boxes (taped closed)

SUCCESS STEP: Ask the student to bring you a ball. Then ask him to bring you another object that is not a ball. (You say, "Bring me something that is not a ball.") Praise a correct response. If the student is not successful, have him bring you the ball again.

PROCEDURE:

1. Have the objects sitting on the table near you so the student has to move to give them to you. Have the student identify the ball. Then ask him to find another ball on the table and give it to you. Have him roll both balls between his hands so he can see and feel the roundness.
2. Have the student give one of the boxes to you. Identify it as a box and point out its sides and corners. Ask the student if he can find another thing on the table that is like this box. Have him touch the sides and corners of the new box and compare them to the first box.
3. Repeat the procedure with the tubes. Have the student feel that the sides are curved but not completely round like the ball. Have him put his fingers in the cylinders.
4. Take one of each item and set the rest on the table. See if the student can bring you a similar shape as you hold your shapes up.
5. Have the student look around the room for other balls, boxes, or tubes. (Make sure that a shape is there for him to find.)
6. If he needs to learn the terminology, tell him that he can also call a ball a *sphere,* a box a *cube,* and a tube a *cylinder.* Do not expect him to give the correct label consistently without a lot of repetition.

DIG GAME

MATERIALS:

- One ball
- One cardboard tube
- One box (taped closed)
- A large box filled with packing bubbles or newspaper to hide the shapes
- A blindfold

PROCEDURE:

1. Hide the ball and another of the three-dimensional shapes in a large box and fill it with packing peanuts, tissue paper, newspaper, or something else that will hide the shapes from view.
2. Blindfold the student.
3. Have the student dig for the ball. (Call it a sphere, if he is working on that vocabulary.) Help him to feel the roundness of the ball if he has trouble.

4. Repeat with digging for the box (cube) or tube (cylinder).

5. This is not as easy a task as it seems. The student has to picture the shape in his mind and distinguish it from the others and then feel for it with only his fingers. Do not spend much time on the activity if the student seems quite frustrated.

GENERALIZATION INTO DAILY ACTIVITIES:

- Continue to point out different shapes in real-life objects. Encourage your student(s) to point out shapes on the playground or in the neighborhood.

- When your child is drawing with large chalk on the playground or driveway, challenge him to draw circles, squares, triangles, and rectangles. Or draw a hopscotch game and see if he can recognize the shapes that are part of the game.

- When serving sandwiches at home, ask everyone if they would like their sandwich cut into squares, rectangles, or triangles. Or when serving crackers with soup, ask if they'd prefer the round or square crackers.

- If your older child or adult is cooking on his own, tell him which recipes call for round, vs. square, vs. rectangular pans (perhaps mark it in his cookbook or on his recipe cards). If your younger child helps you when you are cooking, ask him to get you the round pan or the flat rectangular pan, etc.

Software for Exploring Shape Concepts

Although many software titles include activities designed to help children identify and match shapes, most of them unfortunately include the word "preschool" in the title. These obviously would not be good choices for older students who are aware of what is and is not age appropriate. The exceptions are some of the Edmark titles, now available from Riverdeep (www.riverdeep.net):

- *Mighty Math Zoo Zillions* (explores 3-dimensional shapes as well as early addition and subtraction skills, number lines, and skip counting by 2's, 5's, and 10's)
- *Mighty Math Carnival Countdown* (explores different levels of sorting, addition and subtraction, shapes, place value, and comparisons)

Some of the titles marketed for preschoolers currently available include:

- *Millie's Mathhouse* (lets students build houses out of shapes, matching patterns provided, and also is a good option for students who need to learn number recognition, size discrimination, early addition and subtraction, and other early math skills)
- *Jumpstart Preschool* (Knowledge Adventure)
- *Disney's Mickey Preschool* (Disney Interactive)
- *Curious George Preschool* Learning Games (Simon & Schuster Interactive)
- *Reader Rabbit Preschool* (Learning Company)
- *Awesome Animated Monster Math* (Simon & Schuster Interactive)

- If your students are learning about maps and globes at school, make sure they understand the connection between hemispheres on the globe and the sphere shape they have learned about. "A hemisphere means half of a sphere or ball. Do you see how the globe would look like half a ball if we cut it down this line?"
- If you are eating at a restaurant or somebody else's house, comment on the shape of the ice cubes in your drinks. Are they really ice *cubes?* Or are they rounded, so they really shouldn't be called cubes? If you remember the days when ice cubes were really cube shaped, mention that (unless your children groan when you tell them how things were in the old days!)

Patterns

In general, patterning is the process of discovering auditory, visual, and motor regularities (Charlesworth & Radeloff, 1991). Much of mathematics can be described as problem solving to find number patterns. If you have taught skip counting by 2's, by 5's, and by 10's, you have helped your student(s) find a pattern in the numbers. There is also a pattern in counting the numbers from 20 to 100 that you should have covered in earlier lessons.

Teachers sometimes teach about patterns with colors, shapes, puzzles, and other visual objects. Research is not clear that teaching pattern discrimination with colors and other objects transfers to finding patterns with numbers. Since this book concentrates on survival math skills, only patterns with numbers will be taught.

NUMBER PATTERNS

OBJECTIVE: The student will be able to recognize a repeating pattern with two or more different numbers and create a repeating pattern using two or more numbers.

MATERIALS:
- Black marker
- 15 index cards, cut in half, with the numerals 2, 3, 4, 5, and 6 written in black marker on 6 cards each

SUCCESS STEP: Ask the student to bring you two cards with the number 1 on them. Then ask him to give you two number 3 cards. Praise correct responses.

PROCEDURE:
1. Arrange the cards the student has brought you into a line showing 1, 3, 1, 3. Ask him if he see something the same about the numbers in the line. He may have difficulty figuring out what you mean, so pick the cards up and put them down in a line saying, "1, 3, now again, 1, 3." See if the student can recreate the pattern. Say, "First, I put down a 1, then I put down a 3. What do I put down next?" See if he directs you to put down a 1 and then a 3.

2. If the student tells you to put down a 1 and 3 next, see if he can repeat the pattern with another 1 and 3. Tell him he has made a *pattern*. The numbers repeat (or are the same), making a pattern.

3. Make another repeating pattern line using two other numeral cards. If the student is successful in recreating it, try one with three digits repeating.

4. When the student is secure in recognizing the patterns, see if he can make a repeating pattern of two digits on his own.

5. If the student has difficulty making number patterns, you can color each number a different color. The discrimination of pattern will now be done using color, which is easier than numbers. When he is successful with the colored cards, fade out using the colors by gradually writing the numbers with less color and more black, until the cards are just black and white.

6. For older students who seem to do well with the idea of patterns, you could play a game where you deal out the 30 number cards to 2 players and see who can make the most patterns out of their cards.

FINDING PATTERNS IN A NUMBER CHART

OBJECTIVE: The student will be able to point out the number patterns in the 1-50 (or 1-100) chart found in Appendix B.

MATERIALS:
- The 1-50 chart from Appendix B (page 332)
- The 1-100 chart (page 333)

SUCCESS STEP: Ask the student to name the first and last numbers on the chart. Praise correct answers.

PROCEDURE:
1. Have the student touch and count off the numbers 1-10 on the top row of the numbers chart. Show the student what a row is on the chart and relate the word *row* to some rows that he is familiar with, such as rows of chairs in school, rows of tiles on the floor, rows of stars on the American flag, or any other rows of objects that are in his environment.

2. See if the student can see the same numbers in the units (ones) place in the second row. Have him point to the numbers and say them. (You can also have him color all the same numbers the same color to help him see the pattern. For instance, all the 1's are green; all the 2's are red, etc.)

3. See if you can get him to see that the same numbers are in the units (ones) place in the third row.

4. See if he can detect the same pattern in the fourth and fifth rows.

5. On another occasion, have him read the numbers in the tens place on the second, third, fourth, and fifth rows.

6. Alternate steps 2-4 with step 5 on another day until the student is secure with each pattern on separate days.

7. See if he can point out the patterns of both the units and the tens in the same lesson period.

8. Try using the 1-100 chart for picking out patterns, if seeing many numbers does not daunt the student.

CHAPTER 20

Money

Pre- /Post Checklist

Can the student:

1. _____ Identify 1, 5, 10, and 20 dollar bills.

2. _____ Match the above bills to an item that would be about that cost.

3. _____ Skip count $5's, $10's, and $20's to $100 in currency.

4. _____ Demonstrate the concepts of paying and receiving.

5. _____ Count pennies to 20, labeling the answer as cents.

6. _____ Read prices that have both dollars and cents.

7. _____ Round off money amounts to the next highest dollar.

8. _____ Use the next highest dollar strategy for prices that have both dollars and cents.

9. _____ Use money to buy one item, then several items.

10. _____ Identify commonly used coins.

11. _____ Identify the value (amount of money) of commonly used coins.

The area of money handling is, perhaps, the most important use of mathematics for all of us—including students with Down syndrome and other concrete thinkers. The ability to handle money is certainly a survival skill in modern life. Students with disabilities can learn to handle money with a calculator and support from home or from the community.

In my opinion, one of the barriers that keeps students with disabilities from succeeding with money is the fact that we spend so much of their early years in identifying coins, learning their worth, combining them to make needed amounts, and counting them, counting them, and counting them. Coins are not the simple first choice for learning about money. Coins are often difficult for the student because:

- Their size does not reflect the amount they are worth (nickel bigger than dime, etc.).
- We show coins in two confusing ways—using a slashed "c" or as numbers after a decimal point.
- Naming the numbers to the right of the decimal point does not follow the same pattern as naming the numbers to the left of the decimal point.
- Most calculators delete the 0 at the end of a number so that $.80 becomes .8 —causing confusion for children who have little or no understanding of decimals.

In addition, it often does not make sense to spend a great deal of time teaching how to count coins because:

- Many students have already figured out that they can skip this counting of coins by paying with a dollar bill and letting the cashier figure out the change.
- Many vending machines display how much money you have inserted so you don't have to figure out the amount yourself.
- Many cash registers display the amount of money you should get back in change, or even automatically release your change down a chute so the cashier doesn't even have to count it out.

I think that we have always started teaching with coins first because we figured that young students would have more experience with coins. That is not necessarily true in our inflated economy. Students are engulfed in ads and pictures about items costing more than just change.

In this book, we begin by teaching about currency because it is much easier, and because we can teach strategies to pay for most things with currency. We do teach what the coins are and what they represent, but there are no activities related to counting change or finding how many ways you can use coins to get $0.85 in this volume.

One group of older students with Down syndrome told me that they don't use coins for anything but vending machines. Even with vending machines they usually use quarters, only dealing with nickels or dimes as they receive them in change. The students also said, "The other coins don't always go in the vending machine right. Quarters are heavy, and we can hear them plunk into the machine, and then we get our Cokes."

Most school-aged children don't have much use for pennies. The average American will not bother to bend down to pick up a penny on the sidewalk.

The areas covered regarding money in this volume are:
- **Currency**
  - ▾ Currency identification (sorting)
  - ▾ Beginning functional use of money
  - ▾ Skip counting with money
  - ▾ Concept of cents
  - ▾ Reading dollars and cents prices
  - ▾ Next highest dollar strategy
  - ▾ Purchasing items
  - ▾ Using the calculator for money handling
- **Coins**
  - ▾ Recognition
  - ▾ Values of coins

American Currency

American currency is rather difficult to identify compared to the various colored currencies of other countries. There is a different picture of a man on each bill, but the coloring is the same, and one must look at the details to distinguish one person from another. Students may have difficulty seeing the difference between the one and the ten dollar bill because the numerals look similar against the dark, detailed background. The United States government has started issuing the twenty dollar bill with subtle blue and peach colors added to the green background, and will be adding color to the fifty and one hundred dollar bills too; however, the traditional bills will still be legal and used for quite a long period of time (U.S. Bureau of Engraving and Printing, 2003.)

MATCHING AND RECOGNIZING CURRENCY

OBJECTIVE: The student will be able to identify a one, five, ten, and twenty dollar bill.

MATERIALS:
- A set of realistic one, five, ten, and twenty dollar bills, such as:
  - ▾ *Hands on Money* from www.AttainmentCompany.com or 800-327-4269, around $30.
  - ▾ *Money Tray* from www.pcicatalog.com or 800-594-4263, around $20
  - ▾ Other less expensive realistic play money
  - ▾ Of course, you can use real money if you are teaching just one student or your own child

SUCCESS STEP: Show the student a one and a five dollar bill. See if she can identify either bill. If not, tell her what they are, then, have her handle the bills and repeat their value. Praise her "money skills."

PROCEDURE:

1. Now see if the student can already name the ten and twenty dollar bills (as well as the one and five). Show her each bill and see if she can tell you what it is. If she can, skip this identification procedure and skip down to step 7.

2. *Matching:* Put a one and a five dollar bill in front of the student. Then show her another one dollar bill and see if she can match that bill to the one dollar bill in front of her. If she does not, explain the features of the one dollar bill and have her point to them on the bill in front of her.

3. If she matches the one dollar bills, repeat the matching with the five dollar bills using the same one and five dollar bills in front of her.

4. Practice matching one and five dollar bills by presenting her with a one or five dollar bill in random order.

5. Repeat the matching procedure with the ten and twenty dollar bills. If you are using real currency, do not mix the new, colored twenties with the old twenties.

6. Lay all four denominations of bills in front of the student and ask her to match a bill that you hold from the four choices. Repeat until she seems secure in the procedure.

7. *Recognizing:* Now ask her to listen to you and point to the bill you are talking about. This task is more difficult because she does not have a visual cue and because she has to decide from a brief spoken phrase. At random, say clearly the name of one of the four bill choices. Praise her for the correct choice. If she is incorrect, pull the incorrect bills away from her, leaving the correct bill close to her hand and repeat the request. Practice recognizing all four bills using the above procedure.

8. To accomplish the objective, the student only has to be able to recognize all four types of bills correctly. However, you may want to see if she can *name* each bill correctly.

Beginning Functional Use of Currency

Because we are emphasizing the functional use of money in this book, we want to make sure that students have an awareness of the value of each denomination of currency in regard to buying items that are familiar to them. Your student(s) does not have to learn actual prices of items, but she should be able to roughly estimate what the different denominations can buy. It is important that you use pictures or names of things that are important to the student. Some suggestions will be given, but you should individualize the selection for the student or small groups of students.

INTRODUCING THE CONCEPT

OBJECTIVE: The student will indicate that she has some idea of what the four denominations of bills ($1, 5,10, and 20) can buy by matching pictures or words with the appropriate amount of currency.

MATERIALS:
- Realistic play money
- 12 index cards with pictures of items (such as from sales fliers) that cost roughly 1, 5, 10, or 20 dollars glued to them. (Find 3 pictures for each denomination, e.g., a small bag of French fries or small ice cream cone for $1, a birthday cake, playground ball or Burger King combo for $5, a disposable camera or movie ticket and small popcorn for $10, or a music CD, video, or baseball cap for $20.)

SUCCESS STEP: Have the student help you set up the index cards showing the $1 and the $10 items. Put them up against glasses or mugs so that they are standing up like you would see them in the store. Praise the student for her help.

PROCEDURE:
1. Give the student a one and a ten dollar bill. Pretend you are a store clerk, and she is the customer.
2. Show her several items that are for "sale." Ask her to choose one. Then ask her whether she is going to pay with a one or a ten dollar bill. If she is correct, exchange the money for the appropriate index card. If she is incorrect, laugh and say, "Try again." If she needs assistance after several trials, you can say, "That's too much" or "That's not enough." Repeat with the rest of the $1 and $10 items.
3. Repeat the procedure at another session with the $5 and $20 items.
4. When you think that she understands the concept, you may play store with all the items.

This exercise is more of an awareness exercise than a specific training. We want her to learn that some items cost more than others and that some denominations of currency are worth more than others, but she is not supposed to be learning the relative value of the different bills at present. The student should be reminded of the usefulness of money while working on all the activities in this chapter.

Skip Counting with Money

Although this book emphasizes the importance of using a calculator, counting currency is one skill that is worthwhile for students with disabilities to learn to do without a calculator. Using a calculator at the same time you are handling money can be cumbersome, especially if you are actually buying something at a store. Your students may be able to count their money accurately without using a calculator if they are able to skip count by 5's, 10's, and 20's. Skip counting is done when the student names only some of the numerals in a consistent pattern. For example, we can count by 5's saying "5, 10, 15, 20." The skill is useful in counting money and in understanding multiplication.

Skip counting by 2's, 5's, and 10's was introduced in Chapter 9, More Counting Skills. If the student passed the objective at that time, briefly review the skip counting as used with money at this time.

COUNTING BY TENS

OBJECTIVES: The student will be able to count by 10's to $100.

MATERIALS:
- 5 bundles (with 10 each) of straws or sticks for each student.
- 5 ten dollar bills in play money for each student.
- 10 one dollar bills in play money

SUCCESS STEP: Ask a student to bring you one bundle of straws or sticks (with 10 items in it). Praise her.

PROCEDURE:
1. Give each of the students 5 bundles of straws (10 in each). Count them out as you put each bundle down, "10, 20, 30, 40, 50."
2. Ask them to recount to see if you counted right. Have them *chant* as they put down each bundle,"10...20...30...40...50." Repeat as necessary.
3. If your students do not understand that a ten dollar bill is worth as much as 10 one dollar bills, demonstrate that for them now. Explain that the ten dollar bill is like 10 one dollar bills bound together as they have done with straws. Point out all the 10's in the corners of the ten dollar bill and show them where it says "ten dollars." You may want to put 10 one dollar bills together with a paperclip and exchange it for a ten dollar bill. Repeat as necessary.
4. Now model counting ten dollar bills to $50. Have the students repeat with their ten dollar bills. As you are practicing counting ten dollar bills to $50, occasionally stop and check to see if the student remembers that 1 ten dollar bill is the same as 10 one dollar bills. Trade the student a bundle of 10 one dollar bills for a ten-dollar bill every once in a while and see if she can still count by 10's to $50.
5. Have the students work in pairs and put their 5 bundles with the other person's 5 bundles so they both can count to 100 by 10's.

Varying Manipulatives

Sometimes students get tired of using manipulatives for math. I have found that changing the type of counters you are using makes it more interesting. Straws, sticks, toothpicks, licorice, raisins, and stick pretzels have been used successfully. For items that cannot be bundled together, you can put 10 items into a small plastic bag that zips closed.

One time I ended up doing a small group math lesson at McDonald's. As you might have guessed, we counted French fries.

COUNTING BY TWENTIES

OBJECTIVE: The student will be able to count by $20's to $100.

MATERIALS:
- 5 twenty dollar bills in play money for each student

PROCEDURE:

1. If your student(s) was able to understand that a ten dollar bill is the same as 10 one dollar bills, she should also be able to grasp that a twenty dollar bill is the same as 20 one dollar bills. Check to make sure. Show her a twenty dollar bill and ask her, "How much is this worth?" If she answers incorrectly, show her the 20's on the bill. You may also give her several bundles of 10 one dollar bills and ask her to show you how much the $20 bill is worth.

2. If you really want to make sure she understands the relative value of currency, show her a twenty dollar bill and a stack of 10 one dollar bills. Ask, "Which would you rather have?" Exchange the twenty dollar bill for 20 one dollar bills if she answers incorrectly, so she can see that you get an even bigger stack of ones for a twenty dollar bill.

3. When you are sure the student understands how much the twenty dollar bill is worth, tell her you will show her how to count twenty dollar bills. Count out five twenty dollar bills for each student, "20, 40, 60, 80, 100."

4. See if the students can chant the numbers back when they recount the money themselves. If they can't remember the sequence, try showing them how counting by 20's is similar to counting by 2's. Write 2, 4, 6, 8, 10 on a chalkboard or paper, and show them how you just add a zero after each number to get 20, 40, 60, 80, 100. If they know the cheer, "2, 4, 6, 8, who do we appreciate?" you could try teaching them the response, "20, 40, 60, 80, we appreciate that lady!"

5. If the student can count by 10's but is having difficulty with counting by 20's, you may want to have her use her skill with counting 10's to count twice on the $20 dollar bill. For example, show her how to make two touch points on the $20 dollar bill. Have her touch Jackson's left eye and say "10" and touch his right eye and say "20." On the next bill, she can touch one eye and say "30" and touch the second eye and say "40," etc. The student only has to count by 20's to 100 at this time.

COUNTING BY FIVES

OBJECTIVE: The student will be able to count by $5's to $100.

MATERIALS:
- 10 five dollar bills in play money for each student
- A number line from1 to 20 with spaces 1" apart
- Index cards

PROCEDURE:
1. Try to teach counting five dollar bills by having the student chant 5, 10, 15, etc. as she touches or moves each bill. If she can count by 5's correctly, you can just practice in this manner. Frequently, students have more difficulty counting by 5's than by 10's because there are more numbers to remember and because of the alternation between numbers ending in 5 and then 0. If they need additional visual assistance, use the number line first introduced in Chapter 9, More Counting Skills.
2. Using a number line (from 1 to 20 with multiples of 5 highlighted) and a small object, show the student how the object jumps from 5 to 10 in one jump and repeat for from 10 to 15. Ask the student if she can guess where the object will jump next. Praise her if correct.
3. Repeat jumping the object from 5 to 20, counting by 5's.
4. Using pairs of students (or teacher and student), have one student make the object hop by fives as in #2 above while the other student puts down one five dollar bill for each hop. Then reverse the tasks.
5. Have each student put down 4 five dollar bills while slowly counting "5, 10, 15, 20" without use of the number line. The teacher should write the numbers as the student says them so the students can see the numbers written. Repeat as necessary. Let one student write the numbers on paper or the chalkboard, if possible.
6. Model having the object jump beyond the number line, saying "25, 30, 35, 40, 45, 50." Put down index cards with the numerals, 25, 30, 35, 40, 45, and 50 to extend the number line beyond 20. Show the student how to make the object jump on the number line by fives (from 5 to 20), and then jump the object on the numeral cards to 50.

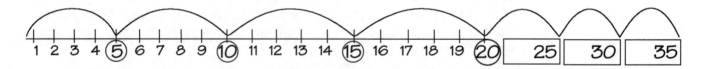

7. If the student is still unable to skip count to 50, make a 1 to 50 number line and show the jumps to 50 on the number line.
8. Using pairs of students, have one student count slowly by 5's to 50 (or as far as she can) and have the other student put a five dollar bill down each time the other student counts. Then reverse the tasks.

Counting by 5's may be difficult, but it is very useful for counting money. Practice as a quick exercise for subsequent sessions to maintain the skill.

GENERALIZATION INTO DAILY ACTIVITIES: Now the student should be able to apply skip counting to real money or realistic play money. Often, having the student put bills in a wallet or purse will make the situation seem more realistic. The adult says, "Here's your wallet. How much money do you have in your wallet?" The student skip counts the bills out loud so the adult can check the accuracy. Students using the realistic play money usually enjoy handling and counting big bills like $10's and $20's.

For now, do not mix the denominations of bills (e.g., 2 twenty dollar bills and 1 five dollar bill). Just use all $10's or $20's, etc.

Count the Jumps

Remember to have the student count the jumps, not the squares or spaces, on the number line. Children often have difficulty remembering whether to count the square they are on at the beginning or the square that they land on. If they get in the habit of counting the jumps, they will not be confused.

MONEY FAT MAT GAME

OBJECTIVE: The student will practice counting currency and exchanging 10 one dollar bills for 1 ten dollar bill.

MATERIALS:

- A Fat Mat from Appendix B for each student (page 336)
- Money Total Slips from Appendix B (page 374)
- Dice
- Realistic one and ten dollar bills
- A timer or watch
- Calculator

PROCEDURE:

1. Give each student a Fat Mat from Appendix B (the headings will say *Ones* and *Tens)*. The teacher or facilitator acts as the bank and keeps the one and ten dollar bills in order to hand them out during the game. Each student rolls one die and the one with the highest number starts first.
2. If the student rolls a 1, 2, or 3, the banker (teacher or older student) gives her 1, 2, or 3 ten dollar bills. She places them on the Fat Mat under the tens column. Rolling a 4, 5, or 6 gets her 4, 5, or 6 one-dollar bills. After the game has been demonstrated, the student must place the bills on the Fat Mat by herself.
3. Whenever the student gets 10 one dollar bills, she needs to exchange them for a ten dollar bill with the banker, or that $10 does not count for her score.
4. Set the timer for 15 to 20 minutes. The player who has the most money when the timer rings, wins. If a player has 10 or more single dollar bills on her

mat, she does not get to count that money in her score. One purpose of the game is to make sure the student knows that 10 single dollars is the same amount as a ten dollar bill.

5. Much of the value of this game comes from the student adding up her final money count. The teacher should demonstrate how to use the Money Total Slips from the Appendix to figure up the total amount.

6. The student should count the number of $1's and place the number in the space provided. Then the student should skip count the number of $10's and put the total in the space provided. Using the Money Total Slip, the student should add up the totals with the calculator. The banker should check the slips carefully for accuracy.

7. When the students are first learning to total their money, the banker should go through the procedure with each student individually, even if the others have to wait. This game will serve as an introduction to counting up various denominations of bills.

Skip Counting with the Calculator

Some students may not be able to reliably use skip counting with money. Other students may be able to skip count the money needed for most real-life transactions in stores, but may find it helpful to count larger sums (such as from their banks) with a calculator. Teach your students that when they use their calculators for adding money, they should write down the value of each bill on paper before doing the addition so the amounts can be checked. They may also want to cross out each number once they have added it, so they can recover if they lose their place when punching in a long series of 5's or 10's.

Practice punching out the 5's, the 10's, and the 20's on the calculator. For example, have the students punch in the number 5 on their calculators. Then have them punch in the addition sign (+) and look at the window to see the answer. Continuing adding 5's until the answer in the window shows 100. Repeat with adding 10's and then 20's in the same manner.

Practice in Money Handling Situations

At this point, you could retry the "Beginning Functional Currency" activity described above, this time "selling" items on index cards for multiples of $10 or $5. For instance, give your student(s) some ten dollar bills, and price items such as radios or clothing for $30 or $40 and see if she can count out the bills to "buy" the items.

Now is also the time to regularly play the *Earn and Pay* game from the assessment in Chapter 4. This game gives such a great deal of practice in skills that will translate into actual money handling skills in the older child, adolescent, and young adult that it should be played daily while you are working on the skills in this chapter. The entire game, including the final money counting, is designed to take less than 15 minutes, once the students have thoroughly learned it.

Skills used in the game:
1. Sorting
2. Skip counting by 5's and 10's
3. Simple money concepts of paying and receiving money
4. Next highest dollar strategy
5. Simple subtraction to find change needed (with a calculator)
6. Simple addition (with a calculator)

For convenience, the instructions are summarized again in this chapter.

EARN AND PAY GAME

MATERIALS NEEDED:
- Earn and Pay game from page 302, pasted onto the center of a file folder
  OR
- Monopoly Junior or Budget Town
- Currency: $1, $5, $10, $20 bills – realistic-type play money
- Die
- Game markers (small buttons, tokens, pennies, etc.)

PROCEDURE:

1. Copy the game board from Appendix A and paste the pages on the inside of a file folder. Color some of the game board, if possible. If you are going to use the board several times, it would be wise to laminate it.
2. Cut out the Earn and Pay cards. Photocopy the Pay cards on one color of paper and the Earn cards on another color, or paste them onto different colored construction paper. You should be able to tell the Pay cards from the Earn cards when they are placed face down. Put the cards face down on the game board as indicated.
3. Give each player: 5 $1's, 2 $5's, 3 $10's, 2 $20's = $85.
4. Have the players throw the die and the highest number starts first.
5. The first person rolls the die and moves her marker that number of spaces. The space landed on will be either a Pay space or an Earn space. The player picks up the top card from either the Pay pile or the Earn pile and receives or pays the amount listed on the card.
6. The corner squares involve some kind of direction, such as lose a turn or go back 2 spaces. When players move up or back following one of those directions, they do *not* pay or earn what is on that square.
7. The first person to reach the finish line is Winner I. She must throw the correct number to land on the Finish Square.
8. Winner II is the person who has the most money left.

GENERALIZATION INTO DAILY ACTIVITIES:

- Think of an item that the student would really want that costs about $20. Show her the item in the store or in a catalog and talk about the price. Tell her you are going to pretend that she has saved up her own money to buy it. Let each student count the currency up to $20 and pretend that she is buying the item. Parents might actually have the student buy the item, if practical.

- Parents, let your child count the currency in your wallet at various times during the week (under supervision, of course). You may want to have her just count the $20's, $10's, $5's, separately. Counting real money (currency) is a great motivator for many individuals.

- Of course, getting your own money is an even greater motivator than counting other people's money. Give your child an allowance in currency, have her do jobs to earn currency, or do both.

    My children always had an allowance that they received just for living in our family. They also had jobs that were part of their duties in the family, but the allowance was not tied to the jobs. As they got older, we increased the allowance, but they also had to buy lunches and other things out of it. If they wanted extra money, there were certain jobs they could do, such as sweeping out the garage, that we paid extra for. That way, they did not expect to get paid for everything they did around the house, but they also had a chance to earn extra money when they wanted it.

- Parents, see if you can encourage your child to save up for a real item that costs $10-15. Have her save a little more than the item will cost and change the money into five dollar bills. If she is too young to save the money, you can save $5 a week in a clear jar until you have accumulated enough five dollar bills. You will be showing the purpose of skip counting in a real situation. Do not use coins at this time.

Reading Money Amounts with Dollars and Cents

Before learning to round off to the next highest dollar, the student needs to be able to understand the difference between dollars and cents. She also needs to be able to recognize money amounts written as dollars and cents using the decimal point.

UNDERSTANDING "CENTS"

OBJECTIVE: The student will be able to count up to 20 pennies, using one-to-one correspondence and labeling the amounts as cents.

MATERIALS:

- 20 or more pennies for each student
- Several one dollar bills (real or realistic play money)
- Jar
- Pencil and paper for the teacher to write numerals on
- Index cards with numbers 1-20 on them, if needed.

SUCCESS STEP: Hold up a penny and ask the student what it is. Praise her if she says "a penny" or "one cent."

PROCEDURE:

1. Have the student count 10 pennies and drop them one by one into a jar or some other container that will make a noise as the pennies are dropped.
2. Tell the student that she now has 10 *cents* in the jar. "Ten pennies make up 10 *cents*."
3. Empty the jar and have her drop in 13 pennies. Then ask, "How many cents do you have in the jar?" Repeat the activity using different amounts of pennies, emphasizing the word *cents* each time.
4. Reverse the activity and have the student count the pennies as you or another student drops the pennies in the jar. Have the student tell you how many cents are in the jar. If the student is nonverbal, have her point to cards that have the numerals from 1 to 20 on them. Even if the student is verbal, showing her the numerals will strengthen the visual learning capacity.
5. To make sure she knows the difference between cents and dollars, give her a couple dollars and a couple pennies and see if she can tell you how many dollars and how many cents she has.

READING PRICES UNDER $10

OBJECTIVE: The student will be able to read prices under $10 that have dollars and cents, reading the decimal point as "and," reading the tenths and hundredths as a two-digit number, and ending with the label "cents."

MATERIALS:

- Two matching sets of 10 index cards with prices (in dollars and cents) written on them such as $2.48 and $1.44. Do not make prices that have less than 10 cents. Make the decimal point twice as large as normally written.
- Two matching sets of 5 index cards that have prices (in dollars and cents) with cents amounts from 1 to 9, such as $4.03 and $9.06.
- Place value chart for dollars and cents (page 375)

SUCCESS STEP: Put 5 index cards with the prices out on the table or desk and ask the student to point to one card that has both dollars and cents on it. Any one that she points to will be correct.

PROCEDURE:

1. Show the student the features of the price on a card. Tell her that the big dark circle or point is like the brick wall on Number Street (see Chapter 10 Place Value). It is the fence between the whole numbers or dollars that we have been working with and the pennies or cents. After the big decimal point, we start counting the cents, and there will only be two digits (e.g., .23) that tell us how many cents there are. Use the place value chart that shows dollars and cents from Appendix B to illustrate visually.

2. Model reading several prices for her. Do not use any prices with less than 10 cents at this time.

3. Show the student one index card at a time from the set with cents amounts over 10 cents. Ask her to point to a card on the table that is just like the one you have shown her. She can take the card in her hand while she is looking for the match. Then you model the number that should be spoken. The important part of this matching exercise is to have the student pay attention to the details of the dollars and cents on the cards.

Notating Cents

At this stage, we do not recommend teaching the alternate way of showing cents with the slashed "c." The slashed "c" is used less frequently than decimals in daily life, and it can be very confusing for students to encounter two entirely different ways of expressing cents during early money learning activities.

4. Repeat the procedure with the other 5 price index cards. If possible, have the student match with all 10 cards resting in front of her.

5. Model reading the prices on all the price index cards that she has matched. See if she can read those prices correctly after hearing your model. You will be practicing reading other prices later in the activity.

6. If the student has trouble reading prices, try covering the decimal point and cents with an index card. For example, if the price is $5.78, cover all but the $5 with the card. After she says "five dollars," slide the card over so the decimal point is revealed, and prompt her to say "and" when she sees it. Finally, reveal the 78 and prompt her to say "cents" after she reads the numbers.

7. Next use the index cards that show prices of several dollars and 1 to 9 cents. Explain that there always have to be two places to the right of the decimal point (or wall) when we are working with money. If there are no tenths, you have to put a 0 in the tens place. This is usually a difficult concept and can best be learned by showing a variety of examples.

8. Again model reading the prices and see if the student can read them correctly after hearing your model.

9. After the student is secure in reading prices, show her some prices that are written incorrectly, such as $2.5 or $5.6 and ask her what is wrong with them. See if she can tell you that there must be *two* numbers after the decimal point. If not, tell her you need two numbers, and show her how you can't tell whether $2.5 means $2.50 or $2.05, because you can't tell where the 0 should go. This concept will be reviewed in the next volume.

10. If she is successful with correcting the prices above that need another digit, show her some prices with 3 digits after the decimal point and see if she can tell you what is wrong. Help her understand that you can only have 99 cents.

> *Kayli counted up the currency and coins in her bank, then informed her mother that she had "3 dollars and 150 cents." Although she knew the values of the coins and currency, she hadn't learned that you can only have 99 cents; one penny more and you have a dollar.*

PLACE VALUE PRICES (ACTIVITY SHEET)

MATERIALS:
- Place Value Prices sheets from Appendix B (page 376)
- Chalkboard and chalk or paper and marker

SUCCESS STEP: Have the student write a dollar sign on the chalkboard (or point to a dollar sign that you have written within a group of other signs).

PROCEDURE:

1. Write some prices with dollars and cents (under $9.99) on the chalkboard and model reading the prices. Review with the students that you should:
   - Read the dollars first
   - Then read the decimal point as "and"
   - Finish reading the cents as a two-digit number
   - End with the label "cents."

   $9.24 is read **9 dollars**...**and** (for decimal point or wall) **twenty-four** (for the two-digit number on the right side of the decimal point or wall) **cents** (as the label).

2. Have the students repeat each part of the price after you have modeled it. Then see if the students can read some of the prices on their own activity sheets. Praise successful efforts. This is not an easy task. Repeat this activity using other prices you have made up. Spend extra time on the prices that have dollars and cents that are 9 and under. Remind them that they have to have the zero as a placeholder or the amount of money is wrong. Do not go beyond $9.99 for the prices at this time.

3. Sometimes students are not able to read dollars and cents accurately using the method described above. You may try to teach them an alternate way of reading prices. That is, have them read the prices as the first numeral, the decimal point, and then the two-digit numeral that describes the cents. For example, $4.67 would be read *four, point, sixty-seven* dollars. Some people use this method for reading numerals regularly because they believe it is easier for other people to understand the entire numeral. When I am reading numbers with decimals for a student to punch in the calculator, I often use this simple system for reading numbers because the student can accurately hear what should be entered in the calculator.

4. Have the students punch in the prices on their activity sheets on the **calculator.** Show them how to put in the decimal point. Emphasize the importance of putting in the decimal point accurately. Check the windows on their calculators to see they are correct each time.

5. When the students are reading prices under $10 accurately, introduce higher prices (under $50) to see if they can extend their learning to larger numbers.

GENERALIZATION INTO DAILY ACTIVITIES: Parents, whenever you are with your child in a store, restaurant, etc. that has items for sale, look for meaningful ways to engage your child in reading prices. For example:

- If your child asks you to buy a certain brand of cereal, cookies, etc. at the grocery store, say, "Maybe. How much does it cost?" (and show her where to read the price) or, perhaps, "No way! Look how much it costs!"
- At restaurants where the prices are posted on a menu board, enlist your child's help in reading the prices. "I can't see how much the drinks cost. Can you?"
- If your child asks you to buy her something that you aren't inclined to buy her at the moment (such as a CD, toy, book), show her the price and suggest she save up for it. "See, it's $14.95. You can buy it for yourself when you have a little more money saved."

At school, you could visit the cafeteria or school store (if there is one) and practice reading prices for desired items there.

Writing Money Amounts

For now, I recommend writing dollars alone (without any cents). For example, write $5, not $5.00. It makes the learning simpler and less confusing. Traditionally, five dollars is written as $5.00 to make lining up the dollars and cents easier when doing paper and pencil addition or subtraction. When using the calculator, we don't have to worry about lining up the numbers underneath each other as long as we are accurate in entering the numbers in the calculator. Later, you can teach the student that $5.00 is another way of showing that there are 5 dollars and no cents, but that we enter just $5 on the calculator because it is faster and easier.

Next Highest Dollar Strategy

Although in this book we advocate working with currency before we work with coins, there is no escaping decimals in dealing with money in the real world. The students will see many ads and commercials that give prices with cents—for example, $1.25 or $19.95. An important strategy to teach when working with money is that of rounding numbers to the next highest dollar. If the students understand the next-highest-dollar strategy, they can pay without knowing the exact value of the coins needed.

Many people use the next-highest-dollar strategy without being aware of it. I drive up to the window at Burger King and order a Whopper and fries. The clerk tells me that my order costs $2.89 and to drive to the next window. Do I get out my change purse and fumble to get $.89 cents in change? No! I hand the clerk three dollars and let her give me back the change. When time is short, many of us use the next-highest-dollar strategy.

Although you probably know the rules for rounding a number to the *closest* dollar, only the *highest* dollar strategy will be taught here. Students who are concrete thinkers often have trouble when several options are given for different situations. Rounding down to the closest dollar might result in the student trying to buy something and not having enough money to pay for it—a very embarrassing situation for any of us.

> *Scott has figured out that most things that he buys cost under $20. There-fore, he keeps just 1 twenty dollar bill in his wallet. Then if he wants to buy anything, he just hands the clerk his $20. He says that it keeps him from being embarrassed by not having enough cash to pay for an item.*

ROUNDING UP TO THE CLOSEST DOLLAR

OBJECTIVE: The student will be able to round off to the next highest dollar for prices under $49.99.

MATERIALS:

- A large teacher number line (1 to 20) or a straight line on the chalkboard that is marked off in 20 equal parts.
- A number line (1 to 20) for each student (not a ruler)
- Six prices under $20 written on index cards or on a chalkboard where all can see ($1.11, $9.08, $12.10, $17. 62, $6.10, $18.12)

SUCCESS STEP: Have the student read the price on one of the index cards. Model the correct price if she is incorrect and have her repeat. Praise success.

PROCEDURE:

1. Hold up the first index card and read off the price ($1.11). Ask the students to pretend they only have dollar bills and no coins. Then ask how many dollars they would need to buy something that costs $1.11. If they say "one," say, "OK, one dollar is enough to pay for the one dollar part of the price" (and cover the $1 with your hand). But what about this eleven cents left over?" Then tell them you are going to show them how to always know how many dollars they need to buy something.
2. Using the teacher's number line, go through each of the six prices and point to approximately where the price is on the number line by looking at the teacher's model. Have students look for the next higher number on the line and point to it

on the teacher's number line. Tell them this is the next highest dollar. Explain that you can give the next highest dollar to the clerk in the store, have enough money to pay the price of the item, and maybe get back change. Write the next highest dollar amount next to the exact price on the chalkboard.

3. Ask the students if they can see a pattern in how we figure the next highest dollar. You may need to help them see that the next highest dollar is always one more dollar than the dollar amount in the price. You may also show then that they just need to look at the numbers to the left of the decimal, say that number, and then count up one to find the next highest dollar.

4. Give a number line to each of the students. Go over where the X's (the real price) will be on their number lines for every price. Then let them find the next highest dollar for each price and write it on the paper (or circle it, if writing is a problem).

5. On another occasion, have them locate the same prices on the number line themselves and then determine the next highest dollar.

6. Repeat as often as necessary for them to internalize the rule for next highest dollar.

7. You may want to laminate the number lines. Then the students can use a washable marker and mark the prices and next highest dollar amounts of all the problems on their worksheets. They then can wash it off to use another day.

COUNTING MONEY AND ROUNDING UP

OBJECTIVE: The student will be able to count how much money she has and determine the next highest dollar.

MATERIALS:
- Six or more pieces of light-colored card stock or construction paper
- Play money dollars and pennies to tape to the cardstock. Use amounts under $20 and make your number of pennies manageable (no more than 12).
- Next-Highest Dollar Practice sheets from page 378

PROCEDURE:
1. Put the pieces of paper and money in front of the student at a table or at several learning stations around the room.

Season wrote the numbers quite confidently until she got to a card that had 2 dollars and only 4 pennies. At first she wrote it as $2.4, but decided that looked strange. Then she wrote the amount as $2.40 so she had two places in the cents.

Her teacher asked her to read the number and she read 2 dollars and 40 cents. "But I don't really have 40 cents or pennies," she said. The teacher then showed her how to write 4 cents using decimals with a 0 in the tenths (dimes) place—$2.04.

Forgetting the 0 when there are no tenths is a very common error when writing money amounts.

2. Give each student an answer sheet. Tell them to count the money on the cards and write the exact amount in the first column. Then write the next-highest-dollar amount in the second column.

3. Repeat this activity using different amounts until students are secure in finding the price and the next highest dollar amount.

SHOPPING ACTIVITY

OBJECTIVE: The student will be able to figure out the next highest dollar using a pretend shopping scenario.

MATERIALS:

- Advertisements that show dollars and cents in the prices
- Garage sale money labels, adhesive printer mailing labels, or Post-It notes

PROCEDURE:

1. Tell the students that you are going to make it easier for them to pay at a store by having them give the clerk the next highest dollar.

2. Show them some ads (usually grocery) for products that cost several dollars and up to $.99 cents in addition to dollars.

3. Tell them that some advertisers want us to think their product is cheaper by putting a lower dollar amount and then adding 99 cents to the dollars. Ask them how close 99 cents is to the next highest dollar.

4. If they don't know, tell them there are 100 cents in a dollar. Then have them count with you from 90 to 100, pausing after 99 (you don't say the 100) to make sure they know 100 comes after 99. Then ask them again how close 99 is to 100 (or a dollar).

5. Explain that no one can sneak a 99-cent trick on them any more. They have caught on to the trick.

6. Let the students change some prices in the ads to the next highest dollar. Have them write the new price on a blank printer label, Post-It note, or garage sale sticker and paste it over the old price.

7. Give the students some realistic play currency ($1, $5, $10). Have them look at the ads with the whole dollar amounts and take turns "buying" items with the play money.

8. Repeat the pretend shopping with different ads for items under $49.

GENERALIZATION INTO DAILY ACTIVITIES:

- At this stage, the student should be able to purchase one item by giving the clerk the next highest dollar. School students should be able to buy one item at the school store or one item of food without direct assistance from an adult. The adult does need to plan with the student and check the amount of money she is carrying. Frequent experience with purchasing items using the next highest dollar strategy is necessary to maintain the concept.

- Do not expect the student to be able to buy more than one item when she accompanies you as you do your regular shopping. Make sure that she has many successful experiences with purchasing one item before she has to purchase several items. At first, you can ensure success by giving your child exactly the number of dollars she needs to use the next-highest-dollar strategy. For example, if she is buying a loaf of bread that costs $2.30, you would give her $3 and, if necessary, prompt her to give all three bills to the cashier when told the price. Later, you can give her an extra dollar or two and watch to see whether she hands over the whole amount to the cashier or counts out the bills correctly.

- Families might consider "charging" various amounts of play (or real) money (currency only) for the children to "rent" home videos or DVDs or to "buy" dessert at dinnertime. You could give the child some play money and say, "That will be $2.11 for the cake and ice cream." She would then need to give you $3 (with prompting, if necessary) to get her dessert. Make sure that if you make one child in the family pay for such things, you make her brothers and sisters do it too!

Sales Tax

What about tax? In the next volume of *Teaching Math*, we will teach how to figure state tax using the calculator. In this volume, the students are not ready to do that type of multi-step process. In addition, some states do not have state sales tax, some states do not charge on essentials such as food, and other states have various rates of state sales tax, which further complicates explaining how to figure tax. Generally, I just explain to students that we pay money on each item to the governor for state tax. Therefore, to be sure they have enough, they always have to have $1 or more over the price of the item.

Using the Next-Highest-Dollar Strategy to Purchase More than One Item

If you have been regularly playing the *Earn and Pay game*, you have already been teaching a multi-step process similar to what is needed for buying several items. At the end of the game, the student has been skip counting the amount of money in each denomination of bills—e.g., 5, 10, 15 dollars in five dollar bills. When each denomination has been counted, the student has been adding the subtotals to get the total amount of money. There is a skip counting process and then an addition process needed to get the total.

To purchase several items, the student needs to go through a similar multi-step process. She needs to add the exact prices of the items she wants to buy (with a calculator) to find a total amount needed. Then she needs to count the money that she has. After figuring both totals, she decides whether she has enough money to buy the items.

SHOPPING ACTIVITY FOR TWO (OR MORE) ITEMS

OBJECTIVE: The student will be able to add (on the calculator) the prices of two items that she wants to purchase, count her available money, and determine whether she has enough money to buy the items.

MATERIALS:
- Newspaper ads, flyers, or catalogs
- Index cards and a marker so the prices can be visually listed for student
- Realistic play currency—2 or 3 ten dollar bills (adjust the amount of money depending on the prices in the flyers or catalog)

SUCCESS STEP: Let the student look through the ads or catalog and find two things that she would like to purchase. Praise her for finding two items. Note: Specific items to buy have not been listed in the Materials section. Having items that the student would really like to buy will help her learn the skill faster and make the sessions more fun.

PROCEDURE:
1. Give each student 2 or 3 ten dollar bills (or the amount you have decided is enough).
2. When she has marked or cut out the items she desires from the catalog or ads, have her add the amounts (on the calculator) to get a total.
3. Have her count the money you have given her.
4. Then have her tell you which amount is bigger—the total price of the items she wants or the amount of money that she now has. Expand upon the activity by making other similar situations. At this time, make up only situations where she has enough money. Let her pretend to buy the items.
5. When she is secure in the situations where she has enough money, introduce a situation where she does not have enough money. (You may need to take back some of her play money.) If she does not have enough money, she can't purchase the items. Do three situations or more in which she does not have enough money. Hopefully, she will get a little upset at not being able to buy what she wants. Then you can say to her, "How much more money do you need to save so that you can buy what you want?" If she does not know that this situation calls for subtraction, show her on paper how you figure the answer.
6. This subtraction situation was introduced in Chapter 16, Using Whole Number Subtraction. However, determining how much more money is needed is one of the most difficult uses for subtraction that children learn. Have the students practice many of these how-much-more-money-do-I-need situations until, at least

when dealing with money, they will automatically subtract the smaller number from the larger to find the answer.

7. The multi-step process discussed above may be too difficult for some students now. Find out what step(s) is not clearly understood by having the student talk through the various steps out loud. If her communication skills are limited, you may have to explain each step and ask her to indicate whether the step is right or wrong. If she still has difficulty knowing how much more is needed, focus instead on achieving the objective of adding the prices of two items and seeing whether she has enough money to buy both of them. Volume 2 of *Teaching Math* will review the how-much-more-money-is-needed situation again.

GENERALIZATION INTO DAILY LIFE: The preceding lessons have taught the basic skills for using money to purchase one or more items. Since this is such a crucial skill for daily living, students need both regular practice in using the calculator to solve these kinds of problems and also real-life situations in which they pay for real things. Home and school need to work together to give ample practice so the skill becomes part of long-term memory. Also essential are real occasions to buy items and thus motivate the student to learn this vital skill. Do not have her buy more than 2 or 3 items at this stage.

Other books and workbooks are probably going to be needed for the student to get the practice she needs. However, many of the current texts and workbooks are crammed with coin exercises when students with Down syndrome and other concrete learners would be better served by learning how to make purchases with currency. You will therefore either need to carefully preview any workbooks before you buy them or else make up your own problems involving buying one or two items.

At first do the problems together, being careful to show the actual numbers to the student in clear, rather large numerals. Explain each problem at first, simplifying the language and directions. When the student seems secure with adding multiple items and finding how much more money is needed to buy an item, you may try to give her a commercially designed worksheet and see if she can read the word problems and work out the answers with little assistance. More work on using money will be given in the next volume.

Introducing Coins

At this time in the students' math experiences, they will be taught the name for each coin, how to recognize the coins, and the value of each coin. They will not be asked to learn the equivalents of one coin to another (for example, 5 nickels are the same as 1 quarter). This skill will be covered in the next volume. While your students are learning about coins, they should continue to practice the next-highest-dollar strategy for purchasing items.

COIN RECOGNITION

OBJECTIVE: The student will be able to recognize pennies, nickels, dimes, and quarters (perhaps also half-dollars, if they are used in your area), giving the proper name and value for each coin.

MATERIALS:
- A light-colored mat or piece of construction paper to put the money on
- Pennies, nickels, dimes, and quarters, plus $1 in currency
- Index cards and a marker

SUCCESS STEP: Throw some pennies on the mat. Ask the student what they are. Praise her for the answer *pennies, cents,* or *money.*

PROCEDURE:
1. Talk to the student about the pennies. Show her the pictures on each side of the coin. Point out that Lincoln, the man on the coin, has a short beard. The building on the other side has a flat top. Talk about the color of pennies. Tell her that no other coin has this reddish brown color.
2. Then show her some nickels. Use the name *nickel* frequently when describing the nickel. The building on the nickel has a round dome top. The man on the other side has a ponytail hanging low on his head. Talk about the nickel's silver color.
3. Give the student some pennies and nickels. Put a penny and a nickel at the opposite ends of the math mat. Cover one of the coins with your hand and ask the student to put a coin just like the coin that's still showing on the mat next to your coin. Reverse the coin that you are covering and have her match the other coin. Repeat as often as needed.
4. Put out four coins (just pennies and nickels) widely separated on the mat and have the student put the matching coins right beside your coins.
5. Practice with just the pennies and nickels until she is secure in that understanding.
6. Now show the student a dime and a quarter and point out their features. Be sure to point out how small and thin the dime is and how it usually has ridges on the side. Roosevelt doesn't have a beard or a pony tail either. Describe the quarter as a heavier and bigger coin than the others. The markings on the quarter can be tricky because Washington has the same hairstyle as Jefferson and the states on the "tails" side of the commemorative state quarters are different on different quarters.
7. Repeat the matching procedure from steps 3 and 4 with dimes and quarters on the mat.
8. Mix up all four coins on the mat and have her match them again.
9. Ask each student separately to point to or give you each of the four types of coins you name. If the student is not correct, review previous instruction on matching. Then model the names of the coins at several sessions until the student can identify each.
10. The three commonly used silver coins are usually difficult for the students to distinguish. If your student is having trouble telling them apart, you may want

to back off and only talk about the quarter, the dime, and the penny for now. The penny is a different color, so students usually recognize it first. The quarter is large and heavy, while the dime is small and thin. Practice the distinctions between the quarter and the dime in a variety of ways:

- Glue a real quarter onto an index card and do the same with a dime. Have the students line their quarters on the table beneath the index card with the quarter and do similarly with the dimes.
- Blindfold the student and see if she can tell the difference between the quarter and the dime by feeling each of them.
- Drop a quarter or a dime on the floor and tell her if she correctly identifies it while standing up, she can have it.

11. When the quarter and dime are securely learned, you may then reintroduce the nickel.

COIN SORTING GAME

OBJECTIVE: The student will practice quickly distinguishing one coin from another.

MATERIALS:

- A plastic sandwich bag for each student
- 3 or 4 pennies, dimes, and quarters (nickels, if the student can distinguish them) for each student

PROCEDURE:

1. Pair the students up and give them (mixed up in a plastic bag) 3 or 4 of each type of coin.
2. Have one student sort the coins into piles and have the other student check the piles. The student who sorts the coins should identify the piles (e.g., the pennies, the dimes, etc.).Then reverse the roles.
3. Then start the game by having them put all the coins back in the plastic bag. Only one person of the pair sorts. The first pair to finish sorting puts both hands in the air and shouts, "Done." The teacher then checks the piles. If there are no mistakes, that pair wins. If you are just working with one student, you can play against her, perhaps putting one hand behind your back because you are such an expert (and to give the student a chance to win).
4. Play the game again, reversing the roles.

Coin Values

As mentioned at the beginning of the chapter, learning coin values can be very difficult for all children, in part because their sizes do not match up with their values. Why *is* the dime smaller than the penny and the nickel if it is worth more? And, unlike currency, where dollar amounts are marked prominently in the corners, coins do not all spell out their value in plain language. Your student(s) may take quite a while (months or years) to be secure in understanding coin values. Gradually, though, as they have practice using real money and come to equate certain coins with certain functions (such as using a quarter to get a gumball out of a machine) they will likely master this knowledge.

Adding up a handful of change, especially mixed change, can be an even larger stumbling block for children with Down syndrome and other concrete learners. Book 2 will provide more activities to help with teaching the values and equivalents (5 nickels = 1 quarter).

INTRODUCING COIN VALUES

OBJECTIVE: The student will be able to tell (or point out) how many cents each of the four common coins is worth.

MATERIALS:
- Index cards
- Penny, nickel, dime, quarter

SUCCESS STEP: Show the student a penny and ask her how much it is worth (or ask, "How many cents is this?"). If she doesn't remember, review "Understanding 'Cents'" activity on page 278.

PROCEDURE:
1. Using the actual coins, teach the student the value ($.25, $.05, etc.) for each coin. As you are talking about the value, write the number (use decimals) on an index card. Put the card down where the student can see and put the proper coin next to the number.
2. Remove the coins from the index cards and see if the student can put them back on the appropriate index cards.
3. Repeat several times. If the student can match the coins with their values, try putting the index cards down in a different order to make sure she is not just remembering what order to put the coins down in (rather than recognizing value). If the student cannot match the coins with their values, try working on just two coins' values for a time or teach her some of the mnemonics from page 293.

TRADING COINS GAME

OBJECTIVE: The student will understand the relative value of pennies, nickels, and dimes by trading pennies for nickels and dimes.

MATERIALS:
- A muffin tin with pennies and nickels for the Banker
- A die
- Half of an empty egg carton for each student with 5 openings circled with a marker

PROCEDURE:

1. Have the students take turns rolling the die. The Banker gives them as many pennies as the number rolled on the die. The idea of the game is to end up with as few pennies as possible but as many nickels as can be traded for.

2. When the student gets five pennies, she *must* trade the pennies in to the Banker for a nickel. As soon as she puts a penny in each of the marker-circled pockets of the egg carton, prompt her to trade them for a nickel. The student with the most nickels at the end of about 10 minutes is the winner. However, if she has 5 pennies that she did not trade for a nickel, she can't be a winner.

3. The game can also be played using pennies and dimes. Do not mix dimes and nickels at this stage in the learning.

GENERALIZATION INTO DAILY ACTIVITIES: Remember, at this stage we are not teaching the student how to figure out the value of several coins (other than pennies). We do want her, however, to be able to recognize the coins, so if a cashier asks her if she has a nickel she can answer correctly. We also want her to become secure in the values of the coins so that she will later be able to determine the value of several coins, as discussed in the next volume. Here are some ideas that parents can use to help their child gradually learn about coins:

- If your child wants to buy a gumball from a machine, tell her she needs a quarter. Hold out several coins in your hand and let her pick the right one. Likewise, if she is buying something from a vending machine, you could say, "You need 3 quarters" and see if she can pick them out of your hand. (Again, you are not asking her to figure out that 3 quarters equal 75 cents).

- Count 50 pennies to put in a roll. Talk about how you have 50 cents at the end.

- Let your child feed the parking meter, just for practice handling coins. Tell her to put a dime (or ten cents) in for you.

- Start a collection of state quarters as a family activity. Let your child help look for new designs in your change and put them into the folder so she gets used to the variety of designs on the backs of the quarters.

- Consider getting a coin sorter bank so your child can drop in a penny or nickel and watch it roll down to the appropriate slot. Say, "Here's a dime for your bank," or, "Here's ten cents for your bank" to practice coin names and values.

- If she brings change to buy milk at school, make sure she knows which coins she needs (e.g., a quarter and a dime). Let her pick out the correct coins from a handful of change occasionally.

- Borrow or buy the computer program *Basic Coins* (Attainment) that has various levels of basic coin recognition and values (about $60).

Coin Mnemonics

The poems below are widely used to teach coin values to young people. As far as I know, the author is unknown (but I will be happy to give credit to the author in the next printing, if I am incorrect). It may help some students to say these as chants.

Penny, penny	Nickel, nickel
Easily spent.	Thick and fat.
Copper brown	You're worth five cents,
And worth one cent.	I know that.
Dime, dime	Quarter, quarter
Little and thin.	Big and bold.
I remember	You're worth 25,
You're worth ten.	I am told.

You could also try these songs that one mother made up to help her child remember the coin values:

The Nickel Song
(To the tune of Bingo)
There was a girl who had a bank
And filled it full of nickels
1, 2, 3, 4, 5 … 1, 2, 3, 4, 5 …
1, 2, 3, 4, 5
There's 5 cents in a nickel.

The Dime Song
(To the tune of My Darling Clementine)
One, two, three, four
Five, six, sev-en
Eight, nine, ten cents in a dime

One, two, three, four
Five, six, sev-en
Eight, nine, ten cents in a dime.

The Quarter Song
(To the tune of the Farmer in the Dell)
A quarter's 25
A quarter's 25,
Hi, ho, the derry-o
A quarter's 25.

CHAPTER 21

Standards-Based Mathematics Learning

In the United States of America, most states have now developed standards for reading and mathematics. These academic content standards provide a clear indication of what students should know at the various grade levels. Accountability for student learning according to these standards will be accomplished by testing all students, except for a very few students with severe cognitive disabilities who will use an alternate assessment. The "No Child Left Behind" Elementary and Secondary Education Act of 2001 (NCLB) has phased in requirements for states to adopt standards and then to do regular assessment based on these standards. Students' learning will be organized around these standards, even when students have disabilities and are still concrete learners.

Most of the states have based their math standards on the recommendations made by the National Council of Teachers of Mathematics (NCTM) in 1989 or the more current revisions of the NCTM standards. These standards are based on the following areas:

- Number and Operations Standard (number sense and computation)
- Measurement Standard (various attributes of items and how measured)
- Geometry Standard (two- and three-dimensional shapes and spatial concepts)
- Algebra Standard (understanding patterns, problem solving with algebraic symbols)
- Data Analysis and Probability Standard (collect, organize, and display data; probability)
- Mathematical Processes Standards
  - ▼ Problem Solving
  - ▼ Reasoning and Proof
  - ▼ Communication
  - ▼ Connections
  - ▼ Representation

What Do These Standards Mean for Students Who Are Concrete Learners?

Typical students learn most of the computation skills (addition, subtraction, multiplication, and division) by the end of fourth grade. Using the calculator, many students with Down syndrome and other concrete thinkers can learn to use the basic principles of computation in elementary school. Of course, this does not mean that they will have learned the math facts. If we spend the time that is usually devoted to having students memorize all of the math facts to instead teach them how to use the calculator and how to set up problems, concrete learners might become quite competent in math.

Public schools do not always teach about the functional uses of math in the general curriculum. That is, although they teach students *how* to add, subtract, multiply, and divide, they do not usually spend much time teaching them *when* to use these operations in daily life. Now that NCLB requires schools to show that most students with disabilities are making progress in the general curriculum, it may be even harder to find time to work on everyday math skills in inclusive classrooms. Parents and teachers will have to make sure that students are able to apply the math skills they learn in school to functional uses at home and in the community.

Where Do the Objectives in This Book Come From?

The objectives used in *Teaching Math* come from a variety of books about teaching mathematics. Some of the most useful were:

Bird, Gillian and Buckley, Sue. *Number Skills for Individuals with Down Syndrome (four modules)*. Southsea, Hampshire, UK: Down Syndrome Educational Trust, 2001.

Fosnot, Catherine and Dolk, Maarten. *Young Mathematicians at Work: Constructing Number Sense, Addition, and Subtraction*. Portsmouth, NH: Heinemann, 2001.

National Research Council. *Adding It Up: Helping Children Learn Mathematics*. Washington, DC: National Academies Press, 2001.

Reys, Robert E., Lindquist, Mary M., Laubdin, Diana V., Suydam, Marilyn N., and Smith, Nancy L. *Helping Children Learn Mathematics*. 7th ed. Hoboken, NJ: Wiley, 2003.

Smith, Susan Sperry. *Early Childhood Mathematics*. 2nd ed. Needham Heights, MA: Allyn & Bacon, 1997.

Thornton, Carol A. *Teaching Mathematics to Children with Special Needs*. Upper Saddle River, NJ: Prentice Hall, 2000.

As you can see, the majority of books I used are about mathematics instruction for typical children. The final objectives and format are modeled after the math standards as reflected in the NCTM guidelines. Ohio mathematics standards were developed during the time that I was writing this book, so I was able to compare the curriculum presented here with the Ohio standards.

The computation objectives or indicators of the Ohio standards were very similar to the objectives in *Teaching Math*. The techniques for teaching them are different, however. I needed to slow up the procedures somewhat. For example, the Ohio standards had the first grade student counting forward from 1 to 100, backward from 100 to 1, and counting forward or backward from any number between 1 and 100 (Ohio Department of Education, 2002). *Teaching Math* has the student count forward to 30 at first, only later progressing to 100. *Teaching Math* does not have the student count backwards from 100 at all, choosing only 20 as the starting point. Our students usually learn things more slowly and are more easily confused with large numbers.

When looking at the details of a standard, I used the "so what" criteria to determine the emphasis. By "so what," I meant that I asked myself, "If the student learns that concept, so what? How useful will it be in his life?" In general, the standard of Number Sense is covered in great detail in all the chapters of *Teaching Math* because it forms the foundation for further math learning.

The Measurement Standard is covered in Chapter 18, Measurement, and also in Chapter 6, Prenumber Concepts, when discussing classification. The Geometry and the Algebra Standards are covered in Chapter 19, Shapes and Patterns. The Algebra Standard is also used in the problem solving addressed in Chapter 14, Using Whole Number Addition, and Chapter 16, Using Whole Number Subtraction. The Data Analysis Standard is covered in Chapter 6, Prenumber Concepts, Chapter 12, Ordering and Comparing Numbers, and Chapter 18, Measurement. The Mathematical Process Standards were incorporated into both the addition (13 and 14) and subtraction (15 and16) chapters and the money chapter (20).

Because of the frequent practice of teaching both addition and subtraction together, it is suggested that students participating in the regular classroom follow the progression that is followed in that classroom. Therefore, when they are tested, they will have had the same exposure to addition and subtraction as their typical peers. However, if the student is older or has not caught up with students working on grade level, it may be important to teach addition thoroughly and then go on to subtraction.

The Importance of Individualizing Math Instruction

Although the school climate in the United States is strongly focused on achieving academic content standards, we need to remember that students with disabilities have the right to an **Individualized** Education Program. While the achievement of academic content standards is very important as a part of schooling, our students need many functional math skills for daily living that are not taught directly in most academic curriculums. Therefore, functional skills such as money management, shopping, telling time, etc. should be taught in upper elementary grades and in secondary classrooms with frequent practice to maintain them. Parents and teachers may need to advocate strongly for goals related to these skills to be included in the IEP, especially in school districts where there is a great deal of emphasis on "teaching to the test." If some schools do not provide enough instruction on functional math skills, parents can teach them in real-life situations that will really show their importance.

Writing Individualized Math Goals

Parents and teachers can base student IEP goals on the objectives in this book. However, the objectives given in *Teaching Math* are not complete *instructional* objectives as written in IEP's. You must add the **conditions** under which the objective will be learned. Also crucial is designating the **criteria** that can be measured and will indicate whether the student has accomplished the objective.

For example, an objective in this book is:
The student will be able to read prices under $10 that have dollars and cents.

An instructional objective would be:
*In the school general classroom and cafeteria (**conditions**), Scott will read prices having dollars and cents accurately, using the word "and" for the decimal point for 9 out of 10 prices on three separate occasions (**criteria**).*

Another objective is:
The student will listen to numerals 11 to 19 given orally and match them with the correct written numerals.

As an instructional objective for the IEP it could be expressed:
*In the general classroom and at home, Scott will be able to point (**conditions**) to the named teen numbers (from 11 to 19) correctly for 3 out of 4 consecutive math sessions and at least once at home (**criteria**).*

The No Child Left Behind act requires that *all* students must be tested—most with a state-standardized test and only those with the "most significant" cognitive disabilities with an alternate assessment. The decision as to which type of assessment your child should take must be made individually by his IEP team, including you, the parents. Not all state alternate assessments are the same, so no specific advice can be given for each concrete learner.

In general, some parents of students with disabilities feel it is very important for their child to take the regular assessments, in order to make the school more accountable for how much progress he or she makes each year. They may have experienced, or heard about, situations where children with disabilities were allowed to make little or no academic progress year after year, with no repercussions for the school district. Other parents of students with disabilities feel that it may be too frustrating for their children to take the regular assessments, and that if their children score very low each time they take the test, it will not provide a good indication of what they are learning and what needs to be emphasized in future instruction.

Students who are progressing in the general classroom are supposed to be assessed by the standardized test that is keyed to the knowledge taught in that general classroom. If your student is to be assessed with the standardized test, he should have accommodations such as the use of the calculator, an alternative or augmentative communication device, extended time, an answer sheet with more space for answers, or instructions read aloud to him, as part of his assessment. Those accommodations need to be part of the student's IEP. A comprehensive list of accommodations that are allowed in different school systems across the U.S. is available at: www.ldonline.org/ld_indepth/special_education/peer_accommodations.html

Conclusion

Since learning math skills can be more difficult for students who are concrete learners, it is crucial to optimize the learning environment for them so they can make as much progress as possible. The ideal situation for these students would be to be given access to the general education math curriculum with additional support in the form of tutoring or one-on-one instruction tailored to their individual needs. In addition, they would be involved in hands-on, interesting math learning activities at school. Also, the school would encourage parents to be active partners in their children's learning, and supportive families would help their children learn at home with games and concrete activities such as those in this book. As a team, parents and teachers would ensure that students with Down syndrome and other concrete learners had early and frequent success with math concepts and activities so that they felt like competent math learners. There is no telling how much a student might learn if only parents and teachers would work together to help him learn in ways that are truly meaningful and motivating to him.

Appendix A: Assessment Materials

Get a cold.
Lose one turn.

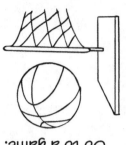

PAY $

Go to a game.

EARN $

Mow the lawn.

Babysit.

PAY $

Go to an
amusement park.

EARN $

EARN $

Get birthday gift
of money.

FINISH

START

PAY $

Buy toys or items
for collection.

PAY $

Go bowling.

PAY $

Buy

EARN $

PAY $

Buy a video.

EARN $

Sell stuff at a garage sale.

Missed the bus. Go back 2 spaces.

PAY $

EARN $

Sell lemonade.

PAY $

Go to the movies.

pizza.

EARN $

Get a prize for most cookie sales.

EARN $

Clean the basement.

Did a good deed. Go ahead 2 spaces.

PAY $ $ 10	PAY $ $ 15	PAY $ $ 25
PAY $ $ 13	PAY $ $ 26	PAY $ $ 35
PAY $ $ 40	PAY $ $ 30	PAY $ $ 8

PAY $	PAY $	PAY $
$ 15	$ 10	$ 21
PAY $	PAY $	PAY $
$ 20	$ 10	$ 11
PAY $	PAY $	PAY $
$ 8	$ 20	$ 22

EARN $	EARN $	EARN $
$ 10	$ 15	$ 20
EARN $	EARN $	EARN $
$ 13	$ 16	$ 30
EARN $	EARN $	EARN $
$ 21	$ 18	$ 8

EARN $	EARN $	EARN $
$ 12	$ 10	$ 14
EARN $	EARN $	EARN $
$ 20	$ 7	$ 11
EARN $	EARN $	EARN $
$ 8	$ 20	$ 9

PAY $	PAY $	PAY $
$ 10	$ 5	$ 8
PAY $	PAY $	PAY $
$ 11	$ 2	$ 7
PAY $	PAY $	PAY $
$ 9	$ 10	$ 8

PAY $	PAY $	PAY $
$ 4	$ 10	$ 11

PAY $	PAY $	PAY $
$ 7	$ 9	$ 11

PAY $	PAY $	PAY $
$ 8	$ 4	$ 3

EARN $	EARN $	EARN $
$ 10	$ 5	$ 2
EARN $	EARN $	EARN $
$ 4	$ 6	$ 7
EARN $	EARN $	EARN $
$ 9	$ 3	$ 6

EARN $	EARN $	EARN $
$ 6	$ 10	$ 5
EARN $	EARN $	EARN $
$ 4	$ 7	$ 11
EARN $	EARN $	EARN $
$ 3	$ 2	$ 9

Type	No. of bills	Amt. of money
$1		
$5		
$10		
$20		
$50		

Type	No. of bills	Amt. of money
$1		
$5		
$10		
$20		
$50		

Type	No. of bills	Amt. of money
$1		
$5		
$10		
$20		
$50		

Type	No. of bills	Amt. of money
$1		
$5		
$10		
$20		
$50		

Type	No. of bills	Amt. of money
$1		
$5		
$10		
$20		
$50		

Type	No. of bills	Amt. of money
$1		
$5		
$10		
$20		
$50		

M	A	T	H
9	14	22	37
3	19	21	31
10	18	20	39
4	11	25	33
7	13	27	35

M	A	T	H
2	15	23	36
5	19	25	34
10	12	26	37
8	17	20	38
7	13	27	31

M	A	T	H
6	14	24	35
3	18	29	33
10	11	26	37
9	19	21	30
5	16	23	32

Calculator Antics Worksheet

$$\begin{array}{r} 47 \\ +18 \\ \hline \end{array} \qquad \begin{array}{r} 23 \\ +20 \\ \hline \end{array} \qquad \begin{array}{r} 89 \\ +11 \\ \hline \end{array}$$

$$\begin{array}{r} 79 \\ +50 \\ \hline \end{array}$$

The answers use all the numbers from 1 - 9.

T	I	M	E
3:30	11:15	5:00	1:00
7:45	4:15	6:30	10:15
2:00	7:30	1:15	8:45

T	I	M	E
2:00	4:15	6:30	8:45
3:30	7:30	1:15	1:00
7:45	11:15	5:00	10:15

Times to be called out by the teacher: T-7:45, T-2:00, T-3:30   I-7:30, I-4:15, I-11:15   M-1:15, M-5:00, M-6:30   E-10:15, E-1:00, E-8:45

T	I	M	E
2:00	4:15	6:30	10:15
7:45	11:15	5:00	8:45
3:30	7:30	1:15	1:00

T	I	M	E
7:45	7:30	1:15	1:00
2:00	4:15	5:00	8:45
3:30	11:15	6:30	10:15

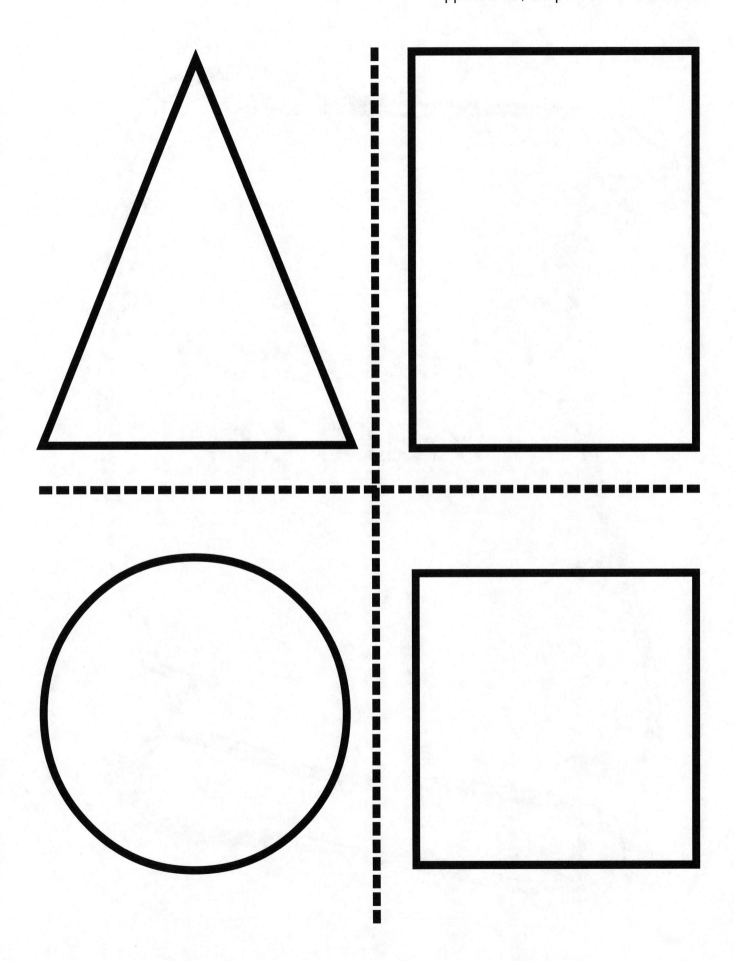

Obedience
Master

Appendix B: Teaching Materials

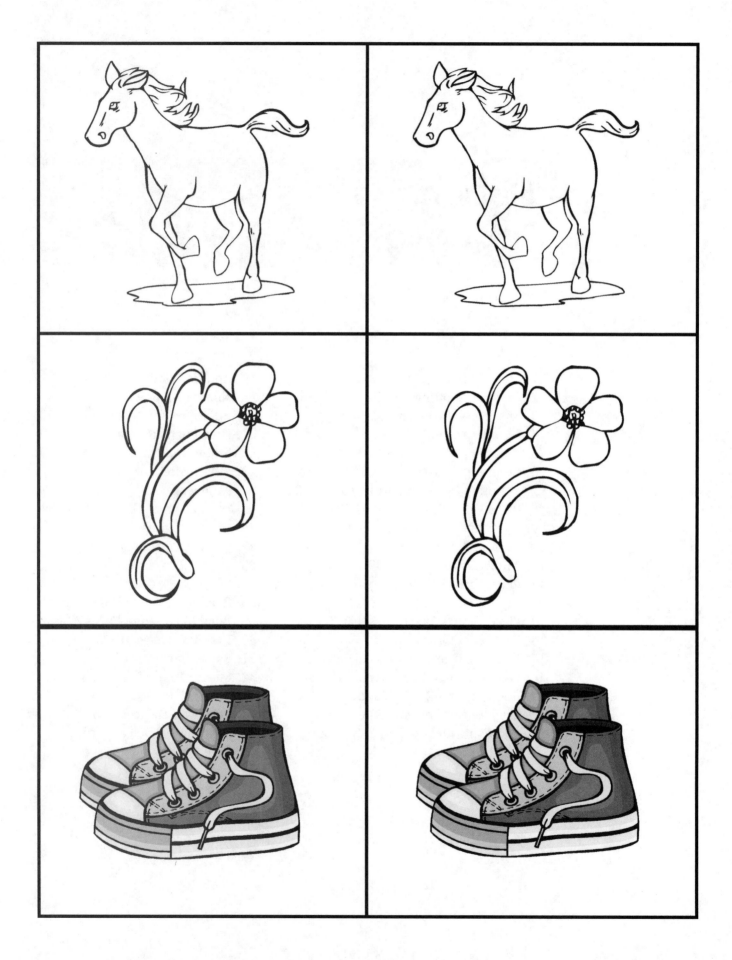

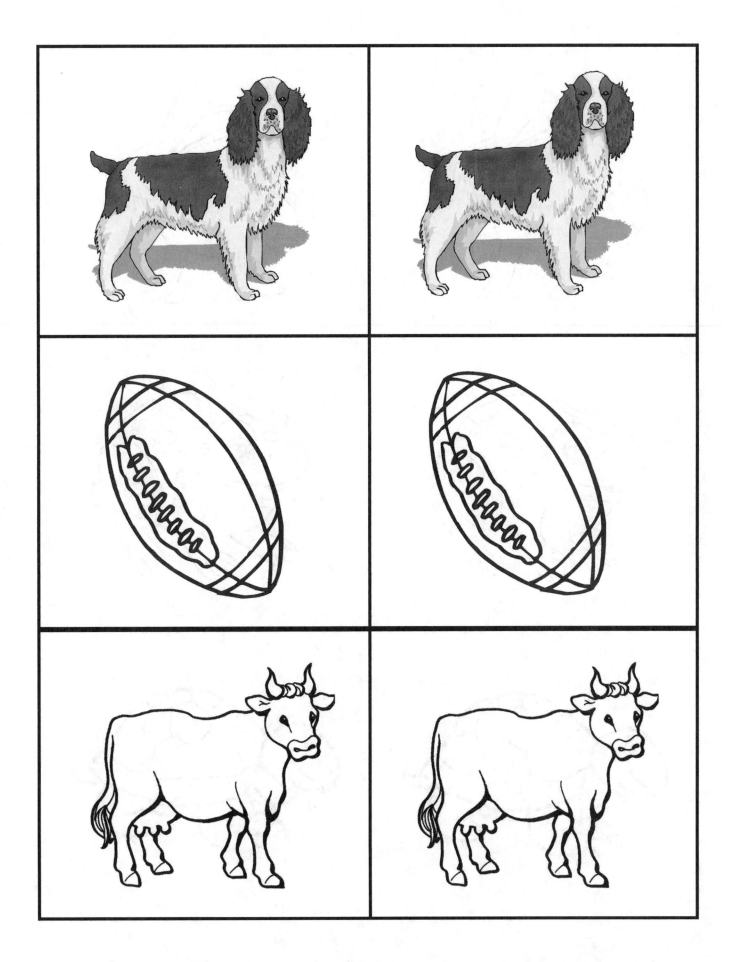

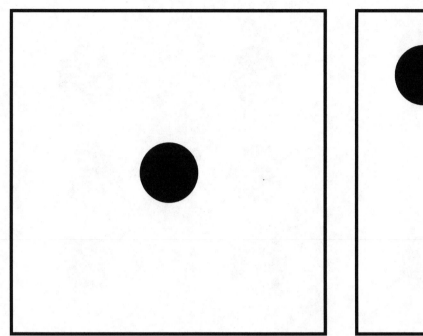

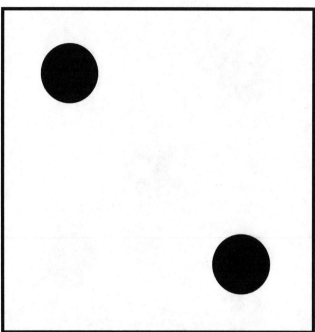

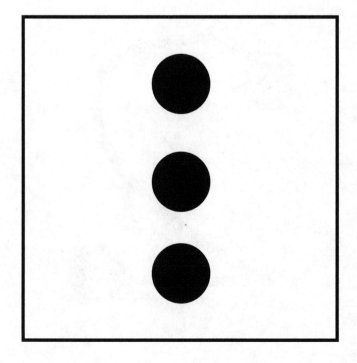

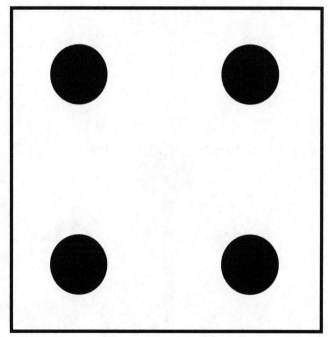

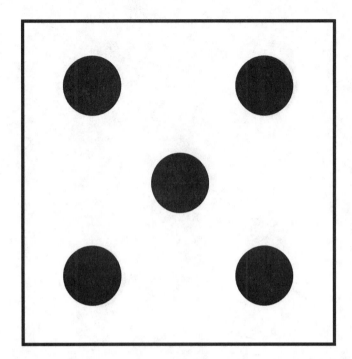

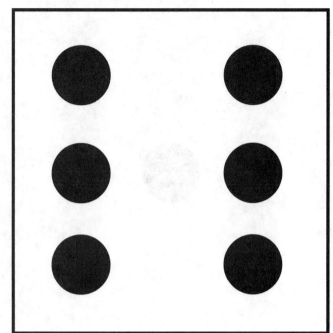

From Dots to Numerals

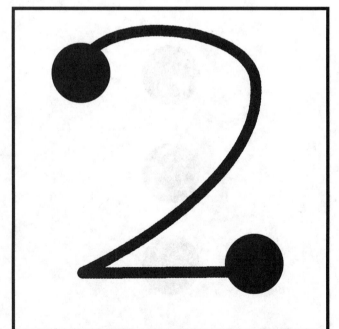

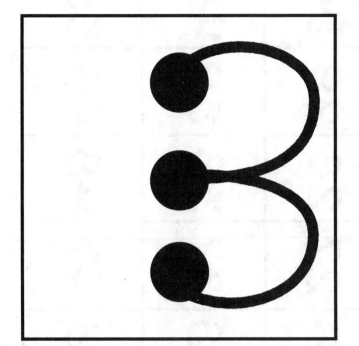

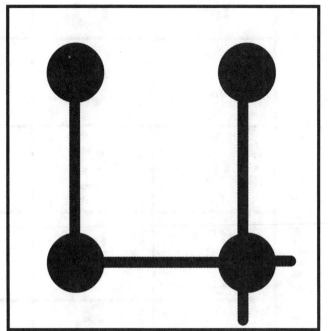

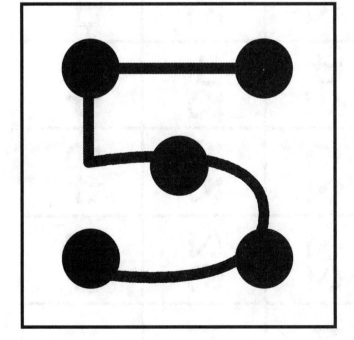

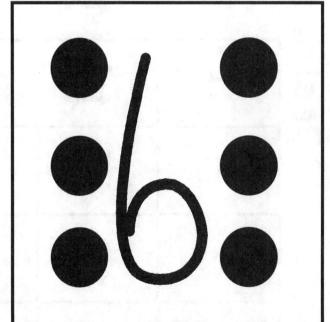

Missing Number Chart

1	2	3	4	5	6	7	8	9	10
11	12	13	14	15	16	17	18	19	20
21	22	23	24	25	26	27	28	29	30
31	32	33	34	35	36	37	38	39	40
41	42	43	44	45	46	47	48	49	50

51	52	53	54	55	56	57	58	59	60
61	62	63	64	65	66	67	68	69	70
71	72	73	74	75	76	77	78	79	80
81	82	83	84	85	86	87	88	89	90
91	92	93	94	95	96	97	98	99	100

Number Lines

1. Cut each line of ten out separately. You will then have 4 strips of ten. Start using just the numbers from 1 - 10. As the student progresses, add another line for the numbers 1-20.

1	2	3	4	5
11	12	13	14	15
21	22	23	24	25
31	32	33	34	35
41	42	43	44	45

2. Paperclip or Velcro the narrow cell which follows each of the *tens* to the next number sequence. You can then have a paper line from 1 - 40.

6	7	8	9	**10**	
16	17	18	19	**20**	
26	27	28	29	**30**	
36	37	38	39	**40**	
46	47	48	49	**50**	

Counting by Tens

1	2	3	4	5	6	7	8	9	10
11	12	13	14	15	16	17	18	19	20
21	22	23	24	25	26	27	28	29	30
31	32	33	34	35	36	37	38	39	40
41	42	43	44	45	46	47	48	49	50

Counting by Fives

1	2	3	4	5	6	7	8	9	10
11	12	13	14	15	16	17	18	19	20
21	22	23	24	25	26	27	28	29	30
31	32	33	34	35	36	37	38	39	40
41	42	43	44	45	46	47	48	49	50

Counting by Tens to 100

1	2	3	4	5	6	7	8	9	10
11	12	13	14	15	16	17	18	19	20
21	22	23	24	25	26	27	28	29	30
31	32	33	34	35	36	37	38	39	40
41	42	43	44	45	46	47	48	49	50
51	52	53	54	55	56	57	58	59	60
61	62	63	64	65	66	67	68	69	70
71	72	73	74	75	76	77	78	79	80
81	82	83	84	85	86	87	88	89	90
91	92	93	94	95	96	97	98	99	10

You may want to try and see if the students can handle all the detail of a 100's chart. Make sure that they are very secure with using 1 - 50 chart before you start to continue the pattern of counting by 10's from 51 - 100.

HUNDREDS Grown-ups	TENS Teens	ONES Kids	DECIMAL POINT WALL

<u>T</u>eens (Tens) and <u>K</u>ids (Ones)

Look at each number below. Draw a **red** circle around all the Teens (Tens). Draw a **blue** circle around the Kids (Ones). The student can just scribble the color over the number if it is difficult to draw a circle.

. 1 2	. 3 4
. 9 1	. 4 3
. 3 9	. 8 7
. 5 1	. 6 3
. 2 8	. 5 6
. 9 5	. 4 5
. 4 6	. 2 1
. 7 7	. 1 7
. 1 9	. 1 4

Fat Mat

Tens	Ones (units)

1 2

3 4

5 6
7 8

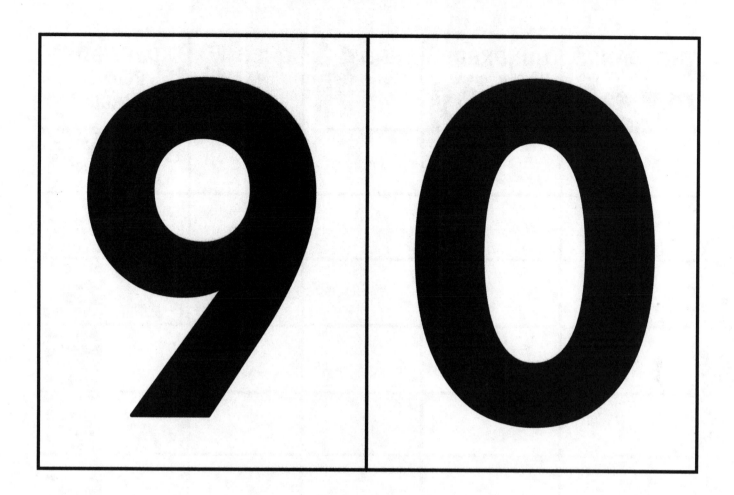

THOUSANDS More Grown-ups	HUNDREDS Grown-ups	TENS Teens	ONES Kids	DECIMAL POINT WALL
				•
				•
				•
				•
				•
				•
				•
				•
				•
				•
				•

Place Value -- Thousands

	Thousands	Hundreds	Tens	Ones
1.				
2.				
3.				
4.				
5.				
6.				
7.				
8.				
9.				
10.				

In a Line Game Board

Cut apart columns. Tape #6 to #7 to form a line from 1-12.
(This page makes two boards.)

1	7	1	7
2	8	2	8
3	9	3	9
4	10	4	10
5	11	5	11
6	12	6	12

Shortcuts to Addition

Adding Zero

When you add 0 to any number, the answer is the same number. If you add nothing to 5, the answer is 5. If you add nothing to 8, the answer is still 8.

1	2	4	6	5	3	7	9	8
+0	+0	+0	+0	+0	+0	+0	+0	+0

0	0	0	0	0	0	0	0	0
+5	+3	+9	+6	+1	+8	+2	+7	+4

Adding 1 to Any Number

When you add 1 to any number, the answer is the next highest number you can count. If you add 1 to 7, the next number higher is 8. So, 7 + 1 = 8. If you add 1 to 2, the next higher number is 3. So, 1 + 2 = 3.

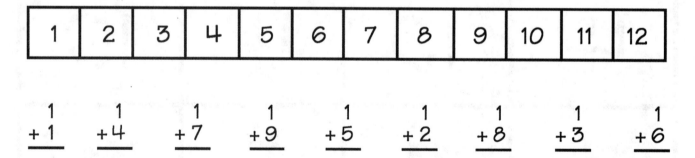

1	1	1	1	1	1	1	1	1
+1	+4	+7	+9	+5	+2	+8	+3	+6

4	2	7	9	5	8	6	3	1
+1	+1	+1	+1	+1	+1	+1	+1	+1

Name: _____

Date: _____

Addition of 3 Double- and Single-Digit Numbers

$$
\begin{array}{r} 17 \\ 2 \\ +\ 1 \\ \hline \end{array}
\qquad
\begin{array}{r} 3 \\ 11 \\ +\ 4 \\ \hline \end{array}
\qquad
\begin{array}{r} 13 \\ 3 \\ +\ 2 \\ \hline \end{array}
\qquad
\begin{array}{r} 9 \\ 9 \\ +\ 1 \\ \hline \end{array}
$$

$$
\begin{array}{r} 11 \\ 5 \\ +\ 1 \\ \hline \end{array}
\qquad
\begin{array}{r} 1 \\ 6 \\ +\ 6 \\ \hline \end{array}
\qquad
\begin{array}{r} 9 \\ 8 \\ +\ 3 \\ \hline \end{array}
\qquad
\begin{array}{r} 14 \\ 2 \\ +\ 4 \\ \hline \end{array}
$$

$$
\begin{array}{r} 1 \\ 8 \\ +\ 11 \\ \hline \end{array}
\qquad
\begin{array}{r} 10 \\ 0 \\ +\ 3 \\ \hline \end{array}
\qquad
\begin{array}{r} 4 \\ 9 \\ +\ 7 \\ \hline \end{array}
\qquad
\begin{array}{r} 2 \\ 1 \\ +\ 16 \\ \hline \end{array}
$$

Answer Sheet

Addition of 3 Double- and Single-Digit Numbers

```
   17          3         13          9
    2         11          3          9
 + 1        + 4        + 2        + 1
 ────       ────       ────       ────
   20         18         18         19
```

```
   11          1          9         14
    5          6          8          2
 + 1        + 6        + 3        + 4
 ────       ────       ────       ────
   17         13         20         20
```

```
    1         10          4          2
    8          0          9          1
 +11        + 3        + 7        +16
 ────       ────       ────       ────
   20         13         20         19
```

Name: _____

Date: _____

Addition with 2- and 3-Digit Numbers

```
   3 1 9          5 1 4
 + 6 6 1        + 1 1 7
 ▢▢▢            ▢▢▢
```

```
   4 7 9          2 2
 + 1 0 4        + 1 9
 ▢▢▢            ▢▢
```

```
   3 8      6 6          5 4 6
 + 5 3    + 2 8        + 2 6 3
 ▢▢       ▢▢           ▢▢▢
```

```
   7 7      5 5 9          2 9
 + 1 9    + 4 0 0        + 3 6
 ▢▢       ▢▢▢            ▢▢
```

Answer Sheet

Addition with 2- and 3-Digit Numbers

```
    3 1 9              5 1 4
  + 6 6 1            + 1 1 7
    9 8 0              6 3 1
```

```
    4 7 9              2 2
  + 1 0 4            + 1 9
    5 8 3              4 1
```

```
    3 8          6 6            5 4 6
  + 5 3        + 2 8          + 2 6 3
    9 1          9 4            8 0 9
```

```
    7 7          5 5 9            2 9
  + 1 9        + 4 0 0          + 3 6
    9 6          9 5 9            6 5
```

Name: _____

Date: _____

Addition with 3- and 4-Digit Numbers

```
    3  8  2          3  7  5  1
+   3  9  1      +   2  0  6  1
_____  _____
```

```
    5  6  2  9          3  8  6  9
+   2  1  7  0      +   4  1  2  0
_____    _____
```

```
    1  1  7          2  7  7  3
+   2  3  6      +   3  1  0  0
_____  _____
```

```
    6  3  9  5          3  8  0  1
+   3  2  0  4      +   2  1  1  8
_____    _____
```

Answer Sheet

Addition with 3- and 4-Digit Numbers

```
    3 8 2              3 7 5 1
  + 3 9 1            + 2 0 6 1
    7 7 3              5 8 1 2


    5 6 2 9              3 8 6 9
  + 2 1 7 0            + 4 1 2 0
    7 7 9 9              7 9 8 9


    1 1 7                2 7 7 3
  + 2 3 6              + 3 1 0 0
    3 5 3                5 8 7 3


    6 3 9 5              3 8 0 1
  + 3 2 0 4            + 2 1 1 8
    9 5 9 9              5 9 1 9
```

Name: _____

Date: _____

Addition with 3- and 4-Digit Numbers

```
    3 5 0              5 2 3 4
  + 2 7 9            + 2 1 8 9
```

```
    2 9 3 1              6 3 5 7
  + 2 0 6 3            + 1 6 3 2
```

```
    1 8 5              4 3 0 5
  + 1 6 4            + 1 0 5 7
```

```
    2 4 6 9              4 9 3 9
  + 4 6 6 1            + 2 0 4 0
```

Answer Sheet

Addition with 3- and 4-Digit Numbers

```
    3 5 0              5 2 3 4
  + 2 7 9            + 2 1 8 9
    6 2 9              7 4 2 3


    2 9 3 1              6 3 5 7
  + 2 0 6 3            + 1 6 3 2
    4 9 9 4              7 9 8 9


    1 8 5              4 3 0 5
  + 1 6 4            + 1 0 5 7
    3 4 9              5 3 6 2


    2 4 6 9              4 9 3 9
  + 4 6 6 1            + 2 0 4 0
    7 1 3 0              6 9 7 9
```

Addition Story Problems — with Drawings

1. I have 5 footballs.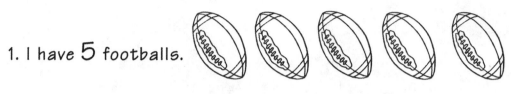

I found 2 more footballs in the garage.

Count the number of footballs. The total number of footballs is _____ .

---

2. There are 6 gym shoes in my closet.

I bring 4 more gym shoes to my closet.

I have (how many?) shoes in my closet _____ .

---

3. I have 4 boots to wear.

My dad bought me 2 new boots.

Count all my boots. How many do I have now? _____

4. I have **1** dog.

My best friend has **3** dogs.

Together, we have _____ dogs.

_____

5. I have picked **4** flowers.

My mother picked **6** flowers.

The total number of flowers is _____ .

_____

6. We have **4** trees in our back yard.

We have **3** trees in our front yard.

How many trees do we have in our front and back yard together? _____

7. I have 4 small sailboats.

I race them in the creek. My best friend also has 4 boats.

We have (how many?) _____ boats altogether.

---

8. In our living room, we have 7 candles.

Mom bought 3 new candles.

Now we have (how many?) _____ candles.

---

9. I have 3 pieces of candy.

My sister has 2 pieces.   My brother has 5 pieces.

We have (how many?) _____ pieces of candy altogether?

Drawing or Stamping-Out Story Problems

Note: *The following problems should be explained one by one by the teacher. The student is not supposed to do the problems by reading this sheet. Read or tell one problem and demonstrate how to draw or stamp the number of items and then count to find the total.*

1. In the school baseball game, Ellen's team made 7 points. Tom's team made 5 points. Who won the game? How many total points were made in the game?

2. Doug's mother baked 36 chocolate chip cookies for the class party. Greg's older sister baked 17 sugar cookies and Rosie baked 24 peanut butter cookies for the party. The total number of cookies for the class party was _____.

3. Jake had 7 fish in his fish bowl. One of the fish gave birth to 20 baby fish. Jake now has _____ fish in his fish bowl. He needs to get a bigger fish bowl!

4. Sandy and Nancy went on a picnic. They ate 4 sandwiches, 2 apples and 3 brownies all together. How many things did they eat at the picnic? (Question format used)

5. At the zoo I saw 20 monkeys climbing in the trees. Four monkeys were playing in the water. How many monkeys did I see altogether? (Question format)

6. On a summer campout, we went searching for red rocks. James found 23 red rocks, Jeff found 15 red rocks, and Stephanie found 16 red rocks. How many red rocks did James, Jeff and Stephanie find altogether? (Question format)

7. Kathy found 15 white shells on the beach. She also found 7 colored shells. How many shells altogether did she find? (Question format)

8. Paul built a sand castle on the beach. He used 11 pails of wet sand to build his castle. He then used 2 pails of dry sand to make the walls of the castle look smooth. How many pails of sand did he use for the sand castle? (Question format)

9. Nate caught the football and ran 34 yards. Then he ran 23 yards for a touchdown. How many yards did he run altogether? (Question format)

10. In another game, Nate ran 13 yards with the football. The next play he handed off the football to Mark, and Mark ran for 21 yards. How many yards did Nate and Mark run altogether? (Question format)

11. Leslie ate 11 pancakes on Saturday morning. DeDe ate 3 pancakes. How many did they eat altogether? (Question format)

The word *question format* in parentheses indicates that the problem may be harder for the student to understand because the subject and verb order is changed by using the question format.

Name: _____

Date: _____

Subtraction with 2-Digit Numbers

$$
\begin{array}{r} 50 \\ -11 \\ \hline \end{array}
\qquad
\begin{array}{r} 81 \\ -75 \\ \hline \end{array}
\qquad
\begin{array}{r} 75 \\ -69 \\ \hline \end{array}
$$

$$
\begin{array}{r} 10 \\ -10 \\ \hline \end{array}
\qquad
\begin{array}{r} 93 \\ -25 \\ \hline \end{array}
\qquad
\begin{array}{r} 34 \\ -19 \\ \hline \end{array}
$$

$$
\begin{array}{r} 86 \\ -61 \\ \hline \end{array}
\qquad
\begin{array}{r} 33 \\ -25 \\ \hline \end{array}
\qquad
\begin{array}{r} 76 \\ -76 \\ \hline \end{array}
$$

Answer Sheet

Subtraction with 2-Digit Numbers

$$
\begin{array}{r}
50 \\
-11 \\
\hline
39
\end{array}
\qquad
\begin{array}{r}
81 \\
-75 \\
\hline
6
\end{array}
\qquad
\begin{array}{r}
75 \\
-69 \\
\hline
6
\end{array}
$$

$$
\begin{array}{r}
10 \\
-10 \\
\hline
0
\end{array}
\qquad
\begin{array}{r}
93 \\
-25 \\
\hline
68
\end{array}
\qquad
\begin{array}{r}
34 \\
-19 \\
\hline
15
\end{array}
$$

$$
\begin{array}{r}
86 \\
-61 \\
\hline
25
\end{array}
\qquad
\begin{array}{r}
33 \\
-25 \\
\hline
8
\end{array}
\qquad
\begin{array}{r}
76 \\
-76 \\
\hline
0
\end{array}
$$

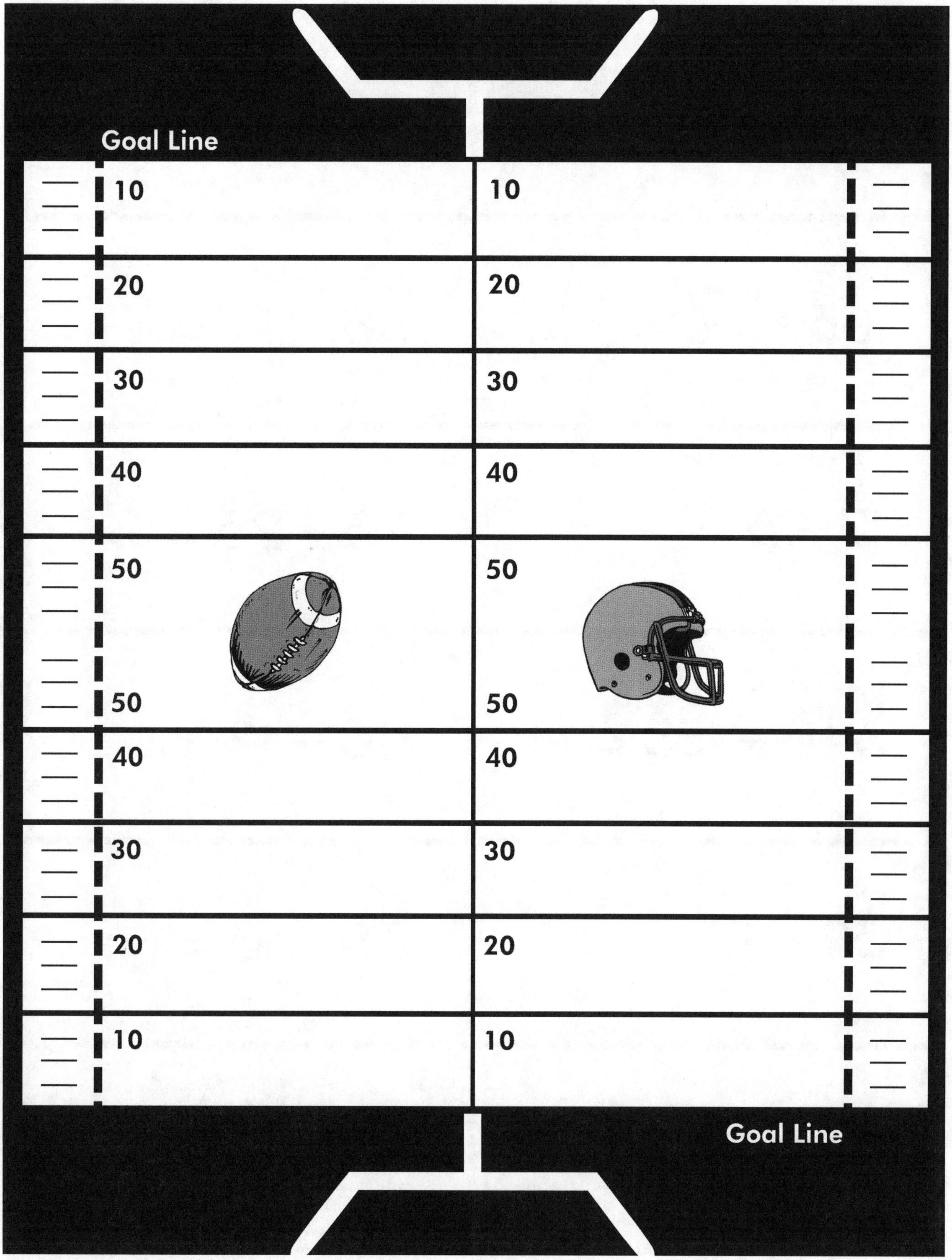

Goal Line

10	10
20	20
30	30
40	40
50	50
50	50
40	40
30	30
20	20
10	10

Goal Line

1 13 − 6 =	2 46 − 4 =
3 135 − 30 =	4 56 − 18 =
5 17 − 8 =	6 76 − 25 =
7 348 − 153 =	8 46 − 12 =
9 39 − 17 =	10 35 − 13 =
11 63 − 31 =	12 69 − 25 =

1 $43 - 6 =$	**2** $22 - 4 =$
3 $105 - 31 =$	**4** $77 - 19 =$
5 $140 - 8 =$	**6** $32 - 24 =$
7 $333 - 192 =$	**8** $82 - 12 =$
9 $35 - 17 =$	**10** $187 - 15 =$
11 $42 - 33 =$	**12** $100 - 23 =$

1 Great run! Go forward 20 yards.	**2** Offsides! Go back 10 yards.
3 Fumble! Ball goes to other team.	**4** Intercepted pass! Ball goes to other team.
5 Completed pass! Go forward 30 yards.	**6** Penalty Holding! Go back 10 yards.
7 Kicked field goal! Score 3 points	**8** Out of bounds. No gain on the play.
9 Completed pass! Go forward 20 yards.	**10** Fumble! Ball goes to other team.
11 Great run! Go forward 20 yards.	**12** Backfield in motion. Go back 10 yards.

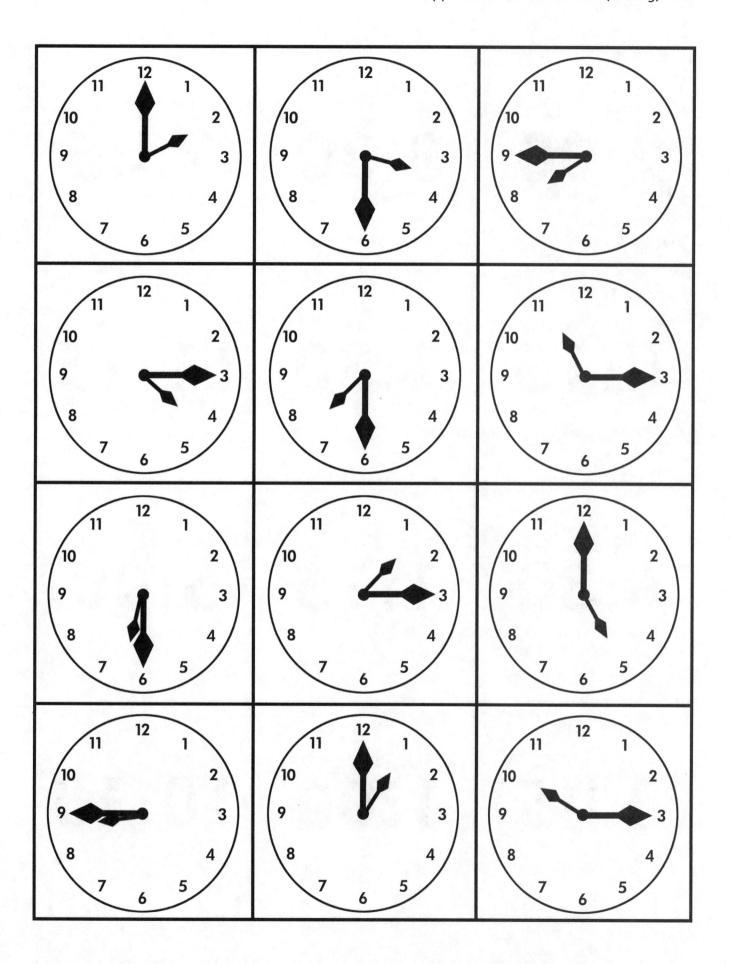

2:00	**3:30**	**7:45**
4:15	**7:30**	**11:15**
6:30	**1:15**	**5:00**
8:45	**1:00**	**10:15**

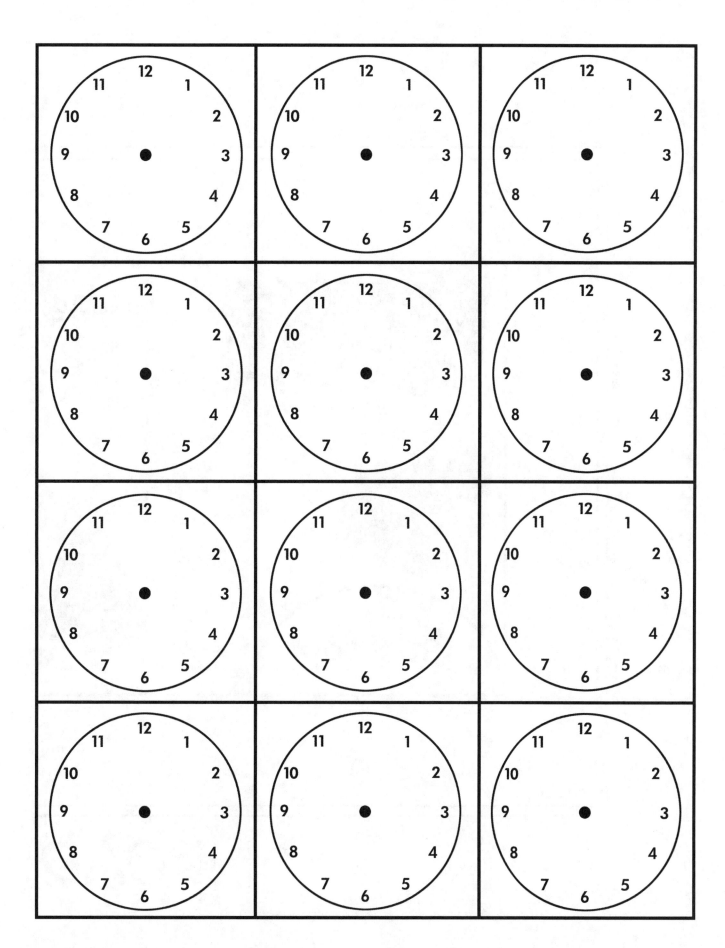

Pit Stop

Stop

ROAD

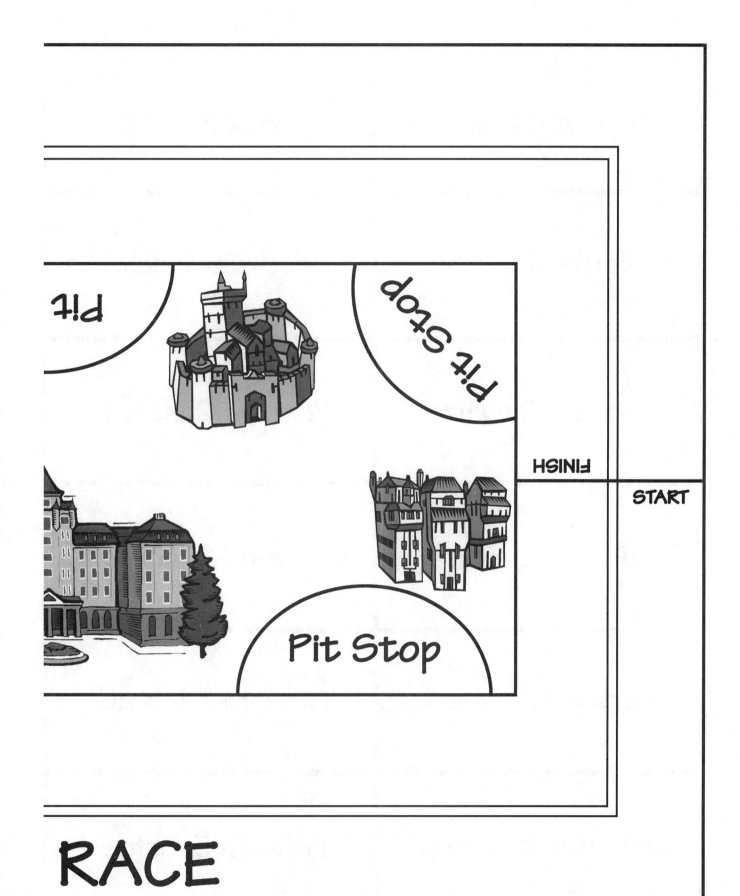

Forward 1 inch.	Forward 1 inch.
Forward 1 inch.	Forward 1 inch.
Forward 2 inches.	Forward 2 inches.
Forward 2 inches.	Forward 2 inches.
Forward 3 inches.	Forward 3 inches.
Forward 3 inches.	Forward 3 inches.

Forward 4 inches.	Forward 4 inches.
Forward 4 inches.	Forward 4 inches.
Go to next pit stop and miss one turn.	Go to next pit stop and miss one turn.
Go to next pit stop and miss one turn.	Go to next pit stop and miss one turn.
Oil on track. Slide back 1 inch.	Oil on track. Slide back 1 inch.
Oil on track. Slide back 1 inch.	Oil on track. Slide back 1 inch.

Forward 5 inches.	Forward 5 inches.
Forward 5 inches.	Forward 5 inches.
Go to next pit stop and miss one turn.	Go to next pit stop and miss one turn.
Go to next pit stop and miss one turn.	Go to next pit stop and miss one turn.
Oil on track. Slide back 2 inches.	Oil on track. Slide back 2 inches.
Oil on track. Slide back 2 inches.	Oil on track. Slide back 2 inches.

Avoid accident.
Slide ahead 2 inches.

Avoid accident.
Slide ahead 2 inches.

Avoid accident.
Slide ahead 2 inches.

Avoid accident.
Slide ahead 2 inches.

Cause wreck!
Slide back 4 inches.

Cause wreck!
Slide back 4 inches.

Cause wreck!
Slide back 4 inches.

Cause wreck!
Slide back 4 inches.

Cause wreck!
Slide back 3 inches.

Cause wreck!
Slide back 3 inches.

Cause wreck!
Slide back 3 inches.

Cause wreck!
Slide back 3 inches.

Road Race Car Pieces

Directions to make cars for the Race Car Game:

1. Photocopy and cut apart on the solid lines, making individual car pieces.
2. Fold on dotted lines.
3. Overlap bottom flaps to make a triangle-shaped stand.
4. Secure bottom with two paper clips.

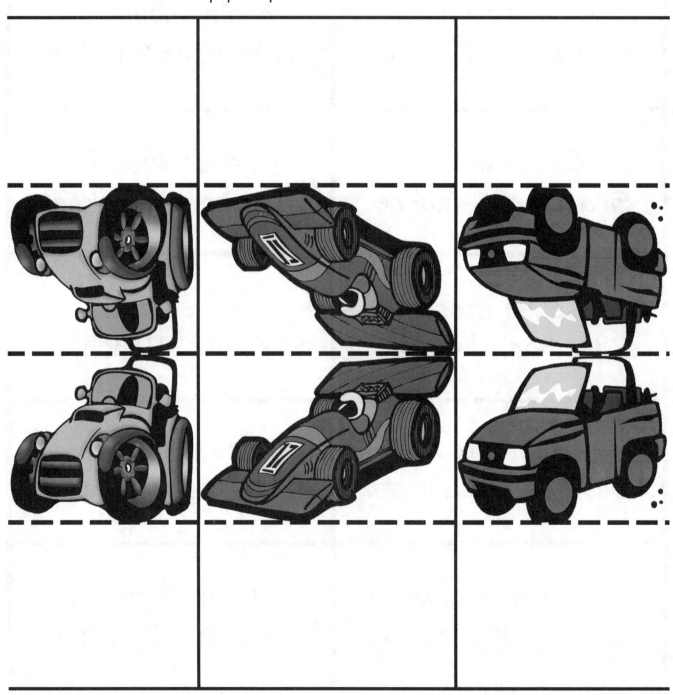

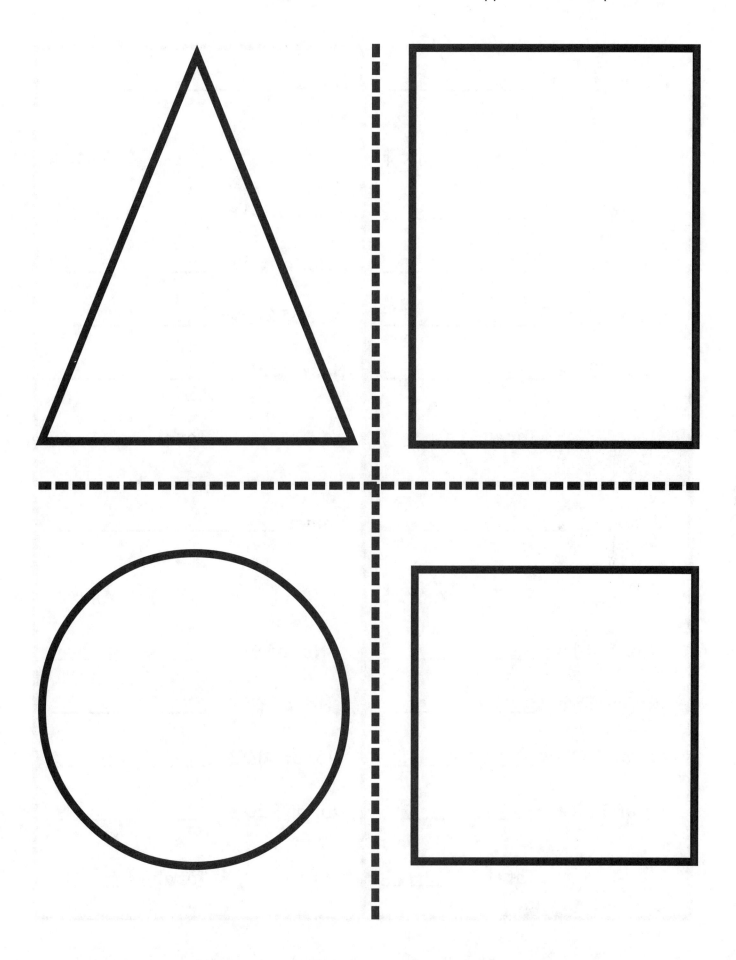

Name: _____

Amt. $

No. of $1's   ____   _____

No. of $5's   ____   _____

No. of $10's   ____   _____

No. of $20's   ____   _____

Total   _____

Name: _____

Amt. $

No. of $1's   ____   _____

No. of $5's   ____   _____

No. of $10's   ____   _____

No. of $20's   ____   _____

Total   _____

Name: _____

Amt. $

No. of $1's   ____   _____

No. of $5's   ____   _____

No. of $10's   ____   _____

No. of $20's   ____   _____

Total   _____

Name: _____

Amt. $

No. of $1's   ____   _____

No. of $5's   ____   _____

No. of $10's   ____   _____

No. of $20's   ____   _____

Total   _____

HUNDREDS	TENS	ONES	DECIMAL POINT WALL		CENTS	
			•			
			•			
			•			
			•			
			•			
			•			
			•			
			•			
			•			
			•			
			•			
			•			

$1.11	$17.62
$9.08	$6.10
$12.10	$18.12
$4.77	$8.23
$1.75	$6.22
$4.03	$1.04

$9.06	$6.10
$11.09	$7.05
$ .25	$ .05
$ .10	$ .50
$ .01	$ .90
$ .75	$ .30

Exact Dollar Amount	Next-Highest Dollar Amount
1.	1.
2.	2.
3.	3.
4.	4.
5.	5.
6.	6.
7.	7.
8.	8.
9.	9.
10.	10.
11.	11.
12.	12.

References

Baratta-Lorton, M. (1991). *Workjobs: Activity-centered learning for early childhood education*. Menlo Park: Addison-Wesley.

Barkley, R. (1992). *ADHD: What can we do?(video)*. New York: Guilford Publications, Inc.

Barkley, R. (1997). *ADHD and the nature of self-control.* New York: Guilford Publications, Inc.

Beninghof, A.M. (1998). *SenseAble strategies: Teaching diverse learners*. Longmont, CO: Sopris West.

Berk, L.E. (2001). *Development through the lifespan* (pp. 221-234*)*. Boston: Allyn and Bacon.

Bird, G. & Buckley, S. (2001). *Number skills for individuals with Down syndrome—An overview*. Southsea, Hampshire, United Kingdom: The Down Syndrome Educational Trust.

Bird, G. (2001). *Number skills development for infants with Down syndrome (0-5 years)*. Southsea, Hampshire, United Kingdom: The Down Syndrome Educational Trust.

Bird, G. & Buckley, S. (2001). *Number skills development for individuals with Down syndrome (5-11 years)*. Southsea, Hampshire, United Kingdom: The Down Syndrome Educational Trust.

Bird, G. & Buckley, S. (2001). *Number skills development for individuals with Down syndrome (11-16)*. Southsea, Hampshire, United Kingdom: The Down Syndrome Educational Trust.

Blenk, K. (1995). *Making school inclusion work: A guide to everyday practice.* Cambridge, MA: Brookline Books.

Bondy, A. & Frost, L. (2002). *A picture's worth: PECS and other visual communication strategies in autism.* Bethesda, MD: Woodbine House.

Bruni, M. (1998). *Fine Motor Skills in Children with Down Syndrome: A Guide for Parents and Professionals.* Bethesda, MD: Woodbine House.

Buckley, S.J., Bird, G. & Byrnes, A. (2001). As quoted in Bird, G. and Buckley, S. (2001). *Number skills for individuals with Down syndrome: An overview.* Southsea, Hampshire, United Kingdom: The Down Syndrome Educational Trust.

Buckley, S. & Bird, G. (1994). *Meeting the educational needs of children with Down syndrome: A handbook for teachers.* Southsea, Hampshire, United Kingdom: The Down Syndrome Educational Trust.

Buckley, S. J. & Sacks, B.I. (1987). *The adolescent with Down syndrome: Life for the teenager and for the family.* Portsmouth: University of Portsmouth, UK.

Buckley, S.J. (1985). Attaining basic educational skills: Reading, writing and number. In D. Lane and B. Stratford (Eds.), *Current approaches to Down syndrome.* London: Holt Saunders.

Charlesworth, R. & Radeloff, D.J. (1991). *Experiences in math for young children,* (pp. 5-7). Albany, NY: Delmar Publishers.

Chilcote, E. & Blaine, J. (1975). *Happy math + happy teacher = happy kids.* Fort Collins: Scott Resources, Inc.

Clements, D.H., Malloy, C.E., Mosely, L.G. & Silbey, R.R. (2002). *Mathematics: PreK – 6 (series), Teacher's guide.* New York: Macmillan/McGraw-Hill.

Copeland, R.W. (1984). *How children learn mathematics.* New York: Macmillan.

De Graaf, E. & de Graaf, M. (1997). Learning elementary maths: Case study of a Dutch boy. Workshop presented at the Down Syndrome World Conference, Madrid, Spain.

Ebeling, D.G., Deschenes, C. & Sprague, J. (1994). *Adapting curriculum and instruction in inclusive classrooms: A teacher's desk reference.* Bloomington: Institute for the Study of Developmental Disabilities.

Feingold, A. (1965). *Teaching arithmetic to young children.* New York: John Day Company.

Feldman, C. & Peckham, B. (2000). *Looking into math: Teacher's guide, Books 1, 2, 3.* Ridgewood, New Jersey, Public Schools. Cambridge: Educators Publishing Service.

Fowler, A.E. (1995). Linguistic variability in persons with Down syndrome. In L. Nadel & D. Rosenthal (Eds.), *Down syndrome: Living and learning in the community.* New York: Wiley-Liss.

Fredericks, H.D. (2001). Education from childhood through adolescence. In Pueschel, S.M. (Ed.), *A parent's guide to Down syndrome: Toward a brighter future.* Baltimore: Paul H. Brookes Publishing.

Freeman, S.F.N., & Hodapp, R.M. (2000). Educating children with Down syndrome: Linking behavioral characteristics to promising intervention strategies. *Down Syndrome Quarterly, 5 (1),* 1-9.

Gray, C. (2000). *New social stories.* Arlington, Texas: Future Horizons.

Greenes, C., Immerzeel, G., Schulman & Spungin, R. (1989). *Math Gems: Sparkling activities for early childhood classrooms.* Allen, Texas: DLM Teaching Resources (no longer available).

Hammeken, P.A. (1996). *Inclusion: 450 strategies for success.* Minnetonka, MN: Peytral Publications.

Hembree, R. & Dessart, D.J. (1986). Effects of hand-held calculators in precollege mathematics education: A meta-analyhsis. *Journal for Research in Mathematics Education, 17,* 83-99.

Hodgdon, L.A. (1995) *Visual strategies for improving communication: Practical supports for school and home.* Troy, MI: QuirkRoberts Publishing.

Horstmeier, D. (2000). Communication. In Pueschel, S. (Ed.) *A parent's guide to Down syndrome: Toward a brighter future.* Baltimore: Paul Brookes Publishing.

Hunt, N. (1967). *The world of Nigel Hunt: The diary of a Mongoloid youth.* New York: Taplinger Pub. Co.

Irwin, K.C. (1989). The school achievement of children with Down's syndrome. *New Zealand Medical Journal, 102 (860),* 11-13.

Kilpatrick, J., Swafford, J. & Findell, B. (Eds.) (2001). *Adding it up: Helping children learn mathematics.* Center for Education. Washington, DC: National Academy Press.

Klein, P.S. & Arieli, M.(1997). Mediated learning and its application to the enhancement of mathematical abilities and children with Down syndrome. *Journal of Developmental Disabilities and Learning Disorders, 1,* 299-319.

Kliewer, C. (1998). *Schooling children with Down syndrome: Toward an understanding of possibility.* New York: Teachers College Press.

Kumin, L. (2003). *Early communication skills for children with Down syndrome: A guide for parents and professionals.* Bethesda, MD: Woodbine House.

Kumin, L. (2001). *Classroom language skills for children with Down syndrome: A guide for parents and teachers.* Bethesda, MD: Woodbine House.

Liautaud, J. (1996). *Addition the fun way.* Sandy, UT: City Creek Press.

McClannahan, L. & Krantz, P. (1999). *Activity schedules for children with autism: Teaching independent behavior.* Bethesda, MD: Woodbine House.

Miller, J.F., Leddy, M. & Leavitt, L.A. (1999). *Improving the communication of people with Down syndrome.* Baltimore: Paul H. Brookes Publishing Co.

National Council of Teachers of Mathematics (2000, 1989). *Professional standards for teaching mathematics.* Reston, Va.: NCTM.

Nye, J. & Bird, G. (1996). Developing number and maths skills, *DownsEd News,* 6(2), 1-7.

Ohio Department of Education (2003). *Academic content standards: K-12 mathematics.* Columbus: Center for Curriculum and Assessment, ODE.

Olsen, J.Z. (1998). *Handwriting Without Tears.* Potomac, MD: Handwriting without Tears (p. 39-44).

Reys, R., Suydam, M.N. & Lindquist, M.M. (1995). *Helping Children Learn Mathematics.* Boston: Allyn and Bacon.

Rynders, J., Abery, B.H., Spiker, D., Olive, M.L., Sheran, C.P. & Zajac, R.J. (1997). Improving educational programming for individuals with Down syndrome: Engaging the fuller competence. *Down Syndrome Quarterly, 2* (1), 1-11.

Seagoe, M.V. (1964). *Yesterday was Tuesday, all day and all night.* Boston: Little, Brown Publishing.

Semple, J.L. (1986). *Semple math: Level I, teacher's manual.* Attleboro Falls, MA.: Stevenson Learning Skills, Inc.

Sharp, D. & Martin, R. (1982). *Bucket math book.* Lansing, MI: M-R Publications (no longer available).

Shepperdson, B. (1994). Attainments in reading and number of teenagers and adults with Down's syndrome. *Down Syndrome Research and Practice, 2* (3).

Shoecraft, P. (1984). *Math games and activities, Vol. I.* Palo Alto: Dale Seymour Publications.

Smith, S.S. (1997). *Early childhood mathematics.* Boston: Allyn and Bacon.

Stainback, S., & Stainback, W. (1992). *Curriculum considerations in inclusive classrooms: Facilitating learning for all students.* Baltimore: Paul H. Brookes Publishing Co.

Stephens, T.M. (1973). *Instructional activities based upon specific math skills.* No longer available.

Stevenson, N. (1998). *Stevenson language skills program: Basic blue level manual.* Attleboro Falls, MA: Stevenson Learning Skills, Inc.

Thornton, C.A. (2000). *Teaching mathematics to children with special needs.* Menlo Park: Addison-Wesley Publishing Company.

Wolpert, G. (1996). *The educational challenges inclusion study.* New York: National Down Syndrome Society.

Zaner-Bloser Handwriting '03 (2003). Columbus, OH: Zaner-Bloser.

Resources

BOOKS

MATH ACTIVITIES

American Education Publishing. *The Complete Book of Math Games.* Columbus: McGraw-Hill Children's Publishing, 2001.

American Education Publishing. *The Complete Book of Math (Grades 3-4).* Columbus: McGraw-Hill Children's Publishing, 2001.

American Education Publishing. *The Complete Book of Math (Grades 1-2).* Columbus: McGraw-Hill Children's Publishing, 2001.

American Education Publishing. *The Complete Book of Time and Money.* Columbus: McGraw-Hill Children's Publishing, 2001.

Hohmann, C. *High/Scope, K-3, Curriculum Series: Mathematics.* Ypsilanti, MI: High/Scope Press, 1991.

Hopping Good Cents: A New Method for Teaching the Counting of Money. Austin, TX: Pro-Ed, 1999.

Johnson, Virginia. *Hands-on Math: Manipulative Activities for the K-1 Classroom.* Cypress, CA: Creative Teaching Press, Inc., 1994.

Kaye, Peggy. *Games for Math: Playful Ways to Help Your Child Learn Math from Kindergarten to Third Grade.* New York: Pantheon, 1987.

Schiller, Pam & Rossano, J. *The Instant Curriculum: 500 Developmentally Appropriate Learning Activities for Busy Teachers of Young Children.* Beltsville, MD: Griffin House, 1990.

Stenmark, Jean Kerr, Thompson, Virginia & Cossey, Ruth. *Family Math.* Berkeley, CA: Lawrence Hall of Science, 1986.

COUNTING BOOKS

There are so many counting books on the market, you can find a book to match almost any child's interests. This section includes only a very small sample of books available. Books listed here are included because they are either counting books with a twist (for example, backwards counting), because they may be especially appropriate for children with Down syndrome, or because they may be more appropriate for older children and young adults who could benefit from looking at counting books.

Baker, Keith. *Big Fat Hen.* Orlando, FL: Harcourt Brace, 1997.
A simple counting book in which bright-colored, humorous pictures illustrate the rhyme, "One, two, buckle my shoe" (only up to "Nine, Ten, a big fat hen"). May be a useful rhyme for teaching rote counting.

Bang, Molly. *Ten, Nine, Eight.* New York, NY: Greenwillow, 1996.
A bedtime book in which a father and daughter count backwards from 10 to 1.

Brown, Ruth. *Ten Seeds.* New York, NY: Alfred A. Knopf, 2001.
Big bold pictures show what happens to 10 seeds after they are planted. They are carried away one by one by an ant, a pigeon, a slug, etc. Excellent for counting backwards from ten.

Gerth, Melanie. *Ten Little Ladybugs.* Santa Monica, CA: Piggy Toes Press (Intervisual Books), 2001.
Molded plastic ladybugs on each page give kids something to touch while they count. You begin with 10 ladybugs on the first page and each subsequent page has one fewer.

Girnis, Margaret. *1 2 3 for You and Me.* Mortons Grove, IL: Albert Whitman, 2001.
This book is illustrated with photos of children with Down syndrome, who pose with interesting objects, people, and animals in quantities from 1 to 20.

Johnson, Stephen T. *City by Numbers.* New York: Puffin, 2003.
A good book for older learners working on number recognition, this book contains realistic paintings of city scenes in which numbers are formed by objects in the scenes (e.g., the 8 is made from two round trash cans as seen from above).

MacDonald, Suse. *Look Whooo's Counting.* New York, NY: Scholastic, 2000.
Baby owl learns to count by encountering various numbers of creatures that look like numerals. For instance, there are 8 spiders that are shaped like 8's. A good book for reinforcing rote counting to 10, as each time the owl encounters something to count, she starts from 1 to count.

Major League Baseball 1 2 3. New York, NY: Dorling Kindersley Publishing, 2001.
Clear, colorful photos of baseball-related items, from 1 baseball to 10 baseball caps.

Marzollo, Jean & Wick, Walter. *I Spy* series. New York: Cartwheel Books, various dates.
Books in the *I Spy* series feature "picture riddles"—full color spreads of photos of many different objects with rhyming instructions to spy things such as 5 clothespins or buttons or pencils. For students who are not overwhelmed by busy pages, the books can also be helpful in teaching about categorizing (for instance, finding the specified number of Christmas ornaments, when none of the ornaments look alike). The *I Spy Little* series of books are simplified

board book editions with fewer objects per page and easier instructions. *I Spy Little Numbers* might be especially useful for students learning to recognize their numbers.

NFL Football 1 2 3. New York, NY: Dorling Kindersley Publishing, 1999.
   Photos of football-related items to count.

BOOKS THAT GO UP TO 100 OR BEYOND

Lee, Chinlun. *The Very Kind Rich Lady and Her One Hundred Dogs.* Cambridge, MA: Candlewick Press, 2001.
   On each page, some of the rich lady's dogs are introduced by name, until at the end, she calls them all in for dinner by name (all 100 of them).

Nolan, Helen. *How Much, How Many, How Fat, How Heavy, How Long, How Tall Is 1000?* Tonawanda, NY: Kids Can Press, 2001.
   This book explores different ways of looking at 1000—when is 1000 a lot and when is it a little?

Schwartz, Stephen. *How Much Is a Million?* New York: HarperTrophy, 1993.
   A good book to help child visualize how much a million actually is.

Sloat, Teri. *From One to One Hundred.* Upper Saddle River, NJ: Scott Foresman, 1995.
   This book offers many interesting objects to count on each page, from 1 to 10 and then by tens to 100. Numbers are shown as numerals and also written out in words.

Soderberg, Erin. *Count to 100 with the NBA.* New York: Scholastic, 2002.
   Count basketballs, basketball players from 1 to 10 and then by tens to 100.

OTHER MATH BOOKS FOR CHILDREN

Burns, Marilyn, editor. *Hello Math Reader* series. New York, NY: Scholastic, various dates.
   The *Hello Math* series offers books with story lines that focus on a variety of math concepts, followed by a few follow-up activities to try at home. They are written on various levels, from Preschool to Grade 3. For students who love reading but are not too fond of math, they can be a good way to sneakily introduce or reinforce math concepts. For example, *Even Steven and Odd Todd* (by Kathryn Cristaldi) explores the concept of even vs. odd numbers with an amusing story about two cousins, one of whom always wants even numbers of things (such as pizza slices), and the other of whom wants odd numbers. *Monster Money* shows cute monsters buying pets for coin combinations (clearly depicted) that add up to ten cents. Some books in the series may be too wordy or complex for some children with Down syndrome; look before you buy.

Carle, Eric. *Papa, Please Get the Moon for Me.* New York: Simon and Schuster, 1991.
   When a child asks her father to get the moon for her, he gets a very *long* ladder (a foldout illustrates how long it is) to climb up to the moon, which is very *big* (again, a foldout shows what "big" means). *High* and *small* are other concepts illustrated in this brightly colored book for young children. (The author's classic book, *The Very Hungry Caterpillar,* is excellent for teaching beginning counting, with holes to touch and count to see how many things the caterpillar ate each day.)

Christian, Cheryl. *How Many?* Starlight Books, 2001.
This book provides good illustrations of "one more" for young children. Sample text: "Here are two puppies. Here is one more puppy. How many puppies can you see?"

Dodds, Dayle Ann. *The Shape of Things*. Upper Saddle River, NJ: Scott Foresman, 1996.
Basic shapes are shown by themselves and incorporated into colorful pictures of everyday objects.

Duke, Kate. *One Guinea Pig is Not Enough*. New York, NY: Puffin, 2001.
One lonely guinea pig keeps on searching for more guinea pigs to play with in this amusing story that illustrates the concept of "one more" or counting on by ones up to twenty.

Duke, Kate. *Twenty Is Too Many*. New York, NY: Dutton, 2000.
This sequel to the previous title illustrates the concept of "one less" or subtracting by one, as one by one, something happens to the twenty guinea pigs who start out on a sailboat.

Hoban, Tana. *Is It Larger? Is It Smaller?* New York, NY: HarperTrophy, 1997.
Clear photos of everyday objects that illustrate relative sizes.

Hoban, Tana. *So Many Circles, So Many Squares*. New York, NY: Greenwillow, 1998.
Colored photos of common objects that are shaped like circles or squares.

Leedy, Loreen. *Measuring Penny*. New York, NY: Henry Holt, 2000.
This picture book explores the concepts of self-measurements vs. standard measurements as the narrator uses items such as dog biscuits, cotton swabs, and rulers to figure out how big and heavy her dog is, how much it eats, etc.

Miller, Margaret. *Big and Little*. New York, NY: Greenwillow, 1998.
Clear photographs highlight the contrast between big and little balls, girls, hats, and other everyday objects.

Murphy, Stuart J. *MathStart Series*. New York, NY: HarperCollins, various dates.
The *MathStart* series consists of illustrated books, each intended to teach one basic math concept. Books are available on three levels (Level 1/Ages 3 up, Level 2/Ages 6 up, and Level 3/Ages 7 Up). Some of them may be too wordy or have plots that are confusing for students with language delays, but others provide good, clear visual explanations of concepts. For example, *Missing Mittens* (2001) provides a good explanation of even vs. odd numbers. Preview individual books in the series at a library or bookstore to judge their appropriateness.

SOFTWARE

Attainment Company
P.O. Box 930160
Verona, WI 53593-0160
800-327-4269
www.attainmentcompany.com
Products include *Match Time* and *Basic Coins* software.

Barnum Software
5191 Morgan Territory Road
Clayton, CA 94517
800-553-9155
www.barnumsoftware.com
The Quarter Mile, good software for drilling math facts at the learner's own pace.

Don Johnston
26799 W. Commerce Dr.
Volo, IL 60073
800-999-4660
www.donjohnston.com
Access to Math (math worksheet program) and *Big:Calc* (onscreen talking calculator).

Education.com
310-649-8007 (customer service)
877-268-6197 (orders)
www.education.com
Source for Knowledge Adventure software, including the *Math Blaster* series. The website includes an online "game room" with math games to try (at www.education.com/blaster/games).

EdVenture Software
203-299-0291 (fax)
www.edven.com
Gold Medal Math, software for drilling math facts.

IntelliTools, Inc.
1720 Corporate Center
Petaluma, CA 94954
800-899-6687 (US); 800-353-1107 (Canada)
www.intellikeys.com
Programmable adaptable keyboards (IntelliKeys), touch screens; some math software designed for individuals with disabilities focusing on early concepts.

Mayer-Johnson Company
P.O. Box 1579
Solana Beach, CA 92075
858-550-0084; 858-550-0449 (fax)
www.mayer-johnson.com
Makers of Boardmaker software and other products featuring the Picture Communication Symbols®.

Riverdeep
500 Redwood Blvd.
Novato, CA 94947
415-763-4700
www.riverdeep.net
Distributors of products by Edmark (such as *Millie's Math House*), as well as software by the Learning Company and Broderbund. Some free demos are available online.

SOURCES OF TEACHING MATERIALS

Attainment Company
P.O. Box 930160
Verona, WI 53593-0160
800-327-4269
www.attainmentcompany.com
    Realistic play money; money-related board games for older students.

Bingo Materials
    See websites on page 41.

City Creek Press
P.O. Box 900880
Sandy, UT 84090-0880
800-585-6059
www.citycreek.com
    Publishers of *Addition the Fun Way* and *Times Tables the Fun Way*.

Different Roads to Learning
12 W. 18th St.
New York, NY 10011
800-853-1057
www.difflearn.com
    Products for helping children with autism learn, including early sorting/categorizing and shape activities that would be useful for children with Down syndrome.

Down Syndrome Educational Trust
The Sarah Duffen Centre
Belmont St.
Southsea, Hampshire
England PO5 1Na
enquiries@downsed.org
www.downsed.org
    Numicon materials for teaching numeracy, as well as many monographs on math skills and other issues in people with Down syndrome.

Generaction Inc.
7707 Camargo Road
Cincinnati OH 45243
877-771- TIME
    Makers of the Time Timer mentioned in Chapter 17.

Handwriting Without Tears
8001 MacArthur Blvd.
Cabin John, MD 20818
301-263-2700
www.hwtears.com
    Multisensory products for teaching printing of letters and numbers, as well as cursive writing.

Innovative Learning Concepts
6760 Corporate Dr.
Colorado Springs, CO 80919
800-888-9191
www.touchmath.com
    Makers of the TouchMath series of teaching products.

Learning Resources
380 N. Fairway Dr.
Vernon Hills, IL 60061
800-222-3909
www.learningresources.com
    Many good math games, calculators, manipulatives, blank dice, workbooks, and other teaching materials.

Onion Mountain Technology
74 Sextons Hollow Rd.
Canton, CT 06019
860-693-2683
www.onionmountaintech.com
    This company specializes in assistive technology. Offers many varieties of calculators, including talking and printing calculators, the Money Calc, and the Coin-u-lator; the Time Timer; clock stamps, number and operation stamps; etc.

PCI Educational Publishing
P.O. Box 34270
San Antonio, TX 78265
800-594-4263
www.pcicatalog.com
    Realistic play money, calculators, Time Dominoes, math board games, software.

Remedia Publications
15887 N. 76th St., Ste. 120
Scottsdale, AZ 85260
800-826-4740
www.rempub.com
    Workbooks designed for special education students with a real-world focus.

Stevenson Learning Skills
8 Commonwealth Ave.
Attleboro Falls, MA 02763
800-343-1211
www.stevensonsemple.com
    Publishers of the Semple Math program, which uses mnemonic devices to help students master basic math concepts.

Texas Instruments
http://education.ti.com/educationportal
    Student calculators by Texas Instruments.

MATH GAMES

Many of the games referenced in this book (such as those by Milton Bradley) are easily found in most toy stores. Here is contact information for some companies that carry math games that may not be as widely available in stores. Many of the companies in the section above also carry educational games.

Discovery Toys
www.discoverytoysinc.com
> Educational toys and software.

Dragonfly Toys
291 Yale Ave.
Winnipeg, MB R3M 0L4
Canada
800-308-2208
www.dragonflytoys.com
> Specializes in learning toys that are appropriate for children with special needs.

Gamewright
www.gamewright.com
> Many of Gamewright's card games involve using math skills in a fun way. For example, Rat a Tat Cat involves trying to get four cards with the lowest total possible; Dish It Up and Blast Off are matching games; Fowl Play is a counting game.

International Playthings
75D Lackawanna Ave.
Parsippany, NJ 07054
973-316-5883 (fax)
www.intplay.com
> This company makes a number of board games, card games, and puzzles that use early math skills. For example, Campbell's Counting Noodles and Puppy Play both use early counting skills; Fishing for Numbers uses counting skills, number recognition, and early addition skills; Spin-a-Shape calls for early shape recognition skills.

Jax Ltd.
141 Cheshire Lane
Minneapolis, MN 55441
763-449-9699
www.jaxgames.com
> Has a variety of educational games, including How Tall Am I? (which introduces children to using a ruler) and The Game of Chips (a game involving matching spots on dice to numerals).

Learning Resources
380 N. Fairway Dr.
Vernon Hills, IL 60061
800-222-3909
www.learningresources.com
> Learning Resources has games that help children learn a variety of math skills, including addition, subtraction, multiplication, and division; money skills; time telling; fractions.

Ravensburger
1 Puzzle Lane
Newton, NH 03858
603-382-3377
www.ravensburger.com/rag/com/presse/usa/index/html
  This German toy company has many high quality educational games, many of which focus on math concepts. They include Buggo (number recognition and counting), Colorama (matching colors and shapes), Number Race (addition and subtraction), and lotto games.

WEBSITES WITH MATH ACTIVITIES & WORKSHEETS

Some of these sites require payment to access some or all of the activities available. Again, this is only a small sample of what's available.

Funbrain
www.funbrain.com

Improving Education Inc.
www.onlineworksheets.org

KidsDomain Family Resource
www.kidsdomain.com

LearningPlanet
www.learningplanet.com

Math Fact Café
www.mathfactcafe.com

MathStories.com
www.mathstories.com

SchoolExpress
www.schoolexpress.com

Schoolhouse Printables
http://schoolhouseprintable.tripod.com

SuperKids Math Worksheet Creator
www.superkids.com/aweb/tools/math

ORGANIZATIONS

Autism Society of America
7910 Woodmont Ave., Ste. 300
Bethesda, MD 20814
800-328-8476
www.autism-society.org

Canadian Down Syndrome Society
811 14th St. NW
Calgary, LA T2N 2A4
www.cdss.ca

Math Forum @ Drexel
3210 Cherry St.
Philadelphia, PA 19104
www.mathforum.com

National Council of Teachers of Mathematics
1906 Association Dr.
Reston, VA 20191
703-620-9840
www.nctm.org

National Down Syndrome Congress
1370 Center Dr., Ste. 102
Atlanta, GA 30338
800-232-6372
www.ndsccenter.org

National Down Syndrome Society
666 Broadway
New York, NY 10012
800-221-4602
www.ndss.org

Positive Behavioral Intervention & Supports Technical Assistance Center
Behavioral Research and Training
5262 University of Oregon
Eugene, OR 97403
541-346-2505
www.pbis.org

Rehabilitation Research & Training Center on Positive Behavioral Support
rrtcpbs@fmhi.usf.edu
http://rrtcpbs.fmhi.usf.edu.statement.htm

Index

About the Author

DeAnna Horstmeier, Ph.D, is an Instructional Resources Consultant at a special education regional resource center in Columbus, Ohio, where she provides educational assistance to parents and educators in teaching strategies and materials for students with special needs. She also presents at and facilitates series on Cognitive Disabilities and on Autism Spectrum Disorder at the center. She has taught at the Ohio State University in both the areas of special education and speech, language, and communication. Her publications include *Ready, Set, Go–Talk to Me: A Handbook for the Teaching of Prelanguage and Early Language Skills Designed for Parents and Professionals* (with James D. MacDonald) and various chapters in other professional publications. She is the mother of a young adult son with Down syndrome, whose needs for independent living skills placed her on the road to finding ways to teach useful math in a hands-on manner.